Principles of construction law

Principles of construction law

Michael Patrick O'Reilly

Longman
Scientific &
Technical

Longman Scientific & Technical
Longman Group UK Limited
Longman House, Burnt Mill, Harlow,
Essex CM20 2JE, England
and Associated Companies throughout the world.

British Library Cataloguing in Publication Data
A catalogue record for this book is available from the British Library

ISBN 0582 215854

Set by 5 in 10/11pt Baskerville
Printed and Bound in Great Britain
at the Bath Press, Avon

Contents

Table of statutes

Table of cases

Table of cases

Abbreviations

The abbreviations used for case citations are found in standard lists (e.g. those in the current Law Yearbook). They are referenced in most specialist libraries by their abbreviations. Abbreviations for cases, specialist reports and other references are as follows in this book:

For case citations

AC	Appeal Cases
All ER	All England Reports
BLR	Building Law Reports
B&S	Best and Smith Reports
CA	Court of Appeal
Ch App	Chancery Appeals
Ch D	Chancery Division
CILL	Construction Industry Law Letter
Constr LJ	Construction Law Journal
CP	Common Pleas
C&P	Carrington and Payne Reports
DLT	Dominion Law Times
E&B	Ellis and Blackburn Reports
EG	Estates Gazette
ER	English Reports
Giff	Giffard Reports
H&C	Hurlston and Coltman Reports
HL	House of Lords
H&N	Hurlston and Norman Reports
IR	Irish Reports
KB	King's Bench
LGR	Local Government Reports
Ll Rep	Lloyd's Reports
LR	Law Reports
M&W	Meeson and Welsby Reports
NY Supp	New York Supplement
NZLR	New Zealand Law Reports
QBD	Queen's Bench Division
SC	Scottish Cases
TLR	Times Law Reports
WLR	Weekly Law Reports

Others

ICE	Institution of Civil Engineers
JCT	Joint Contracts Tribunal
RIBA	Royal Institute of British Architects
RICS	Royal Institute of Chartered Surveyors

Preface

In writing this book I wished to produce a short work in which the presentation of the detailed rules of law would take second place to an exposition of the fundamental principles involved. Hence the title: 'Principles of Construction Law'.

The book originated as a compilation of the material which I taught in a variety of undergraduate and postgraduate courses at the University of Nottingham and on the Construction MSc course at Loughborough University of Technology. I decided to publish my notes in the present form when I was unable to refer my students to a single inexpensive book which covered all my lecture material. As I began to write, I realised that this book would also be of use to practising construction professionals and I have expanded the material so that it would be of maximum benefit to that readership. It will also, I believe, be of assistance to lawyers whose experience of construction law is limited.

The standard texts *Keating* and *Hudson* (see bibliography for details of all books and other materials referred to in the text) deal with issues relating to contracts with far more authority than I could hope to do. This is a much shorter book and aims to summarize the principal elements of the law of construction. The major texts assume an understanding of the legal system and the law. I have designed this book to be a beginner's text since construction students and indeed many practising construction professionals have no prior knowledge of the law, except as citizens. Through this book I also wished to familiarise them with a wider variety of topics than are dealt with in the major texts; in particular I wished to discuss tortious obligations in some detail and also to give them an introduction to international issues in construction law. I should also like to mention the book *Construction Law* by John Uff, now in its fifth edition. Dr Uff's book deals with a wide range of topics and includes short commentaries on the main standard forms of contract. There is, I believe, a fundamental difference in approach between my work and his; he aims to cover a wide field (and does so admirably) whereas my prime objective is to provide a fundamental understanding uncluttered by detailed rules and conditions from standard contracts.

In this book I have aimed to present the basic law and to illustrate it with the words of the judges so that the reader may see the way in which legal rules are formulated. The quotations and the case histories are selected as much for their clear language and their obvious bearing on practical problems in construction as for their weight as precedent. Accordingly, there are as many, if not more, passages from the judgments of the Official Referees as there are from the Law Lords. I make no excuse for this.

I would like to thank Dr Mick Mawdesley, Dr Andrew Newport, Mr Arthur O'Reilly and Miss Anne Dennett, each of whom read through and commented critically on the text in preparation. They have pointed out many faults; needless to say, any errors or misunderstandings which remain are wholly my responsibility. I would also like to thank Miss Rachel Ramsden and Miss Selina Willis for helping me to prepare the manuscript and proofs.

Most thanks, however, go to Professor Stephen Brown and all the students and staff of the Department of Civil Engineering at Nottingham University for providing me with the stimulation, facilities and space to write this book. I dedicate this book to them all.

Michael P O'Reilly
Nottingham,
September 1992

A note on the arrangement of the book

This book has been arranged into four parts.

Part 1, 'Introductory Topics', contains three chapters, each concerned with background material or introductory aspects of construction law. They are also concerned with a number of aspects relating to the general legal system which are important for or affect construction law, including the legislation affecting construction.

The second and third parts deal respectively with the laws of Contract and Tort, the two major constituents of construction law. Contractual obligations arise when two parties make an agreement; tortious obligations arise independently of agreement. Thus, if a contractor and a landowner agree that for a certain sum of money the contractor will build a house a contract comes into existence. If the contractor builds the house but the owner refuses to pay, then the contractor's claim is for breach of contract. However, if the house subsequently collapses and thereby damages property on a neighbour's land, that neighbour's claim (either against the building owner or the constructor or both) will be in tort. This is because the obligation not to damage the neighbour's property arises independently of an agreement to which the neighbour is a party.

In Part 2, 'Contract', Chapters 4 to 8 deal with general principles and Chapter 9 to 16 deal with specific aspects of contract law relating to construction. This part of the book contains thirteen chapters, approximately half the book, reflecting the overriding importance of contracts in construction law.

Part 3, 'Torts in Construction', contains five chapters. The topics dealt with here are important for an overall understanding of the subject but the coverage is less detailed than that of the section on contracts since, in practice, the law of tort plays a less significant role in construction law.

Part 4, 'Miscellaneous Topics in Construction Law', contains six chapters dealing with a variety of topics. Some of these are relevant both to contractual and tortious aspects of construction law; some deal with topics which could not satisfactorily be included within either.

Part 1

Introductory Topics

Introduction: the construction industry and construction law

1.1 The scope of this book

The construction industry can justifiably claim to be one of the most important operating in the national and international economies, both because of the (large proportion of national and world income devoted to construction) and also on account of the vital role played by the construction industry in maintaining the infrastructure which underpins our current civilisation. In construction, as with all commercial activities, it is important for the continued prosperity of the industry, and its ultimate beneficiaries, the public, that the parties involved should understand the obligations that they assume when working within that sector. Construction law is that branch of commercial law which deals with the construction process and the rights and obligations of the parties involved in or affected by it.

There are a range of activities which occur during the construction process but which are not dealt with in detail in this book. For example, during the preliminary stages of the project employers may buy or lease the site; in the case of a local or statutory authority, they may acquire it by compulsory purchase. They will also obtain relevant planning consents from the planning authority. During the construction phase, intellectual property rights regarding equipment (patents) and designs (copyright) must be considered, and insurance, safety obligations and employment relations are often important. Following construction, the works must often be maintained in a good and safe condition by law (e.g. roads under the Highways Act 1980). The matters just mentioned are treated in this book as ancillary to the principal construction activity and are covered either in outline only or not at all, although the practising construction lawyer must understand their implications.

Parties involved in construction owe, potentially at least, duties or obligations to a large number of others. For instance, a contractor will owe an important duty to the employer to construct the works in accordance with the specifications and drawings. He will also owe a duty to the occupiers of neighbouring land not to interfere unreasonably with their use of their land. Further, he will owe a duty to visitors to the site and indeed to passers-by to take reasonable care for their safety.

One of the features of construction is the large degree of interaction between the various parties involved so that a single event or activity can affect a large number of people or companies. Hence the mistake or default of one individual or firm can have considerable and wide consequences; those affected will wish to know whether, to what degree, and on what basis they can recover against the party in default for the losses they sustain and, indeed, to what degree they themselves may be liable for the losses which are caused by others. These questions will be addressed in the chapters which follow.

1.2   An introduction to the construction industry

1.2.1   Sectors within the construction industry

The term 'construction industry' is an umbrella term covering a wide range of activities which involve construction. A number of classifications are currently used. The main distinction is between the civil engineering and the building sectors. In practice it is often difficult to categorise a particular project as either civil engineering or building and most projects will have an element of both.

Civil engineering
This involves work associated with the 'basic infrastructure' including roads, tunnels, bridges, harbours, coastal and river engineering, water supply, sewers and power stations. Much of the work in the civil engineering sector tends to be large scale in terms of the capital value of the projects, the volumes of materials involved and the expected working lifetimes of the completed works.

Building
This includes both commercial buildings and domestic dwellings. The focus in building work tends to be on building details and the services and finishes provided within the building. The structure of the building often accounts for less than half the capital construction cost.

Other categories
A number of types of work are considered by many to fall outside both the civil engineering and building categories even though they would normally be considered to fall within the construction industry's range of activities; these include demolition, the construction of process plants (factories, chemical plants, materials handling plants), landscaping works (general landscaping, golf courses) and shipbuilding.

The description of the sectors presented above is designed solely to assist in understanding the way in which the industry perceives itself. From a legal point of view, however, it is not usually of any intrinsic legal significance whether a piece of work falls within one sector or another. The only situation where the classification of the work may be important in law is where parties agree to contract on 'the relevant standard form' or other similar wording; in this case the type of work will often define the form of contract to be used since different standard forms of contracts tend to be used in different sectors.

1.2.2   Parties involved in construction

Note: The term 'party' used throughout this book means simply 'person, organisation, partnership, company or corporation'.

Those involved in the construction industry have traditionally been divided into three major classes: employers, consultants and contractors. The traditional role of these parties is as follows.

Employers

The employer is the party who commissions or promotes the project. The employer generally owns the building or structure which forms the subject matter of the construction, and may be operating in the public sector (e.g. local authorities or government departments) or in the private sector (e.g. home-owners or commercial companies). Employers may be experienced in construction work (e.g. companies which specialise in building development) and may have the skills to design and supervise construction activities 'in-house'. Alternatively, they may rely heavily on consultants to advise them.

While the term 'employer' will be used in this book to describe the party who owns/commissions the project it should be noted that there are a wide range of terms in current usage to describe the party which commissions and promotes the work. The term 'client' is often used by consultants to describe the employer as he or she will usually also be their professional client for the consultancy advice they provide. The term 'promoter' is also widely used in the industry to describe the employer; in the contracts published by the Institutions of Chemical, Electrical and Mechanical Engineers the term 'purchaser' is used. However, 'employer' is used by the main civil engineering and building contracts.

Consultants

Consultants comprise all those who provide advice on or in relation to the project. They include architects, engineers and surveyors. The role or responsibilities of these consultants will depend on the terms of their 'brief', that is their agreement with their client. Most consultants belong to a professional institution, such as the Institution of Civil Engineers or Royal Institute of Chartered Surveyors. However, anyone may, in the UK, describe himself or herself as an engineer or surveyor. The term 'architect' is the only protected name in the UK; by the Architect's Registration Act 1938 no one may practise as an architect unless registered by the Architect's Registration Council. In many foreign countries, descriptions such as 'engineer' are also protected. The traditional roles of each of these groups of professional advisers are as follows.

Architects   Architects provide overall advice on building works, scheme designs, detailed design of building layout, coordination of services (e.g.

water supply and ventilation) and supervision of building works. They will also provide advice on the commissioning of specialist designs, suitable forms of contract and the suitability of contractors: see, for instance, *R v Architect's Registration Tribunal, ex parte Jagger* [1945] 2 All ER 131 at 134, where the Divisional Court considered the typical functions of architects.

Engineers   These may undertake a variety of roles. Civil engineers provide the same services as an architect in respect of civil engineering works (i.e. major infrastructure projects such as roads, water supply, harbours, bridges, etc.). Civil engineers who work in the building sector (often called structural engineers) tend not to take the coordinating role in the construction but to work with the architects to provide detailed designs for load-bearing elements of the building. Service engineers provide a range of design services including electrical supply, ventilation, light and water supply. Mechanical engineers will be used as consultants in respect of machinery to be installed in buildings or in civil engineering works.

Surveyors   The term 'surveyor', like the term 'engineer', tends to be used to describe a range of consultants who provide services in connection with construction. A quantity surveyor is employed to ascertain the likely cost of construction by examining the materials used, their costs, the quantities required and any aspects of the construction process which may affect the cost. Before the work is let, he or she will often draw up bills of quantities, these being tables of the various items of work necessary to complete the project, together with their quantities. During the works the quantity surveyor will 'measure' the works (that is compute the amount of work of each description in the bill of quantities which the contractor has completed and hence calculate the payment due at that stage by reference to the contract terms) and monitor expenditure with a view to maintaining some degree of control over it. Structural surveyors are used to examine the structural characteristics of a piece of construction work. Setting-out surveyors (often called setting-out engineers) use surveying instruments to indicate the precise location on site of each element of the works so that everything fits together and can be coordinated in the available space.

Contractors
Contractors physically construct the works. Traditionally, contractors have operated under what might be called 'build-only' contracts (also called the 'conventional' or 'traditional' arrangement) and their function has been to translate designs and drawings provided by an engineer or architect on behalf of the employer into a physical structure. In recent years alternative types of contracts such as 'design and build', where the contractor takes an active role in the design process, have become increasingly important.

Contractors range in size from major international contractors whose turnover is expressed in billions of pounds sterling per annum to small specialist contractors and domestic builders. The major contractors normally act as 'main contractor' for large projects; that is they take on the overall responsibility for the construction. The smaller contractors either work only on minor projects (for example domestic builders constructing a house extension) or undertake specialist elements of the work on large projects as subcontractors to the main contractor (for example, plastering subcontractors, joinery subcontractors, etc.).

Recent developments in the structure of the construction industry
In recent years economic and organisational changes have occurred which have tended to blur the distinction between the groups described above. For instance, much construction work is now designed and constructed by the same party, so that the contractors now employ design personnel who would traditionally have been employed by independent consultancy firms. Also, contractors are now increasingly becoming interested in project promotion, including financing the projects they construct with their revenue being generated by charging the user, for example, by tolls; in such cases they exhibit many of the characteristics of the employer under the traditional classification system.

1.2.3   The typical arrangement and progress of construction works

The typical development and progress of construction projects needs to be understood, at least in outline, if the law relating to construction is to be put into its proper context. The parties to a construction project may, in general, agree to organise the works to be constructed in any way they consider appropriate. Two types of arrangements have already been mentioned: build-only and design and build. These, and other common contractual arrangements, are described in detail in Chapter 4; but it is worthwhile understanding at this stage the typical procedures used in order to gain an appreciation of the way in which the construction industry operates.

The project commences when the employer perceives the need to commission some work of construction. He appoints one or more consultants to advise him on the design of the works and its likely and potential costs. If, after receiving this advice, the employer decides to pursue the project, he may ask the consultants to prepare detailed designs, drawings specifications and all the other things necessary so that a contractor, when one is appointed, will know exactly what to construct. Alternatively, if the employer wishes the project to proceed on a design and build basis, that is with the contractor assuming the responsibility for detailed design, he will ask his consultants to devise general scheme drawings and specifications which indicate requirements such as the layout of buildings, aesthetic requirements and standards of performance.

When the designs are sufficiently advanced a number of contractors are asked to provide quotations ('to tender') for the works. In the case of a design and build project the contractor's tender will include design ideas combined with a quotation for the all-in price for designing and constructing the works, all in accordance with the general requirements of the employer. The employer, on the advice of his consultants, selects the contractor who has submitted the most attractive quotation. Possession of the site is then delivered over to the successful contractor, who commences construction. A finish date for the construction is usually agreed.

The construction is usually supervised by a consultant, who assumes the role known in the industry as that of 'certifier'. For civil engineering works a civil engineer will usually be the certifier; for building it will normally be an architect; for process plants, a chemical engineer; for landscape work, a landscape architect; and for shipbuilding, a naval architect. The certifier normally acts to safeguard the employer's interests but in some matters he or she must act fairly as between the employer and the contractor; for instance in contracts where the contractor is to be paid in stages throughout the project duration it will be the certifier who decides on the correct amount to be paid at each stage. In making decisions of this nature the certifier must act fairly to both parties.

2

An outline of some aspects of the legal system

2.1 Introduction

This is a book about construction law. However, construction, as with all activities which we undertake, must be performed within the context of the overall legal system which governs our lives. It is necessary, therefore, to understand the basic features of the legal system. This chapter sets out the basic law relating to a number of topics which have an important bearing on construction law and which, therefore, need to be understood. These topics may be introduced as a series of questions.

How are laws made and published?
Unless we are able to identify a rule as a law, which binds us, we cannot know whether or not we are obliged to comply with it. In Section 2.2 we shall see that the three principal sources of law are statutes made by Parliament, laws made by the European Community and the decisions of the courts; whether or not a rule has legal force will depend on whether or not it has been made in the appropriate manner prescribed for each of these types of law. In addition it is a fundamental rule of a free society that laws be published and we shall also briefly see in Section 2.2 the process by which the public can become aware of the laws which come into existence.

Who has 'personality' in law?
Only 'persons' are entitled to act in law. Thus only a person may make a contract or commit a crime. The law's definition of 'person' comprises both natural persons (human beings) and artificial persons (corporations). Within the category of artificial persons, foremost, in terms of numbers, are companies registered under the Companies Acts 1985 and 1989. These companies are able, for instance, to enter into contracts, commit torts and in some cases to commit crimes. The question asked here is important since the object of commercial law, in the end, is to establish liabilities and enforce rights. It is, therefore, important to know against whom such liabilities may potentially be established and against whom such rights may be enforced. This matter is dealt with in Section 2.3.

Who is competent/entitled to represent another?
Often, one person represents another; the former is termed the 'agent', the latter being the 'principal'. It is, for instance, impossible for an artificial person to act without being represented by an agent. The question posed here and examined in Section 2.4 relates to the authority of the agent; under what circumstances, for example, is a company bound by the agreements purportedly made on its behalf by a person who claims to be its agent?

For how long is a person liable at law for his or her default?
The term 'default' used here does not imply any moral culpability; it means any failure at law, including such matters as breaches of contract. The aim of construction law is to identify the circumstances under which those who work in, and are connected with, the construction industry are liable for their defaults. The law, however, also limits their liability in terms of time. It would, for example, be unjust for an architect, engineer or contractor to remain liable forever for their negligent designs; accordingly the law places time limits on the ability of a wronged party to bring a legal action. These are dealt with in Section 2.5.

What are the principal sources of information in construction law?
While this book provides a significant amount of information on construction law it is sometimes necessary to obtain a more authoritative statement of the law and on occasions it will be necessary to refer to the primary sources. Section 2.6 explains where this information may be obtained.

2.2   The framework of the law

It is traditional to refer to the framework of the law which operates in this country as the 'English legal system'. However, since 1972, the UK has become gradually integrated into the European Community and the rules and laws of the Community are becoming increasingly applicable in the UK. Consequently, it is somewhat misleading to refer to the framework of law in operation as 'English' as many important provisions derive directly from European legislation.

2.2.1   States and countries: the UK and England

A clear distinction must be drawn between 'states' and 'countries'. In law, a state is an independent sovereign entity occupying an area of territory ruled exclusively by a government and/or legislature which is generally accepted as having effective control over that territory. A country is simply a territory within which the laws are everywhere the same.

The United Kingdom is a state. The government/legislature based in London has full authority and sovereignty over the whole of the UK territory, that is England, Wales, Scotland and Northern Ireland. However, the laws are not the same everywhere in the UK; there are three legal countries, namely England and Wales, Scotland and Northern Ireland. In addition there are other territories, such as the Channel Islands and the Isle of Man, which have a status which is difficult to categorise.

In this book the law presented will be the law of England and Wales, though for the vast majority of the material dealt with in this book the rules are the same everywhere in the UK. Hence they will apply also to Scotland and Northern Ireland. Indeed, many rules of contract and tort are also the same in other Commonwealth jurisdictions such as Canada, New Zealand, Australia and Hong Kong, and cases from these jurisdictions are regularly cited in English courts as evidence of what the English law is.

2.2.2   The English legal system: general background

The constitution
Many states have comprehensive, written constitutions. These constitutions are the primary documents of the state and all questions of the authority of the various law makers, courts and executive government are decided by, or in accordance with, the constitution. In the UK there is no written constitution and so the questions of the authority and powers of the various organs of state are a matter of convention and tradition. Suffice it to say that, for our purposes, Parliament is recognised as the supreme law-making body. It is said to be 'sovereign' in that it is entitled to make or unmake any law it wishes. Any other sources of law, for example judicial decisions or European legislation, have force and effect because, and only because, Parliament has assented to them having such effect.

Legislation/statutes
Parliament makes laws by passing legislation, known as 'statutes' or 'Acts of Parliament' (the two terms are synonymous), in a traditionally specified sequence comprising three 'Readings' of the draft statute (the 'Bill') in each of the Houses of Parliament, the Commons and the Lords, followed by the Royal Assent (the Queen's affirmation). The statute is then published by Her Majesty's Stationery Office (HMSO) and may be purchased by the public from any HMSO outlet. The statute is given a name by which it may be identified. Examples which are dealt with in this book include the Defective Premises Act 1972 and the Building Act 1984.

In addition to the legislation passed directly by Parliament there is a category of law, known as 'subordinate legislation', which has the same status as that passed by Parliament but which is formulated by others under the power of a statute. An example is given by the Building Regulations which are not formulated by Parliament itself; they are, however, given direct statutory effect by Section 1 of the Building Act 1984.

Judicial decisions
Whenever a point of law is covered by the words of a statute, the law is conclusively as stated in that statute. In practice, however, only a small proportion of working commercial law is contained in detailed statutes and so the courts (the judiciary) also have an important law-making role. Their law-making function is important in two situations:

- where the point of law at issue is not dealt with by statute: this applies to the majority of the law relating to construction
- where the statute is unclear in its meaning or scope, the judges have to decide upon its meaning or whether or not it applies in a given situation.

In each of these cases the judges must interpret or develop the law to deal with the matter before the court. The gradual accretion of a coordinated system of legal rules is facilitated by the 'doctrine of precedent' which operates in England. This doctrine presupposes the existence of a hierarchy of courts, and the present system of civil courts (i.e. excluding criminal courts) and their position in the hierarchy is shown in Figure 2.1.

The doctrine requires that a court dealing with a point of law must decide it in the same way as previous courts which are superior to it in the hierarchy of the courts.

In the field of construction law, judge-made law ('case law') is extremely important because the relevant principles of law are not covered by statute to any great extent. Rather, they have been developed in the last two centuries by countless successive decisions of the courts. Accordingly, when a point of law is disputed, the parties will make reference to previously decided cases which are similar or analogous to the issue currently in dispute.

The court system

Small claims are normally dealt with by the County Court. 'Small' in this context means less than about £50 000 (see the High Court and County Court Jurisdiction Order 1991, SI 1991/724). The courts do have powers to transfer cases involving greater sums to the County Court. Disputes involving large sums are dealt with by the High Court. The majority of disputes of a construction nature will be dealt with by judges known as 'Official Referees'. They do not have full High Court Judge rank, but preside over construction and other similar disputes as part of the High Court's business.

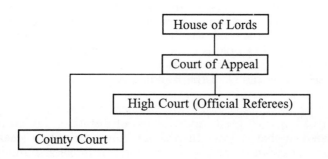

Fig. 2.1: Civil courts relevant to construction

Decisions of either the County Court or the High Court may be appealed to the Court of Appeal. Appeal to the House of Lords is 'with leave' only; that is to say the Court of Appeal or House of Lords must allow the appeal to be heard, basing its decision on the importance of the issues in dispute.

County Court and High Court disputes are normally heard by a single judge. Court of Appeal and House of Lords matters are usually heard by three and five judges respectively, though for important cases more judges (always an odd number) may be involved.

Since case law is of great importance in the formulation of construction law it is necessary to understand the basic principles to be used when relying on a previous decision. These principles may be summarised as follows.

First, the statements concerning the law contained in the recorded judgment of a court can be divided into two constituents. The first component, the *ratio decidendi,* contains the legal rule or rules which is/are applied in reaching the decision. The second component, the *obiter dicta,* are discussions and observations of a general nature which are not a necessary part of the court's decision. In practice, the judgment of a court comprises one or more decisions, one from each of the judges involved. These are in fact 'essays' written by the judges and are often more than twenty pages in length. They contain such matters as the relevant facts, the background law, a record of the contentions made by the parties during the hearing and any other material which the judge feels it helpful to include. Judges, however, rarely identify the *ratio decidendi* in their own decisions and hence lawyers must attempt to distill it out from the written judgments by analysing the necessary stages in arriving at the final decision. Much court time is taken up with lawyers arguing about which part of a previous judgment actually constitutes the *ratio decidendi.*

Second, the *ratio decidendi* of a 'court of record' (i.e. the High Court, the Court of Appeal and the House of Lords) is not merely a statement of opinion about the law; it is a statement of the law. This might be contrasted with the situation in countries which have a codified system of law (which includes most continental European countries) where the law is in the code and the decision of the judge is an opinion concerning the law.

Third, there is a hierarchy of courts of record. The decisions of a High Court judge can be overruled by the Court of Appeal. Likewise the House of Lords can overrule decisions of the Court of Appeal. This means that a *ratio decidendi* from the decision of the House of Lords prevails over a *ratio* from the Court of Appeal or the High Court. Since the House of Lords is at the summit of the hierarchy its decisions are the most authoritative.

Fourth, there are a number of courts which do not fit into the hierarchy. These include the courts of foreign countries which have legal systems based on the English model (e.g. Canada, New Zealand) and the Privy Council, a special court which hears appeals from the colonies and some former dependencies. The decisions of these courts are described as 'persuasive' rather than 'authoritative'; this means that a court is not bound to follow them but that they should be seriously considered by the court.

2.2.3 European law

One aspect of the framework of law applicable in the UK which has had a profound effect on the English legal system and continues to become yet more important is European law, the law generated by the European Community.

The European Community: general introduction
The European Economic Community (EEC) was established in 1957 by the six original member states who signed the 1957 Rome Convention. The EEC was designed, according to the Preamble to the treaty, 'to lay the foundations of an ever closer union among the peoples of Europe'. The United Kingdom, as well as Ireland and Denmark, joined the Community in 1973 and the European Community treaties were incorporated into UK law through the European Communities Act 1972. Following the accession of Greece in 1979 and Spain and Portugal in 1986 there are now twelve member states. In 1986 the twelve member states signed the Single European Act (SEA) which was designed to create a single internal market by the end of 1992. In February 1992 the member states signed the Treaty on European Union (the Maastricht Agreement) designed further to strengthen the union of the Community. However, the treaty must be ratified by member states and at the time of writing (September 1992) its future is not absolutely assured. Several referenda have so far been held in European member states. Popular endorsement for the treaty has been formally recorded in Ireland and France, but the Danes have voted against it. The Danish government has nonetheless committed itself to the idea of the European Community and to getting a revised treaty endorsed by its people. The British government has recently committed itself to getting the treaty ratified in or before early 1993 (which will involve obtaining Parliamentary consent). The situation is, however, extremely fluid.

The UK's accession to the European Community profoundly affected the basis of our legal system because the laws made by Europe can prevail over those made by the UK Parliament and thus the theory of parliamentary sovereignty which was discussed in Section 2.2.2 can no longer be said fully to apply. These changes are important both practically as well as theoretically because the scope of authority of the European legislative machine is extremely wide, covering not only economic but social issues as well. It is, in theory, perhaps not too late for the UK to withdraw; however, the pull of Europe is, in serious practical terms, ineluctable with withdrawal meaning economic and developmental isolation. And so, with little option but to proceed with Europeanisation, the basis of the UK's traditional sovereignty is being gradually transferred to the authorities of the Community with the result that the law-making authority of the UK Parliament is being increasingly diminished. Parliament may still make or unmake whatever laws it wishes with the following provisos; first, those laws must be such as to incorporate European Community directives into UK law; and second, no laws may be introduced which conflict with European Community laws or policies. In *HP Bulmer Ltd v J Bollinger SA* [1974] Ch 401, Lord Denning accurately predicted the long-term effect of the European treaties when he observed that

> the Treaty is like an incoming tide. It flows into the estuaries and up the rivers. It cannot be held back.

The institutions of the EC
In this section the principal organs of the European Community and their various functions and powers will be discussed. Four principal institutions were established by Article 4 of the EEC Treaty: the European Parliament, the Council [of Ministers], the Commission and the Court of Justice.

The European Parliament   The European Parliament is composed of elected members from each of the member states and its principal functions are advisory and supervisory. The Council must seek Parliament's opinion before a Regulation of the Council is issued regarding certain subject matters. While the Council is not obliged to follow the advice, a Regulation issued before such advice is obtained is a nullity (*Roquette Frères SA v Council*, Case 138/79). Since the introduction of the Single European Act, Parliament has also a right to object to legislation; if it continues to do so, the Council may still pass it but must do so unanimously and within three months.

Parliament exercises direct political control over the Commission and commissioners must reply to its questions. The Council of Ministers is not, however, subject to parliamentary control, but is subject to significant supervision. The President of the Council is obliged regularly to address the Parliament and the Parliament reports on and debates the activities of the Council.

The Council of Ministers   The Council consists of representatives of the member states, nominated by the governments in each member state. It has a fluctuating membership; when matters relate to economic policy, finance ministers will participate; when matters of the most fundamental importance are discussed Heads of State may attend. When Heads of State meet, as they do twice yearly, the Council is called the European Council. The Council's task is 'to ensure that the objectives set out in this Treaty are attained' (Article 145). It has power to take final decisions in respect of most secondary legislation. Because of this important role, the systems whereby the Council reaches its decisions are crucial. Generally, voting is either on a basis of unanimity or by 'qualified majority' whereby each state's vote is weighted. The UK, France, Germany and Italy are each accorded ten votes, eight for Spain, five for Belgium, Greece, the Netherlands and Portugal, three for Denmark and Ireland and two for Luxembourg; the required minimum vote for a qualified majority is fifty-four out of the seventy-six available. In general, the Council has attempted to achieve unanimity and it is exceedingly rare for a vote to be forced.

The SEA, however, has extended the areas where voting may proceed on the basis of qualified majority including most of the legislation required to complete the internal market.

The Commission   The Commission consists of seventeen members, two from the UK, France, Germany, Italy and Spain and one from the other member states, who are chosen on grounds of general competence and unquestionable independence. They must 'neither seek nor take instructions from any government or from any other body' (Merger Treaty, Article 10). They have three main functions:

- to initiate action: all important Council decisions begin upon proposals by the Commission although the Council is able to request the Commission to undertake 'any studies which it considers desirable for the attainment of the common objectives'
- to ensure, by action in the European Court if necessary, that member states comply with EC law
- it is the executive of the European Community: once the Council has enunciated general policy, it falls to the Commission to implement that policy by legislation (which must be endorsed by the Council to become law).

The Court of Justice   The court is the supreme authority on questions of European law. While the UK courts use the doctrine of precedent the Court of Justice uses 'teleological methods'. Lord Diplock, in *R v Henn* [1981] AC 850, said: 'It seeks to give effect to what it conceives to be the spirit rather than the letter of the Treaties; sometimes, indeed, to an English judge, it may seem to the exclusion of the letter'. The Court consists of thirteen judges, one from each member state and a President. The Court is assisted by six Advocates-General. All are chosen from people of unquestionable independence. The function of the Advocates-General is to present detailed submissions to the judges analysing the relevant issues. When the court receives the submission it makes its decision in a short statement and so the main exposition of the law is to be found in the submissions of the Advocates-General.

There are a number of means whereby the Court of Justice may be seised of a matter. These include actions against member states such as *The Commission v Ireland* (Case 45/87) 44 BLR 1, which provides a good and accessible example of the application of European Community competition law to construction.

There is also an important route whereby individual litigants may find themselves before the Court of Justice. The basis of the court's jurisdiction in this case is provided for by Article 177, which provides

> The Court of Justice shall have jurisdiction to give preliminary rulings concerning:
>
> (a) the interpretation of this Treaty;
> (b) the validity and interpretation of acts of the institutions;
> (c) the interpretation of the statutes of bodies established by an act of the Council, where those statutes so provide.

Where such a question is raised before any court or tribunal of a member state, that court or tribunal may, if it considers that a decision over the question is necessary to enable it to give judgment, request the Court of Justice to give a ruling thereon.

Where any such question is raised in a case pending before a court or tribunal of a member State, against whose decisions there is no judicial remedy under national law, that court or tribunal shall bring the matter before the Court of Justice.

The court does not, therefore, operate as an appeal court; rather it provides preliminary rulings which the national courts apply. The court does not interfere in the decisions concerning which matters are to be referred; it cannot act unless there is a request from a national court. The court has interpreted the term 'any court or tribunal' used in Article 177 very widely provided there is an element of public participation in the tribunal; where, however, in a shipbuilding case, the arbitration agreement excluded recourse to the ordinary courts the arbitrator was, according to the Court of Justice, not 'a court or tribunal' – *Nordsee Deutsche Hochseefischerei GmbH* (Case 102/81).

Any relevant court or tribunal is entitled to request the Court of Justice to provide a ruling; but by Article 177, any court, such as the House of Lords, against whose decision there is no judicial remedy under national law is obliged to refer the matter to the Court of Justice.

Sources of European law

By virtue of the European Communities Act 1972, European law is directly applicable in the UK. Section 2(1) of the ECA 1972 provides

> All such rights, powers, liabilities, obligations and restrictions from time to time created or arising by or under the Treaties ... are without further enactment to be given legal effect in the United Kingdom.

The sources of European law are as follows:

1 *Treaties*   the Treaties establish the institutions of the European Community and contain the basic principles of the Community.
2 *Regulations*   these are made by the Council of Ministers or by the Commission. They are directly applicable to all member states and are binding on them without further enactment.
3 *Directives*   these are issued by the Council of Ministers or the Commission and are addressed to member states. Directives state the result which must be achieved but leave the means of attainment to each individual member state.
4 *Decisions*   decisions of the Council of Ministers and the Commission are specific determinations addressed directly to specific states or legal persons in the Community and they bind only those to whom they are addressed.
5 *Judgments of the European Court of Justice*   these judgments represent the court's view on individual disputes relating to the interpretation of Community law.

Section 2(2) of the ECA 1972 gives the UK Government power to make subordinate legislation to enact European Directives which are not directly applicable in the UK. Section 2(4) and the European Communities (Enforcement of Community Judgments) Order 1972, made under it, makes provision for the enforcement of Judgments of the European Court and Decisions of the Council.

European legal measures of particular relevance to construction
At the present time, European law impinges only to a slight extent on the construction industry but its influence is rapidly increasing. Much of the law in this field may be thought of as variations on two principal themes. The first of these, the 'level playing field' thesis, requires that citizens and companies from all member states should have identical opportunities to compete in every member state; this is effected by allowing full access to the markets of other countries and by making Community-wide standards so that the possibility of discrimination in favour of, or against, specific Community nationals on the basis of the superiority, or inadequacy, of specific national standards is avoided. Second, there is a strong consumer protection theme running through the legislation.

Much of the European law which is of most direct effect in the construction sector has been in the form of secondary legislation (Directives) of recent origin, many of which have been explicitly incorporated into UK law as UK parliamentary legislation. Examples of laws or possible future laws which will have an effect on construction law include public construction procurement, the applicable law of the contract, consumer protection law, safety regulations, construction products and harmonised liability laws for professionals.

These are very briefly outlined in Chapter 3, which deals with the legislative background to construction.

2.3 Legal personality

In construction the main actors are corporations (which include companies), partnerships and individuals. However, only a person or some entity with the same legal status as a person may, for instance, enter into a contract or commit a tort. The law recognises two categories of legal person: natural persons (i.e. human beings) and corporations. Nothing more need really be said about natural persons except that they will not normally be held liable for their breaches of contract unless they are over 18 years old at the time of making the contract.

2.3.1 Corporations and companies

Corporations may be created by charter or by statute, and this class includes local authorities and universities; or they may be created as companies by registration under the Companies Acts. Corporations are legally distinct from their members. Thus while a company is owned by its shareholders, it is, in law, an independent person. Therefore, the liabilities of the companies do not devolve upon the shareholders; creditors must sue the company itself rather than the shareholders if they wish to seek redress against the company. The distinction here is particularly important when the corporation is a limited (limited liability) company in liquidation for here the personal liability of the shareholders is limited to the value of the initial stake in the company allotted to them. The directors of the company also escape liability for the company debts provided they have not been reckless or fraudulent in their dealings.

There are very few situations where directors or shareholders can be made personally liable. Under the Insolvency Act 1986, if a company goes into insolvent liquidation and a director knew beforehand that there was a reasonable prospect that this may happen, the court may order the director to make a personal contribution to the company's assets.

2.3.2 Non-incorporated associations

A number of situations often arise in connection with the construction industry in which the legal personality status of an organisation is not immediately clear; in particular, in construction, this is so in the case of partnerships and 'joint ventures'. These are examples of non-incorporated associations which are groups of persons (natural or legal or both) which act together but do not form a corporation.

Partnerships
Many firms of consulting engineers, architects and surveyors exist as partnerships. These firms do not have independent legal personality although the fact that an organisation exists as a partnership has some legal consequences. The partnership must sue and be sued as a collection of individual natural persons in the same way as any other unincorporated association although, because of its special status as a partnership, it may sue or be sued through any partner, all of whom are jointly and severally liable for the activities of the partnership. The Partnership Act 1891 should be consulted for details.

Joint ventures
Two or more companies may form a 'joint venture' whereby they join forces to undertake a project. This practice is particularly common on very large projects and on overseas work where many employers insist on joint ventures being used. The principal reason for this is risk-reduction; the more companies involved, the greater the distribution of the risk of major losses.

There are two principal approaches adopted by construction companies who wish to enter into a joint venture. First, they may create a separate company to deal with joint venture business. This allows the joint venture to act as an independent legal person even though that independent person is wholly owned by the principals of the joint venture. Alternatively, the joint venturers may make a simple agreement to share the profits of the adventure between them in some agreed proportion in which case the law treats them as two separate legal persons who act in concert. They will, in this case, both be jointly and severally liable for the debts of the joint venture. This means that contracts made with third parties must be honoured by either party, so that if one of the joint venturers becomes insolvent the other will be liable for all the debts incurred in the adventure even if they are attributable to the default of the other joint venturer. Likewise, a payment of a debt related to the adventure by a third party to one of the joint venturers will clear that debt; the third party will not have to investigate the proportion of the debt owed to each joint venturer.

2.4 Agency

In the commercial world most decisions are made by agents; and most contracts are made and broken by agents. For instance the statement 'Company A and Company B entered into a contract' means that authorised representatives from A and B agreed, on behalf of A and B respectively, that A and B would be bound by the contract. In the law of agency, the authorised representatives are known as agents and the companies whom they represent are the principals.

The central question relating to agents concerns their authority. For example, the canteen manager of a construction company A may be authorised to order food and kitchen supplies on behalf of A, but would not normally be authorised to enter into a construction contract. On the other hand, the Managing Director would normally be authorised to enter into contracts on behalf of A over the full spectrum of A's activities.

Three principal types of agents' authority are often described as follows.

1   *Actual authority*   if a principal expressly authorises an agent to undertake some work on its behalf, that agent is said to have actual authority.
2   *Usual authority*   a principal cannot seek to avoid his or her obligations under a contract on the grounds that the agent which made the contract was not actually authorised if it is usual for a person in that position to be authorised to that degree. The classic example is that of the managing director, who is usually authorised to enter into contracts in every field of that company's activities.
3   *Ostensible or apparent authority*   when a principal puts another forward in circumstances where it appears that that other has the requisite authority, that other may bind the principal even though he has no actual authority or someone of his status would not normally have that degree of authority (i.e. he has no usual authority). This happens because the principal has clothed him with ostensible or apparent authority.

Common examples of agents employed in the construction industry for whom questions of authority are often raised include site agents and the certifier.

Site agents

A site agent is usually the contractor's agent on the site (he will normally be called the project manager on a major project). His usual authority will normally extend to purchases of site materials, commissioning site services and other things incidental to the site and the detailed construction. He will not normally be authorised to agree alterations to the contract, although his company may clothe him with such actual authority.

The certifier
Persons such as the engineer under the ICE Contract, the architect under the JCT Contract and the supervising officer under the GC Works contract have certifying roles under those contracts and also act in many functions as the employer's agent. The scope of the certifier's authority is usually set out clearly in the contract conditions. Normally he or she will, under the terms of the contract, have authority to order variations to the works in specified circumstances. But, generally speaking, engineers, architects and other certifiers will not be authorised to vary a contract on behalf of their clients. For example, in *Toepfer v Warinco* [1978] 2 Ll Rep 569 at 577 Mr Justice Brandon said: 'it is well-established that an architect or engineer has no implied authority from the building owner by whom he is employed to vary or waive the terms of a building contract'. Some construction contracts deal specifically with the authority of the certifier. For instance Clause 2(i)(c) of the ICE 6th Edition Contract provides: 'Except as expressly stated in the Contract, the Engineer shall have no authority to amend the Terms and Conditions of the Contract nor to relieve the Contractor of any of his obligations under the Contract'.

2.5   Limitation periods at law

2.5.1   General

The period during which aggrieved parties may sue for their damage is known as the 'limitation period'. When this has expired, aggrieved parties may no longer enforce their rights by legal action except in cases involving fraud by the potential defendant. The limitation period runs from the time at which the 'cause of action' arises and the rule is that the appropriate proceedings, which, in the case of High Court litigation means the issue of the Writ from the Registry, must commence before the limitation period expires.

2.5.2   Limitation in civil actions

For civil law actions, limitation periods are imposed by the Limitation Act 1980. The two types of actions most commonly used in construction law, based respectively on breaches of contract and on duties arising under the law of tort, each have periods of limitation of six years from the point in time at which a cause of action arises. The rule is modified in one important case, namely contracts 'under seal'. A contract under seal is one made with special formalities; the rules applicable for this are discussed in Section 2.5.3.

There is, however, a significant difference between tort and contract limitation which stems from the definition of the 'cause of action' in each case. For contracts, the cause of action arises at the time of the breach. In the case of a construction contract this means the time at which, under the contract, the contractor is no longer entitled to remedy the defective work: see Section 2.5.3. In the case of a consultancy contract the breach occurs at the last time when the defective work can reasonably be rectified (since the consultant has a continuing duty to remedy his errors while it is possible for him to do so). In tort, however, the cause of action normally does not accrue until some damage occurs. If the damage takes five years to manifest itself then the limitation for the action in negligence is, for practical purposes, five years longer.

Until 1988, the longer effective limitation period available in tort was extremely important in construction law since defects often take several years to come to light and the contractual limitation period has often expired before the damage is fully understood. In 1988, however, in *D&F Estates v The Church Commissioners* [1989] AC 177, the House of Lords decided, in effect, that defects in buildings were not to be the subject of tortious actions unless physical damage occurred to property other than the building itself. Since the most important category of claim was for damage to the building itself, the law of tort and its advantageous limitation period became less important.

Despite this change in the law there is still one area where the possibility of a longer limitation period in tort than in contract is still of considerable importance; that is when the recommendations of a professional person result in loss. In Chapters 16 and 18 it will be seen that professional people may often be liable in the tort of negligence for statements they make in the course of their professional activities. If they make a statement to their client (with whom they have a contract), which results in loss for their client, they may thereby incur simultaneous contractual and tortious liabilities. The law is unclear in such a case as to whether the client may pursue parallel actions in contract and tort and hence, in effect, take advantage of the longer limitation period available in tort. In the recent High Court case of *Nitrigin Eireann Teoranta v Inco Alloys Ltd* [1991] 2 All ER 854, Mr Justice May refused to consider an argument that a tortious remedy was unavailable simply because a contract existed. Such a matter, he said, could only be decided by the House of Lords. Nonetheless, general principles expounded by the courts in recent years suggest that when a contract exists then any remedy sought should be sought under that contract alone. For example, in *Tai Hing Cotton Mill v Liu Chong Haing Bank* [1986] AC 80 at 107, the Privy Council said

> Their Lordships do not believe that there is anything to the advantage of the law's development in searching for a liability in tort where the parties are in a contractual relationship. This is particularly so in commercial relationships. ... their Lordships believe it to be correct in principle and necessary for avoidance of confusion in the law to adhere to the contractual analysis: on principle because it is a relationship in which the parties have, subject to a few exceptions, the right to determine their obligations to each other, and for the avoidance of confusion because different consequences do follow according to whether liability arises from contract or tort, e.g. in the limitation of action. Their Lordships do not, however, accept that the parties' mutual obligations in tort can be greater than those to be found expressly or by necessary implication in their contract.

However, when the contractual obligation involves the provision of advice or of services where the client relies upon the skill of a professional, it is thought that that professional may still owe a concurrent and co-extensive duty in contract and negligence. For example, in *Midland Bank Trust Co v Hett, Stubbs & Kemp* [1979] Ch 384, Mr Justice Oliver held that a co-extensive contractual and tortious relationship could exist. In that case a solicitor who had failed to exercise proper care in handling some papers (registering an option on a farm purchase) was held liable more than six years after the negligent act which constituted the breach of contract. The above quoted words of the Privy Council are not, in legal theory, capable of overturning the rule developed in *Midland Bank* and so professional people whose negligent work causes their client a loss may well be subject to parallel actions in both contract and tort and therefore be exposed to the longer limitation period offered by the law of tort (negligence).

The fact that the rules relating to the limitation period when a professional is involved are different from other situations seems difficult in principle but appears to be the law. This matter will need reconsideration in the light of the Privy Council decision in *Tai Hing Cotton Mill*.

2.5.3 Particular aspects of the law relating to limitation

Contracts under seal
Parties may enter into an agreement with special formalities known as a contract 'under seal', also called a 'deed'. In former times it was necessary for such a contract to be sealed with wax, hence the name. The requirements of the law at present are less exacting. A document is a deed if it makes it clear on its face that it is intended to be a deed and complies with Section 1 of the Law of Property (Miscellaneous Provisions) Act 1989. In the case of an individual making the deed, that person must sign the document, have it witnessed and show by his or her conduct that the person intends to be bound (this last aspect is known, somewhat confusingly, as 'delivery'). If a company makes a deed, two directors or one director and the secretary must sign it on behalf of the company. Seals in the sense of a wax seal or indenting seal are no longer required.

The main effect of having a contract under seal is that the limitation period runs for twelve years rather than six. In construction the importance of this derives from the fact that many defects which occur in buildings take years to manifest themselves; any investigation into the causes of a defect will also take time. The brevity of a six-year period causes many sound claims for defective design and construction to be unenforceable. Therefore an additional six years on the limitation period is of considerable benefit to employers and those who have rights under building contracts. In terms of practical advice, employers under building contracts should generally seek to have their construction contracts made under seal, while contractors should seek to avoid this.

Fraud and concealment
Section 32 of the Limitation Act 1980 provides that where the defendant has been fraudulent, and this has affected the plaintiff's knowledge of his or her right to make a claim against the defendant, the period of

limitation does not run until the plaintiff has, or could reasonably have had, knowledge of his or her cause of action. Thus in *Gray v T P Bennett & Son* [1987] 43 BLR 63 the contractor, in breach of his contract, cut back concrete outstands designed to support brickwork; this was deliberately concealed from the architect, engineer and clerk of works. Accordingly, the limitation period did not begin to run until the brickwork began to move thereby indicating that there was a defect in the support system. In order for Section 32 to operate, however, the defendant must have a 'guilty conscience'; if the concealment results from mere incompetence or a mistake on his or her part the normal limitation rules apply.

The point in time at which a cause of action arises when the claim is based on the contractor's defective work
The question of when the breach of contract occurs and, hence, the time from when the limitation period runs, causes some difficulty in construction contracts because of their long duration. Suppose, for instance, that a contractor on a very large project installs a beam on 1 January 1980 and completes the project on 1 January 1986; if the employer takes possession on 2 January 1986 and immediately notices that the beam is defective, is he prevented from suing the contractor for the defective beam since it is more than six years since the installation? Lord Diplock, in *P and M Kaye v Hosier & Dickinson Ltd* [1972] 1 All ER 121, developed the idea of the 'temporary disconformity' which suggests that where the party who has performed the defective work remains in a position where he may rectify it, for example if he is a contractor who continues to have possession of the site, the defect is not automatically to be treated as a breach. Rather, it is to be treated as a disconformity, but one which the employer may expect to have rectified before the contractor hands over possession to the employer; hence the qualification 'temporary'. The breach then consists in the contractor giving possession to the employer without rectifying the defect. Accordingly, in the example of the defective beam, it would appear that the breach occurred at the beginning of 1986 so that the owner has until the end of 1991 to sue. This temporary disconformity idea has received some criticism and subsequent courts have not always followed it in the format proposed by Lord Diplock. In *Antino v Epping Forest District Council* 53 BLR 56, for instance, in the context of a criminal action for breach of the Building Regulations, it was held that a breach of the Building Regulations could occur before the overall works were complete (see Section 3.3).

The fifteen-year longstop for negligence actions
The Latent Damage Act 1986 provides that no negligence claim may be brought more than fifteen years after the breach of duty. The protection offered by this rule is likely, on occasions, to be of value to professionals.

2.6   Sources of information in construction law

The principal sources of law are statutes, European legislation and the decisions in contested cases. The question addressed in this section is how an individual may come to know what the law is.

2.6.1 Primary sources

Statutes are published by Her Majesty's Stationery Office (HMSO) and copies of all statutes are available at HMSO outlets. In practice, lawyers obtain information on statutes from a series known as Halsbury's Statutes in which statutes are arranged in subject order and which is frequently updated by supplementary volumes. Copies of European legislation may also be obtained through HMSO outlets.

The judgments from contested cases are reported in a variety of publications. A variety of series of general law reports are published. When citing a case (that is when referring to it as authority for a legal proposition), it is usual to provide its abbreviated citation reference, indicated for each series in parentheses below. The important general series of case reports include the official series, a set being produced annually for each division of the Supreme Court (QB for Queen's Bench Division, Ch for the Chancery Division and AC for appeal cases heard in the Privy Council and House of Lords). A number of important unofficial series are also published including the Weekly Law Reports (WLR), the All England Law Reports (All ER) and The Times Law Reports (which are normally abridged).

While construction lawyers frequently consult these general series of reports, they also tend to rely heavily on specialist series. These include specialist construction law series such as the Building Law Reports (BLR), the Construction Law Reports (Con LR), the cases in the *Construction Law Journal* (*Constr LJ*) and those in the *Construction Industry Law Letter* (*CILL*) as well as more general commercial law series such as Lloyd's Reports (Ll Rep).

2.6.2 Secondary sources

In addition to the primary sources many books and articles have been published which provide opinions on and analysis of the law. The two leading practitioners' general textbooks are *Keating's Building Contracts* (5th edition by Sir Anthony May, 1991) and *Hudson's Building Contracts* (10th edition edited by Ian Duncan Wallace QC, 1970: a new edition is expected shortly). In legal theory these texts should not be cited as authority on the law but they are regularly used in court 'as strong evidence of the law'; which often amounts to much the same thing in practice. Less detailed texts are also available for a more general readership including *Construction Law* by John Uff QC (5th edition, 1991).

Articles on recent developments in the law are also published in the *Construction Law Journal*, the *Construction Industry Law Letter* and the *International Construction Law Review*. Articles of interest to construction lawyers are also published in the wider legal press.

Details of the books and articles referred to here and elsewhere in the book can be found listed in the bibliography, together with details of additional texts and materials of potential value to the reader.

2.6.3 Information on standard form contracts

In Chapter 4 it will be seen that standard form contracts (i.e. standard printed conditions of contract worded so that they are applicable to a wide range of contractual situations) are widely used in the construction industry. Copies of all the commonly used standard domestic forms (i.e. for use in the UK) are published in one collection in *Emden's Construction Law* together with some commentary. Much practical construction law involves applying the terms of contract and in order to do this the meanings of the terms have to be determined. Detailed commentaries on these standard forms are available in order to assist with this. They show how the terms of the contract interrelate with one another and offer advice on the best approach to a variety of contractual problems. The best known examples are Max Abrahamson's book *Engineering Law,* which is a commentary on the Institution of Civil Engineers (ICE) contract, and Ian Duncan Wallace QC's commentaries on a variety of standard form contracts. Many general construction law texts also contain commentaries. Keating and Uff both deal with the standard building (JCT) contract and the standard civil engineering (ICE) contract. The reader who wishes to buy a commentary of a particular construction contract should be careful to check that the commentary deals with the correct edition.

A review of statutory provisions affecting construction work

3.1 Introduction

In Chapter 2 it was seen that the highest ranking source of English law is the legislation passed by Parliament. A large number of statutes are passed each year. These tend to be concerned with matters of general public importance. Therefore, it is not surprising that a number of aspects of construction which affect the public, or are of general importance, are subject to statutory requirements. Among the most important of these requirements are

- the requirement that planning permission be obtained before any development occurs
- the requirement that any building work complies with the Building Regulations
- the requirement that any work performed is undertaken in conformity with the safety legislation
- the requirement that any work performed is undertaken in conformity with the pollution control legislation.

As well as the legislation relating to the above topics, a large number of other statutes are of importance in particular instances. For example, works involving highways must be undertaken in full compliance with the requirements of the Highways Act 1980 and the New Roads and Street Works Act 1991; the destructive power of water impounded in reservoirs means that special responsibilities are laid upon 'supervising engineers' by the Reservoirs Act 1975. In addition, many statutes such as those relating to companies (for example, the Companies Acts 1985 and 1989 and the Insolvency Act 1986) and taxation (for example, the Finance Acts passed each year) are of great practical importance in the construction industry. They are, however, important in all spheres of commerce and hence will not be dealt with here.

In this chapter planning law and the Building Regulations will be briefly covered. Safety and pollution control legislation will be merely touched upon as will European legislation, which is becoming increasingly important in the construction industry. It should, however, be stressed that all these areas of law are highly technical and the short exposition presented below cannot hope to convey fully the detailed requirements for any given situation.

3.2 Planning permission

3.2.1 Development and the need to obtain planning permission

In the UK the general rule concerning any new development work is that it is disallowed unless the relevant planning permission is obtained. This places the obligation on the developer to obtain the relevant permission unless legislation is in place which automatically grants the permission. If required, planning permission must be obtained from the relevant planning authority. In the case of a local development the planning authority is the local/district council. For major schemes the county councils are the planning authorities. If the local authority refuses to grant planning permission there is an automatic right of appeal to the Secretary of State for the Environment.

The same procedures are followed in obtaining planning permission whether the developer is a major developer or a householder seeking to extend his or her house. The only exceptions are where the developer is authorised by statute to undertake the development.

The term 'development' is defined in Section 55 of the Town and Country Planning Act 1990 as 'the carrying out of building, engineering, mining or other operations in, on, over or under land, or the making of any material change in the use of any buildings or other land.'

Section 336 defines terms such as 'building' and 'land' and, in general, it may be said that all works of construction except the most minor do-it-yourself tasks involve 'development' according to this definition. However, Section 55 makes a number of significant exceptions. For example, it states that works which do not materially affect the external appearance of a building and works of highway maintenance do not constitute development.

The 1990 Act itself grants planning permissions in certain instances so that there is no need to make an application to the local planning authority. These situations are set out in a Development Order made by the Secretary of State, the current one being the Town and County Planning General Development Order 1988 (SI 1813). The classes of currently permitted development include certain modifications to the curtilage of dwelling houses and certain works by local authorities and statutory undertakers.

3.2.2 Applications for planning permission and appeals

If planning permission is required, as it will be for most commercial projects, an application is made to the local planning authority. The authority will consider the application with due regard to the interests and amenities of the locality and the community and, in particular, will consider the application in the light of the 'Development Plan', a document which the local authority produces from time to time stating its aims and ambitions relating to development generally in the locality.

If planning permission is granted it may be subject to conditions or for a limited duration. Work on the project must then normally commence within five years or else the permission lapses. The permission is part of the right over the land and, upon the sale or other disposition of the land, the permission passes to the purchaser.

If planning permission is refused or is subject to conditions which the applicant feels are unnecessary, the applicant may make an appeal to the Secretary of State within six months. In such a case the Secretary of State may direct that an inquiry is heard before an inspector so that representations may be heard from local people.

3.2.3 Control

Development without permission or in contravention of conditions imposed in the permission will normally result in the local planning authority serving an enforcement notice (Section 172). The authority need not serve such a notice; but if they wish to do so they need normally to serve it within four years of the works being constructed. The notice will state the grounds of complaint, the steps required for their rectification and the period in which the offending developer has to comply. The steps required may include demolition.

An appeal against an enforcement notice (which includes an implied application for planning permission) may be made to the Secretary of State. It is an offence under the criminal law to refuse to comply with an enforcement order.

3.3 Compliance with the Building Regulations

In order to secure the health and safety of people in buildings, and others who may be affected by them, a series of statutes has been enacted whereby Building Regulations have been published which are enforced by local authority inspectors. All buildings which are constructed must comply with the current Building Regulations. The current legislation in this field is the Building Act 1984. This statute is essentially in the same form as its predecessors such as the Public Health Act 1936, although it introduces a number of novelties including the designation of 'Approved Inspectors'; these are private individuals who may perform building control functions traditionally reserved to the local authorities. The current Building Regulations (1991) are given the force of law by Section 1 of the Building Act.

Historically, building control in London has been governed by separate rules from the rest of Britain. However, the system in London is now being brought into line with the provisions of the general legislation.

Two principal points are raised by the building control regulations: first, the liability of the building control officials for failures to act competently, and second, the criminal liability of those who perform work which fails to comply.

3.3.1 Liability of the building control inspectors

The obligations of the building control inspectors are considered in general terms in *Murphy v Brentwood* [1990] 3 WLR 414 (discussed in Chapter 18) and in the context of an Approved Inspector in *NHBC Building Control Services Ltd v Sandwell Borough Council* 50 BLR 101. *Murphy v Brentwood* overturned the House of Lords' earlier decision in *Anns v London Borough of Merton* [1978] AC 728 that a local authority in the exercise of its building control function was liable in negligence for economic losses suffered if it failed to undertake that function properly.

3.3.2 Criminal liability

Section 35 of the Building Act 1984 provides

> If a person contravenes any provision contained in building regulations he is liable on summary conviction to a fine not exceeding level 5 on the standard scale and to a further fine not exceeding £50 for each day on which the default continues after he is convicted.

In *Antino v Epping Forest District Council* 53 BLR 56, it was held that the builder (and presumably the culpable designer, developer, etc.) was guilty of an offence in relation to each and every element of the work at the point in time at which they purported to finish such element of work. The court said

> In our judgment building works, unless very confined in scope, are not to be regarded as an indivisible whole for the purpose of the Regulations. A part or parts of the building works may be regarded as having been carried out when the builder purports to have completed them. This will no doubt be the case in respect of every part of the works when practical completion stage is reached. But the builder will also purport to have carried out any part of the works when that part is complete and the builder is proved to have no intention of remedying such defects in that part as contravene the Regulations.

3.4 Miscellaneous legislation affecting construction

3.4.1 The safety legislation

Work, whether or not it be construction work, must be undertaken in conformity with the safety legislation. In addition to general rules concerning safety, detailed safety regulations are laid down specifically for various industries and processes including the construction industry and many of the operations which are carried out as part of construction. Recently, European directives have been enacted which affect the safety precautions which must be undertaken in connection with construction. However, despite the large volume of rules and regulations in force the construction industry has always had and continues to maintain an appalling record of deaths and reportable injuries.

The health and safety legislation which is applicable to construction work consists of two principal statutes and a large amount of subordinate legislation made under the power of the principal statutes, appearing as the Construction Regulations and other published regulations. The two principal statutes are the Factories Act 1961 (for the purposes of which, construction sites are to be treated as notional factories) and the Health and Safety at Work etc. Act 1974.

Historically, health and safety at work legislation has developed piecemeal with legislation being passed to cover particular industries or situations or classes of worker. The rules laid down were not consistent. This situation caused disquiet among workers' organisations and in 1970 matters came to a head when a Private Member's Bill was introduced into the House of Commons aimed at including workers in implementing safety prevention policy; the Bill was withdrawn when a committee chaired by Lord Robens was set up to report generally on health and safety at work. The committee reported in 1972; its principal recommendation was that the mass of existing legislation be replaced by a single statute applying to all persons at work, which statute would be expressed in simple, easily understood rules and with the emphasis being placed on safe systems of work rather than upon technical standards. The result was the Health and Safety at Work etc. Act 1974. Although the intention was to replace all previous legislation with this statute, the Factories Act 1961 continues in force and it is under this latter legislation that many of the most important regulations which have a direct bearing on the construction industry have been made.

In the context of safety, the Occupiers' Liability Acts 1957 and 1984 also merit a mention. These statutes make all those who are in occupation of any land, including building sites, liable to take reasonable care to ensure the safety of those who come onto the land. If reasonable care is not taken and damage ensues, those occupying land will be liable for injuries sustained by those who are lawfully on the site and to some extent for trespassers. The occupiers of a building site will normally include both the employer and the main contractor and any other person who has control over that part of the site where the damage occurs.

3.4.2 Environmental control legislation

A number of statutes control noise and set limits on other pollution. This legislation includes the Public Health Act 1936, the Control of Pollution Act 1974 (which provides a local authority with power to control noise and proposed methods of working on site) and the Environmental Protection Act 1990. An example of the operation of the 1974 Act is to be found in *City of London Corporation v Bovis Construction Ltd* 49 BLR 1.

3.4.3 European legislation

Many European Directives have recently been proposed, published or enacted as part of the European Community's drive to create a Single Market. Such a market requires that the internal rules of each member state which may affect the competitiveness of the people in that state relative to people from other states are harmonised. Construction, which is one of the largest players in the European economy, has featured significantly in these proposals and changes.

Some of the Directives which have been issued have been enacted as UK statutes (e.g. the Consumer Protection Act 1987). In addition Conventions signed by EC members have been enacted (e.g. Contracts (Applicable Law) Act 1990). However, as the creation of a Single Market approaches, the rate of change is increasing and new developments are occurring all the time. Brief notes on the legislation which has already been passed and on that which is proposed in the near future are given in the following sections. The reader should appreciate, however, that at the present time (mid-1992) a large number of developments are currently underway and the account presented is necessarily incomplete.

Generally applicable European laws

The applicable law of the contract   Whenever the contractual situation involves more than one country the question of which country's laws govern the contract arises. English law has developed a series of rules to deal with this problem. However, the Contracts (Applicable Law) Act 1990, enacted as a result of a Community treaty, the Rome Convention 1980, has now superseded English law; the rules relating to the applicable law of the contract are dealt with in detail in Chapter 27.

Consumer protection law   As a result of a Community Directive each member state was required to enact consumer protection legislation with specific consumer protection rules. The UK enacted the Consumer Protection Act 1987, which is drafted widely enough to cover domestic house construction.

European legislation closely connected with the construction industry

Public construction procurement   Rules are currently being established to ensure that companies from all member states will have an equal opportunity to contract for the construction, maintenance, etc. of major public works in all other member states.

Construction products   A Directive published at the end of 1988 requires member states to enact legislation dealing with the safety of construction and the harmonisation of construction product specifications. These Construction Products Regulations became law in the UK in 1991.

Harmonised liability laws   It has been accepted in principle by the European Parliament that the laws relating to the liabilities of construction professionals, construction companies and other parties in the construction industry should be 'harmonised' across the Community. The Community is currently studying the ways in which this may be achieved.

Safety   New Directives are being brought into effect which will require more active consideration of safety at all stages of construction, from design to completion.

Part 2

Contracts

4

An introduction to contracts in the construction industry

4.1 General

The vast majority of construction work and work ancillary to construction, such as the design of construction works and the provision of construction advice, is performed under contract. The small amount of work which is undertaken in the absence of a contract is usually so conducted either in the expectation that a contract will at some stage come into existence (but where none, in fact, eventuates) or alternatively in the belief that a contract is already in existence (but none actually exists).

The term 'contractor', which is in common use in the construction industry to describe the party who actually constructs the project works, tends to focus attention on the employer–contractor relationship. But normally all the subcontractors and suppliers will be operating under contract as well. Further, it is not only the physical building work which is performed under contract; consultants will also normally be appointed under contract. In addition, there may be a series of additional contractual obligations existing within the construction setting, known as direct warranties. These are dealt with in Section 13.2.3.

In this book the term 'construction contract' means a contract in which the physical construction of the works is the principal obligation. This definition excludes contracts made with advisers or consultants which are termed 'consultancy contracts' in this book and are governed, in some respects, by different principles. The basic rules of contract law apply to both construction and consultancy contracts and these basic rules are explained in Chapters 5 (formation of contracts), 6 (contract terms) and 7 (ending of contracts).

4.2 Subcontracts

One important and very common aspect of construction contracts, though not of consultancy contracts, is the use of subcontractors to carry out parts of the work. The typical scheme will entail the employer letting the work to a main contractor who in turn sublets it to a subcontractor.

A subcontract is as much a contract as is the main contract and is subject to exactly the same requirements as any other contract. The prefix 'sub-' does not refer to any legal inferiority; it merely denotes its position in a contractual chain.

Subcontracts are of considerable significance in the construction industry. They are specifically dealt with in Chapter 13. However, the contents of the present chapter are equally relevant to subcontracts as they are to main contracts.

4.3 The function of contracts

A contract is, in broad terms, a device whereby rights and obligations are created between two or more persons, namely the parties to the contract, and a basis for the enforcement of those rights. On a more detailed level, the contract will

- provide statements and definitions relating to the scope of the work to be undertaken, the standard of work required, the payment terms, the time in which work should take place and other similar considerations.
- provide mechanisms to allow the work to be controlled and regulated if a variety of events should occur. For instance, if there is a possibility that the employer may wish to vary the design or to alter the construction programme, the parties may write into their contract what the position is to be concerning additional payments and extensions of time for completion of the work.
- provide a statement concerning the risks which each party assumes under the contract. Construction is inherently very risky and significant cost and time overruns are frequent. For instance, poor ground conditions often cause additional costs and time to be expended; it is important, therefore, in any contract which features construction in the ground that the contract should state who is to bear the risk of these overruns in cost and time.

4.3.1 The general rule concerning contracts

The English law of contract was developed mainly during the nineteenth century when the prevalent philosophy was economic liberalism. It was fashionable, at that time, to allow complete freedom of contract and moral justification for this attitude was provided by the writings of Adam Smith and other economists. The result is a law of contract in which the golden rule is: 'whatever the parties have agreed, in circumstances where it is clear that they intended the agreement to bind them, the law will enforce that agreement through the courts'. This rule implies that the parties to a construction contract are entirely at liberty to choose whatever terms and obligations they wish to govern their agreement and, indeed, with a few minor exceptions, this provides a satisfactory summary of the situation. The exceptions mentioned are of little consequence in commercial construction or consultancy contracts and relate principally to dealings with consumers and employment contracts: however, see the effect of the Unfair Contract Terms Act 1977 discussed in Section 24.3.2.

4.3.2 Classification of construction contracts

The term 'construction contract' in this book means a contract under which the works are to be constructed. These are, of course, not the only contracts which arise during the construction process; many consultants (e.g. designers, engineers, architects and surveyors) will be appointed under contract. These consultancy agreements will be considered in Chapter 16.

Since the parties are free to contract on whatever commercial basis they wish, and because the construction scenarios that can be conceived are infinitely various, it is not surprising that a wide range of contractual arrangements and contract types have been developed and are currently in use in the construction industry. There are a number of ways in which they may be categorised; the following three methods of classification are suggested. Each focuses on a different aspect of the employer–contractor relationship.

Classification of contracts according to the scope of the contractor's obligations

Build-only contracts   These are the construction contracts which have, traditionally, been used in the industry. The contractor is given the detailed drawings and specifications and must build exactly what is shown. He assumes no responsibility for the design of the works.

Design and build contracts   Here the contractor is engaged not only to construct the works but also to design them. The contract will normally include a statement of the employer's requirements; but providing the contractor stays within these requirements he can design and build according to his own wishes. The advantage of this arrangement for the employer is that a single party, namely the contractor, carries out the work whereas in the traditional arrangement the design and the construction are separated. Accordingly, under a design and build contract there is only one person from whom to seek redress if the work is badly done. This not only presents an administrative advantage but also helps the employer to ensure that the finished product will be fit for its purpose (see Section 11.2.5). From the contractor's point of view the design and build method is attractive because the contractor can design the works for ease of construction; this not only facilitates construction but also often produces a cheaper price for the employer because of the enhanced efficiency.

Design, build, operate and transfer   In many situations, particularly where the project relates to high technology plants or projects in less developed countries, it is useful for the contractor to provide staff who will operate the plant for a specified period after the completion of construction during which skills relating to the running of the works are transferred to the local management and labour force. This enables them to operate the plant without a long-term dependency on a foreign company's or nation's technological expertise.

Finance, design and build, operate and transfer   In this contract arrangement the contractor acts essentially as a developer. Normally, the contract will include a licence or a concession for the contractor to operate a piece of infrastructure and to charge tolls or other rates in order to recover his initial capital expenditure and to make a profit. This form of contract is becoming increasingly popular. Recent examples include the Channel Tunnel and the new Dartford and Severn crossings.

Classification of contracts according to the method of remuneration
See Section 9.3 for a discussion of the effect of the classification of the contract on the price payable for the work.

Lump sum contracts   Here the contractor is paid a fixed price for a fixed piece of work. There will usually be provisions in the contract whereby the employer can include variations to the works and here the contractor will be paid an additional or reduced sum relative to the original fixed contract sum depending on the extent to which the variations comprise an increase or decrease in the work to be done. Often a 'bill of quantities' or a 'schedule of rates' will be included in the contract for the purpose of valuing variations but their inclusion in this form of contract should be contrasted with re-measurement contracts (described below) where the bill/schedule forms the fundamental basis for payment of all monies whether they relate to the original scope of works or variations.
    Lump sum contracts are often used

- where the extent of the work is reasonably clear (e.g. standard buildings constructed from readily available materials using conventional techniques).
- where the employer wishes to be reasonably sure of the price in advance of construction. In some cases the employer wishes to construct the works as cheaply as possible. In others he is prepared to pay a premium to ensure that his maximum financial obligation is sensibly defined in advance. This latter policy is particularly prevalent amongst employers such as domestic home-owners and small institutions and companies where any price changes could cause financial embarrassment, and in these cases a lump sum approach has advantages.
- where the employer wishes to use the design-build format it is usual to agree to a lump sum remuneration system. This makes sense because the essence of the design and build arrangement is that the contractor will use all his skill to produce the most efficient outcome and the best incentive for this is a lump sum contract.

If the circumstances outlined in these three points are present, then a lump sum arrangement is likely to be appropriate. If the converse circumstances obtain, then, of course, this suggests that other forms of remuneration should be used. Whenever works are likely to provide unexpected surprises (e.g. where a significant element of the works is to be executed below ground level) lump sum contracts generally require contractors to accept a greater risk than, say, a measurement or cost-plus contract. Also, large institutions are often concerned with the keenest out-turn price rather than with certainty of price and these employers will usually adopt a re-measure or cost-plus system of remuneration which are described below.

Re-measurement (or admeasurement or measurement) contracts   Here the contract refers to rates given in terms of money per unit of work for work which falls into a particular classification. The classifications may be provided by simple descriptions such as 'excavate soil for foundations' or the work may be closely defined by reference to a 'method of measurement'. In the example just given, 'excavate soil for foundations', it is not clear from the description whether the rate is to include for removing the excavated soil from the site or for supporting the sides of the excavation or for preparing the excavated surfaces to accept the concrete which will form the foundations; one of the functions of a method of measurement is to clarify the scope of standard descriptions.

During the currency of the project the total units of work in each classification is measured at intervals and payment is made in accordance with the measured value (the measurement may be a physical measurement on site or calculations from drawings showing the progress of the works). Usually the tendering process is conducted on the basis of anticipated quantities of work, thus producing what is normally referred to as the 'tender estimate'. But the 'contract price', that is the actual value of the contract as it will turn out, is unknown at the outset because the actual quantities of work are unknown until the project is complete and the measurement process has been finalised.

A re-measurement contract requires a 'schedule of rates' or 'bill of quantities' to be drawn up. These documents contain lists of agreed prices. In the case of a bill of quantities there is also a list of quantities. It is usually a term of the contract that if the quantities change significantly from those in the bill then those rates are rendered inapplicable and the certifier or other named person will need to 're-rate', that is to determine a new rate. In the case of a schedule of rates contract, a list of quantities is not usually provided. Schedule of rates contracts are typically used for contracts where the scope of the work is unknown in advance, such as in the case for maintenance contracts in which a contractor agrees to undertake such maintenance as will become necessary in a particular area during a specified time.

Cost-plus contracts   Here the contractor is reimbursed for all his or her reasonable expenses and outgoings in connection with the scheme together with an additional sum representing the contractor's fee. This scheme of remuneration presents few risks for the contractor and, in addition, makes the employer vulnerable to cost and time overruns. Consequently a variety of techniques have been developed to deal with this and to put the employer into a more protected position. One solution is the use of 'target contracts' whereby there is a target out-turn price and a target completion date. If the contractor exceeds the cost or time target he pays a penalty on his fee. If he performs the work at a keener price or faster than the target he receives a bonus on his fee. This induces the contractor to work as efficiently as possible. However, the employer must employ his or her own staff to ensure that quality is not compromised by the contractor's enthusiasm to achieve an efficient outcome.

Classification of construction contracts according to the project organisation
Some contracts are drafted to operate within a particular project organisation scheme. Contracts and subcontracts and, if appropriate, direct warranties within this scheme are often co-ordinated (or 'harmonised') so that the responsibilities of all the parties are explicitly set out and the risks borne by each are clearly defined. Examples of the various organisation types commonly employed are management contracting and construction management.

Management contracting   This involves the entirety of the work being let to the 'management contractor' who then subcontracts all of it to 'trade contractors'. The management contractor's role is to manage the project on behalf of the employer rather than to construct the works even though the management contractor's position *vis-à-vis* the employer is, in purely contractual terms, similar to that of a contractor under a traditional construction contract. In order to promote efficient management by the management contractor a risk-sharing arrangement may be operated; a target price cost-plus remuneration scheme is a typical method of achieving this.

Construction management   Here the employer employs the contractor who will construct the works directly but the work is controlled by a specialist construction management company, also directly employed by the employer. This is similar in basic arrangement to the traditional construction system where a certifier appointed by the employer administers the contract. When a construction management team is employed, however, more than one contractor is often employed by the employer, the contractual and management systems tend to be significantly more sophisticated and there will often be a much greater interventionist coordinating role for the construction manager than for the typical certifier under a traditional construction contract.

4.3.3   Standard form construction contracts

The Banwell recommendations
In 1964 Sir Harold Banwell chaired a committee which produced a report entitled *The Placing and Management of Contracts for Building and Civil Engineering Work* (HMSO 1964). One of the principal recommendations of the Banwell Report was that

> A common form of contract for all construction work, covering England, Scotland and Wales, is both desirable and practicable. As a first step, the differences which appear in the various standard conditions for building work and civil engineering work respectively should be examined by all those concerned, including government departments, in order to produce one set of standard conditions for each. The special requirements of Scottish law or

of public bodies should be met by agreed additions or alternatives rather than by separate sets of conditions. Once this has been achieved, a joint form for all construction work should be negotiated.

In other words there should, eventually, be just one standard form contract covering the whole of the construction industry. This recommendation has some merit but it has been all but ignored by the industry and a plethora of standard forms are currently in use. The reason for this is that different employers and, indeed, different contractors, have a wide range of views on the proper approach to construction and risk-sharing during the construction process. Many contractors now favour design and build contract obligations which give them additional freedoms to organise and plan the works; but such obligations are incompatible with the traditional view which places the independent architect or engineer as the director of construction. These incompatibilities and the wide range of views on the most appropriate way to conduct construction will ensure that a diversity of standard forms continues to be used.

The advantages of standard form contracts
Many types of contracts are produced as standard forms by a wide variety of organisations. There are clear advantages in using standard form contracts, rather than drafting one for an individual project (often known as 'home-drafted contracts'). These include

1   *Cost*   it is very expensive to draft a contract specifically for a project; in certain circumstances it becomes economic to do so when a contract is unusual, but not normally in the case of fairly standard projects.
2   *Contractor's confidence*   many contractors are uneasy about signing home-drafted contracts: it involves them in significant time wasting and legal expenses to have it checked thoroughly.
3   *Errors*   the best drafted documents contain errors and ambiguities. By using a standard form, the document will at least have been considered by a panel of senior professionals and hence be less prone to error. Also court decisions and articles on standard form clauses help to clarify any difficulties.

Alteration and amendments to standard form contracts
It is very unusual for parties to contract on the basis of an unamended standard form. The usual practice is to use the printed form as a basic 'template' and to add, omit, substitute or revise the clauses to suit the particular requirements of the parties (and principally the employer). In many instances, however, it is not a good idea to amend the standard forms, because however inept or unsuitable the existing clauses may be, there is a high risk that the new clauses will affect the overall scheme of the contract in ways which cannot readily be foreseen.

4.3.4   Typical components of construction contracts

There are a large number of standard form contracts available to those who promote construction work. They provide for a range of contract types, remuneration methods, organisation types and other factors. However, while many standard form contracts seem superficially to be very different from one another, they all tend to address the same questions; it is the way in which they deal with these questions that creates the difference. It is important to understand the principal issues dealt with by contracts since new contracts appear regularly and these can be evaluated only in terms of the way they deal with these issues. The following elements will be found in all standard form contracts whether they be for a small domestic house extension contract or a major international highway.

A statement of the work to be undertaken

The statement will describe the scope of the contractor's obligations. It will state whether he is to be responsible for the design of the works or whether he is to work to a design supplied to him. It will indicate the size, layout, and other features of the proposed works, usually by reference to documents or drawings. A 'specification' is also normally included which defines the materials to be used and the required quality of workmanship. Further, it may deal with ancillary matters such as who is to provide various facilities such as power supply, the reinstatement of the site and so on. The definition of the scope, standard and design obligations are likely to be much more detailed in the case of major commercial projects than for small domestic contracts and the scope is often set out in suites of drawings and lengthy specifications.

A statement concerning time and access obligations

The employer will wish to have the work undertaken at a convenient time and reasonably quickly. The time for completion and the time when the contractor may have access to the site generally or to specific areas of the site will be stated clearly, perhaps by reference to a drawing or programme. Furthermore, the employer will be keen to know exactly who will have access to the site and he might therefore require the contractor to give notice concerning personnel and subcontractor attendance on site, perhaps with some power to restrict entry to certain individuals.

A statement concerning the terms of payment

The contractor and employer will wish to ensure that the price (or a sensible mechanism for determining it) is agreed in advance. The contractor may also wish to receive advance payments and stage payments and, while advance payments are rare in the commercial sector, stage payments are usual. Frequently the contract will also provide for 'retention monies', sums to be deducted at the time of payment from the sum which will ultimately become due to the contractor under the contract; the retained monies will be used by the employer to ensure the contractor's full compliance with the contract and to cure any defects which occur in the works during a specified period after the ostensible completion of the works.

Variations

Often, during the currency of a project, additional work to that originally described in the contract appears worthwhile or necessary. For instance, the employer may wish to have additional works carried out in a part of the site where the contractor already has resources available. Or the contractor may, during the work, uncover conditions, such as corroded fabric in an existing building, in circumstances where it makes sense for the contractor to rectify the problem there and then rather than to get someone else in to do the work. Such variations to the work are extremely common in all construction and it is very useful to write a statement concerning variations into the contract stating the basis on which varied work is to be paid, and who is to value any varied work.

Insurance

The question of who is to insure the contractor's equipment which is left on the premises during the work and who is to insure against damage to other property, including the works themselves, which is suffered as a result of negligence, bad work or fire and other risks should be stated clearly in the contract.

Disputes

In the event that disputes arise it is often useful to write into the contract a scheme for dealing with those disputes. For instance, disagreements may, in the first place, be referred to a named individual for his or her decision; if this decision is unacceptable to the parties then the contract may contain an arbitration clause so that the matter may be dealt with by a private tribunal rather than taking the dispute to the courts.

Subcontractors

Significant subcontracting is used in major projects: in order to control this on behalf of the employer there tend to be provisions for allowing, forbidding and nominating subcontractors. Subcontractors can be divided into two classes, nominated and domestic subcontractors. Nominated subcontractors exist under certain forms of contracts where the employer is entitled to specify who the contractor employs as a subcontractor in certain circumstances. For instance, if the employer wishes the air-conditioning to be provided and installed by a particular manufacturer, he will (providing he is so entitled by the contract) make that manufacturer a nominated subcontractor. Most subcontractors are domestic subcontractors; they are chosen and taken on by the main contractor to suit the main contractor's convenience. Most contracts have a provision whereby if a contractor wishes to appoint a subcontractor he must obtain the permission of the employer; in some cases the employer has a right to object to any subcontractor without stating his reasons, in some cases the employer must not object unreasonably.

Others

Construction contracts also often contain a number of provisions relating to the following matters.

1   *Forfeiture clauses*   the employer may wish to have the right to terminate the construction project or the contractor's involvement in it in certain circumstances, such as when the contractor becomes insolvent.

2   *Property in plant clauses*   in order to safeguard his interests in the event
of the contractor failing to proceed with the work, the employer will
often insist on provisions in the contract whereby he, the employer,
will take a property right in the plant and material brought onto site
for the execution of the works.

3   *Bond obligations*   in order to provide security for the employer in the
event of a default by the contractor, the contract often requires the
contractor to obtain a 'bond' in favour of the employer. The bond is
an irrevocable undertaking by a third party (usually a bank) to pay
the employer a sum, which is stated in the bond, upon some specified
event. This event is typically related to an act of serious default by the
contractor, but the bond is usually worded so that the event which
triggers the payment is a 'call on the bond' by the employer, that is
a bona fide claim by the employer to be entitled to the bond money.
The bank, on the specified event, must pay the agreed sum; however,
the bank will be able to claim an indemnity from the contractor,
so that it is the contractor who ultimately pays. The bond device is
efficient for the employer in that the money is readily and quickly
obtainable from a solid financial institution and remains obtainable
even if the contractor goes into liquidation. The bond is a contract
which is collateral to the construction contract and as such is outside
the scope of this book. The Court of Appeal considered a number of
aspects of the law relating to bonds in *IE Contractors Ltd (formerly GKN
Contractors Ltd) v Lloyds Bank plc and Rafidain Bank* 51 BLR 1.

4.4   Consultancy contracts

Consultancy contracts tend to be less detailed than construction contracts.
Under a consultancy contract it is inappropriate for detailed specifications
and standards to be incorporated as would be the case in a construction
contract and the provisions relating to the contract requirements in
consultancy contracts are correspondingly shorter.

Typically the obligation under a consultancy contract is to perform the
consultancy work with reasonable skill and care and the principal function
of the documentation is to define those matters which fall within the scope
of the consultant's obligations and to set out the payment terms. As with
construction contracts, a number of standard form contracts are available
for consultancy works and the reasons for the use of standard forms
for consultancy work are identical to those suggested for their use in
construction contracts. Standard forms are issued by a variety of interested
institutions. The Association of Consulting Engineers, the Royal Institute
of British Architects and the Royal Institute of Chartered Surveyors
produce standard forms of appointment for engineers, architects and
surveyors respectively.

The rules relating to consultancy contracts are dealt with in detail in
Chapter 16.

5

Formation of contract

5.1 Introduction

5.1.1 The importance of the 'formation' question in construction

Most construction and construction-related work, such as the supply of construction services, construction advice, design services and materials, is performed under contract. The contract sets out the rights and duties of the parties including, for instance, the standard of work required and other matters which the parties have agreed. Sometimes the contract will have detailed terms; sometimes it will be contained in a short letter or conversation. Often, the existence of a contract is beyond dispute and usually both parties are in agreement about the terms it contains. However, this is not always the case.

This chapter deals with how and when contracts come into existence. If no contract is formed, the legal effects may be very different from the situation where a contract is formed and, indeed, many practical construction law problems involve a consideration of whether and, if so, when, a contract has come into being.

The complexity of building and civil engineering work means that protracted negotiations are often conducted before the work commences and, indeed, negotiations concerning the precise basis on which the work is to be performed often extend well into the construction period and, sometimes, beyond. The parties will frequently 'haggle' and the terms on offer at any particular time will change during the course of the negotiations. The terms governing the contract will be those 'on the table' at the time when the contract comes into existence and hence, in an environment where the terms on offers are changing rapidly, the contractual rights and obligations of the parties under the contract will be a function of the precise time at which the contract is formed.

5.1.2 A note on the use of the word 'contract'

In general construction industry parlance, the term 'contract' is synonymous with 'project' or 'scheme'. An engineer or architect might therefore ask 'which contract are you working on?', meaning 'which project?' For the lawyer, however, a contract is a set of rights and obligations created by agreement. When a contract comes into existence, the rights and obligations of the parties are then fixed and the lawyer speaks of the contract being 'concluded', 'formed' or 'made'. Since, for the lawyer, the term 'contract' relates to the agreement, while for the engineer or architect it means 'project' it is quite possible for a lawyer to say 'the contract has been concluded' and at the same time for an engineer to say 'the contract is about to begin', both referring to the same factual situation.

5.2   Formal requirements for the formation of contracts

It is widely believed that a contract needs to be created in some formal manner; some believe that it needs to be in writing, others that it needs at least some formality such as the shaking of hands, while others believe that witnesses are necessary. In fact, no formalities are required in the vast majority of cases. There are some exceptions such as contracts for the transfer of rights in land which need to be evidenced in writing; but in general contracts may be made orally or, indeed, purely by gestures. An example of the latter is where a newspaper is bought from a street-vendor without exchange of words.

5.3   Agreement: the basis of contract

The principal requirement for the formation of a contract is agreement made with an intention to create legal relations; that is the parties to the contract must be in agreement, first, as to the terms of the agreement, and second, that those terms are to be legally binding upon them.

There is also a third condition, known as the requirement for 'consideration'; this means that both parties to the contract must contribute something to it. However, it is often argued that the requirement for consideration is simply an alternative test to the intention to create legal relations. The requirement for consideration will be discussed in Section 5.9.

5.3.1   Agreement to be legally bound

In *Rose and Frank Co v Crompton Brothers* [1925] AC 445 Lord Justice Aitken said: 'To create a contract there must be a common intention of the parties to enter into legal obligations, mutually communicated expressly or impliedly'. In practice it is presumed that, in a commercial context, the parties intend to enter into legal obligations; while, in making social arrangements, it is presumed that there is no intention to create legal relations. These presumptions may be defeated if a clear intention to the contrary is shown to exist, but it is very rare for such a claim to be made in the case of construction industry contracts.

5.3.2   Agreement and the two-stage test

The word 'agreement' suggests the simultaneous coming together of minds. Viewed in this way, agreement appears to be a single event and, therefore, capable of analysis only on this basis. However, this causes practical difficulties. For example, what is to happen if one party subsequently claims that he changed his mind shortly before the agreement allegedly came into being?

The law aims, in general, to uphold the agreements made by commercial people and to create certainty in commercial life. In order to improve this certainty, and to facilitate the analysis, the law prefers not to look upon agreement as a single occurrence but to infer it using a two-stage approach: offer and acceptance. The basic principle is as follows. Once an offer has been made it may be accepted by the party to whom it is addressed. If it is unconditionally accepted there is agreement and a contract has come into existence.

A number of important matters arise when considering how this principle might be applied in practical situations and these are dealt with in the sections which follow.

5.3.3 Objectivity in contract

The formation of contract is analysed objectively. The term 'objective' used in this context refers to a viewpoint which is neutral and may be contrasted with the term 'subjective'. The latter refers to a view which is that of a particular individual. Take for example an offer by A which reads: 'Dear B, I will build you a house according to the plans and drawings I saw at your office for £30 000'. If B writes back saying 'I accept', a contract comes into being. However, supposing that two days later A says 'I apologise, but I genuinely meant to offer to build you the house for £40 000; it would be impossible for me to build it for £30 000', what is the situation? If A is being honest then, viewed from a subjective viewpoint, there is no agreement. However, from an objective point of view, there is no doubt about the terms of the contract; the offer was to build the house for £30 000. Because the law deals objectively, A is required to build a house for that price. See *Tamplin v James* (1880) 15 Ch D 215, for an example of the operation of this principle.

The law's approach, then, is to look at the outward manifestations, determined objectively, rather than to attempt to speculate about the state of mind of the parties, determined subjectively. In other words, the law asks whether reasonable persons would have considered the words and actions of the parties to constitute a clear offer and a clear acceptance. If so, the parties have a contract even if both parties subjectively intended to contract on a different basis.

5.3.4 Offers, counter-offers and acceptances: general principles

The following terminology is used when discussing offers: the offeror is the person who makes the offer and the offeree is the person to whom the offer is addressed.

The unconditional acceptance of an offer
Once an offer is made, the person to whom it is addressed may accept it while it subsists. If the acceptance is unconditional, a contract comes into

existence. The terms of the contract are those contained in the offer which has been accepted.

The life of an offer

Clearly, an offer may be accepted only while it exists. It may be destroyed in a variety of ways; it may be withdrawn by the offeror, may lapse, be superseded by a subsequent offer (by the offeror or by the offeree) or be rejected by the offeree.

1   *Withdrawal*   the offeror may withdraw the offer at any stage before he or she hears that the offeree has accepted the offer.
2   *Lapse*   an offer will lapse at the time stated in the offer, if any. Thus, an offer expressed 'to remain open until noon tomorrow' will lapse at that time. If no time is stated in the offer, it will lapse after a reasonable time: in the case of a contract for perishable goods or stocks and shares in a fast moving market, the time will be short, whereas for major construction projects several weeks may well be allowed before the offer lapses.
3   *Supersession*   an offer will be superseded if the offeree seeks to change the offer. If for instance a contractor offers to construct a bridge for £1 million and the offeree replies 'no, we will only pay you £800 000', this constitutes a counter-offer which supersedes the first offer, so that the first offer no longer exists. There is now, however, a new offer (£800 000) available for acceptance by the original offeror. In negotiations for contracts many counter-offers may be tendered before an acceptance is made.
4   *Rejection*   a rejection destroys the current offer but provides nothing for the offeror to accept.

5.3.5   Typical stages in agreeing construction industry contracts

The process of the formation of construction contracts is often difficult to analyse. Protracted negotiations are the rule rather than the exception. In many cases, however, the end result is made clear by the fact that parties jointly execute (i.e. write or compile) a formal document containing the agreed terms, and this often obviates the need to look to the detailed history of the formation of the contract. In many other cases, however, the situation is not clarified in this way. The formation even of a straightforward construction contract may proceed in the following stages:

1   *Invitation to tender*   this is generally a pre-offer invitation (an 'invitation to treat') in which the employer invites one or more contractors to tender quotations for a specified piece of work.
2   *Tender or quotation*   this is generally an offer by the contractor to undertake the work for the sum quoted and upon the conditions contained in his offer.
3   *Letter of intent*   upon receipt of tenders, the employer will often write to the successful tenderer in terms such as 'we intend to place a firm order with you shortly' and it may continue 'please commence works

as soon as possible'. Such a communication does not generally rank as an acceptance because it is not unconditional.

4 *Acceptance*   this is the unconditional acceptance of the tender.

The qualification 'generally' is required in the first three cases because in some cases an invitation to tender can be an offer although, generally speaking, the tender itself will constitute the offer; a tender can, in some cases, however, be an invitation to treat or even an acceptance; and a document expressed to be a letter of intent usually has no binding effect but it may be an acceptance if it contains words which signify that the offer to which it refers is being accepted unconditionally. The important point to note is that the law looks to the words used in a document or statement, not just to the description of the document, although the description may, of course, assist in ascertaining the meaning of the document as a whole. Thus while the use of the term 'tender' may suggest that an offer is being made, the true test to be applied is: what is the true effect of the words contained in the tender given the circumstances in which it is provided?

Consultancy contracts are generally formed with less stages than construction contracts. This may be because firms of consultants such as architects, engineers and surveyors expect, and are expected, to contract on standard forms of contract produced by their professional bodies. Further, those standard forms are generally straightforward since professional designers and consultants are engaged not to comply with specifications but to compose them, even the 'specification' for their own detailed performance, limited only by the normal requirement that they exercise reasonable care and skill. Consequently, relatively little haggling occurs and it is generally a straightforward matter to prove the existence and content of a consultancy contract.

5.4 Offers, tenders and invitations to tender

5.4.1 Distinguishing between offers and invitations to tender

It is important to distinguish between an offer and an invitation to tender. An offer is an expression by the offeror that he is willing to be bound by the terms of his offer providing the offeree is also willing to be bound. An offer is accepted by simply communicating a willingness to be bound or, if the offer demands it, by complying with whatever conditions are laid down in the offer. An invitation to tender, on the other hand, is a request that an offer be made.

If an employer writes to a series of contractors in the following terms: 'We hereby invite tenders for the work shown on the appended drawings and described in the appended specification', then this appears clearly to be an invitation to tender, not an offer. If however the letter were to continue 'we will accept the lowest tender', then the situation has changed. This communication may be regarded as an offer which will be accepted by the contractor who complies with the terms of the offer, that is the contractor who submits the lowest tender in the appropriate form.

This analysis is clearly illustrated by the case of *Spencer v Harding* (1870) LR 5 CP 561. Here the defendants wrote to a number of interested parties, including the plaintiff, in the following terms: 'We are instructed to offer to the wholesale trade for sale by tender the stock-in-trade of Messrs G Eilbeck and Company.... The stock may be viewed up to Thursday, the 20th instant, in which day at 12 o'clock noon precisely the tenders will be received and opened'. The plaintiff submitted the highest tender, but the defendants refused to transfer the stock to them. The court was invited by the plaintiff to find that the notice in the instant case was an offer, and was accepted by submitting the highest tender, and that accordingly the defendants were in breach of contract in refusing to effect the transfer of the stock. Mr Justice Willes did not agree:

> I am of opinion that the defendants are entitled to judgment. The action is brought against persons who issued a circular offering a stock for sale by tender, to be sold at a discount in one lot. The plaintiffs sent in a tender which turned out to be the highest, but was not accepted. They now insist that the circular amounts to a contract or promise to sell the goods to the highest bidder, that is, in this case, to the person who should tender for them at the smallest rate of discount .... If the circular had gone on, 'and we undertake to sell to the highest bidder'... there would have been a good contract in respect of the persons. But the question is, whether there is here any offer to enter into a contract at all, or whether the circular amounts to anything more than a mere proclamation that the defendants are ready to chaffer for the sale of the goods, and to receive offers for the purchase of them. In advertisements for tenders for buildings, it is not usual to say that the contract will be given to the lowest bidder, and it is not always that the contract is made with the lowest bidder. Here there is a total absence of any words to intimate that the highest bidder is to be the purchaser. It is a mere attempt to ascertain whether an offer can be obtained within such a margin as the sellers are willing to adopt.

It will be exceedingly rare for words to be included in an invitation to tender in the construction industry which will make it into an offer. One recent example, involving share transfers, is found in *Harvela Investments Ltd v Royal Trust Company of Canada Trust* [1986] AC 207 where a vendor of shares requested tenders from prospective buyers of those shares. In the request there was an undertaking to accept the highest tender. In construction, however, the employer's decision is influenced by a number of considerations, not just the price quoted, and so this type of undertaking is hardly ever to be found. Often, indeed, there is a clause to the opposite effect which states that the employer does not undertake necessarily to award the contract to the lowest or to any tenderer. Accordingly, documents referred to as 'invitations to tender' are most unlikely to be offers.

5.4.2 Keeping offers open

Since an offer may be withdrawn at any stage prior to its acceptance, it follows that whenever a tender is an offer it should be capable of being withdrawn at any stage until it is accepted, even if it is expressed to remain open for a longer time. This, indeed, is the current rule adopted by the English courts. Accordingly, someone who has submitted a tender can withdraw it one minute before the announcement of the name of the successful tenderer. If, of course, the tender is properly construed as an acceptance (because the invitation to tender was an offer and the tenderer provided the successful tender) no withdrawal is possible as the contract has already been concluded.

There are a number of devices which an employer who invites tenders can use to ensure that a tender, once it is submitted, is not, in practice, withdrawable. The employer may, for instance, require the contractor to enter into a collateral contract at the time he submits the tender, the terms of which are that, if the tender is withdrawn, and, as a result, the employer must employ a more expensive contractor, that loss will be recoverable as damages under the collateral contract. This renders the withdrawal of a tender which the employer wishes to accept as equivalent to refusing to construct the works once the contract has been awarded.

5.5 Responses to an offer

5.5.1 General

Whenever an offer is made, it is open to the person or company to whom it is made, the offeree, to accept it, thereby concluding the contract. In order to create the contract, the acceptance must comply with certain rules. It must be made before the offer lapses, is withdrawn or is superseded; it must be in the form stipulated, if any, in the offer; and it must be unconditional.

In the construction industry the analysis of offer and acceptance is often complex. There are a variety of responses that an offeree might make to an offer, including the following.

1 *Rejection of the offer* the effect of a rejection is to cause the offer to cease to exist. Once rejected, an offer cannot be accepted unless the offeror makes the offer once more.
2 *Request for a clarification of the offer* when the offeree asks for a clarification, this leaves the offer intact, but has no other effect.
3 *A counter-offer* this is an offer by the offeree to contract on a different basis from that which has already been proposed. If, for instance, A says to B 'I will build the wall for £100' and B replies 'OK, but I'll only give you £95', B's response is not an acceptance but a counter-offer as it is a conditional acceptance. A now has an opportunity to decide whether or not to accept B's counter-offer. A common form of counter-offer arises where the offeree makes a conditional acceptance, subject to a condition to be fulfilled by the offeree. For example, the employer in a construction project often 'accepts' an offer subject to the contractor obtaining a bond in a specified form. While such responses are often said to be conditional acceptances their legal description is as a counter-offer as they bring no legally binding obligations into existence and they have all the characteristics of an offer by the employer which can be accepted by the contractor simply by obtaining the bond in favour of the employer.
4 *A letter of intent* the offeree might state an intention to accept the offer unconditionally in the future. This is not a counter-offer as there

is nothing for the offeror to accept and may be regarded as a 'letter of intent'. The letter of intent may read: 'we intend to accept your offer within the next two weeks ... please commence preparatory work'. The reasons for writing such a letter are numerous, but often involve the uncertainty in obtaining financial backing. Often financiers wish to analyse the price breakdown and study the details of the proposed construction methods before committing themselves, which, in turn, means that employers cannot accept tenders as soon as they would like.

5   *Unconditional acceptance*   in this case a contract comes into being. While lawyers generally use the term 'acceptance' to mean the unconditional acceptance of an offer which causes a contract to come into being, the term is also used to mean an acceptance 'subject to contract'. However, such an 'acceptance' is, in its legal effect, no more than a letter of intent. An example of such usage in the context of a construction contract is found in *M Harrison & Co (Leeds) Ltd v Leeds City Council* 14 BLR 123 where Lord Justice Megaw remarked

> In 1965, tenders were invited, both for the main contract and for the sub-contract steelwork. The contractors tendered for the main contract. Their tender was over £1,115.00. It was accepted. The main contract, *which was to be made* between the tenderers whose tender was accepted and the employers *would include* relevant contractual provision as to sub-contracts. [Emphasis added]

Clearly the judge is here talking of an acceptance which does not rank as the unconditional acceptance required to bring the contract into being.

5.5.2   Apparently inconclusive negotiations and the formation of contract

The complexity of construction contracts, in terms of the technical specification and logistical arrangements as well as the financial aspects, means that it is very common for the formation of the contract (if any) to be prefaced by lengthy and detailed negotiations. In some cases the discussions which take place before the contract is eventually formed will include instances of each of the species of response described in Section 5.5.1.

Often it will appear that the negotiations are inconclusive and that there is no clear offer which is unconditionally accepted. The question arises whether or not a contract then comes into existence at all. In practice, the law does not require *absolute* agreement and, provided that the parties are in substantial agreement, a contract will come into existence.

One situation that regularly occurs is where the parties exchange correspondence, each party stating in his correspondence that the contract is to be on his own standard terms. Often substantial agreement is made concerning the subject matter of the contract but it is unclear as to whose terms govern the transaction. This is known as the 'battle of the forms' and the courts will analyse this situation as best they can using the principles of offer and acceptance. The practical difficulties involved in this are illustrated by a number of well-known cases such as *Butler Machine Tool Co Ltd v Ex-Cell O Corporation (England) Ltd* [1979] 1 WLR 401. The approach of the Official Referees' courts when considering questions of formation when there is a long series of negotiations is illustrated by the case of *Chichester Joinery v John Mowlem* 42 BLR 100.

Sometimes the parties commence operations in accordance with a draft contract before the contract has been finally agreed, and the question arises whether an acceptance can be made by conduct, that is by acting in accordance with the draft agreement. The courts look not only at the words used by the parties in their communications but also at the circumstances surrounding those communications and the activities of the parties and the courts may, in appropriate circumstances, infer acceptance from conduct alone. In *Brogden v Metropolitan Railway Co* (1877) 2 App Cas 666, for example, the transaction concerned the supply of coal and coke for the Metropolitan Railway Company. A draft agreement was drawn up by the railway company and sent to Brogden, the supplier, for signature and completion. By the draft agreement a specified amount of coal was to be supplied at a specified price. Brogden signed it but left other parts of the draft agreement blank, including dates. The railway company manager put the draft in a drawer and formal contracts were never exchanged. When the railway company requested coal, however, it was supplied on the terms set out in the draft agreement. But Brogden later refused to supply more coal and the railway company sued for breach of contract. Brogden denied that there was a contract. Lord Blackburn said

> If the parties have by their conduct said, that they acted upon the draft which has been approved of by Mr Brogden, and which if not quite approved of by the railway company, has been exceedingly near it, if they indicate by their conduct that they accept it, the contract is binding.

The House of Lords held that in this case the contract had indeed been accepted by conduct. In the case of construction contracts, however, one should be cautious before assuming that a contract comes into being on the basis of conduct simply because a contractor commences work on site or the employer pays in accordance with rates included in a draft agreement. Often parties will continue to negotiate after the works are begun and, in that situation, payments or work performed are unlikely to cause the agreement to become binding.

5.5.3 Letters of intent

At the end of pre-contract negotiations it often happens that a contract is not finally concluded but that the party who is entitled to accept the offer made by the other issues a 'letter of intent'. This is a statement which informs the other that the offeree intends to accept the offer. In some cases the offeree will also suggest to the offeror that the offeror should commence work.

The status of 'letters of intent' was considered in *British Steel Corporation v Cleveland Bridge and Engineering Co Ltd* [1984] 1 All ER 504. The dispute in that case concerned steelwork for a bank in Saudi Arabia. Cleveland

Bridge Engineering (CBE) was the subcontractor for the steel fabrication. The parties began negotiations during the course of which a letter of intent was issued by CBE. Mr Justice Goff considered the effect of such letters of intent:

> Now the question whether in a case such as the present any contract has come into existence must depend on a true construction of the relevant communications which have passed between the parties and the effect (if any) of their actions pursuant to those communications. There can be no hard and fast answer to the question whether a letter of intent will give rise to a binding agreement: everything must depend on the circumstances of the particular case.

5.6   Essential terms

It is sometimes suggested that express agreement is required regarding certain essential matters, such as the price of the work, before a binding contract can come into existence. However, contracts often come into existence without the parties even discussing the terms upon which the work is to be carried out. In such a case, the terms of the contract may often be implied, the terms being that the standard of work will be of a reasonable quality, the time for performance will be a reasonable time and the rate of remuneration will be a reasonable rate: see the Supply of Goods and Services Act 1982.

It may be, however, that in some cases, terms such as the price are so fundamental that no agreement can occur until they are expressly agreed. This possibility is explored further in Section 9.2.2.

5.7   Certainty of terms

5.7.1   Uncertain terms the basis of an agreement

One important matter relating to the question of formation of contract is the question of imprecise and/or meaningless terms. Since such terms seem to strike at the idea of agreement, parties might be tempted to use them as a vehicle in order to avoid their contracts. In *Scammel v Ouston* [1941] AC 251, for instance, a term in a contract for the purchase of a motor vehicle read 'this order is given on the understanding that the balance of the purchase price can be had on hire-purchase terms over a period of two years'. The House of Lords held that this sentence was 'so vaguely expressed that it cannot, standing by itself, be given a definite meaning – that is to say, it requires further agreement to be reached between the parties before there would be a complete *consensus ad idem*'. There was no such thing as 'usual terms' in the context and so there was no contract because the necessary element of agreement was missing.

5.7.2   Uncertain terms which can readily be severed

The courts will, however, always try to uphold an agreement. In *Nicolene v Simmonds* [1953] 1 QB 543, for instance, Lord Denning dealt swiftly with an attempt to avoid an agreement:

This case raises a short, but important, point which can be stated quite simply: the plaintiffs allege that there was a contract for the sale to them of 3000 tons of steel reinforcing bars, and the seller broke the contract. When the buyers claimed damages the seller set up the defence that there was no contract at all. The material words are: 'We are in agreement that the usual conditions of acceptance apply.' There were no usual conditions of acceptance at all, so the words are meaningless. There is nothing to which they can apply. On that account it is said that there was never a contract at all between the parties. In my opinion a distinction must be drawn between a clause which is meaningless and a clause which is yet to be agreed. A clause which is meaningless can often be ignored, whilst still leaving the contract good; whereas a clause which has yet to be agreed may mean that there is no contract at all, because the parties have not agreed on all the essential terms. . . .

In the present case there was nothing yet to be agreed. There was nothing left to further negotiation. All that happened was that the parties agreed that 'the usual conditions of acceptance apply.' That clause was so vague and uncertain as to be incapable of any precise meaning. It is clearly severable from the rest of the contract. It can be rejected without impairing the sense or reasonableness of the contract as a whole, and it should be so rejected. The contract should be held good and the clause ignored. The parties themselves treated the contract as subsisting. They regarded it as creating binding obligations between them; and it would be most unfortunate if the law should say otherwise. You would find defaulters all scanning their contracts to find some meaningless clause on which to ride free.

5.7.3   Specifications lacking in detail

An area where lack of certainty may cause a contract to be void is where a contract to undertake work is extremely loosely specified, particularly where it is let on a fixed price basis. This is discussed in *Southway Group Ltd v Wolff and Wolff* 57 BLR 33. In that case the works were significant in volume but were not specified in any detail. Lord Justice Parker explained the situation as follows:

The specification of the works to be done . . . was described by [counsel for the employer] as threadbare. The description is in my view fully justified. It was headed 'outline specification' and occupied a little over two pages . . . . This was, it must be remembered, a fixed price contract with a specification so lacking in detail that there was an almost infinite number of detailed specifications which could be said to fall within it. Indeed so lacking in detail was it that [counsel] indicated that, had it been open to him, he would or might have contended that the contract was void for uncertainty. For my part I consider that such a contention would have had considerable force.

5.8   Mistake

5.8.1   Introduction

It sometimes happens that parties make an 'agreement' either on the basis of mistaken facts or on the basis of a common misunderstanding. These two situations may be described as involving a mistake which potentially operates to prevent any real consensus from being formed.

While the law does recognise that a 'mistake' may, in the right circumstances, operate to prevent a contract from coming into existence, the scope of the term 'mistake' must be understood. In particular it should be noted that mistakes which relate to the motivation of either party are not sufficient to enable the contract to be challenged. For instance, contractors on ground-work projects often submit low bids believing that the ground conditions will be good which belief turns out to be mistaken; or they may enter into a contract for the demolition of a building mistakenly believing that the materials in the building are valuable and can be salvaged and sold at a good profit, whereas in fact those materials have been removed many years previously. Neither of these situations will be sufficient to enable the contractor to avoid his contractual obligations.

5.8.2 Mistake concerning the existence of a basic fact

On occasions, parties will make an agreement upon the assumption that some particular state of affairs exists, but where, in fact, that state of affairs does not exist. An example is where the parties agree on a building refurbishment contract for a building in a remote location and, unbeknown to them both, the building has already been destroyed or demolished. An important question here is whether a contract comes into existence or not, or alternatively, whether the non-existence of the assumed facts constitutes a breach of contract by the party who promoted a belief in their existence.

Professor Smith in his book *The Law of Contract,* (1989) suggests that the most appropriate method of analysing problems where there is a mistake by both parties as to the existence of a fundamental fact is to classify the factual situation into one of the following three classes:

- A impliedly promised B that the thing existed or would continue to exist
- A impliedly promised B that he had taken reasonable care to find out whether it existed
- A and B proceeded on a common assumption, for which neither was more responsible than the other, that the thing existed.

If the situation is of the first type, the non-existence of the fundamental fact will be a breach of contract by A. This will also be the case if the situation is of the second type *if* A has failed to take reasonable care to appraise himself of the facts. In either of those cases B may sue A for breach of contract if the basic condition is not fulfilled. If the situation is of the second type and A has taken reasonable care to appraise himself of the facts or if the situation is classifiable within the third type then A is not in breach and the contract is rendered void *ab initio* for mistake, that is to say it never came into existence; no effective agreement has been reached.

5.8.3 Mistake due to a common misunderstanding

The law of contract insists that all questions be treated objectively; that is to say the actual intention of the parties is never relevant. However, there are circumstances where the actions of the parties during the agreement are motivated by two distinct but reasonable beliefs concerning some element of the project, so that it would be quite wrong to say that a binding agreement had come into existence. The key here is that there must be a genuine ambiguity so that, objectively, no consensus could be found. The leading case is *Raffles v Wichelhaus* (1864) 2 H&C 906 where two parties made an agreement concerning the cotton cargo of a ship called *The Peerless* which was to leave Bombay. There were, in fact, two ships called *The Peerless*, both leaving Bombay that autumn, one in October and one in December, both with cotton cargos; the buyer thought his cargo would leave in October, the seller thought that the cargo would leave in December. The court held that there was no consensus and no contract.

Situations similar to those in *Raffles v Wichelhaus* may readily arise in construction contracts. If, for example, an agent of the employer makes an oral contract, perhaps over the telephone, with a contractor for the performance of some small element of preparatory works it is not difficult to imagine a common misunderstanding arising concerning the location of the works.

5.9 Consideration and intention to create legal relations

5.9.1 Introduction

Agreements may be made in a variety of circumstances. The courts have had to distinguish between two principal types of agreements: those which give rise to legally enforceable duties and obligations and those which do not. The former agreements are contracts; the latter are merely unenforceable promises. The underlying question posed by the courts is 'have the parties the requisite intention to create legal relations?' but because this question presents difficulties because of its vagueness and the possible need to consider the subjective intention of the parties, they have framed an alternative question which is considered to provide an objective test similar to that of 'intention to create legal relations': they ask 'has consideration been provided?'

The classic definition of 'consideration' is given in *Currie v Misa* [1875] LR 10 Ex 162:

> A valuable consideration, in the sense of the law, may consist either in some right interest, profit, or benefit accruing to the one party, or some forebearance, detriment, loss or responsibility, given, suffered or undertaken by the other.

In order for an agreement to be enforceable, both parties must provide consideration. In a construction contract the contractor agrees to build and the employer agrees to pay each; is providing consideration. The contractor provides the building work (strictly speaking, he provides the *promise* to build) and the employer provides the promise to pay.

The law is not concerned with ensuring that contracts are fair but that they were intended to be binding. An extreme example will illustrate this: A offers £1 to B for B's car which is worth £30 000 and B accepts; A now owns the car. If B refuses to deliver it, then A can sue B for the loss he has suffered because of B's breach of contract, namely £29 999. If, however, B had agreed to let A have the car for nothing, rather than £1, then A would not have been able to sue because he would have provided no consideration and there would have been no binding contract. The law is not, therefore, concerned with the adequacy of the consideration, but with the legal sufficiency of it. £1 is clearly inadequate for an expensive car; but in law it is sufficient.

5.9.2 Consideration and privity

The doctrine of consideration and the rule concerning privity of contract, which will be discussed in detail in Chapter 13, are closely linked. The doctrine of privity says that only those who have a contract with a party X may sue X for a contractual remedy. Consequently, a contract between two parties, A and B, cannot be sued upon by a third party C, even though the principal purpose of the contract might be to benefit C. This may be restated, to the same effect, using the terminology of the doctrine of consideration: C has provided no consideration to the contract and hence cannot sue upon it.

5.9.3 Can an agreement to perform an existing contractual obligation be consideration?

The question whether or not an existing contractual obligation can be sufficient consideration is one which has long been uncertain; there are decisions which come to a range of conclusions on this point. The question is of some practical importance in the field of construction law. It often happens, for instance, that one party is behind schedule on a project and other parties involved who are affected by his lack of progress agree to help him out to enable him to meet his contractual commitments. They may promise him additional payments if he accelerates back onto his originally agreed programme. But if he does accelerate, what obligation is there for them to pay in accordance with their promise? Surely the party who has accelerated his work is not doing something additional to what he had already agreed to do? What consideration has he provided?

An example of this is found in the case of *Williams and Roffey Bros v Nicholls (Contractors) Ltd* [1990] 2 WLR 1153. The plaintiff was a carpenter. The defendant was the main contractor under a building contract. The plaintiff was engaged by the defendant to undertake the carpentry work in twenty-seven flats in a specified time for £20 000. In fact, the price was too low and the plaintiff got into financial difficulties. These difficulties put the defendant at risk under his contract with the employer for late completion and so the defendant agreed to pay an enhanced rate if the plaintiff would perform in accordance with his earlier agreement. A dispute arose concerning these extra payments. The question which the court had to decide was: was the varied agreement supported by consideration? If so, what was the consideration? Lord Justice Glidewell said after a review of the cases:

> Accordingly following the view of [judges in previously decided cases] . . . the present state of the law on this subject can be expressed in the following proposition: (i) if A has entered into a contract with B to do work for, or

to supply goods or services to, B in return for payment by B, and (ii) at some stage before A has completely performed his obligations under the contract B has reason to doubt whether A will, or will be able to, complete his side of the bargain; and (iii) B thereupon promises A an additional payment in return for A's promise to perform his contractual obligations on time; and (iv) as a result of giving his promise, B obtains in practice a benefit, or obviates a disbenefit; and (v) B's promise is not given as the result of economic duress or fraud on the part of A; then (vi) the benefit to B is capable of being consideration for A's promise, so that the promise will be legally binding.

It is therefore my opinion that on his findings of fact in the present case, the judge was entitled to hold, as he did, that the defendant's promise to pay the extra £10 300 was supported by valuable consideration, and thus constituted an enforceable agreement.

5.10 Formalities and sealed contracts

Some contracts, notably those of surety, guarantee and for interests in land need to be evidenced in writing; otherwise they are unenforceable. Excepting these, contracts may be in any form; they are equally binding whether they are made orally or by a highly formal sealed document.

Many standard form contracts currently used in the construction industry entitle one or both parties to require the other to execute the contract under seal. Before being sealed the contract is known as a 'simple' contract or a contract 'under-hand'. When sealed the contract is said to be 'a specialty', 'a deed' or 'under seal'. The effects of executing a contract under seal are as follows:

- the limitation period (i.e. the time following a breach of contract in which the innocent party is entitled to sue) is extended from six to twelve years
- by virtue of a special rule, contracts under seal do not have to be supported by consideration
- the 'doctrine of merger' operates in many instances to erase the existence of the former simple contract. Accordingly if the sealed contract contains a term which contradicts a term in the simple contract the sealed version will prevail unless it can be shown that it was included by mistake.

5.11 Variation of contract

Whenever parties have agreed a contract they are bound by its terms. However, at any stage after making the contract, they may agree to modify or vary the terms or, indeed, to discharge the contract altogether. In order to vary the contract the same legal elements are required as are required to form a contract in the first place, namely agreement, an intention to be legally bound by the variation and consideration.

5.11.1 Variations to the contract distinguished from variations under the contract

Many construction contracts contain provisions enabling the employer to vary the scope, layout, nature and quantities of work to be performed by issuing a notice or instruction to the contractor. There are usually also provisions in the contract which require these variations to be valued and for the overall price to be adjusted. Such 'variations' are not 'variations to the contract'; rather, they are 'variations under the contract' since the contractual agreement between the parties is not altered by the variation. The contract remains as before. What changes is the work which is to be performed under the contract. It is important to distinguish between 'variations under the contract' and 'variations to the contract'. Only the latter require agreement and consideration. The former require only that the proper procedures set out in the contract (e.g. issuing a variation order) are followed.

5.11.2 Agreement

As with the formation of the original contract, the agreement to vary the contract is achieved by offer and acceptance.

5.11.3 Agreement obtained by duress

The agreement must be genuine and not obtained by duress. Many cases are recorded where a contract has been part-performed and one party uses a leverage it has obtained by that part-performance to extract a variation to the contract terms which are to his benefit. In such cases the 'innocent party' may either affirm or avoid the new arrangement created by the variation. In *North Ocean Shipping Co Ltd v Hyundai Construction Co Ltd and another* [1979] QB 705, for instance, a shipbuilding company agreed to build a ship, payment to be made in US dollars. When the dollar was devalued by 10 per cent the shipbuilders insisted that payments be increased by 10 per cent to account for this. The owners refused but the shipbuilders threatened to stop construction if payments were not made on the increased basis. The owners, who were negotiating a lucrative deal for letting out the ship when it was completed, agreed to pay the increased sums. When the work was finished the owners claimed not to be liable to pay the additional 10 per cent. Mr Justice Mocatta said

> I think the facts found in this case do establish that the agreement to increase the price by 10 per cent reached at the end of June 1973 was caused by what may be called 'economic duress'. The Yard [the shipbuilders] were adamant in insisting on the increased price without having any legal justification for so doing and the owners realised that the Yard would not accept anything other than an unqualified agreement to the increase . . . . If it be right to regard this as having been reached under a kind of duress in the form of economic pressure, then what is said in *Chitty on Contracts,* 24th ed. (1977), vol. 1, para. 442, p. 207 to which both counsel referred me, is relevant, namely, that a contract entered into under duress is voidable and not void:

>> . . . consequently a person who has entered into a contract under duress, may either affirm or avoid such contract after the duress has ceased; and if he so voluntarily acted under it with a full knowledge of all the circumstances he may be held bound on the ground of ratification, or if, after escaping from the duress, he takes no steps to set aside the transaction, he may be found to have affirmed it.

Thus in *North Ocean Shipping v Hyundai* the variation was obtained by economic duress and hence was voidable. In fact, the owners were found to have affirmed the variation by failing to inform the shipbuilders promptly that they would challenge the agreement after the duress had been lifted and hence they became liable to pay the increased amount.

5.11.4 Consideration

The question of whether or not consideration supports the variation appears to be more likely to cause problems in the case of a variation of contract rather than its original formation. This is normally because one party agrees to an enhanced performance of his or her own obligations if the other will provide a proper contractual performance; for example, in *Williams and Roffey Bros v Nicholls (Contractors) Ltd* [1990] 2 WLR 1153 the main contractor agreed to make an enhanced payment to the subcontractor if the latter completed on time. The problem was addressed at some length in *North Ocean Shipping v Hyundai* and in the leading modern case of *Williams and Roffey Bros v Nicholls (Contractors) Ltd* [1990] 2 WLR 1153, discussed in Section 5.9.

6

Contract terms: general considerations

6.1 Introduction

Parties, as we saw in Chapter 5, often trade offers and counter-offers which contain terms. Some of these terms will find their way into the contract which is eventually agreed, while others will not. Those terms which will, in fact, form part of the contract are the terms contained in the unconditionally accepted offer. The first task which a contract lawyer must undertake when the contract arises from a series of negotiations is to identify the offer which is unconditionally accepted and hence to identify the terms which it contains. These terms are the express terms of the contract.

Even when it is possible to identify completely the terms of the agreement a significant number of additional related questions must be addressed and these are dealt with in this chapter.

In a series of negotiations the parties may make representations to one another which will be relied upon by the other party when agreeing the contract. One task of the contract lawyer is to determine which of such statements are to be terms and which are to be 'mere representations' which have no contractual effect (but may have consequences for the contract). This question is answered by reference to the objective intention of the parties (see Section 6.3).

In many contracts the express terms, those which have been expressly agreed, do not cover the whole of the subject matter of the contract and it is necessary to imply terms on the basis that, if the parties had thought about it, they, themselves, would have agreed those terms. The topic of implied terms is dealt with in Section 6.4.

Traditionally, the courts have divided terms into two categories: conditions and warranties. A breach of a condition entitles the innocent party to terminate the contract, while the breach of a warranty allows the innocent party to sue for damages only. It is a question of some importance, therefore, to decide which terms are conditions and which are warranties (see Section 6.5).

Further, it is necessary to have regard to the possibility that the terms of the contract may be supplemented by a 'collateral contract' formed during the negotiations (see Section 6.6).

Once the terms of the contract have been defined there remains the question of the meaning of those terms. The contract may, for instance, contain contradictory terms or terms which are difficult to understand. This process of determining the true meaning of the contract in law is known as the 'construction' of the contract, from the verb to construe (see Section 6.7).

6.2 The terms of the agreement

6.2.1 General

Once the offer and acceptance have been identified, the terms of the contract may be ascertained. Since an acceptance is the unconditional acceptance of the offer, the terms are those set out in the offer. One difficulty which arises, however, is that offers and counter-offers will frequently be exchanged without setting out the full offer word-for-word. Often it will be assumed (the law applies an objective test) that terms of a previous offer are to be carried over into the new offer. Clearly, if the new offer contradicts a preceding offer in some respect, then the later offer destroys the former insofar as it is inconsistent with it. But terms advanced during early negotiations may never be contradicted and the question arises whether or not they will survive the negotiations to become a term of the contract; or alternatively whether they will be a subsidiary representation. This matter is discussed in Section 6.3.1.

Frequently, the terms agreed are subsequently set out in a formal document acknowledged (and sometimes sealed) by both parties. The terms are, then, generally those included in that formal document. This is a convenient method of attaining a high degree of certainty about what terms are and are not in the contract. It will be difficult for either party subsequently to challenge the document as not representing the intention of the parties except in narrowly defined situations where the document sets out a term in a form which is clearly not in accordance with their prior agreement. In such a case the party wishing the document to be amended to correspond accurately with the agreement will seek 'rectification'. Sometimes the party can show a collateral agreement to supplement the principal agreement (see Section 6.6) which avoids the need to challenge the document.

6.2.2 Recitals

Some formal contracts contain a series of recitals before the substantive terms are set out. These typically begin with the word 'WHEREAS' and may outline the background to the contract. For instance, the contract document may begin: 'WHEREAS the Employer is desirous of having new prestige headquarters constructed, NOW it is HEREBY AGREED . . .'. The words setting out the employer's desire to have a new headquarters building do not form part of the terms. Often the recitals will, however, contain definitions (e.g. the precise identity of the parties) and to this extent they may have contractual effect.

6.2.3 Incorporation by reference

The terms which form a contract need not be spelt out word-for-word in the agreed document or spoken in the case of an oral agreement. It is quite sufficient if a document containing the terms is stated to be part of the agreement. In this case the terms are said to be 'incorporated by reference'. An example would be:

Contractor   1 April 1992: We offer to construct the works set out in the drawings and specifications supplied by yourselves for the sum of one million pounds sterling, in accordance with the enclosed priced bill of quantities, and all in accordance with the current edition of the ICE Conditions of Contract.

Employer   2 April 1992: We accept your offer.

Here the ICE Conditions of Contract current at 1 April 1992 (i.e. the 6th Edition 1991) are incorporated into the agreement; thus if, for example, a dispute arises the arbitration provisions of Clause 66 of that standard form contract will govern the dispute resolution process.

It is quite possible and, indeed, common to have second- and third-remove incorporation. If a document A is incorporated into the contract which specifically incorporates document B, which in turn specifically incorporates document C, then the terms of C will form part of the contract, as well as those of A and B. Often, it happens that there are inconsistencies in these various documents in which case the general rule is that terms in an incorporating document take precedence over those in an incorporated document.

6.3 Mere representations and misrepresentations

During the process of negotiating a contract many statements may be made by each party in order to inform the other party relating to aspects of the subject matter of the contract and generally to induce the other to enter the contract on the terms beneficial to the person making the statement. Such statements may become contract terms but they need not, in which case they are said to be 'mere representations', the epithet 'mere' being added to indicate an inferiority relative to a statement which becomes a term.

A typical, and common, example of where a statement might be a mere representation in the case of a construction contract is where the contractor is supplied with a site investigation report containing borehole information with the tender documents, which report is expressed to be 'for information only'. If the report is not included in the list of documents which form the contract it will not become an express term. If the borehole information is accurate, no problem arises. But if inaccurate, the contractor may experience significant difficulties resulting in lost time and money because of his reliance on that borehole information. The contractor may then rightly ask whether he has any remedy for this 'misrepresentation' and, if so, what?

In this section two matters will be dealt with. First, which statements become terms and which are 'mere representations'? Second, if the statement is a mere representation, and it is inaccurate (a 'misrepresentation') can the party to whom the statement is addressed (the 'representee') obtain redress against the person who makes the statement (the 'representor') and, if so, under what circumstances?

6.3.1 Terms and mere representations

The question whether or not any statement will become a term of the contract depends on the objective intention of the parties. In order to determine whether they intended the statement to become a term or for it to remain as a mere representation all the surrounding circumstances must be taken into account. A number of 'indicators' have been advocated. The first is applicable when the contract is reduced to writing; if the statement is not in the written terms then it will not normally be a term of the contract. The second indicator relates to the time at which the statement is made; if it is uttered as part of the preliminary negotiations then it is unlikely to survive into the contract. The third indicator focuses on the relative knowledge of the parties; if one party is in a position of superior knowledge and he makes a statement in circumstances where he must be taken to know that the other will be relying upon that statement, that suggests that the statement will become a term. These indicators, however, are, as the name suggests, simply indicative and exceptions are commonly found in the decided cases.

Indicator 1: when a contract is reduced to writing no terms are likely to be found outside the written document
The rule that, when a contract is reduced to writing, it contains all the terms may be upset in a number of situations. First the party who alleges an overriding term which is not included in the written document may claim that that overriding term is contained in a 'collateral contract' (see Section 6.6). Or, the party may claim that the term was omitted from the document by mutual mistake of both parties and that the document should be 'rectified' to include the term alleged. But there are instances of where the courts have allowed an oral term to survive the compilation of an agreed document. In *Birch v Paramount Estates Ltd* (1956) 16 EG 396, for example, the plaintiff bought a house from the defendant developer who, at the time, was still constructing the house. The developer said that the plaintiff's house would be as good as the 'show house' which the plaintiff visited. In fact the house the plaintiff bought was not as good as the show house and this was held by the court to be a breach of contract even though the written agreement contained no reference to the show house.

Indicator 2: if the statement is made in preliminary negotiations it is unlikely to be a term
Clearly a statement will become a term only if it is included in the final offer; but the process of offer and counter-offer rarely involves the parties in reciting each and every potential term whenever an offer is advanced. Many terms survive tacitly, though tenaciously, through the negotiations and if a term is fundamental enough to the purpose of the contract it

may well survive from the early negotiations. In *Schawel v Reade* [1913] IR 81, for instance, the contract was for the sale of a stud stallion. The plaintiff buyer visited the horse and began to examine it. The seller said 'You need not look for anything; the horse is perfectly sound' and the buyer ceased his examination. The sale was concluded more than three weeks later. The questions for the jury were, first, did the seller represent to the buyer *at the time of the contract* that the horse was sound? And if so, did the buyer rely upon that statement? The jury found that the representation survived to the time of the contract and that the buyer had relied upon it. Accordingly, the representation became a term of the contract, so that when the horse proved unfit for stud purposes this was a breach of contract. The House of Lords supported this decision.

Indicator 3: if one party has special knowledge, his or her statement on matters within the sphere of his or her expertise are likely to be terms
The test of relative knowledge in deciding whether or not a statement becomes a term is relevant only when the statement is one of fact as opposed to statements of opinion. The latter are, in principle, insufficient to become terms and, accordingly, the other party should not rely upon them. However, where the opinion is presented in circumstances where the representee is entitled to believe that the opinion has been formed with reasonable skill and care then there may be an undertaking, which will be a contract term, not that the opinion is correct, but that it has been formed reasonably. An example of this is given by *Esso Petroleum Co Ltd v Mardon* [1976] QB 801 where a petrol company represented to a prospective tenant of a filling station that, in their opinion, a certain volume of sales would be reached. In fact their opinion was a significant overestimate. The court held that, even though the statement was expressed as an opinion, it was given by one in a superior position of knowledge so that there was an undertaking by the petrol company that the opinion had been made with reasonable skill and care. That undertaking had been broken and the tenant was able to recover damages.

6.3.2 Misrepresentation

A mere representation which is inaccurate is termed a 'misrepresentation'. If one party represents that a certain factual state of affairs exists and the representee has been induced to enter into the contract by that representation then, if the represented state of affairs does not exist, the plaintiff may sue for the misrepresentation. Misrepresentation is not a contractual action; it is, in the modern law, a mixture of tort and the application of the general and ancient principles of 'Equity', modified and added to by statute law. However, while not being a contractual remedy in theory it relates to contracts in such a way that it is properly dealt with in a contractual context.

For representees to prove a successful case in misrepresentation they must show

- that they were induced to enter into the contract on the current terms by the misrepresentation
- that it was reasonable for them to rely upon the misrepresentation.

Prior to 1967 there were two distinct types of misrepresentations, fraudulent and innocent misrepresentation. Fraudulent misrepresentation was dealt with by the tort of deceit and arose whenever a misrepresentation was made when the representor did not believe in the truth of the representation. The remedy for deceit was damages. Innocent misrepresentation, where the representor believed in the truth of the representation which turns out to be inaccurate, was not treated by the courts of common law as giving the representee any remedy at all; however, the courts of equity (which until the last quarter of the nineteenth century operated a parallel system of justice to that provided by the courts of the common law) allowed the innocent party to rescind the contract since equity felt that it would be wrong even for a wholly innocent party to benefit from his misrepresentation. This position was changed somewhat by the case of *Hedley Byrne & Co v Heller & Partners* [1964] AC 465 which allowed a party to recover damages when the representation had been made negligently; but this was available to the representee only when the two parties were in a 'special relationship' and it did not cover the general case of negligent misrepresentation.

The position was not satisfactory. An action for negligent misrepresentation was rarely possible. In order to gain a remedy for fraudulent misrepresentation all the difficulties associated with proving fraud arose. If the action was characterised as innocent misrepresentation the remedy might not be of any assistance; rescission, that is a return of the position of all parties to their pre-contract state, may readily be achieved in the case of contracts such as sales of goods, but construction projects do not enable this to be accomplished with ease. The law was changed to assist the representee in the Misrepresentation Act 1967.

The primary provisions of this Act are contained in Section 2. Subsection 2(1) provides

> (1) Where a person has entered into a contract after a misrepresentation has been made to him by another party thereto and as a result thereof he has suffered loss, then, if the person making the misrepresentation would be liable to damages in respect thereof had the misrepresentation been made fraudulently, that person shall be so liable notwithstanding that the misrepresentation was not made fraudulently, unless he proves that he had reasonable grounds to believe and did believe up to the time the contract was made that the facts represented were true.

This subsection creates a right of action which is sometimes called 'negligent misrepresentation'; however, unlike an action under the rule in *Hedley Byrne v Heller,* there is no need to show that the elements of the tort of negligence are present. All the representee has to show is that if the representation had been fraudulent it would be actionable, which, in effect, widens the scope of the tort of deceit to cover even careless misrepresentations. It is as though all misrepresentations were deemed to have been made fraudulently, without imputing to the representor the stigma of fraud, unless the representor can prove that they were made wholly innocently. 'Wholly innocently' here means that the representor did believe the statement both at the time he made it and at the time the contract was entered into and that he had reasonable grounds for that belief.

The second subsection of Section 2 deals with the problem of rescission, which was the normal remedy for misrepresentation before the 1967 Act. Subsection (2) provides that the court or an arbitrator may declare that the contract shall continue to exist even if the representee has already declared the contract to have been rescinded. And, when a contract is declared to subsist, as will be the case in almost all construction and consultancy actions in which misrepresentation is alleged, the tribunal may award damages in lieu of rescission. This, then, will be the normal, indeed almost the invariable, remedy in construction cases. Subsection (2) reads:

> (2) Where a person has entered into a contract after a misrepresentation has been made to him otherwise than fraudulently, and he would be entitled, by reason of the misrepresentation, to rescind the contract, then, if it is claimed, in any proceedings arising out of the contract, that the contract ought to be or has been rescinded, the court or arbitrator may declare the contract subsisting and award damages in lieu of rescission, if of opinion that it would be equitable to do so, having regard to the nature of the misrepresentation and the loss that would be caused by it if the contract were upheld, as well as the loss that rescission would cause to the other party.

6.4   Implied terms

When a contract is made it will include a number (sometimes a large number) of agreed terms. The question to be addressed in this section is whether and, if so, in what circumstances terms may be implied into the contract when they have not expressly been agreed. Terms will be implied in three distinct situations:

- where they are implied by statute
- where they must be implied in order to give the contract business efficacy
- where the express contract that the parties have agreed does not cover the matter which eventually becomes the subject of dispute, and the court attempts to define 'usual practice' to determine the intention of the parties.

6.4.1   Terms implied by statute

A number of statutes affect the contents of commercial contracts. For instance, the Supply of Goods and Services Act 1982 implies into all contracts for the supply of services (which include construction and consultancy contracts) obligations to perform the work with reasonable skill and care; to transfer property which is reasonably fit for the purpose for which it is required; to do the work in a reasonable time; and to pay a reasonable remuneration for that work. These implied terms can be overridden by express terms in the contract.

6.4.2   Terms which are necessary for business efficacy

In *The Moorcock* (1889) 14 PD 64, the defendants agreed for consideration that the plaintiff could unload his ship at the defendants' wharf. When the tide ebbed the ship was grounded, as expected by both parties, but unexpectedly (for the plaintiff at least) there was a ridge of hard ground beneath the wharf which damaged the ship. The contract contained no express terms regarding the state of the ground beneath the wharf but the plaintiff sued on an implied term that the wharf was suitable and succeeded. The court decided that the business efficacy of such a contract required such a term to be implied. Lord Justice Bowen said of the purpose of implying terms:

> In business transactions such as this, what the law desires to effect by the implication is to give such business efficacy to the transaction as must have been intended at all events by both parties who are business men; not to impose on one side all the perils of the transaction, or to emancipate one side from all chances of failure, but to make each party promise in law as much, at all events, as it must have been in the contemplation of both parties that he should be responsible for in respect of those perils or chances.

Similar considerations as applied in *The Moorcock* may apply to some aspects of construction and consultancy contracts. A construction contract may, for instance, refer in detail to specifications, time obligations for completion and to payment. But it may not say that the contractor is to have access to the site. If the contractor was refused reasonable admission to perform the works it is likely that the court would imply a term that the contractor is to have adequate access consistent with the terms of the contract (see Section 12.3). Such a term is necessary to make the contract work, to give it 'business efficacy'.

On occasions, however, parties attempt to have a term implied where business efficacy often does not require such an implication. In such situations a term will not be implied. For instance, subcontractors may claim that they are entitled to have sole possession of some parts of the site at certain times even though the contract is silent on the point. In building construction, electrical, mechanical, ventilation, and other subcontractors often work in the same general area at the same time. They tend to interfere with one another's progress and this causes them to work less efficiently than if they were working alone. In most situations, where subcontractors claim sole possession (or more usually, additional remuneration for the disruption experienced), they are claiming that such a term is necessary to give the contract business efficacy. This may be proved in some situations but this will only rarely be so.

The basic position adopted by the courts regarding implied terms is that their role is to interpret the contract, not to make it for the parties. Thus the court will not imply terms simply because they appear reasonable or sensible. Lord Justice Mackinnon in *Shirlaw v Southern Foundries* (1926) [1939] 2 KB 206 at 227 said in a well-known passage

> that which in any contract is left to be implied and need not be expressed is something so obvious that it goes without saying; so that, if, while the parties were making their bargain, an officious bystander were to suggest some express provisions for it in their agreement, they would testily suppress him with a common 'Oh, of course!'

In *Trollope & Colls v North West Metropolitan Regional Health Board* [1973] 2 All ER 260, Lord Pearson said

The court does not make a contract for the parties. The court will not even improve the contract that the parties have made for themselves no matter how desirable the improvement may be. The court's function is to interpret and apply the contract which the parties have made for themselves. If the express terms are perfectly clear and free from ambiguity, there is no choice to be made between different possible meanings: the clear terms must be applied even if the court thinks that some other terms would have been more suitable. An unexpressed term can be implied if and only if the court finds that the parties must have intended that term to form part of their contract: it is not enough for the court to find that such a term would have been adopted by the parties as reasonable men if it had been suggested to them; it must have been a term that went without saying, a term *necessary* to give business efficacy to the contract, a term which though tacit, formed part of the contract which the parties made for themselves.

6.4.3 Usual implied terms

Construction is a complex process and the contracts which regulate it tend to be detailed. In some cases, however, the contract may be a simple agreement with very few express terms and the question arises whether, in such cases, there is a body of 'usual terms' which can be implied into the contract. If, for instance, a contract price is agreed on a project where the construction period is two years, but no mention is made of stage payments, does this mean that the employer does not have to pay anything until the end of the works? It does not seem, on the business efficacy view, that any such implication is necessary but several judicial statements appear to suggest that a term to this effect might, nonetheless, be implied (see Section 9.5). When deciding whether payment was to be made in stages or as a single sum at the end, the court would certainly have regard to the usual practice in the industry to fill the gap.

Another way of justifying the inclusion of 'usual practice' in a contract by implication is by styling it a 'trade custom', that is that the custom of the relevant trade which is so well-known and widely used that the parties may be presumed to have contracted on that basis. Lord Blackburn in *Tucker v Linger* (1883) 8 App Cas 508 said

> The custom, when proved, is to be considered as part of the agreement: and if the agreement be in writing, though the custom is not written, it is to be treated exactly as if that unwritten clause had been written out at length.

Usual practice in the construction industry in the context of the usual obligations of the employer and contractor under a construction contract will be discussed in Chapters 9 to 14. A note of caution should, however, be sounded lest it be thought that terms can very easily be implied using 'usual practice' or 'trade custom'. In the modern construction industry the role of trade custom as a source of implied contract terms has, it is submitted, diminished greatly. The modern trend is for parties to make or adopt novel schemes covering every aspect of the work, its administration and its payment, so that it would, in today's world, be difficult to say exactly what represented a custom.

The parties may, of course, exclude the operation of any rule of usual practice or trade custom either expressly or impliedly by agreeing on terms inconsistent with the custom.

There are many instances of where the court have implied terms into construction contracts; one of the most detailed reviews of the type of term that may be implied in the context of construction is provided by *London Borough of Merton v Leach* 32 BLR 51. In this case it was held that there were to be implied terms that the employer would not hinder or prevent the contractor from carrying out his obligations under the contract, that the architect (who in this case had the responsibility to provide the design information) would cooperate with the contractor, that the information he provided would be correct and that the architect would carry out his duties with reasonable competence. It should be clearly understood, however, that each situation and each contract will have its own peculiarities and so it is not possible to say whether the same terms would be implied into a similar but slightly different contract. Primary reliance should always be placed on the basic principles.

6.4.4 Terms will not be implied simply because they are reasonable

It is important to appreciate that a court will not imply a term on the basis that it is reasonable to do so or would have seemed a wise provision to include when viewed in hindsight. This is clearly brought home in the case of *Thorn v Mayor of London* [1876] AC 120. The contractor, Thorn, had rebuilt Blackfriars Bridge. The drawings which were prepared by the engineer showed that the foundations were to be built using caissons. In fact this method proved impracticable and the contractor was forced to use another method; this new method was much more expensive than caissons would have been. There was no express term in the contract to the effect that the works could be constructed using caissons and the contractor therefore attempted to show an implied term to this effect. Lord O'Hagan said

> It is unfortunate that they [the contractors] should be subjected to such serious loss; but I do not think that your Lordships can intervene to save them from the results of their own improvidence, by making, for the parties, a contract which they never contemplated, and inserting in it a warranty of which no one ever thought.

6.5 The status of terms

Traditionally the law of contract has sought to divide terms into two categories: conditions and warranties. Conditions are important terms. Their breach is thought of as being so serious as to undermine the purpose of the contract and the law has, following the breach of condition, entitled the innocent party to elect whether to continue with the contract or to treat it as being at an end. Accordingly if, in the case of a construction contract, the contractor is in breach and the breach in question is a breach of condition, the employer is entitled to terminate the agreement, hire another contractor to perform the work in full accordance with the specification and then to sue the offending contractor for any resulting damage, including the cost of rectifying the first contractor's work and employing the second contractor.

According to the traditional analysis, terms which are not conditions are warranties. A breach of warranty does not entitle the innocent party to terminate the agreement. He or she must continue with the work and sue for damages.

The classification into conditions and warranties depends upon a true construction of the contract (see e.g. *Bettini v Gye* (1876) 1 QBD 183) and not upon the description applied in the agreement. In *L Schuler AG v Wickman Machine Tool Sales Ltd* [1974] AC 235, the House of Lords said that simply because a term was called a condition that, of itself, did not make it one. It was, they said, necessary to determine its importance by construing the whole contract. Unfortunately there is no hard and fast rule which can be used to classify terms into the two categories; however, it is quite clear that 'conditions of contract' are rarely conditions in the sense that their breach automatically entitles the innocent party to end the contract.

Recently, the courts have been increasingly reluctant to force terms into the rigid categories of conditions and warranties. The difficulty of such a categorisation in complex contract obligations, such as appear frequently in construction contracts, is readily demonstrated. If, for example, a contract contains a term that the works must be carried out strictly in accordance with a specified safety code then, according to the traditional analysis this must be a condition or a warranty. But it is not difficult to imagine, on the one hand, a trifling oversight and, on the other, a serious and deadly infraction of the rules. Likewise with specification terms. If crushed rock for road construction is to comply with a specification grading envelope, then this is, according to the traditional analysis, either a condition or a warranty; but while the provision of a completely different material in large tracts of the work may strike at the purpose of a contract in which this work forms a substantial component, it is equally possible to imagine a slight disconformity which will have no real effect on the performance of the work at all.

In the *Hong Kong Fir Shipping Co Ltd v Kawasaki Kisen Kaisha* [1962] 2 QB 26 the Court of Appeal had to consider a charterparty (a type of contract in which the charterer 'hires' the ship from the owner). The charterparty required the ship to be in a seaworthy condition. The ship as delivered was, however, not in a good condition and the engine-room staff were not very competent. After a number of delays the charterer repudiated the contract. They claimed that the owner's breach of the seaworthiness term was a breach of a condition. The Court of Appeal, however, was reluctant to decide whether or not the term relating to seaworthiness was a condition or a warranty. Lord Justice Upjohn illustrated the reason for their reluctance as follows:

> If a nail is missing from one of the timbers of a wooden vessel, or if proper medical supplies or two anchors are not on board at the time of sailing, the owners are in breach of the seaworthiness stipulation. It is contrary to common sense to suppose that, in such circumstances, the

parties contemplated that the charterer should at once be entitled to treat the contract as at an end for such trifling breaches.

It is submitted that identical considerations apply to virtually all terms in construction contracts, and that, therefore, terms will be 'innominate terms', terms whose precise classification will depend on how, and in what circumstances, they are breached. However, the categorisation into conditions and warranties is still important in allowing the parties to create an entitlement to end the contract upon the breach of specifically mentioned terms. If the parties have, by express words, or by some other device which clearly points to that same conclusion, indicated that a particular term is of such importance that a breach, even an insubstantial breach, will cause the innocent party to be entitled to terminate the contract then that term will be a condition.

If the terms in a construction contract are to be described as 'innominate', the focus will be diverted away from the nature of the term onto the nature of the breach. In recent years the use of the phrase 'fundamental breach' has developed to describe a breach which is sufficiently serious that the innocent party is justified in refusing to render further performance. A fundamental breach, then, has the same consequences as the breach of a condition. The question of the termination of a contract on the grounds that the other party has been in breach of a condition or has committed a fundamental breach is dealt with in Section 7.4.

6.6 Collateral contracts

The general rule is that once a contract has been reduced to written form a party may not attempt to show that an oral term was also agreed which is inconsistent with any of the written terms. This rule can be, and is regularly, evaded by the device known as a collateral contract. Here the term which is allowed to be proved is not a term of the principal contract but of a contract operating in parallel to it. For example, in *De Lassalle v Guildford* [1901] 2 KB 215, the Court of Appeal had to consider a claim for breach of contract by a tenant under a lease for a house. The lease was silent about the drains but the alleged breach of contract was that the drains were not in good order. However, the evidence was that the tenant had refused to sign the lease until he had received an undertaking that the drains were in good condition. The court held that there were two contracts. The first contract was the lease. The second was a collateral contract in which the landlord promised that the drains were in good order, thereby allowing the tenant to supplement the written terms of the lease. The consideration supplied by the tenant for the collateral contract was his entry into the lease agreement. The tenant successfully sued upon the collateral contract.

The device of the collateral contract may often be useful in situations where parties contract on standard forms where the terms are agreed simply because they are in the standard document which they do not wish, for whatever reason, to alter. In such cases significant oral undertakings may be given which supplement the contract terms in the standard form and these oral undertakings may form terms in an enforceable collateral contract. A collateral contract will not, of course, come into being unless the person giving the undertakings has the authority to do so.

6.7 Construction of contract terms

6.7.1 The need to construe contract terms

It often occurs that the documents which form the contract are agreed upon by both parties but that

- a dispute arises about the meaning of a term
- two or more terms exist which appear to contradict one another.

The role of construction (i.e. of construing the document) in these situations is to identify the true legal meaning and effect of the words used. This does not involve any recourse to the subjective intentions or views of the parties either before or after making the contract. The law of contract is quite clear on this point; the contract is to be construed objectively.

6.7.2 A common sense construction

While the words used by the parties are paramount, constructions which offend against common sense are not readily adopted by the courts. In *Antaios Compania Naviera SA v Salen Rederierna* [1985] 1 AC 191 Lord Diplock said: 'I take this opportunity of restating that if detailed semantic and syntactical analysis of words in a commercial contract is going to lead to a conclusion that flouts business common sense, it must be made to yield to business common sense.' This common sense approach to construction of terms was used by Judge Thayne Forbes in *Davy Offshore Ltd v Emerald Field Contracting Ltd* 55 BLR 1. He recited arguments made by counsel for the plaintiff contractor and the defendant employer regarding the construction of the contract – in particular regarding what was included within the contractor's obligations. He then said (p. 45–6):

> In my opinion, [counsel for the contractor]'s submissions to the contrary are based on an interpretation of words and terms of the contract which is contrary to the repeatedly expressed intention and purpose of the contract read as a whole, namely that the entire responsibility for design and for ensuring that the work and facilities comply with Appendix O is placed with DOL [the contractor]. To adopt the words of Lord Diplock in *The Antaios,* in a detailed and comprehensive commercial contract such as this one, the construction argued for by [counsel for the plaintiff] flouts common sense. In my judgment it must yield to [counsel for the defendant]'s contractual construction which is the one I consider accords with the business common sense of this design and construct contract.

6.7.3 Negotiations and the factual matrix

In order to facilitate the objective construction of the contract, the parties are allowed to adduce evidence of the 'factual matrix' surrounding the formation of the contract by showing details of the pre-contract negotiations. The negotiations, themselves, however, insofar as they indicated the intention or perception of the parties involved may not be adduced, for their subjective views are not relevant. Only those parts of the evidence which indicate the factual matrix are to be taken into account. When the contract is in writing, evidence of negotiations is inadmissible because the positions that parties adopt may change during the negotiations. In *Prenn v Simmonds* [1971] 1 WLR 1381 Lord Wilberforce also ruled that evidence of the parties' intentions, or of their contemporary view on the meanings of words and phrases was inadmissible:

> The words used may, and often do, represent a formula which means different things to each side, yet may be accepted because that is the only way to get 'agreement'. The only course then can be to try and ascertain the 'natural' meaning. Far more, and indeed, totally dangerous is it to admit evidence of one party's objective – even if this is known to the other party . . . . In my opinion, then, evidence of the negotiations, or of the parties' intentions . . . ought not to be received, and evidence should be restricted to evidence of the factual background known to the parties at or before the date of the contract, including evidence of the 'genesis' and objectively the 'aim' of the transaction.

On occasions, the meanings of the words used require that extrinsic evidence be adduced. A good example is provided by *The Bank of New Zealand v Simpson* [1900] AC 183. Here, an engineer was employed to design a railway and manage its construction. His estimate for the cost was £35 000. The contract was contained in a letter written by the engineer to the bank. The engineer's fee for the work was to be calculated in accordance with the formula set out in the letter and there was a supplementary fee payable as follows: 'I should be allowed another $1\frac{1}{2}$ per cent on the estimate of £35 000 in the event of my being able to reduce the total cost of the works below £30 000'. The actual cost of construction turned out to be some £28 000. The cost of land, engineer's fees and other costs, however, brought the overall total to more than £43 000. But the engineer contended that since the total cost of construction was less than £30 000, he should receive an additional fee. The contract term quoted thus fell to be construed: did the phrase 'total cost' refer to construction alone or did it include land purchase etc.? Lord Davey said

> It is not, therefore, a mere question of the meaning of the words 'the total cost of the works' standing alone, but the meaning of 'the estimate of £35 000' also has to be considered. The words point to something which was known to and in the contemplation of both parties to the contract, and with reference to which they had contracted; and, in order to construe and apply the contract, you must ascertain what was included in 'the estimate of £35 000' on the reduction of which the contract depended. Extrinsic evidence is always admissible, not to contradict or vary the contract, but to apply it to the facts which the parties had in their minds and were negotiating about.

6.7.4 The rules of construction

The basic rules of construction are very simple: the words are to bear their ordinary natural meaning and any conflicts, ambiguities and so on are to be resolved by asking what would a reasonable person appraised of the factual matrix at the time of making the contract consider the meaning to be. There are some supplemental rules which have been derived by the courts. For a useful and accessible summary see *Kitson's Sheet Metal v Matthew Hall* 47 BLR 90 at page 104. A number of the rules of construction are outlined briefly below.

Order of precedence when terms are incorporated by reference
Of importance in construction is the rule that where a contract document incorporates other terms by reference, the incorporating document generally takes precedence over the incorporated document. Often the best evidence of the contract is to be found in a letter which makes reference to a standard form contract and contains other terms. If any of the terms set out in the letter conflict with the terms in the standard form, the terms in the letter will normally prevail, unless there is an indication in the contract that some other scheme of precedence is to operate.

The contra proferentem *rule*
One of the best-known rules of construction is that contracts must be construed *contra proferentem,* that is to say that any ambiguity must be resolved against the party who proffers the document. Thus since provisions in a contract relating to liquidated damages are considered by the courts to be for the benefit of the employer they are to be construed against an employer who puts the contract forward. *Peak v McKinney* 1 BLR illustrates this point. Here the contract contained a liquidated damages clause but there was no provision for an extension of contract duration if some part of the delay was due to the employer's fault; if no such provision was included, the time at which the contract should have been completed was not determinable and so the time from when liquidated damages should apply was unknown. Hence, in this case, the employer was not entitled to deduct any liquidated damages. Lord Justice Salmon said

> The liquidated and extension of time clauses in printed forms of contract must be construed strictly *contra proferentem.* If the employer wishes to recover liquidated damages for failure by the contractor to complete on time in spite of the fact that some of the delay is caused by the employer's own fault or breach of contract, then the extension of time clause should provide, expressly or by necessary inference, for an extension on account of such a fault or breach on the part of the employer. I am unable to spell out any such provision out of [the contract] .... There had clearly been some delay on the part of the corporation [the employer]. Accordingly ... there is no date under the contract from which the defendant's liability to pay liquidated damages could be measured. And therefore none can be recovered.

Another example is furnished by clauses in which the employer or his or her agent is entitled to deduct monies from the contractor's account. Such clauses are clearly for the employer's benefit and are to be construed against the employer. In *Rosehaugh Stanhope v Redpath Dorman Long* 50 BLR 75, the contract appeared to give the employer's agent extensive, even draconian, powers to recover money on demand from the contractor upon an allegation by the agent that the contractor's work had caused the employer a loss equivalent to the sum demanded. Such a power has been described (not by the court) as 'a licence to liquidate the contractor' and the court made it clear that they would exploit any ambiguity in the contractor's favour. Lord Justice Bingham said

> I cannot believe that the parties intended one of them to be subject to a potentially crippling obligation upon a contingency. In any event, I consider these provisions to be ambiguous and so adopt the construction less favourable to the plaintiffs [the employer] whose document it is.

Printed, typed and manuscript writing
Finally, it is worth briefly mentioning a rule of construction which appears to have developed concerning contracts in which the terms are expressed by printed words, by typed words and possibly also by words in manuscript. This often happens in construction contracts where a printed form may be used as the basic document with typed additional or substitute clauses and perhaps with last minute agreements being recorded by hand. The rule, expressed in cases such as *The Brabant* [1967] 1 QB 588, suggests that, all other things being equal, manuscript words prevail over typed words, which in turn prevail over printed words.

7

Ending of construction and consultancy contracts

7.1 Introduction

In this chapter the ways in which construction and consultancy contracts may be 'ended' are discussed. 'Ended', in this context, does not necessarily mean 'eradicated' so that neither party may rely upon its terms in the future. Rather, it means that neither party will have the opportunity to make further performance under the contract without the consent of the other. The contract, as an agreement, however, may often continue in existence; accordingly actions to obtain rights under the contract or to recover damages for breaches of contract may often still be pursued on the basis of the contract agreement. For example, if a construction contract 'ends' because the contractor refuses to perform and the employer appoints another contractor to do the work, the contractor will not be entitled to change his mind and to render the agreed performance; but the employer will be able to sue the contractor on the grounds of breach of contract. Thus, while the contract is dead as far as further performance is concerned, it continues to govern the rights of the parties.

There are, however, a number of situations where the contract, in effect, disappears. An example of this is where the parties vary an existing agreement and in so doing expressly agree that all rights and liabilities under the previous agreement be discharged.

Five principal methods of ending a contract are considered in this chapter:

- performance
- agreement to discharge or vary the contract
- accepted fundamental breach
- termination under the terms of the contract
- frustration.

7.2 Performance

The usual method of ending a contract is by both parties performing all their obligations under it.

The normal rule is that the contract must be performed completely in accordance with its terms. In the case of a construction contract this will mean that the specifications and other contract requirements must be complied with to the letter. In some circumstances, however, a party who has provided a performance somewhat different to that specified may claim that the performance is sufficient. This possibility is examined in Section 11.4.

7.3 Agreement to discharge or vary the contract

An agreement to discharge or vary the contract will operate to substitute a new agreement, or no agreement, for the one formerly in existence. As with formation of contract, any agreement to discharge or vary the contract must be agreed upon by authorised agents of the parties and supported by consideration (see Section 5.11).

When there are obligations as yet unperformed by both parties, sufficient consideration is provided if they agree to discharge the contract by both forgoing the requirement that the other complete his or her contractual obligations. If one of the parties has completed his obligations and he agrees to a lesser performance from the other party then this will not be a binding agreement since no consideration has been given by the party who wishes to tender a lesser performance. In *D&C Builders v Rees* [1966] 2 QB 617, for example, the contractor completed his work and the employer then told him that he would have to accept a sum less than the contract price or else he would receive nothing at all. The contractor signed an agreement accepting the lesser sum and received it. He then sued for the full amount. The court held that the agreement was not binding since it was not supported by consideration and that the contractor was therefore entitled to recover the full contract price.

When a party accepts less than complete performance from the other in return for some undertaking from that other, this is often referred to as an 'accord and satisfaction'. Such agreements are typically made to avoid disputes being litigated or arbitrated and the consideration provided often consists of one party forgoing the right to pursue a bona fide claim.

7.4 Accepted fundamental breach or accepted repudiation

When a party to a contract indicates, either expressly or impliedly, that he or she intends no longer to comply with the contract, the other party (the innocent party) may elect whether or not to continue with his or her own performance of the contract. The party in breach may indicate that he no longer intends to comply with or be bound by the contract in one of two ways:

- by breaching a fundamental term of the contract
- by renouncing the contract, by words or by conduct.

Once such an indication has been given, the innocent party has the right to decide whether or not he or she wishes to continue with his or her performance of the contract. It is important to note the innocent party's right of election here; the contract is not automatically terminated, and will continue to exist if the innocent party affirms it. Hence the title of this section is *accepted* fundamental breach or *accepted* repudiation; that is acceptance by the innocent party of his or her opportunity to refuse further performance under the contract.

7.4.1 Fundamental breach

All breaches entitle the innocent party to sue for damages. But some breaches are considered so fundamental that they also entitle innocent parties to be released from their further performance of the contract if they so wish. Breaches which present the innocent party with this right are called 'fundamental breaches'.

In Section 6.5 the status of terms was discussed, including the classification of terms into conditions and warranties. The basic rule is that, upon the breach of a warranty, the innocent party would not be entitled to terminate the contract, but that, upon the breach of a condition, he or she would. The categorisation of terms into conditions and warranties is traditionally achieved by construing the contract and is not affected by the type of breach which actually occurred. However, following the Court of Appeal's decision in *Hong Kong Fir Shipping Company v Kawasaki Kisen Kaisha Ltd* [1962] 2 QB 26, it seems as though a rigid classification of terms into conditions and warranties may not be the appropriate approach to construction and consultancy contracts. Accordingly, it is perhaps more appropriate to talk in terms of a 'fundamental breach', rather than to decide whether the breach which occurs is a breach of a condition or of a warranty.

The test of whether the breach is fundamental or not appears to be one of impression rather than analysis. The guiding factors are perhaps, first, the importance which the parties would have attached to a breach of the term in question had they directed their minds to the matter at the time of making the contract; and second, how serious are the results of the breach. In the context of construction contracts, where the majority of terms may be breached in such a way so as to cause substantial damage, and also, in ways which produce little damage, it would seem that the second factor is, in most cases, the more important of the two. However, if the parties have attached a special significance to a particular term, the first factor may come into play and, in an appropriate case an insignificant breach of such a term may be considered 'fundamental'.

7.4.2 Repudiatory breach

A repudiation is a breach of contract whereby a party indicates that he or she intends not to perform an important obligation. When the time for the obligation to be performed has not yet arrived, this is often known as an 'anticipatory breach'. The breach consists, not of the failure to perform the obligation but, rather, of the renunciation of the agreement itself. Accordingly, the breach occurs upon the renunciation even though the time for performance is still in the future, and in this case, the innocent party may sue immediately upon the repudiation.

The question whether an indication by a party that he or she will not perform a contract obligation amounts to a repudiation is an important and difficult area in construction law. In the leading case of *Mersey Steel and Iron Co v Naylor Benzon & Co* (1884) 9 App Cas 434 at 438, Lord Selborne summarised the law's approach in the terms set out below:

> You must look at the actual circumstances of the case in order to see whether the one party to the contract is relieved from its future performance by the conduct of the other; you must examine what that conduct is so as to see whether it amounts to a renunciation, to an absolute refusal to perform the contract.

It is clear then that all the surrounding circumstances must be taken into account; but the overriding factor appears to be a consideration of whether there has been 'an absolute refusal to perform the contract'. The situation can be particularly difficult to interpret where the meaning of the contract is unclear and one party refuses to perform an obligation in accordance with the true construction of the contract, believing that some lesser or alternative performance is sufficient. In *Woodar Investment Development Ltd v Wimpey Construction (UK) Ltd* [1980] 1 All ER 571, Wimpey, a construction company, agreed to purchase land from Woodar at some time in the future as specified in the agreement. Wimpey then changed its mind about buying the land because land prices fell dramatically; however, it honestly believed it had a right under the contract to avoid the transaction and sent Woodar a notice of its intention not to complete. Wimpey's belief concerning its right to avoid the deal turned out to be ill-founded, but nonetheless the House of Lords held that there had been no repudiation. Lord Wilberforce said

> in considering whether there has been a repudiation by one party, it is necessary to look at his conduct as a whole. Does this indicate an intention to abandon and to refuse performance of the contract? In the present case, without taking Wimpey's conduct generally into account, Woodar's contention, that Wimpey had repudiated, would be a difficult one. So far from repudiating the contract, Wimpey were relying on it and invoking one of its provisions, to which both parties had given their consent. And unless the invocation of that provision were totally abusive, or lacking in good faith, (neither of which is contended for by [Woodar]), the fact that it has proved to be wrong in law cannot turn it into a repudiation.

7.4.3 Examples of events entitling an innocent party to refuse further performance

The analysis in the above sections makes it clear that all the circumstances must be taken into account in determining whether or not a breach, actual or anticipatory, entitles the innocent party to refuse to perform the contract further. Accordingly, the examples cited below are not to be treated as precedents, but as illustrations only.

Repudiation of a construction contract by the employer

Failure to give possession of the site   The majority of contracts provide for the employer to give such possession to the contractor as will enable him to construct the works. If the contract is silent then such a term will be implied. Failure to give possession at the appropriate time will, consequently, be a breach. Whether or not the breach is serious enough to constitute repudiation depends on the facts. If the employer says, 'I will not give you *any* possession', then this is, no doubt, an anticipatory repudiation entitling the contractor to treat the contract as being at an end.

If, however, the failure to give possession is not complete but partial, or is a delay rather than an outright refusal, then this may not amount to a repudiation. In *Carr v J A Berriman Pty Ltd* (1953) Comm LR 327, for instance, it was decided that delay alone may be insufficient to ground a repudiation unless it is clear that the employer intends not to be bound by the contract.

Failure to pay   Refusal to make a payment will not amount to a repudiation unless the employer evinces, by his failure to pay, an intention not to be bound by the contract. Usually, a failure to make a payment is associated with an honest belief on the part of the employer that he or she is entitled to refuse the payment under the terms of the contract. In *Mersey Steel and Iron Co v Naylor, Benzon & Co* [1884] 9 App Cas 434, for example, deliveries of steel were to be made in instalments with payment for each instalment to be made within three days of the receipt of shipping documents. However, the buyers, on legal advice, postponed payments. The sellers treated the postponement as a repudiation. The House of Lords held that it was not a repudiation since the buyers did not indicate their unwillingness to be bound by the contract. If the amount of payment withheld is so significant that it could not be treated as bona fide this may amount to a repudiation (see e.g. the comments of Lord Wilberforce in *Woodar v Wimpey,* quoted above, where he suggested that if a refusal was 'totally abusive or lacking in good faith' then this may cause the refusal to be a repudiation).

In view of the law expressed above, it is clear that contractors who have not been paid should carefully consider the position before they treat the employer's refusal to pay as a repudiation and elect to treat the contract as at an end. If they treat the contract as being at an end and it subsequently transpires (in litigation or arbitration) that the employer's failure to pay was not a repudiation of the contract, they may find themselves in repudiatory breach on account of their leaving the site and hence liable for substantial damages relating to the cost and delay associated in re-starting the work with a new contractor.

Repudiation of a construction contract by the contractor
Abandoning the site work   If the contractor abandons the site in such a way as to evince a refusal to carry out the work this is clearly a repudiation.

Defective performance   Seriously defective work, sufficient in its extent, and quality to make rectification impossible, or almost impossible, may well amount to a fundamental breach of the contract entitling the employer to treat the contract as being at an end.

Late performance   If the employer is to be entitled to treat the contract as being at an end, the contractor must be in fundamental breach. Generally speaking, terms of the contract relating to time obligations have been presumed not to give rise to fundamental breaches; it is said that 'time is not of the essence', meaning that time terms are not essential terms. Accordingly, unless there is a term in the contract making time of the essence no right to terminate the contract can flow from late performance. Such terms are normally required to be express but can in some cases (e.g. where hand-over must necessarily be before some particular date) be implied.

Because time is not normally of the essence, this may allow the contractor to abuse time obligations and so the law gives parties the power to make time of the essence simply by giving the other a notice stating that time obligations are being treated as essential. The notice, however, must be reasonable in its terms and hence must give the other sufficient time to complete the works in all the circumstances.

Subletting in breach   Construction contracts usually contain terms placing restrictions on the ability of the contractor to subcontract the work. In *Thomas Feather & Co (Bradford) Ltd v Keighley Corporation* (1953) 53 LGR 30 it was held that subcontracting in breach was not, in this case, a repudiation. This, however, is simply an illustration and in appropriate circumstances and with appropriate and clear contract wording, it is submitted that subletting without permission can be a fundamental breach.

Repudiation of a consultancy contract
The grounds which will constitute a repudiation of a consultancy contract will be similar to those which apply to construction contracts. Thus the client will be in repudiatory breach if he or she refuses to grant the consultant access to the site or to necessary information in circumstances where it is clear that the client intends not to be bound by the contract. Similarly, clients will be in fundamental breach if they withhold payment to the consultant in circumstances where clients indicate that they intend not to be bound by the contract. The consultant will be in breach of condition if he abandons the project, performs it so badly that no recovery is possible or is late in his time obligations after a notice has been issued making time of the essence.

7.4.4 Election

It is an important basic rule in contract law that, upon a repudiatory event or a fundamental breach, innocent parties may elect whether to treat the contract as being at an end or whether to continue with their performance of it. If innocent parties elect to treat the contract as being at an end, they may sue immediately for their loss.

Following a fundamental or repudiatory breach, the innocent party may affirm the contract, expressly or impliedly and will, in effect, be saying, 'I wish the contract to remain in force and I wish that we each continue to perform our obligations under it'. After the affirmation, the contract will be available for both parties to sue upon for breaches occurring before and after the fundamental breach.

The rule that the innocent party may affirm the contract may, in some situations, lead to absurdity in the construction context and it is not clear to what extent it applies. The leading case, *White & Carter (Councils) Ltd v McGregor* [1961] 3 All ER 1178, involved a company who supplied litter bins to the council. They were allowed to place advertising plates on the bins and in one transaction they agreed with the defendant that they would, over a period of 156 weeks, fix plates to litter bins to advertise the defendant's business. Payment was to be made in instalments. The whole price became payable if any instalment was still unpaid four weeks after it was due. The defendant, however, after entering into the contract decided not to go ahead with the agreement and they let the plaintiffs know that they would not pay, an anticipatory repudiation. The plaintiffs had, in theory, an option: they could elect to treat the contract at an end and sue for damages, or else they could continue to perform. They chose to continue to perform. The House of Lords held that they were entitled to do this.

The logical extension of *White & Carter v McGregor* appears to be that an employer or client who decides for some reason not to proceed with a project after he or she has entered into an agreement with a contractor or a consultant cannot theoretically cancel unless the contract provides such a right. The contractor can insist on constructing the works which the employer no longer wants; or a consultant can insist on designing buildings or compiling reports which are no longer required. However, in *White & Carter v McGregor,* Lord Reid indicated that his decision may have been based upon two factors which would not be present in normal construction or consultancy situations. First, the contractor in *White & Carter* was able to perform the work without the other party's cooperation, and second, the contractor had an interest in performing the contract because of the default clause which may cause the whole price to fall due early. That Lord Reid used these as possible distinguishing factors is important because the decision of the House of Lords was by the slightest majority of three to two, and this suggests that when these special factors are not present, the decision might well fall in favour of the defendant.

Further, Mr Justice Megarry in *London Borough of Hounslow v Twickenham Garden Developments* 7 BLR 81 decided that *White & Carter* was not applicable where the work was to be performed on the property of the other party. Curiously, however, he then went on to find an implied term in a building contract that the contractor was entitled to remain on the site (and to perform the work) unless and until the employer could show that the contractor was in breach of contract sufficiently to entitle the other to determine the contract (either under the terms of the contract or by breach of condition). This decision was heavily criticised by Mr Justice Mahon in *Mayfield Holdings Ltd v Moana Reef Ltd* [1973] NZLR 309. He could find no grounds for implying the term which Mr Justice Megarry found. He preferred to think that if they were asked at the time of making the contract what they had agreed if the relationship between contractor and employer had broken down they would answer: 'I [the contractor] agree that you [the employer] go ahead and finish the job, and I will sue you for my loss of profit'. The approach of Mr Justice Mahon was preferred (though not cited) by His Honour Judge Bowsher in *Tara Civil Engineering Ltd v Moorfield Developments Ltd* 46 BLR 72.

7.5 Determination under the terms of the contract

The law enforces the agreement of the parties. Accordingly, any determination clauses in the contract will be enforced providing they do not amount to a penalty clause or other species of unenforceable clause. Construction contracts often provide terms entitling the parties to determine the contract on the occurrence of specified events. It is, for example, very common for determination provisions to entitle an employer to terminate the contractor's employment if the contractor falls seriously behind the programme or becomes insolvent.

7.6 Frustration

Frustration of a contract occurs whenever the circumstances surrounding the performance of the contract obligations change so radically that the contract becomes an agreement to do something wholly different from what was envisaged at the time the agreement was originally made. The frustrating event must not be caused by either party. An example of where frustration of contract will occur is where a consultancy contract to design the refurbishment works for a building or the contract to perform the works have to be terminated because the building burns down by accident. Where the supervening event is not so catastrophic, however, the scope of the doctrine of frustration is not so clear and can best be gauged by an examination of the two leading cases, *Davis v Fareham* and *Metropolitan Water Board v Dick, Kerr.*

In *Davis Contractors Ltd v Fareham Urban District Council* [1956] AC 696, it was held that the contract had not been frustrated. Here, a contractor agreed to build seventy-eight houses in eight months. However, the contractor experienced an acute shortage of skilled labour and the work took twenty-two months. The contractor had agreed to build the houses for a fixed sum and in order to increase their remuneration they claimed that the contract had been frustrated and that they were entitled to be paid a reasonable sum for the work which they had done. The House of Lords said that the contract had not been frustrated. While the circumstances which the contractor encountered were different from those which he expected, they were not so radically different as to make the contract one to perform something entirely different from what he had agreed to do.

In *Metropolitan Water Board v Dick, Kerr and Co Ltd* [1918] AC 119, however, the contract was held to have been frustrated. Here, the contractor agreed to build reservoirs within a six-year period. The contract gave the engineer wide powers to extend the time for completion for delay due to 'difficulties, impediments, obstructions, oppositions ... whatsoever and howsoever occasioned'. In 1914 the war broke out and in February 1916 the minister stopped work on the reservoir and ordered the plant and materials to be sold. In November 1917 the work was still in suspension. The House of Lords held that the delay was of such a nature to fundamentally change the circumstances surrounding the contract. The contract had been frustrated despite the engineer's wide powers to extend the contract duration.

An interesting recent decision which involved a consideration of the doctrine of frustration is *McAlpine Humberoak v McDermott International* 51 BLR 34 (1992) CILL p. 747 (CA). This case concerned metalwork construction for the Hutton Tension Leg Platform in the Shetland Basin. The defendant was the main contractor for the deck structure and the plaintiff was subcontractor who was commissioned to undertake certain welding and fabrication work and, in particular, the construction of four 'pallets' to form part of the top deck of the platform. The contract provided for additional payments for variations to the work. The work was let before the design was sufficiently advanced and substantial modifications were made to the design with many additional drawings being issued. The subcontractor was eventually asked to bear the large costs which arose because of inefficiency in design and drawing issue. The works continued to completion as had the works in *Davis v Fareham*. It was held by the judge at first instance that the contract was frustrated because the 'ultimate situation in this case was not within the scope of this contract at the time of its formation on 18th November 1981'. It is difficult to see how this contract was frustrated any more than that in *Davis v Fareham*. An interesting twist in the case is that it was a mere legal fiction that the contract was made on 18 November 1981. It was in fact made on 24 March 1982 and was agreed to have effect backdated to the date of the letter of intent, namely 18 November 1981. The parties apparently knew quite well by March 1982 the way the work was progressing and the subcontractor still signed the agreement. On appeal, the Court of Appeal held that there was no frustration. Lord Justice Lloyd said

> We find ourselves unable to agree with the judge's conclusions that the contract was frustrated. The revised drawings did not 'transform' the contract into a different contract, or 'distort its substance and identity'. It remained a contract for the construction of four pallets . . . . If we were to uphold the judge's finding of frustration, this would be the first contract to have been frustrated by reason of matters which had not only been well known to the parties, but had also been provided for in the contract itself.

Restitution in the absence of a contract

8.1 Introduction

Restitution is that branch of the law which deals, in essence, with a claim by a person, A, that another, B, has been unjustly enriched at A's expense; the claim is for the recovery, the restitution, of the value of the enrichment which B has experienced at A's expense.

A claim in quasi-contract is a claim made under the principles of restitution in situations where a contractual claim would, in the ordinary course of things, be advanced, but because of some failure of the contract to come into existence or to continue in existence, such a contractual claim cannot be advanced. The terminology in this branch of the law is confusing and it is suggested that nothing is to be gained by the continued use of the description 'quasi-contract' but that the phrase 'restitution in the absence of a contract' provides a better statement of the nature and basis of the claim.

One way of describing the quantification of the claim is *quantum meruit* (as much as it is worth). This phrase is in widespread use and will be used in this chapter to describe the quantification generally of a restitution claim.

A variety of situations commonly arise where a restitution claim may properly be advanced because money, property or services have been expended by one person for the benefit of another but where the absence of a contract prevents a contractual claim. Such situations may be divided broadly into two categories:

- where a contract does not come into existence
- where the contract comes into existence but is later avoided or rescinded.

These situations are dealt with in the following sections.

8.2 Where a contract does not come into existence

8.2.1 Where the plaintiff has supplied services in an emergency

It often happens in construction work that a piece of work (e.g. a scaffold or piece of temporary works) becomes unstable or dangerous and action is required to preserve the integrity of the work, other property, or the safety of those in the vicinity. Because these problems often require immediate attention, the person specifically responsible for the work is not always available, or in a position to carry out the preventive work, and, on occasions, another person (whom we shall call 'the intervener') performs the emergency operations. The question arises whether or not the intervener is entitled to claim for this work from the responsible person.

Where the intervener is expressly requested to undertake the work by the person responsible no difficulty arises; the request is sufficient to create an obligation on the part of the responsible person to pay the intervener a reasonable amount for his or her services. Such a request is often sufficient, if acted upon, to bring a contract into existence so that the intervener is contractually entitled to charge a reasonable amount.

When, however, the intervener acts on his or her own initiative the situation is more difficult. In *Falcke v Scottish Imperial Insurance Co* (1886) 34 ChD 235 at 248–249 Lord Justice Bowen said

> The general principle is, beyond all question, that work or labour done or money expended by one man to preserve or benefit the property of another, do not according to English law create any lien upon the property saved or benefited, nor even, if standing alone, create an obligation to repay the expenditure. Liabilities are not be forced on people behind their backs any more than you can confer a benefit upon a man against his will.

Goff and Jones (*The Law of Restitution* by Lord Goff of Chieveley and Gareth Jones, 3rd edition at p. 338 *et seq.*) suggest that the intervener should be entitled to be reimbursed for his or her services in some circumstances and in particular if the intervener is a professional doing a professional job. They put the possible recovery in the following way:

> As a general rule we would prefer to limit the stranger's claim to the sums which he has expended, including the materials which have been used in his attempt to preserve the property. He should recover these expenses even if his intervention is unsuccessful; for it is proper to assume that the defendant would have authorised this expenditure if he had been given the opportunity of doing so. But the courts should reimburse the stranger only for expenses which were reasonably incurred in, and which contributed to, the attempts to preserve the property in an emergency. They should not reimburse him for expenses which no reasonable person would have incurred. Nor should they compensate him, through a restitutionary claim, for any damage which he has suffered through his intervention. A roofing contractor may recover the cost of materials used for repairing the roof but not compensation for the loss of any arm broken while doing so.

8.2.2 Where one person commences work in the expectation that a contract will eventuate

It frequently happens that while parties are still negotiating a contract one of them will commence the work which it is intended will be regulated by the contract. For instance, in the context of construction, the professional team and the contractor will often begin work before the contracts have been agreed. Two principles regarding this situation emerge from the decided cases:

- that the contract, when eventually agreed, will operate to cover all work including that undertaken before the date of the agreement, unless otherwise stated in the contract
- that if no contract eventuates, then the professional or contractor is entitled to be paid by the employer on a *quantum meruit* provided that the work which was carried out was done for the benefit of the employer and at his or her request, implied or express.

A number of points are raised in this context.

Preparatory work

In *William Lacey (Hounslow) Ltd v Davis* [1957] 1 WLR 932 the plaintiffs submitted a tender for the reconstruction of a damaged building. Their tender was the lowest of those received and the defendant employer encouraged them to believe that the contract would be awarded to them. Acting on this encouragement they performed a substantial amount of preparatory work, including calculations and revising estimates, which work was outside the normal work involved when tendering. No contract came into being, however, because the defendants sold the building. The plaintiffs sought to recover the value of the extra work which they had undertaken, even though the defendant had not benefited from that work. Mr Justice Barry held that the plaintiffs were entitled to recover. A similar situation arose in *Marston Construction Co Ltd v Kigass Ltd* 46 BLR 114. Here again, a company had performed preparatory works expecting a contract to come into existence. Although there was no express request that the contractor should perform this preparatory work, Judge Bowsher allowed the contractor to recover because it was performed under a mutual belief and understanding that the contract would be entered into and was performed for the benefit of the employer.

Contractual counter-claims

Contractors often supply goods and services which are accepted by the employer while negotiations are taking place. If no contract eventuates, this situation can operate unfairly for the employer. This is because the supplier of the goods and services can claim a *quantum meruit* for them, but the employer cannot, in theory, make a contractual counter-claim (e.g. for late delivery) because no contract exists. In *British Steel Corporation v Cleveland Bridge and Engineering Co Ltd* [1984] 1 All ER 504 this problem arose. The dispute concerned steelwork for a bank in Saudi Arabia. Cleveland Bridge Engineering (CBE) was the subcontractor for the steel fabrication. The parties began negotiations during the course of which the following 'letter of intent' was issued by CBE:

> Sama Bank – Dammam
> We are pleased to advise you that it is the intention of Cleveland Bridge & Engineering Co. Ltd to enter into a Sub-Contract with your company, for the supply and delivery of the steel castings which form the roof nodes on this project. The price will be as quoted in your telex (Mr. Dorrance to Mr. Roberts) dated 9th February '79 .... The form of Sub-Contract to be entered into will be our standard form of sub-contract for use in conjunction with the I.C.E. General Conditions of Contract, a copy of which

is enclosed .... We understand that you are already in possession of a complete set of our node detail drawings and we request that you proceed immediately with the works pending the preparation and issuing to you of the official form of sub-contract.

British Steel commenced work immediately so as not to delay the delivery dates. They did not have all the drawings and there were lengthy discussions and negotiations concerning the technical specification and the terms of contract to govern the contract. The technical matters were finally resolved but there was little agreement concerning the contract terms. As matters progressed, however, the existence, or not, of a contract became a crucial matter since CBE alleged late delivery of the steelwork; if there was no contract it could not be alleged that the delivery was late since there would be no binding agreement concerning when deliveries should be made. It was argued by CBE that there was a contract. Mr Justice Goff considered the effect of the letter of intent:

> In my judgment, the true analysis of the situation is simply this. Both parties confidently expected a formal contract to eventuate. In these circumstances, to expedite performance under that anticipated contract, one requested the other to commence the contract work, and the other complied with that request. If thereafter, as anticipated, a contract was entered into, the work done as requested will be treated as having been performed under that contract; if contrary to their expectation, no contract was entered into, then the performance of the work is not referable to any contract the terms of which can be ascertained, and the law simply imposes an obligation on the party who made the request to pay a reasonable sum for such work as has been done pursuant to that request.

Mr Justice Goff concluded that in the circumstance no contract came into existence at all and that therefore no damages for breach of contract could be claimed. The effect of this was to allow BSC to claim for the work it had done at CBE's request, but to bar the defendants' counter-claim for damages for late delivery because there was no contract in existence. Against this, academics have argued (e.g. Ball, S N (1983) 99 LQR 572) that this injustice might be remedied by the courts being more willing to find a contract if necessary by supplying essential terms.

8.3 Where the contract ceases to exist

A contract may cease to exist in a number of situations, for example

- where the contract is voidable for mistake and is later set aside (e.g. see *Huddersfield Banking Co Ltd v Henry Lister & Son Ltd* [1895] 2 Ch 273 where Lord Justice Kay said: 'It seems to me that, both on principle and authority, when once the court finds that an agreement has been come to between parties who were under a common mistake of a material fact, the court may set it aside')
- where the contract is voidable because the agreement was obtained by duress but it is avoided by the weaker party once the duress has been lifted
- where the contract is frustrated
- where the contract is rescinded on grounds of misrepresentation.

In the third and fourth situations the legislature has provided statutory rules and powers respectively through the Law Reform (Frustrated Contracts) Act 1943 and the Misrepresentation Act 1967. However, in all cases, the courts will seek to apply, so far as they may, the basic principles of the law of restitution, namely that one person should not be able to benefit unjustly through the expenditure of another.

In regard to the Law Reform (Frustrated Contracts) Act 1943 the leading commentators, Goff and Jones, have said that '[i]n our view the fundamental principle underlying the Act is, quite simply, the principle of unjust enrichment'. For those interested in a judicial analysis of the 1943 Act see *BP Exploration Co (Libya) Ltd v Hunt (No 2)* [1979] 1 WLR 783, [1981] 1 WLR 232 (CA) and [1983] 2 AC 352.

In regard to misrepresentation the common law allowed rescission by a misrepresentee followed by a restoration of benefits provided by each party. In *Newbigging v Adam* (1886) 34 Ch 3 582 at 595 Lord Justice Bowen indicated that, following rescission, there should be 'a giving back and a taking back on both sides', which produces a result in line with the principles of the law of restitution. However, in much construction work, services are often transferred rather than goods or money and restitution, in the same form in which it was rendered, is not possible. In such circumstances, the courts are reluctant to allow rescission (see e.g. *Glasgow and South Western Railway v Boyd and Forrest,* [1915] SC (HL) 20). The enactment of the Misrepresentation Act, however, allows the plaintiff to recover damages in the case of negligent misrepresentation (Section 2(1)) and provides the court with power to order damages in lieu of rescission in the event of an innocent misrepresentation (Section 2(2)). There is, however, no indication in the statute concerning the quantification of the damages. It would seem that a just solution would be to treat the claim as one based on the principles of restitution, thereby putting the plaintiff in the position he would have been in had he not engaged in the contract.

8.4 *Quantum meruit*

The principle of *quantum meruit* is plain and clear. The plaintiff is entitled in the appropriate circumstances to receive a reasonable sum for his or her services. The valuation of that reasonable sum will be a question for evidence, usually expert evidence, or, as often happens in construction, for the decision of an arbitrator qualified in that field.

In some situations, however, services are rendered in the expectation that their remuneration will be greater than a reasonable sum calculated purely on the quantity of work supplied. In *Way v Latilla* [1937] 3 All ER 759, the plaintiff provided valuable information to a company relating to gold mines in Africa in the expectation that he would receive a share in the concession to be awarded to the company. However, no binding agreement regarding payment was ever made though, in Lord Atkin's words: 'the parties had discussed remuneration on the footing of what may loosely be called a "participation" and nothing else'. The plaintiff sued for the value of his services and the court held that he was entitled to a *quantum meruit* based not simply on the number of hours' work and his reasonable charging rate but having regard to the nature of the intended agreement. They said that the plaintiff 'was employed on the basis of receiving a remuneration depending on results'. He was awarded £5000. Similar situations commonly arise in the construction industry, particularly in the field of speculative development work where information concerning future development opportunities is passed on to others on the basis that the remuneration will depend on future profits.

8.5 Miscellaneous mistakes and the bounds of the law of restitution

In some circumstances benefits may be transferred from the plaintiff to the defendant where the law will not require restitution. This is where the enrichment of the defendant is not unjust because the defendant has not encouraged the plaintiff and the defendant cannot return the benefit he or she has acquired.

The following examples illustrate the position at law. The first is taken from Goff and Jones at page 39:

> A builder contracts with a third party whom he mistakenly but reasonably believes owns Blackacre to build a swimming pool on Blackacre. He does so. The third party who has not paid the builder is evicted by the true owner. A sub-contractor contracts with the main contractor to install light fittings in the owner's house. He does so. The contractor is unable to pay him. English as well as American courts will deny the builder and the sub-contractor any restitutionary claim against the owner.

The second comes from Lord Cranworth in *Ramsden v Dyson* (1866) LR 1 HL 129 140–1 cited in *Proctor v Bennis* [1887] Ch D 740 by Lord Justice Cotton:

> If a stranger begins to build on my land supposing it to be his own, and I, perceiving his mistake, abstain from setting him right, and leave him to persevere in his error, a court of equity will not allow me afterwards to assert my title to the land on which he had expended money on the supposition that the land was his own. It considers that, when I saw the mistake into which he had fallen, it was my duty to be active and to state my adverse title; and it would be dishonest in me to remain wilfully passive on such an occasion, in order afterwards to profit by the mistake which I might have prevented.

Payment for construction work performed under contract

9.1 Introduction

When no contract comes into existence, the obligation (if any) to pay for work performed arises under the principles of restitution discussed in Chapter 8. In the great majority of cases, the work is performed under contract. The present chapter deals with payment under the contract.

The principal obligation of the contractor under a construction contract is to perform the agreed work; the principal obligation of the employer is to pay for it. Often, the payment obligations will be set out at length in the contract and, in this situation, the problems which arise generally relate to the construction of the terms that have been agreed rather than the implication of additional payment terms. A number of matters, however, relating to the general principles of construction of payment provisions, merit consideration. In addition, the position at law, in a number of miscellaneous situations such as when no price is expressly agreed or when the employer refuses to pay the full amount claimed by the contractor on the grounds that the contractor already owes the employer some money, will be discussed in this chapter.

9.2 When no price is expressly agreed

9.2.1 A reasonable price

When a contract is agreed but no express terms relating to payment are agreed, the law will imply an obligation for the employer to pay a reasonable price: see the Supply of Goods and Services Act 1982.

9.2.2 Is the price an essential term in construction contracts?

There is some authority for the proposition that a complex construction contract cannot come into existence unless the price is agreed. The rationale for this is that the price is so fundamental that overall agreement, sufficient to create a contract, sometimes cannot be considered to be reached without agreement on price. However, in *BSC v Cleveland Bridge*

Engineering [1984] 1 All ER 504 Mr Justice Goff put the law in the following terms:

> In the course of his argument counsel for BSC submitted that, in a contract of this kind, the price is always an essential term in the sense that, if it is not agreed, no contract can come into existence. In support of his contention counsel relied on a dictum of Lord Denning MR in *Courtney & Fairbairn Ltd v Tolaini Bros (Hotels) Ltd* [1975] 1 All ER 716 at 719, [1979] 1 WLR 297 at 301 to the effect that the price in a building contract is of fundamental importance. I do not however read Lord Denning MR's dictum as stating that in every building contract the price is invariably an essential term, particularly as he expressly referred to the substantial size of the contract then before the court. No doubt in the vast majority of business transactions, particularly those of substantial size, the price will indeed be an essential term, but in the final analysis it must be a question of construction of the particular transaction whether it is so. In the present case, however, I have no doubt whatsoever that, consistently with the view expressed by Lord Denning MR . . . the price was indeed an essential term, on which (among other essential terms) no final agreement was ever reached.

9.3 The contract type: its effect on calculations of total payment due

9.3.1 A note on the classification of contracts

In Section 4.3.2 a variety of classifications for construction contracts based on the method of payment were described; these included lump sum, re-measurement and cost-plus categories. A note of caution relating to such classifications should be sounded here. The legal categorisation of a contract may differ from that into which it appears to fall on first impression. For instance the standard form of building contract (JCT 80) frequently operates with bills of quantities and thus looks, at first glance, as though it may produce a re-measurement contract since there are elaborate provisions for altering the sums due to the contractor under the contract in accordance with the rates set out in the bills. The JCT 80 contract is, however, in law, a lump sum contract. The contractor agrees in essence (see especially Articles 1 and 2 of the Articles of Agreement) to do a defined quantity of work for a fixed sum. The sum may vary under the contract if the work actually carried out is different from that which is set out in the bills of quantities, but the sum is altered from the originally agreed sum rather than re-measured in its entirety. The fact that the price can be changed in a wide variety of situations does not destroy the essence of the lump sum basis of the agreement.

9.3.2 Lump sum contracts

In principle, the simplest form of contract is a lump sum contract. If a contractor agrees to undertake certain works and the employer agrees to pay a certain price, without reference to any particular standard form of contract, a lump sum contract will be created.

In lump sum contracts, the extent of the work to be undertaken for the stated price must be ascertained. The contract price is a sum which covers only the contract works. The contractor is not obliged to perform other works unless there is a term in the contract requiring him to do so; in these cases additional payment will normally be recoverable.

When there are no bills of quantities incorporated into the contract, the scope of the work will be defined on the basis of what work was necessary to carry out those works described in the contract. See, in this regard, *Williams v Fitzmaurice* (1858) 3 H&N 844, discussed in Section 11.2.2.

Where bills of quantities form part of the contract, the contractor is still required to carry out whatever work is required to complete the project but the work in excess of that included in the bills is normally to be classed as 'additional work' and is to be paid for at the billed rates or, if none, at a reasonable rate. In *Patman & Fotheringham v Pilditch* (1904) Hudson's Building Contracts 4th Edition Vol II p. 368, for example, the contract required the contractor to build a block of flats 'according to the plans, invitation to tender, specification and bills of quantities signed by the contractors'. The actual quantities of work exceeded those in the bill and some work was not described in the bill. Nonetheless, the contractor recovered additional payment for those items. The meaning of the bill and the scope of each billed item will be construed in accordance with the general principle of *Williams v Fitzmaurice*, namely that the item will include those things which it is objectively understood to include.

9.3.3 Re-measurement contracts

A re-measurement contract is one where the sums payable are computed by measuring the total quantity of work of each description and paying the billed rate for each unit of work of that description. In a re-measurement contract it is often not a matter of great importance whether or not a piece of work is described in the bill of quantities. If the work is already covered by a item in the bill it must be paid for at that billed rate. If there is no appropriate rate in the bill but there is a mechanism for determining the rate (e.g. the certifier may have to determine a rate having regard to the rates for similar items in the bill), that mechanism is to be activated. If there is no such mechanism, then a reasonable price is to be paid: see *Re Walton-on-the-Naze UDC v Moran* (1905) Hudson's Building Contracts 4th Edition Vol II p. 376. The question of what work is included in each billed item is a question of construing the bill in the light of the overall contract; this process is often made certain by including a Method of Measurement in the contract by which the billed items are drawn up.

9.3.4 Pricing errors in bills of quantities

Pricing errors commonly occur in bills of quantities. The rate is often correctly inserted into the bill, but the computation of the price based on those rates is incorrect. The problem is, in fact, not acute in the case of a re-measurement contract since such an error will disappear on re-measurement. In a lump sum contract, on the other hand, these errors will not disappear and it may not be possible to imply a term that such errors may be corrected. It is, however, impossible to make generalisations about this; the whole contract including the overall scheme of payment must be considered.

9.3.5 Cost-plus and target contracts

A cost-plus contract is one where the contractor is to be repaid his or her costs incurred in performing the work, plus a 'fee'. This fee may, as discussed in Section 4.3.2, be a lump sum, a simple percentage or be adjusted in accordance with the contractor's performance relative to time and money targets. In cost-plus contracts a number of problems may frequently arise, including the definition of the term 'cost' in this context and the question of the employer's obligation to pay for work which is performed in an inefficient or wasteful manner so that its cost is higher than it would have been if performed efficiently.

The definition of cost
Cost-plus contracts often include complex definitions of 'cost'. The meaning of cost is then determined by construing the contract. When the contract is a simple agreement without detail what is the position? The meaning of 'cost', unless otherwise defined, is, it is submitted, the actual cost to the contractor, including internal direct costs, but excluding the cost of general off-site overheads which do not relate specifically to the project.

The employer's liability for the contractor's extravagance
Frequently there are safeguards protecting the employer from having to pay for any extravagance on the contractor's part. Subject to contrary express provisions, the contractor is entitled, it is submitted, to recover all his costs, even if he has not worked with complete efficiency. The test is, it is submitted: has he performed the overall project with the skill and care of a reasonable contractor? If so, he is entitled to be paid for all costs incurred. The fact that an individual item of work was inefficiently performed does not disentitle the contractor from being paid the actual cost to him for that item unless it was performed in a grossly inept or wilfully extravagant manner. Inefficiencies occur on all projects and must be taken to be a normal part of construction to be balanced against those items of work which the contractor performs with better than average efficiency.

9.3.6 Work outside the contract

When the contractor performs work which falls outside the scope of the contract and this work is necessary to complete the contract works and is requested, expressly or impliedly by the employer, it is to be paid for on a *quantum meruit* (see Chapter 8). In modern construction standard forms it is usual for such works to be covered by the variations clause and thus to form part of the varied contract description.

9.4 Entire and severable contracts

9.4.1 Definitions

An entire contract is one in which every element of the obligation forms part of an indivisible whole. The effect of a contract being entire is that, in the absence of express or implied contrary provisions, the party who, in breach, performs only part of his or her obligation cannot sue for payment for that part. The situation is different, of course, where one party is in breach and, as a result of that breach, the other party cannot perform the entirety of the work. Here, the innocent party may sue for that element done as part of the general damages recoverable.

A severable contract is one which can be subdivided. Contracts for the supply of goods or services on an ongoing basis are often severable. Thus if a contractor agrees to supply construction services, if and when required, in accordance with agreed rates over a stated period of time, then each discrete request for the supply of services will create an obligation to pay.

9.4.2 Construction contracts are prima facie entire contracts

In *Modern Engineering (Bristol) Ltd v Gilbert Ash (Northern) Ltd* [1974] AC 689, Lord Diplock said 'a building contract is an entire contract for the sale of goods and work and labour and work done for a lump sum price payable by instalments as the goods are delivered and the work is done'. This suggests that a construction contract is prima facie an entire contract. The effect of this is illustrated in *Sumpter v Hedges* [1898] 1 QB 673. In this case a contractor was contracted to build two houses but he only part completed the work and then left site. It was held that even though the employer had received a considerable benefit from the work which the contractor had done, the contractor could not recover for the benefit supplied as he had not completed his obligations under what was an entire contract.

Clearly there is considerable scope for the abuse by owners of the rule concerning entire contracts: they can allege that some minute proportion of the work was not performed and refuse to pay on that basis. The possibility of such abuse is largely avoided by two factors: one is the doctrine of law known as 'substantial performance', the second is the common practice of using stage payments in construction contracts.

9.4.3 Substantial performance

According to this doctrine a party may sue for work performed provided that he or she has 'substantially performed' it. An example is provided by *Hoenig v Isaacs* [1952] 2 All ER 176. Here, certain works of interior design and furniture making were to be performed. The employer paid some of the agreed price but refused to pay anything like the whole amount on the grounds that some elements of the work were not completed. The court held that the work was substantially complete and that, therefore, the contractor was entitled to the whole cost less the amount representing the cost of repair and completion of the outstanding items.

9.4.4   Stage payments

In practice, many of the problems associated with the failure of the contractor substantially to complete an 'entire contract' are avoided by the use of stage payments. Suppose the contractor in *Sumpter v Hedges* had been paid a sum in advance, which sum was less than the value of the work actually performed. Could the employer have recovered this back from him on the basis that since the contract had not been substantially performed, no payment was due? It seems that the employer would not be entitled to recover the advance payment in total unless he could show a 'total failure of consideration', which in the example proposed could not be proved. If, however, the employer made an advance which was greater than the value of the work actually provided then he would be able to recover the excessive payment under the general principles of restitution as well as damages for breach of contract.

9.5   Implied obligation to make stage payments

It is common practice in the construction industry for payment to be made in stages during the work. The advantages of this to the contractor are that his cashflow is eased and other risks associated with long-term credit are avoided. Further, stage payments provide the contractor with a practical defence against a possible claim by the employer that the contract is entire and that substantial completion has not been achieved (see Section 9.4.4).

The stages provided for in standard form contracts are normally time stages. Often monthly time intervals are used; each month, the value of the payment to be made is assessed. In some standard form contracts, the stages for payment are defined by the proportion of the total work performed.

Often, especially with smaller contracts, the parties may have failed to include any express provisions concerning stage payments. The contractor will often still wish to be paid in convenient stages in order to ease his cashflow. If, however, he is to receive stage payments in these circumstances he must show that there is an implied term to this effect in the contract. He cannot do this on the basis of business efficacy and, hence, should rely on the 'usual practice' in the industry. Some support for this approach is provided by the following dictum by Mr Justice Phillimore in *The Tergeste* [1903] p. 26: 'A man who contracts to do a long, costly piece of work does not contract, unless he expressly says so, that he will do all the work, standing out of pocket until he is paid at the end'. And in *Modern Engineering v Gilbert-Ash* [1974] AC 689 Lord Morris said: 'It is manifest that it would not be reasonable or fair to expect a contractor to wait until

What is a reasonable time is a question of fact to be determined in all the circumstances. If the contractor fails to complete within a reasonable time he will be in breach of contract and he will be liable for any loss which the employer suffers as a result of that breach.

10.2.2   Where a completion date is expressed

Where a completion date is expressed, the contractor will be obliged to complete the contractual work by that date. Most professionally drafted contracts will also contain an 'extension of time clause' to extend the completion date in the event that any matter at the employer's risk hinders the contractor in the performance of the work, or in the event that the employer orders a variation to the works. If the employer delays the contractor in any way and no suitable provision for extending the contract duration is included in the contract, the expressed time obligation will fall and will be replaced by an obligation to complete within a reasonable time. This is often referred to as putting time 'at large': see further Section 10.3.2.

10.2.3   Does the contractor have an obligation to maintain reasonable progress when constructing the works?

A question which often arises is: does the contractor have an obligation to maintain reasonable progress when constructing the works, in addition to his obligation to complete the whole of the works within the contract time (or, if none is stated, a reasonable time)? A reading of the relevant cases and professional textbooks does not provide a clear answer. In *Greater London Council v The Cleveland Bridge Engineering Co Ltd and another* 34 BLR 57, Mr Justice Staughton had to consider whether, and if so, to what extent, such terms might be implied. The contract was for the manufacture and erection of the gates and gate arms for the Thames Barrier. There were 'key dates' described in the contract and liquidated damages were payable as an exclusive remedy if those dates were not met. Clause 19 of the contract allowed the employer to remove the contractor from site and have the work completed by others if the contractor failed to proceed with due diligence and expedition. But the employer contended that there was an additional term to be implied that the contractor was, in any event, to work with due diligence and expedition and that damages would be payable for the breach of such a term. Mr Justice Staughton reviewed the law set out in the leading textbooks:

> There is a difference of view in the textbooks on this problem. *Hudson's Building and Engineering Contracts* (10th Edn), p. 611, has this passage:
>
>> for practical purposes, the implication of a fundamental term requiring due diligence by the builder is more essential to the employer in comparatively lengthy contracts for work done such as building contracts . . . It is submitted that in most building contracts this term is necessary to give the contract business efficacy and that where a builder persists in a rate of progress bearing no relation to a specified or reasonable date of completion, and the employer gives him notice requiring a reasonable rate of progress, if

he then fails to proceed at a reasonable rate he will be evincing an intention
no longer to be bound by the contract and his dismissal would be justified,
notwithstanding the absence of any express term empowering the employer
to determine.

In contrast, *Keating on Building Contracts* (4th Edn), p. 59, says:

It has been suggested that where there is no express provision as to
progress, business efficacy requires the implication of a term that the
contractor will proceed with reasonable diligence and maintain reasonable
progress. It is thought that while such a term may have to be implied
in some cases each contract and its surrounding circumstances must be
considered, and that there is no such rule of general application. It may
well be that in some cases the contractor's only duty is to complete by
the due date.

Mr Justice Staughton then went on to discuss a related point; whether
the contractor is free to plan his work within the project duration as he
pleases. If he is free to plan his work as he wishes this would not square
well with an implied term that he was under an obligation to proceed with
due diligence and expedition. The judge continued

There is, moreover, a general principle applicable to building and engineering
contracts that in the absence of any indication to the contrary, a contractor
is entitled to plan and perform the work as he pleases, provided always
that he finishes it by the time fixed in the contract. That is exemplified
by the case of *Wells v Army and Navy Cooperative Society* (1902) 2 Hudson's
Building Contracts (4th Edn) 346 ... Lord Justice Vaughan Williams said
at p. 354:

in the contract one finds the time limited within which the builder is to
do this work. That means not only that he is to do it within that time,
but it means that he is to have that time within which to do it. To my
mind that limitation of time is clearly intended, not only as an obligation,
but as a benefit to the builder ... in my judgment, where you have a
time clause and a penalty clause, it is always implied in such clauses that
the penalties are only to apply if the builder has, as far as the building
owner is concerned and his conduct is concerned, that time accorded to
him for the execution of the works which the contract contemplates he
should have.

In conclusion Mr Justice Staughton said

If there had been a term as to due diligence, I consider that it would have
been, when spelt out in full, an obligation on the contractors to execute the
works with such diligence and expedition as were reasonably required in
order to meet the key dates and completion date in the contract.

All in all, then, this case suggests that no term for due diligence and
expedition is to be implied. However, it has to be recognised that this
decision was made in the light of a contract which contained key dates for
completion in addition to the overall completion date; it also contained an
express term dealing with due diligence and expedition which was silent
on the question of whether lack of diligence and expedition was a breach.
However, in cases of projects of long duration without intermediate

completion obligations, it is submitted that an obligation for the contractor to proceed with due diligence and expedition may well be implied. But, since it is generally the contractor's right to plan his work as he pleases, he would not be in breach of his obligation to proceed with due diligence unless his work was so slow that no reasonable contractor would work in that manner, given the overall contract obligation.

10.3 Extensions of time clauses

10.3.1 The importance of an adequate extension of time clause

As mentioned briefly in Section 10.2.2 it is most desirable to include an extension of time clause into a construction contract whenever a completion date is set. Otherwise, if the employer causes the contractor to be late, either directly, by ordering extras or, indirectly, by being the party at risk under contract for any factor which delays the contractor, the time obligation will fall and time will be put 'at large'; in other words the contractor's obligation will now be to complete within a reasonable time. In the case of a contract containing a liquidated damages clause this will also lead to the employer losing his right to claim liquidated damages. This is because there will be no directly ascertainable date from which such damages will run.

Because of the need to retain an ascertainable time for completion, most properly drafted construction contracts contain very widely drafted extensions of time clauses to avoid such a possibility. For example, the ICE 6th Edition contract lists a wide range of situations under which the contractor may claim an extension of time and concludes with a 'catch-all' which entitles the contractor to claim in the event of 'other special circumstances of any kind whatsoever which may occur' – Clause 44 (i) (e).

10.3.2 Time at large

When the completion date is no longer applicable and there is no extensions of time clause which covers the cause of the delay, what new time obligations are there upon the contractor?

When the completion date becomes inapplicable, time is often said to be 'at large', a phrase apparently first used by Baron Parke in *Holme v Guppy* (1831) 3 M&W 387 and remarked upon by Lord Justice Lloyd in *McAlpine Humberoak v McDermott International Inc* (1992) CILL 747 at p. 749, where he said: 'Even if time is "at large" (whatever that may mean)'. The idea which the phrase appears to convey is that there is no set time for completion and that the contractor may have as long as he likes to complete. It is clear, however, that whenever a completion date becomes inapplicable the contractor's obligation is to complete in a reasonable time. In *McAlpine Humberoak* the contractor appeared to argue that, once time had been put at large, he could have all the time he wished for, providing there was no positive evidence of culpable delay on his part. The Court of Appeal, however, decided that the contractor should only have a reasonable time to perform. The question of what is a reasonable time is a question of fact and is to be judged in the light of all the surrounding circumstances, including the originally envisaged time, if any, in the contract. In *McAlpine Humberoak* the approach to this computation was clearly seen. Here, the employer had delayed the contractor by issuing drawings and instructions. The last issue was on 11 June but the employer claimed an earlier date as the reasonable completion date. Counsel for the contractor argued that the reasonable completion date could not precede the final drawing issue on 11 June. However, Lord Justice Lloyd said

> Counsel for McAlpine Humberoak submits that, since the extra work is covered by the definition of 'the Work' in clause 1 of the Contract, and since the extra work was not ordered until 11 June, the date for the completion of the contract cannot precede that date. Accordingly McDermott's claim for damages cannot run from 1 May. We do not agree. Here, as we have said, McDermott are claiming unliquidated damages. Obviously they cannot recover damages for any additional delay caused by the extra work. But this was taken care of by the three weeks allowed for by Mr McLauchlan [the employer's surveyor], and by the ten and a half weeks which we are allowing ourselves. If a contractor is already a year late through his culpable fault, it would be absurd that the employer should lose his claim for unliquidated damages just because, at the last moment, he orders an extra coat of paint. On the facts of this case and the conditions of this contract the ordering of extra work on 11 June did not have that effect. McDermott were not deprived of their right to damages.

10.3.3 Extensions of time and the contractor's right to be able to plan his work

Generally, the contractor is entitled to be able to plan his work and a failure by the employer or his or her agent reasonably to grant appropriate extensions of time sufficiently promptly to enable him to do so may represent a further cause of delay. The situation sometimes arises, however, where the extension of time cannot be determined until after the works are completed. If the factors causing delay are outside the employer's control then retrospective extensions of time will be allowed. In *Amalgamated Building Contractors Ltd v Waltham Holy Cross UDC* [1952] 2 All ER 452, for example, the contractor claimed an extension due to difficulties in obtaining labour and materials. Lord Justice Denning said that since this clause operated every day until the works were completed it was, therefore, not possible to decide on the appropriate extension until the works were completed.

10.4 The effect of failure to complete on time

10.4.1 Is time of the essence?

Where the contract does specify a completion date the question arises whether a breach of that term is a breach sufficient to allow the other party to refuse further performance; in other words is the breach of the time terms a 'fundamental breach' (see Section 7.4). When a breach of the time obligation does involve a fundamental breach, time is said to be 'of the essence'.

In cases involving the sales of goods, time has often been held to be of the essence. But the courts have been most unwilling to treat time as being of the essence in construction cases. The difference in approach is, no doubt, due to the fact that if a sale of goods contract is terminated, the goods can readily be returned, while this is not so in the case of a building which automatically becomes the employer's property because it is fixed to his land. If time were of the essence, in a construction contract, the employer could terminate the agreement if completion was just one day late without paying the builder; this unjust result is one that the courts, naturally, wish to avoid.

Although it appears that it is generally to be presumed in construction contracts that time is not of the essence, the courts have allowed the employer to make time of the essence by service of a notice on the contractor, following which he will have a reasonable time to comply: see for example *Carr v JA Berriman Pty Ltd* (1953) Comm LR 327. If the contractor still fails to comply with a reasonable time obligation, the employer may treat the contract as being at an end and refuse further performance. Time may thus be made 'of the essence' by reasonable notice even where it was not 'of the essence' at the time of making the contract. However, if time is not of the essence the employer may still recover damages for the breach of the time obligation. But the rule whereby the employer can serve the contractor with a notice making time of the essence prevents the contractor refusing to complete and is particularly valuable where there are no liquidated damages provisions (see Section 10.5) and where the employer will have difficulty proving a real loss.

10.4.2   Damages for late completion

In many construction contracts the parties agree in advance a sum or rate representing the genuine pre-estimate of the employer's loss should the contractor fail to complete on time. This is termed 'liquidated damages' and is dealt with in Section 10.5.

Where no liquidated damages provisions are included, the normal rules apply; that is to say, if the contractor fails to complete the works by the agreed date, or by a reasonable date if no completion date is expressed (or, if the completion date becomes inapplicable: see Section 10.3), then the employer can recover any losses he or she sustains. The general principles of calculating such losses are discussed in Chapter 22.

10.5   Liquidated damages clauses

10.5.1   Liquidated damages: definition

Liquidated damages are all those fixed sums in contracts which are payable upon the breach of contract by the party. They may be contrasted with 'unliquidated damages' which have not been reduced to a defined sum and are claimable only upon proof of loss in accordance with the principles set out in Chapter 22.

Liquidated damages are used in a variety of situations but most commonly as a fixed remedy for the contractor's delay. They are generally expressed as a certain amount of money per unit of time (e.g. pounds sterling per day).

10.5.2   Do the liquidated damages represent the ceiling of claimable damages?

The decided cases appear to suggest that the incorporation of a liquidated damages clause into the contract means that the maximum claimable remedy is fixed by the level of liquidated damages. Therefore, even if the employer could prove that his actual loss due to the contractor's late completion was in excess of the value of the liquidated damages he is limited to recovering the set value of the liquidated damages.

In *Temloc v Errill Properties Ltd* 39 BLR 30, for instance, the word 'nil' had been inserted as the rate of liquidated damages in a standard printed form of contract. The Court of Appeal decided that this meant that the rate was £0 and that this was 'an exhaustive agreement as to the damages which are or are not to be payable by the contractor in the event of his failure to complete the works on time' (per Lord Justice Nourse).

The value of liquidated damages set must be a genuine pre-estimate of the likely loss which would flow from the late completion. If it is in excess of this, the sum is said to be a penalty, and the liquidated damages provision then fails. In these circumstances, the employer may still recover damages, but to do so he must prove his loss in the normal way. A problem which may arise is that the liquidated damages provision may fall as being a penalty or for some other reason; but because of a turn of events the actual loss suffered by the employer may exceed the level of liquidated damages set. There is some authority for the fact that the employer could in these circumstances recover his full damage. However, it is submitted that it would be inequitable to allow the employer to rely on his own failed attempt at obtaining an excessive level of damages (which is the root cause of a liquidated damages clause failing) to recover a higher sum than that agreed.

10.5.3   Defences to the payment of liquidated damages

The liquidated damages are not a genuine pre-estimate of the expected loss
A liquidated damages clause may not be used to penalise a breach excessively and the sums payable may be no greater than a sum representing a genuine pre-estimate of the likely damages which would normally flow from the breach. Accordingly if it is clear that a liquidated damage clause is a penalty clause then the courts will not enforce it but will treat the damages as unliquidated and will assess them: see *Dunlop Pneumatic Tyre Company v New Garage and Motor Company* [1915] AC 79.

There is a delay caused by the employer and there is no extension of time provision to cover that delay
In *Peak Construction (Liverpool) Ltd v McKinney Foundations Ltd* 1 BLR 111 the employer was responsible for some of the overall delay. However, there was no provision enabling an extension of time to be granted

to compensate the contractor for that delay and the Court of Appeal decided that the entire liquidated damages clause became inoperable as the commencement date for liquidated damages could not be established. When the liquidated damages provisions fail, the employer is still entitled to claim damages but, in order to do so, needs to prove his loss.

There is no date stated in the contract

Most modern standard form construction contracts contain provisions for the time of completion and liquidated damages. Frequently the parties are left to complete the form, by including figures for the completion date and liquidated damages. Sometimes, however, these are only partly completed; the rate of liquidated damages may be included, but no completion date, for instance.

It seems that the courts are most reluctant to assist the employer in imposing liquidated damages. It should follow that the courts will not supply a date for completion when one is not expressly mentioned and, indeed, this appears to have been the case in *Kemp v Rose* 1858 1 Giff 258 at 266. However, in *Bruno Zornow (Builders) Ltd v Beechcroft Developments Ltd* 51 BLR 16 a contract for a residential development had been varied so that the scope of the work was considerably extended but no date for completion was included in the contract. Judge Davies asked

> Is it necessary to imply in this contract a date for completion ... tied to a provision for liquidated damages for breach to give it such business efficacy as the parties must have intended? Or is it unnecessary to imply any such date at all when the contract already provides that the works should be performed with due diligence, when in the absence of an express date for completion, there would, in any case, be implicit in it an obligation to complete within a reasonable time, and failure to do so would, in any event, be remediable by a claim for unliquidated damages? ... In a lump sum contract like this involving a commercial development with an attendant risk of indeterminate loss of profits claim it would, in my view, be commercially unrealistic to suppose that the parties did not mutually intend that it should contain a date for completion linked to the liquidated provision which it already contained .... In my view, therefore, it is necessary to imply in this contract a date for completion.

His Honour then implied a reasonable date for completion based on the facts at the time of the contract.

10.5.4 Sectional completion and liquidated damages

Difficult problems also relate to sectional completion provisions in the contract. A sectional completion requirement not only obliges the contractor to complete the works as a whole by a certain date, but also requires him to complete specified elements of the work at dates before the date for completion of the overall contract. A sectional completion obligation supplemented by liquidated damages provisions related to each section which remains uncompleted at the due date is readily achieved by clear wording in the contract. On occasions, however, parties attempt to create such an obligation simply by inserting words into the liquidated damages clause which indicate a rate per section or element of the work which remains incomplete. In many instances this creates ambiguity when read with other terms in the contract; the requirement that the liquidated damages provisions of the contract be construed *contra proferentem* then results in the employer's intentions being defeated. In *Bramall & Ogden v Sheffield City Council* 29 BLR 73, for instance, the contract for the construction of 123 dwellings was substantially in the JCT 63 form. This form is drafted in the contemplation of a single completion date. Clause 16 of the contract allowed the employer to take over parts of the works which the contractor had completed before the works as a whole were completed, and the clause provided a mechanism for reducing the liquidated damages payable in this event. Sheffield City Council attempted to convert the contract into one for sectional completion where the contractor had an *obligation* to hand over parts of the works at specified times. However, they attempted to achieve this simply by including as the rate for liquidated damages in the Appendix to the contract 'the rate of £20 per week for each uncompleted dwelling'. They did not modify Clause 16, in which the method of calculation could not be operated together with the wording in the Appendix. Hence, applying the rules of construction in *Peak v McKinney* 1 BLR 111, the liquidated damages clause was inoperable and hence unenforceable.

Defining the contract work

11.1 Introduction

The contractor's most important and most obvious obligation is to perform the construction work described in the contract. Many contracts contain an express provision to this effect, but it is not clear that this adds anything to the general obligation. The extent of the contractor's obligations will be determined by construing the terms of the contract. This often involves difficulties which are addressed in this chapter.

Many contracts also contain express provisions which allow the employer to vary the works, either in scope or in specification. These 'variations clauses' are discussed in Section 11.3.

Furthermore, work is often not performed in exact compliance with the contract specification. Such a failure is normally a breach of contract on the contractor's part and the employer is entitled to require the contractor to rectify the work or to pay damages for breach. However, on occasions the contractor will advance an argument justifying the non-compliance. For example, he may claim that what is provided is equivalent to or better than what was required and that the works need not, therefore, be 'remedied' since they are not defective; or he may claim that the employer has granted him a unilateral concession. The potential validity of these arguments is examined in Section 11.4.

11.2 The scope of the contract work

11.2.1 Scope to be determined by construing the contract documents

In major construction projects the scope of the work will normally be set out in the drawings, specifications and bills of quantities. For small projects the scope may often be described in the loose wording of a conversation between the employer and the contractor. In both cases, the contractor is obliged to execute only that work which, on a true construction of the contract, forms part of the contract work. The contractor is entitled to be paid additionally for any work he is asked to perform outside the true scope of the contract as priced.

Contradictions, ambiguities and apparent omissions in the contract documents frequently give rise to problems in defining the scope of the works. Some contracts contain mechanisms for resolving these problems, but in others the solution is found only by construing the contract. Consider, for example, a contract to build a bridge in accordance with certain drawings, specifications and bills of quantities all of which documents have equal status under the contract. The drawings show crash-barriers, hand-rails and lighting but these items are not described in the specification nor in the bills of quantities which list out in detail the anticipated items of work. Does the contractor have an obligation to install the crash-barriers, the hand-rails and the lighting? And if so, must he do it for the original contract price? In many cases, particularly re-measurement contracts, the answer to such questions are not of great financial weight since the rails and barriers will have to be measured and paid for whether or not they originally formed part of the contract. In the case of a contract to do all the work for a fixed price, however, the question is of considerable importance and is answered by construing all the contract documents to determine the true objective intention of the parties.

11.2.2 Contractor to supply all reasonably necessary items to complete

In general the contractor must supply all items which are reasonably to be defined as necessary to complete his obligations. Thus in *Williams v Fitzmaurice* (1858) 3 H&N 844 a builder agreed to make a house and in particular 'to do and perform all the works of every kind mentioned and contained in the foregoing specification, according in every respect to the drawings furnished . . . the house to be completed and dry and fit for occupation by August 1st 1858'. The specification described the floor-joists but not the flooring itself. The builder refused to supply and install the flooring without additional payment. Chief Baron Pollock said

> I had some doubt whether the specification was not to be regarded as the contract between the parties; but upon the whole facts being disclosed it appears to me that no person can entertain any reasonable doubt that it was intended that the [builder] should provide the flooring as well as the other materials requisite for the building and that it was merely by inadvertence that no mention of flooring was made in the specification.

11.2.3 The effect of conditions on site being worse than anticipated

Many modern construction contracts will contain provisions relating to extra payments in the event that the work is more difficult than originally envisaged. However, unless the contract contains such a provision, the contractor is obliged to complete the job he has agreed to perform even though the physical conditions on site are worse than he expected.

In *Bottoms v Mayor of York* (1892) Hudson's Building Contracts 4th Edition Vol II p. 208, the contractor claimed extra payment because the ground conditions were worse than he had anticipated. The court held that on a true construction of the contract the employer had not warranted the state of the ground and hence the contractor could not claim any additional payment. Lord Esher said of the contractor:

> the real reason why he has come to this misfortune, indeed, is that he would go and tender when there was no guarantee given to him as to the kind of soil ... and that he either too eagerly or too carelessly tendered and entered into the contract without any such guarantee or representation on their part, and without due examination and enquiry by himself. That is what has produced the difficulty.

In *Sharpe v San Paulo Railway Co* (1873) LR 8 Ch App 597, the contractor undertook to construct a length of railway. When he commenced work it became clear that the works could not be constructed in the way originally envisaged and the contractor had to redesign the works. The court held that his contract, truly construed, was to construct the complete length of railway whatever difficulties he may encounter and so no additional payment would be recovered for the extra work.

11.2.4 Where the works cannot be accomplished in accordance with the drawings

If the works cannot be accomplished in accordance with the drawings, thereby necessitating a revised method of working or construction, does this revised method fall within the scope of the original agreement? Or is it outside the original scope thereby entitling the contractor to be paid an extra amount if it is more costly to execute than the originally proposed scheme? In *Thorn v Mayor and Commonalty of London* [1876] 1 AC 120, the contractor, Thorn, undertook to take down the existing Blackfriars Bridge and to build a replacement. The 'plans of the intended new bridge and specification of the works to be executed' were to be seen at the office of Joseph Cubitt, the well-known engineer. The plans showed that the works were to be constructed using caissons; Lord Cairns described this technique as being 'somewhat, if not altogether, novel'. There were various statements in the specification such as: '54. The Contractor must satisfy himself as to the nature of the ground through which the foundations have to be carried; all the information given on this subject is believed to be correct, but is not guaranteed', '63. The foundations of the piers will be put in by means of wrought iron caissons, as shown on drawing No. 7' and '77 .... all risk and responsibility involved in the sinking of these caissons will rest with the contractor.' In fact it was impossible to construct the foundations in the manner described. It was necessary to abandon the upper part of the caisson and as a result the tides in the river had a severe effect on the rate and cost of the construction. The contractor claimed additional money because of this difficulty and based his claim upon an implied term in the contract that the work could be performed according to method described in the drawings and specification. The House of Lords were unable to imply any such term and hence rejected the claim. Lord Cairns said

Is it natural to suppose, can it be supposed for a moment, that the Defendants [the City of London] intended to imply any such warranty? My Lords, if the contractor in this case had gone to the Bridge Committee, then engaged in supervising the work, and had said: you want Blackfriars Bridge to be rebuilt; you have got specifications prepared by Mr Cubitt; you ask me to tender for the contract; will you engage and warrant to me that the bridge can be built by caissons in this way which Mr Cubitt thinks feasible, but which I have never seen before in practice. What would the committee have answered? Can any person for a moment entertain any reasonable doubt as to the answer he would have received? He would have been told: You know, Mr Cubitt as well as we do; we, like you, rely on him – we must rely on him; we do not warrant Mr Cubitt or his plans; you are as able to judge as we are whether his plans can be carried into effect or not; if you like to rely on them, well and good; if you do not, you can either have them tested by an engineer of your own, or you need not undertake the works; others will do it.

My Lords, it is really contrary to every kind of probability to suppose that any warranty would have been intended or implied between the parties; and if there is no express warranty, your Lordships cannot imply a warranty, unless from the circumstances of the work some warranty must have been necessary, which clearly is not the case here, or, unless the probability is so strong that the parties intended a warranty, that you cannot resist the application of the doctrine of implied warranty.

In *Thorn v Mayor of London* the House of Lords, however, accepted that if the nature of the work needed to change very radically then the contractor would not be obliged to perform the work. This is not because the contractor is not obliged to perform the contract but because the required work has changed so radically that it does not form part of the contract.

If . . . it was additional or varied work, so peculiar, so unexpected, and so different from what any person reckoned or calculated upon, that it is not within the contract at all, then it appears to me, one of two courses might have been open to him; he might have said: I entirely refuse to go on with the contract . . . I never intended to construct this work upon this new and unexpected footing. Or he might have said, I will go on with this, but this is not the kind of extra work contemplated by the contract, and if I do it, I must be paid a *quantum meruit* for it. (per Lord Cairns)

Note: In some current standard form contracts an express term is included allowing the contractor to be paid if the works cannot be constructed in accordance with the drawings and specifications.

11.2.5 Design obligations and other professional services: the scope of the obligation assumed

Contractors have traditionally assumed a 'build only' role, so that the detailed design is provided to them by, or on behalf of, the employer. In modern contracts, however, there is an increasing tendency for contractors to assume design obligations or to provide other professional services. As with questions concerning the scope of the work which they have contracted to perform, questions of their responsibility for design and other services is to be determined by a true construction of the contract documents. An example of where problems may arise, in this context, is the use of a subcontract which provides: 'The subcontractor hereby assumes the like responsibilities for the subcontract works as the contractor has assumed in respect of the contract works as a whole'. If the main contract is a design and build contract and the main contractor designs the whole works in detail in his own design offices, as was envisaged by both parties, the question may arise whether or not the subcontractor has a contractual responsibility for the design of the subcontract works.

Contractors should be aware of the level of responsibility they undertake in respect of design and other professional services, as well as the scope of the responsibilities. If, for instance, they contract on a design and build basis is the level of their responsibility for the design equivalent to that assumed by a consulting engineer or architect? In general the answer to this is 'no'. It is important to distinguish the provision of design alone (as considered in Chapter 16) and the situation which arises when the provision of design is coupled with a construction obligation. In the former situation, the obligation is to undertake the work with reasonable skill and care. In the latter, the obligation is to provide a result which is reasonably fit for the purpose for which it was intended using materials which are of merchantable quality.

This distinction may readily be illustrated. Suppose the employer wishes to build a paved enclosure with concrete paving flags. If he or she employs a consulting engineer to design the concrete mix, the consulting engineer's obligation is to exercise reasonable skill and care in the design. If the concrete begins to crack because of frost attack the consulting engineer need show only that he acted with skill, not that he achieved the required result. If the employer does not appoint a consulting engineer but lets the project to the contractor on a design and build basis, the contractor cannot plead that he acted with skill in designing the mix. His obligation is to provide a paved surface which is reasonably fit for its purpose. Section 4 of the Supply of Goods and Services Act 1982 requires goods supplied (e.g. concrete paving under the contract described above) to be of merchantable quality and fit for their purpose. However, Section 13 reads

> In a contract for the supply of a service where the supplier is acting in the course of a business, there is an implied term that the supplier will carry out the service with reasonable care and skill.

The courts have taken the view that when construction and design obligations are coupled the contractor's obligation is to provide a product which is fit for its purpose, Section 13 being applicable only to situations in which professional services (and no goods) are provided. In *IBA v EMI and BICC* 14 BLR 1, the litigation resulting from the collapse of the Emley Moor television mast, for example, Lord Scarman said

> in the absence of a clear contractual indication to the contrary, I can see no reason why one who in the course of his business contracts to design, supply and erect a television mast is not under an obligation to ensure that it is reasonably fit for the purpose for which it was intended to be used.

This may seem anomalous since the main contractor under a design and build form of contract who employs a designer to carry out the design will be liable to the employer if the design renders the construction unfit for its purpose, even though the design may have been performed with reasonable skill and care and despite the fact that the contractor will not normally have an action against the designer. The contractor appears to be liable without fault and without a right of action to recover his losses. The solution as far as the contractor is concerned is to ensure that the designer undertakes the like obligations to the contractor in respect of the design as the contractor has undertaken to the owner. This appears to have been achieved impliedly in *Greaves (Contractors) Ltd v Baynham Meikle & Partners* 4 BLR 56, discussed in Chapter 16, but contractors should, to protect themselves, make this an express term of the design contract.

11.3   Variations

The contractor's obligations may change with time. This may happen in two ways. The first is where the contract itself is varied. The second is where the contract provides a mechanism for the scope or specification of the work to be varied and that mechanism is operated.

An important preliminary point to note is that no one may alter the contractor's obligation to complete the works in complete accordance with the existing or current drawings and specification unless they are authorised to do so, either by grant of authority from the employer or by the terms of the contract. The importance of this requirement is frequently overlooked; but it is vital. Generally speaking, for example, engineers and architects will not be authorised to vary a contract on behalf of their clients. In *Toepfer v Warinco* [1978] 2 Ll Rep 569 at 577, Mr Justice Brandon said 'it is well-established that an architect or engineer has no implied authority from the building owner by whom he is employed to vary or waive the terms of a building contract: see *Hudson's Building and Engineering Contracts*, 10th Edition.' While this dictum is, perhaps, too sweeping a generalisation, it does, it is submitted, represent the normal situation.

There is one situation where the employer can be made liable for a variation even though, at the time of the variation, the representative had no authority. This arises where the employer subsequently ratifies the representative's order; in effect the employer clothes the previous acts with authority by adopting them.

11.3.1   Variation of the contract

If the employer (or his or her authorised representative) allows a relaxation to the specification so that a set of mutual benefits (i.e. sufficient consideration) is derived from the relaxation, in circumstances where it is clear that both the contractor and employer intend the relaxation to be binding, then a variation of the contract will ensue so that a compliance with the relaxed specification will be a compliance with the contract. Note, however, a variation can occur only if the agents who negotiate it are authorised to vary the contract.

There is currently some doubt as to what constitutes consideration for these purposes and reference should be made to *Williams and Roffey Bros v Nicholls (Contractors) Ltd* [1990] 2 WLR 1153. Here a subcontractor had agreed to perform certain works by a specified time. The subcontractor was behind schedule and the main contractor offered him an increased price if he completed on time, which the subcontractor did. The question was whether the subcontractor was entitled to the additional price, it being argued by the main contractor that the subcontractor had supplied no consideration to the agreement. The Court of Appeal held that since the main contractor obtained a benefit that was sufficient consideration, hence there was a binding agreement to pay the additional price.

11.3.2 Variation to the scope or specification of the work

The purpose and usefulness of variation clauses
Many construction contracts contain an express power for the employer or his or her agent to vary the scope of the work or the specification of the work (usually with appropriate money and time adjustments). In such cases, the relevant clauses will contain a mechanism for the introduction of the variation and, if that mechanism is operated, the contractor's obligation becomes the performance of the newly defined work. Some contracts contain a term such that if the works cannot legally or physically be accomplished in accordance with the specification then the contractor is entitled to a variation and here the specification may be varied automatically.

Where variations must be ordered in a particular form
In some contracts there are strict rules concerning variations to the contract works or specification. An example of where such rules were not complied with is given by *Forman & Co Proprietary Ltd v The Ship 'Liddlesdale'* [1900] AC 190. Here the employer's 'representative' (the captain of the ship which was being repaired, who was authorised to order variations in writing) expressly requested an oral variation. However, Clause 8 of the contract provided: 'The contractor shall not make any alteration or deviation from the specification agreed upon, nor shall he be entitled to make any charge or claim for extras or for anything whatever beyond the lump sum agreed upon, unless he obtain the written sanction of the captain'. The Privy Council said

> [If] ... such an order [i.e. an oral variation order] was given, the question of Captain Clark's authority comes in ... It appears to their Lordships that the object of Clause 8 was to prevent the contractors from making claims on account of extra work unless they had a written order for it .... The clause was evidently intended as a check on the contractors .... But it was not calculated or intended to enlarge Captain Clark's authority, nor, even, if so expressed, could it have that effect as against his principals. It is now used to justify claims against the defendant [shipowner] for a class of repairs which he had expressly prohibited.

Therefore, advised the Privy Council, since the order had not been given in writing, the employer's representative was not authorised to make the order and hence the employer was not responsible for it.

However, even where the contract provides that no variation will be effective unless ordered in writing, the lack of a written instruction may not be fatal where the primary question relates to whether, or not, the work required is, or is not, within the scope of the original contract. This is particularly so if the contract contains an arbitration clause entitling the arbitrator to review the decisions of the person vested with authority to order written variations. In *Brodie v Cardiff Corporation* [1919] AC 337, for example, a reservoir was to be constructed. The contract provided that 'no extra charges in respect of extra work will be allowed . . . unless such works shall have been ordered in writing by the engineer'. It reinforced this with 'It is to be distinctly understood that the corporation shall not become liable to the payment of any charge in respect of any additions, alterations or deviations unless the instruction for the performance of the same shall have been given in writing by the engineer'. The contract contained an arbitration clause providing for arbitration after the project was complete and entitling the arbitrator to rule 'as to any objection by the contractor to any certificate, finding, decision, requisition or opinion of the engineer'. During the works the engineer required that the construction be done using certain methods and materials. The contractor claimed that this was a variation in the scope of the works. The engineer disagreed and refused to issue an instruction in writing on the basis that his requirements fell within the original scope. At the end of the project, the contractor claimed additional payment, notwithstanding the lack of a written order. The arbitrator awarded a payment and the employer appealed. The House of Lords supported the arbitrator. Lord Finlay said

> The dispute was whether the item was an extra for which an order in writing should have been given, and when the parties agreed the work should be done and that the question should stand over to arbitration, the effect of the contract is that the finding of the arbitrator is to take the place of the order in writing which ought to have been given. Otherwise the postponed arbitration would be entirely useless.

The requirement contained in some construction contracts that variations will not be allowed or paid for unless they be ordered in writing is a device for protecting an employer but enabling him to avoid responsibility for informally discussed or suggested changes to the work. Sometimes, however, it would be most inequitable for the employer to rely on the lack of written instruction or order and, in such cases, payment may be recovered without a written order. For instance, if the employer becomes personally involved with the discussions concerning changes to the scope of the works and he personally orders variations or is present while his representative does so, he may not set up the lack of a written order as a defence. In *Meyer v Gilmour* [1899] 18 NZLR, for example, the requirement for written variation orders was held to be waived on account of the attendance of the employer at the meetings where the oral variation orders were given.

Variations for the contractor's benefit
On the other hand, if the variation mechanism is properly operated, in principle, it does not matter for whose benefit the variation was required. In *Simplex Piling v St Pancras Borough Council* 14 BLR 80 the variation

was requested by the contractor who was contracted to install driven piles capable of carrying a stated load. Pile testing was to be carried out during the work but, surprisingly, the pile capacity fell well short of the contract requirement. The contractor then advised bored piling down to a more competent stratum and the architect, who by the terms of the contract was given wide powers to vary the works, agreed. The court held that the letter in which the architect signified his agreement to change the works constituted an architect's instruction for a variation which under the contract entitled the contractor to receive additional payment. This was so despite the fact that if the architect had not issued a variation instruction in this manner the contractor would have had to undertake this work at his own expense simply to comply with the terms of the contract.

The rule in *Simplex* was clarified in *Howard de Walden Estates Ltd v Costain Management Design Ltd* 55 BLR 124. In this case it was decided that even where the contractual mechanism is followed so that the contractor seems able to recover additional payment (as in *Simplex*), he will not be paid for getting himself out of a situation where he is in breach (or may find himself in breach if no action is taken) if he is put on notice that he will not be paid for that work.

In *Waldens v Costain*, Waldens were the employers for a refurbishment contract and Costains were contractors employed to underpin a wall. Costains failed to undertake the work in accordance with the contract and the wall collapsed. The arbitrator found that their non-compliance was the effective cause of the wall's collapse. Following the collapse, the Architect issued instructions regarding remedial works and, relying on an interpretation of *Simplex*, Costains sought to recover the cost of the remedial works. However, there was an important difference between the facts in *Simplex* and those in the present case: in this case, after the wall had collapsed, a sequence of correspondence arose including a letter dated 27 October 1990, from the architect to Costains, which read:

> ... architect's instructions relating to the collapse of the rear wall to 115 Harley Street have been and will be issued with the prefix DST. The quantity surveyor will be responsible in the first instance for determining whether or not any instruction or part thereof prefixed by DST is payable under the contract. It is generally intended that costs arising from any instruction or part thereof, judged by the quantity surveyor not payable under the contract be excluded from interim valuations unless resolution on the issue of liability shows it to be a matter for which the client [Waldens] is responsible.

The remedial works were in fact carried out under instructions prefixed DST. Waldens argued that this letter recorded a new arrangement which superseded the contractual arrangements. Accordingly, instructions pre-fixed DST fell within this supplementary arrangement and the question of payment for work performed under those instructions was directly related to the question of liability for the collapse.

Judge Newey accepted the argument for Waldens that a supplemental 'agreement' came into existence as set out in the letter of 27 October and that payment was only due to Costains if Waldens had caused the remedial work to be necessary. In the event, since the arbitrator had found Costains liable, no payment was due to Costains. This was different from the situation which existed in *Simplex* where there was no subsequent or additional arrangement and where the instructions must have been issued in accordance with the main contract, which contract entitled the contractor to be paid. One point of some importance is that the judge found that there had been a new 'agreement'. However, the question of the formation of that agreement was not discussed in the judgment. It is submitted, however, that the existence of a new agreement is not important; it is the fact of putting Costains on notice which is important, rather than obtaining their agreement.

The lesson to be learnt from *Simplex* and *Walden v Costain* is that where a contractor is having difficulty in fulfilling his contractual obligations the employer should not issue instructions for the contractor's benefit without first setting out in writing the basis upon which payment will or will not be made.

The permitted magnitude of variations
While many contracts enable the employer expressly to order variations to the work, rarely do they state the magnitude of variations that may be considered to be part of the contract obligation. If, for instance, the contract is originally for the construction of 100km of road, the varied length might reasonably be expected to be between 90 and 110km. But what if more than 500km is ordered?

In *Thorn v Mayor of London* [1876] 1 AC 120 (discussed in Section 11.2.4), it was originally considered that caissons could be used for the foundations but in fact this turned out to be impossible. The question arose whether the varied method of construction which the contractor needed to operate to execute the works were outside the scope of the original contract. Lord Cairns said that if variations, such as might reasonably be contemplated at the time of contract are requested, the employer can insist that the contract rates govern these variations. But the contractor can refuse to perform variations in excess of this quantity or he may claim a reasonable amount for doing them. What was contemplated at the time of the contract is to be determined by objectively construing the contract. In *Blue Circle Industries v Holland Dredging Co (UK) Ltd* 37 BLR 40, a contract was let for dredging works. It was subsequently agreed that the dredged material should be used to form an artificial island and the question subsequently arose whether or not the island formation fell within the original contract scope. The original contract was on the ICE Standard Form which included a variation clause, Clause 51. Lord Justice Purchas said

> In considering whether a particular turn of events comes within Clause 51 of the General Conditions as a variation, as [counsel] correctly submitted, the question must be posed: Could the employer have ordered the work required by it against the wishes of the contractor as a variation under Clause 51? If the answer is 'No' – then the agreement under which such work was carried out cannot constitute a variation but must be a separate agreement. The original dredging contract provided that the spoil from excavating should be deposited in 'areas within Lough Larne to be allocated . . . upon approval by the local authorities'. In the event, as a result of local pressures and the attitude of the licensing authority this term became impossible to fulfil legally. The

only alternatives were dumping at sea or the creation of an artificial bund with the formation of an artificial island. Either of these two solutions were wholly outside the scope of the original dredging contract and therefore had Holland not been willing they could not, in my judgment, have been obliged to accept the work as a variation ... In my judgment [counsel's] submission that the island contract is separate from the dredging contract is correct.

11.4   Non-compliance with the specifications and/or drawings

It frequently happens that construction works are not built in strict accordance with the original specification and there is no properly authorised variation to cover them. Sometimes this arises from a misreading of the contract documents or poor communication between those responsible for interpreting the contract and those who actually perform the work. Sometimes it is deliberate, but as often as not, the deliberate non-compliance is done in the belief that what is actually being provided is as good as what the contract requires. Often, indeed, the deliberate non-compliance is done with the full knowledge and, sometimes, complicity of engineers and architects employed by the employer. If the non-compliance is accidental and is pointed out to the contractor, the contractor usually returns to the affected area and corrects the work; or if this process is likely to be far more expensive than the diminution in value of the works due to the non-compliance, then some financial 'accommodation' will normally be made and the work will remain in its non-compliant state. However, there are situations where the employer or his or her agents are adamant that the work must be re-done in full accordance with the specification and the contractor feels that this requirement is either inequitable or makes engineering nonsense, or both. The question addressed in this section concerns the bases, if any, upon which a contractor may legitimately resist a request to return and correct non-compliant work.

Generally speaking, non-compliance with the contract specification will be a breach of contract on the part of the contractor and the employer is entitled to require the contractor to rectify the defect or, alternatively, to pay damages. However, there are circumstances where the contractor may claim that the employer cannot enforce the strict requirements of the original specification against him. Such a claim may be founded on one of the following bases: first, the contractor may claim that while he has, technically, failed to comply with the details of the specification, nonetheless, the employer has got an equivalent structure to the one he wanted. This may be regarded as a claim of 'equivalent performance'. Second, the contractor may claim that the employer has granted a unilateral concession which he is not entitled to withdraw. The contractor may claim that by his behaviour, the employer (by himself, or through an authorised agent) has waived his right to insist on a strict performance of the contract. Or, the contractor may claim that the action of the employer or his agent may be such as to cause the contractor to expend some resources in performing the works in a particular manner which does not accord with the specification so that it would be inequitable for the employer now to insist on compliance with the specification.

11.4.1 Equivalent performance

If the contractor performs work which is not the stipulated work but claims that the work as done is equivalent to or better than the specified work, the question arises, can the contractual obligation be met by such a performance? The contractor may be claiming that the work as performed is a sufficient performance of the contractual requirement because

- the difference between what is supplied and what was specified is inconsequential; since the law is not concerned with trifling differences (*de minimis non curat lex*) the employer cannot complain
- or, the work performed is different to that stipulated but, nonetheless, it still completely satisfies the employer's needs and purposes under the agreement.

The de minimis *rule*
In the first case the contractor claims the *de minimis* rule applies. The law will not generally concern itself with inconsequential matters. To illustrate how a contractor might rely on this principle consider the case where a contractor agrees to install bathroom fittings manufactured by A and of a type specified in detail; however, the contractor finds alternative fittings which are slightly different from those made by A but which function well, are made of similar materials and look similar. When the employer discovers that the wrong fittings have been supplied can the contractor claim that his performance is sufficient?

It may be that, if the fittings in question are for a bathroom in an expensive house, and, that the employer has specified equipment made by a particular designer, the supply of a similar product is not a non-compliance *de minimis*. If, however, the fittings are for public conveniences the failure may well be *de minimis*. It is suggested that in the latter case the contractor would not be obliged to replace the fittings, while in the former case he would.

A claim that the work supplied is perfectly satisfactory even though it doesn't comply with the specification
In the second case the contractor is claiming that the work performed is equivalent to or better than that specified. In *Forman & Co Proprietary Ltd v The Ship 'Liddlesdale'* [1900] AC 190, the contractor agreed to undertake certain specified repairs to a ship which had been stranded off the coast of Western Australia for a lump sum. They carried out repairs and the ship benefited. However, the repairs performed were not precisely those stipulated; in particular, iron girders were used instead of steel. The contractor, when challenged, said that the iron girders were better than the steel girders specified, and they were more expensive. The Privy Council, however, advised that the contractors were in breach.

It is suggested by some commentators that this case indicates that the law does not recognise a substituted performance as being a sufficient fulfilment of a contract, irrespective of whether the substituted performance is as good as what was contracted for. However, it is submitted that the case does not conclusively support this conclusion: but, neither does it support the opposite conclusion, that a substituted performance is acceptable. The Privy Council (Lord Hobhouse) said: 'As regards the work done no doubt exists but that it was good work and added value . . . to this ship'. However, despite the contractors' claims that what was supplied was as good as what was contracted for, there was a strong technical argument about whether or not that was the case. Reviewing the evidence, and in conclusion, the Privy Council said

> It is also made clear that the substitution of iron for steel not only added to the weight and to the expense, but altered the structure of the vessel – to her advantage, as the plaintiffs [contractors] contend, but, as the defendant [shipowner] says, causing a rigidity in her framework which is a source of danger to her. That is a matter on which opinions vary; but there is no dispute that the alteration is not consistent with the plaintiff's obligation to restore the vessel to her original condition prior to the accident.

If it had been clear that the substituted performance was, without doubt, as good as the performance originally contracted for, then, it may be suggested, the Privy Council's advice may have been that the contract had been complied with sufficiently.

It is submitted, in fact, that a practical approach to these problems should be used. While contracts must, undoubtedly, be complied with, the question of whether any particular work falls within the specification is a matter of construing the agreement in a businesslike manner, without placing undue emphasis on specification details, unless those details can be shown to be materially important. It may be, for example, that where the contract calls for a particular class of product to be used, the words 'or other product which can perform its task just as well' can be read into the contract as part of a businesslike and practical construction of that term. If, for instance, a concrete frame is to be built using concrete of a particular strength and the contractor supplies concrete which is, in all respects, identical to the material contracted for, except that it is stronger, it is thought that this will normally be a compliance with the contract, unless the employer produces a serious argument which shows that the added strength is detrimental to the structure in some material respect. Accordingly, in this case, the term 'Provide concrete of strength $35N/mm^2$' may be construed to mean 'Provide concrete of strength *at least* $35N/mm^2$'.

11.4.2 Employer's unilateral concessions

The effect of a unilateral concession
If the employer, or his or her authorised representative, positively represents to the contractor that the strict specification need not be adhered to, then, even if that concession is purely unilateral (i.e. there is insufficient consideration to create a variation to the contract), the contractor will still be entitled to rely upon it; and if the employer wishes at some later

stage to withdraw the concession he cannot do so without compensating the contractor for any losses caused to the contractor as a result.

Lord Justice Bowen explained the ambit of the rule in *Birmingham and District Land Co v L & N W Rly* (1888) 40 ChD 268:

> if persons who have contractual rights against others induce, by their conduct, those against whom they have such rights to believe that such rights will either not be enforced or will be kept in suspense or abeyance for some particular time, those persons will not be allowed by a court of equity to enforce the rights until such time has elapsed, without at all events placing the parties in the same position as they were before.

Lord Denning in *WJ Alan & Co v El Nasr Export and Import Co* [1972] 2 All ER 127 at p. 140 put the rule (which he called the rule of waiver) in the following way:

> The principle of waiver is simply this: if one party, by his conduct, leads another to believe that the strict rights arising under the contract will not be insisted on, intending that the other should act on that belief, and he does act on it, then the first party will not afterwards be allowed to insist on the strict legal rights when it would be inequitable for him to do so . . . . There may be no consideration moving from him who benefits from the waiver. There may be no detriment to him by acting in it. There may be nothing in writing. Nevertheless the one who waives his strict rights cannot afterwards insist on them. His strict rights are at any rate suspended so long as the waiver lasts. He may on occasion be able to revert to his strict legal rights for the future by giving reasonable notice on that behalf, or otherwise making it plain by his conduct that he will thereafter insist upon them . . . . But there are cases where no withdrawal is possible. It may be too late to withdraw: or it cannot be done without injustice to the other party. In that event he is bound by his waiver: he will not be allowed to revert to his strict legal rights. He can only enforce them subject to the waiver he has made.

The question of authority

Whenever it is claimed that the contractor has been granted a concession, the question of the grantor's authority is properly raised. Such questions are answered in accordance with the general law of agency and the precise circumstances of each situation must be taken into account in determining whether or not a particular person is an authorised agent. In particular if it is claimed that a person is authorised by the contract to make an agreement or to order a variation or to grant a unilateral concession, this matter will be resolved by construing the contract.

Employer's representatives on site   Employer's representatives on site will not usually be authorised to make binding concessions. But they may have implied authority to make a binding concession relating to matters such as those concerning the service of contractual notices if it is they who are authorised to receive the notices under the contract; this after all is a matter relating to the administration of the contract and they have been appointed to administer the contract and should therefore be taken to have the usual authority associated with that position. However, the limits of this authority are, no doubt, narrow and are restricted to administrative matters. See *The Liddlesdale [1900]* AC 190 for a case where the representative had authority to order variations in writing but not, said the Privy Council, unless they were in writing.

Contractors, in fact, often claim that they are entitled to supply a product which does not fully comply with the specification because the employer has employed a site representative to supervise the work and that the representative failed to condemn the work. This line of argument has traditionally received short shrift from the courts who insist that the role of the employer's agent (unless there are contract terms in the contract between the employer and contractor, which express a different intention: see *Ata Ul Haq v City Council of Nairobi* 28 BLR 76, discussed below, for an example of such a case) is to protect the interests of the employer. There are two issues involved here; the first concerns the authority of the representative and the second involves the question of an express grant of a unilateral concession. As already indicated in this section, the site representative is unlikely to have the appropriate authority. A failure to condemn is unlikely to be sufficient to create a binding concession. However, contractors make such claims with such frequency that it is worthwhile briefly reviewing the issues and dicta from the judiciary on this point.

Consider the following example. A road construction contract requires the granular sub-base to be crushed rock from a specified quarry but the contractor is not informed why that particular quarry is specified. He finds a cheaper supply which appears to him to comply with all the normal specification requirements and commences to lay this material, advising the site engineer, who is employed by the employer to supervise the construction, that the material does not come from the specified source. The site engineer makes no comment. The contractor continues to lay the material for three weeks along two kilometres of road. He then receives a letter from the employer indicating that the stone as laid is not in compliance with the contract and showing good technical reasons why the stone from the specified quarry is better than the material which has been laid. The contractor is asked to take out the crushed rock laid and to replace it with material which complies with the specification.

In this case, the contractor may feel that it is unjust for the employer to enforce the contract strictly against him. After all, he might argue, the employer or his agent has indicated, either by silence or by implied representation, that all is well with the work in progress. The courts have, however, emphasised that the employer's agents on site are there for the employer's benefit, not for the benefit of the contractor and in *East Ham Borough Council v Bernard Sunley Ltd* [1966] AC 406 at p. 449 Lord Pearson observed that

> it seems to be unreasonable ... to let [the contractor] shelter behind the architect's failure to detect faults in the course of his visits during the progress of the work. The architect's duty is to the employer and not to the contractor, and the extent of his obligation to make inspections and tests depends upon his contract with the employers and the arrangements made and in the circumstances of the case. *Prima facie* the contractors should be and remain liable for their own breaches of contract, and should not have a general

release from liability in respect of all breaches which the architect should have detected but failed to detect throughout the currency of the contract.

In *AMF International Ltd v Magnet Bowling* [1968] 1 WLR 1028 at p. 1053 Mr Justice Mocatta put the matter even more bluntly and observed

in general an architect owes no duty to a builder to tell him promptly during the course of construction, even as regards permanent work when he is going wrong; he may, if he wishes, leave that to the final stages notwithstanding that the correction of a fault then may be much more costly to the builder than had his error been pointed out earlier.

An example of where the employer's representative on site allowed consistently substandard work is provided by *Ata Ul Haq v City Council of Nairobi* (1959) 28 BLR 76. The contractor claimed that he had been granted a unilateral concession concerning the quality of hardcore in the bases of a series of buildings because the employer's representative had certified eleven bases as complete even though they had been constructed with substandard material. The matter at issue related to a further six bases which were also constructed using the same material as had been used for the previous eleven but for which no certificate had been issued. The Privy Council advised that, on the true construction of the contract, the effect of the certificates was such that the employer could not complain of the eleven blocks already certified. However, damages were recoverable for the six remaining bases for which there was no certificate, since those blocks did not comply with the contract specification. There was no positive concession by anyone with the authority to grant it and, save for the bases where the binding certificates had been issued, the employer was not bound by the conduct of his representative.

A difficult question may also arise in contracts which contain a provision that the work is to be performed not only to a specification but also to the approval of some named representative of the employer and that person is asked specifically to provide an approval for certain work which is in the process of being executed. If approval is given and the work later turns out to be defective, can the contractor rely on the approval as a defence? The approval does not appear to constitute a defence unless the matter was a subjective one upon which the approval could not be challenged. If the matter was a question of the quality of materials, for instance, or some other matter upon which an objective compliance with the specification can be determined, the specification will need to be complied with in addition to the approval being obtained (see, for example, *National Coal Board v William Neill & Sons (St Helens) Ltd* 26 BLR 81). To allow the contractor to circumvent the specification by seeking the approval of the named person would be to require that that named person had authority to vary, and did vary, the contract so that the specification no longer was operative in respect of matters which fell within his approval.

The position regarding subcontracts   Under a subcontract the parties are the main contractor and the subcontractor. A contractor (for example, acting through an agent such as the managing director who will normally have general authority to bind the contractor) may grant a concession to a subcontractor upon which the subcontractor relies. It will not, of course, be open to the main contractor subsequently to claim that he is not authorised by the employer to vary the works or to grant concessions in respect of the works. The question of authority in such a case relates solely to whether or not the main contractor has clothed the agent who granted the concession with authority, rather than with the question whether or not the employer has done so, since the employer is, contractually speaking, a stranger to the subcontract (see Section 13.2). Main contractors often make informal arrangements and grant concessions to their subcontractors and these are often made by directors who may well be authorised to enter into such arrangements.

A note on the terminology relating to unilateral concessions   The terms 'waiver' and 'estoppel' and several others are commonly used in the context of a concession granted; hence some explanation regarding the terminology is required. The first point to make is that there is a considerable confusion over the meaning of all of these terms and, indeed, whether or not and, to what extent, they overlap. Lord Denning talks of 'waiver' in the above-quoted passage from *Alan v El Nasr*. Elsewhere, writers talk of 'estoppel' in similar terms. In *Keating on Building Contracts* 5th Edition at p. 264 it is said: 'Waiver is related to, if not a species of, estoppel'. In *Charles Rickards Ltd v Oppenheim* [1950] 1 KB 616 at p. 623 Lord Denning said

> Whether it be called waiver or forbearance on his part, or an agreed variation or substituted performance does not matter. It is a kind of estoppel. By his conduct he evinced an intention to affect their legal relations. He made, in effect, a promise not to insist on his legal rights. That promise was intended to be acted on, and it was in fact acted on. He cannot afterwards go back on it.

Accordingly, it is not thought that any purpose is served by an analysis of the cases to distinguish between situations described as estoppels, those described as waivers and those otherwise described. It is submitted that the test is identical however one wishes to characterise a unilateral concession and that the test is that quoted from Lord Denning above in *Alan v El Nasr*. In this section the term 'unilateral concession' will be used. The qualifiers 'binding' and 'non-binding' will be used to describe their effect; a binding unilateral concession is one which binds the employer. If the employer wishes to withdraw such a concession he or she must compensate the contractor for the contractor's losses sustained in reliance upon that concession.

Implied unilateral concessions

Consider the following example where the contractor may feel that the employer's conduct was sufficient to establish a binding unilateral concession by implication. A domestic dwelling extension contract requires the walls to be painted white and all windows to be double-glazed. The builder, because he has misread the drawings, paints the walls green and fits single-glazed windows. The employer is on site every day and, although he sees the work in progress, he says nothing. When the builder claims to have completed the work the employer points out the defects and insists that the walls be repainted and windows be replaced with windows which comply. The contractor may feel that this is unfair; he may claim that the employer has, by a failure to condemn, *impliedly* waived his strict rights under the contract.

However, it is submitted that, in general, a binding unilateral concession has to be expressly granted, whether in words or by conduct. It cannot, it is submitted, be inferred by, for example, a failure to condemn work in progress. Work in progress may, in any event, not attain the status of a defect until the contractor no longer has an opportunity to remedy it under the 'temporary disconformity' principle (see Section 2.5.3) and hence it would be unfair on both parties to require the employer to interfere before the shortcoming in the works even attained the status of a defect.

When, however, the representor has a duty to inform the representee that, in his opinion, the works are not being constructed in accordance with the contract, silence may constitute a representation. In *Hopgood v Brown* [1955] 1 WLR 213, for instance, Lord Evershed said that an estoppel may arise 'where one person, the representor, has made a representation to another person, the representee, in words or by acts or conduct *or, being under a duty to the representee to speak or act, by silence or inaction*' (emphasis supplied). Under some contracts, the certifier has an obligation to serve notices on the contractor if, in the opinion of the certifier, the work is not in accordance with the contract in some specified regards; if the certifier checks the works and fails to serve the required notices, the contractor has at least an arguable case that this amounts to a binding unilateral concession. Where the certifier merely has a power, rather than an obligation, to serve the notices, it seems that no concession will be made.

The withdrawal of a unilateral concession

Once a unilateral concession is granted it may be withdrawn without compensation by the service of reasonable notice providing no injustice is done. However, even where withdrawal would cause injustice, the employer is, it is submitted, never prevented from withdrawing the indulgence and requiring the contractor to complete the remainder of the project with specification standard materials or techniques providing he is prepared to compensate the contractor for his losses.

An example of where the courts have given guidance on the withdrawal of a unilateral concession in the middle of a contract is given by *Panoutsos v Raymond Hadley* [1971] 2 KB 473. Here the contract required a buyer of goods to provide a confirmed credit (a device which would ensure that the seller would be paid). The buyer opened an unconfirmed credit (which was not so secure). The seller indicated that he was happy with the unconfirmed credit until he suddenly terminated the contract on the grounds that the buyer had obtained the wrong type of credit. The Court of Appeal said that he could not terminate the contract since the seller was not in breach because the seller had granted him a unilateral concession.

But, said the court, the seller was entitled to insist that a confirmed credit be opened within a reasonable time and if the buyer failed to open the proper credit expeditiously then he would be in breach. In *Charles Rickards v Oppenheim* [1950] 1 KB 616 a purchaser in a contract in which time was of the essence led the seller to believe that he would not insist on the time obligation being enforced. It was held that he could not set up the seller's failure to comply with the time obligation against him; however, an obligation to perform in a reasonable time could be re-established by reasonable notice to the seller.

After an analysis of the cases including *Alan v El Nasr*, Dugdale and Yates ('Variation, waiver and estoppel – a re-appraisal', (1976) 39 MLR 680) concluded

> In the case of a pre-breach representation it should be possible for the representor to revoke the alteration, provided that it is still possible i.e. that the circumstances provided for in the altered terms have not yet occurred. The possibility of such a revocation is the essential difference between an alteration of the terms of contract without consideration and an alteration with consideration which amounts to a variation.

12

The obligation of the employer to cooperate with the contractor

12.1 Introduction

In many instances, the contractor cannot proceed with and/or complete the works without the cooperation of the employer. The work will normally be undertaken on the employer's land and the contractor must be permitted access if he is to do the work. Often, there are several contractors on the site; if the employer has control over them, the question arises, to what extent does the employer have to coordinate the work so that there is sufficient space for the contractor's workfronts? Frequently, the scope and description of the contract works will not be known in their entirety at the time when the contract is let and, in these circumstances, the contractor will be reliant on the employer to supply drawings and instructions during the progress of the works.

Whenever the contractor cannot proceed efficiently with the works without the consent, assistance or cooperation of the employer the question arises: what is the scope of the employer's obligation to cooperate with the contractor? As always, if the contract makes express provision for these matters, those contract terms will prevail. However, such terms are often not expressly agreed and the terms which will be implied in the absence of express provisions will be considered in this chapter.

12.2 The employer's obligation not to interfere with the contractor's performance

There will normally be a term implied into the agreement that the employer will not interfere with the contractor's progress in the sense that he will not *directly* prevent the contractor from performing the work. In *Barque Quilpué Ltd v Brown* [1904] 2 KB 261, for instance, Lord Justice Vaughan Williams observed

> There is an implied contract by each party that he will not do anything to prevent the other party from performing the contract or to delay him in performing it. I agree that such a term is by law imported into every contract.

It often happens that the employer, through acquiescence, or by acting in accordance with some entitlement he has under the contract, will hinder the contractor. This, however, is not considered a direct prevention. Rather it is best viewed as an occupational hazard which is part of the contractor's risk burden under the contract.

The sources of potential 'interference' which may be experienced by the contractor include failures to provide access to the site, sufficient space and workfronts, necessary drawings, instructions and permits, and the failure to institute mechanisms and make appointments necessary for the project to operate (e.g. the appointment of certifiers, nomination of subcontractors etc).

12.3   The employer's obligation to grant access

12.3.1   General obligation to grant access

In *The Queen in Right of Canada v Walter Cabott Construction Ltd* 21 BLR 46 Mr Justice Urie considered the employer's general obligations to grant the contractor access to the site:

> It is fundamental to a building contract that work space be provided unimpeded by others. The proposition of law is succinctly put by the learned author of *Hudson's Building and Engineering Contracts*, 10th Ed. (1970) at p. 318, as follows:
>
> > Since a sufficient degree of possession of the site is clearly a necessary pre-condition of the contractor's performance of his obligations, there must be an implied term that the site will be handed over to the contractor within a reasonable time of signing the contract (see e.g. *Roberts v Bury Commissioners* (1870) LR 5 CP 310 at pp. 320 and 325) and, in most cases, it is submitted, a sufficient degree of uninterrupted and exclusive possession to permit the contractor to carry out his work unimpeded and in the manner of his choice. This must particularly be so when a date for completion is specified in the contract documents.

It is thought that Mr Justice Urie's phrase 'it is fundamental to a building contract' means that it is fundamental in the sense that 'it went without saying' that it was a term of construction contracts that the contractor should have adequate access. If, however, the failure to provide access is prolonged and deliberate then it is also, it is submitted, likely to be fundamental in the sense that it will present the contractor with a right to terminate the contract and to sue for damages.

12.3.2   The degree of access which the employer is obliged to grant

The contract often expresses in some detail the degree and extent of the possession of the site to be granted to the contractor. If it does not, the courts will consider what terms relating to access should be read into the agreement. The following matters may be taken into account.

1   The nature of the works to be undertaken
   For example, a large-scale muck-shifting project may require complete possession of large tracts of the site; ornate joinery fittings, on the

other hand, will require only small areas of access in the immediate vicinity of the workfront as well as access routes for materials so that exclusive possession of the building will not be necessary or reasonable.

2   The factual matrix known at the time of making the contract
If, for instance, a subcontractor knows (or should have realised) that other subcontractors would also be working in the same general area of the site, he cannot complain that he has not been given complete control of that part of the site.

As regards failure to provide adequate space and workfronts there appears to be no presumption in favour of the contractor. In *Kitsons Sheet Metal v Matthew Hall* 47 BLR 90, for instance, Judge Newey made the following comments (at page 108) when construing a clause relating to access:

> I go at once to clause 6(2) which required the defendants to secure the availability for the plaintiffs of work areas and of access to them, but the obligation was qualified by the words 'so far as (they are) able'. The qualification was inevitable in the circumstances, but meant that so long as the defendants tried to obtain areas and access needed by the plaintiffs from [the other persons working on the site] the plaintiff's work could be brought to a complete stop without the defendants being in breach of the contract – or even morally at fault. If, of course, the defendants deliberately failed to make work areas available to the plaintiffs or made insufficient efforts to obtain them, then the defendants were in breach of contract.

12.3.3   Provision of access: a positive obligation to ensure access or an obligation not directly to hinder the contractor's access?

On some occasions access to the site or workfront is impossible because third parties have acted to prevent access, either deliberately or inadvertently; for example, an important access road may be closed to traffic or industrial action may prevent normal access to site. The question here is whether the contractor's inability to gain access in such circumstances is a breach on the employer's part or whether this is a risk to be borne by the contractor. It seems from the cases that the courts tend to treat such occurrences as being at the contractor's risk. For example, in *LRE Engineering v Otto Simon Carves* 24 BLR 131 the contract required that 'access to and possession of the site shall be afforded to the contractor by the [employer] in proper time for the execution of the work'. A physical route onto the site was provided by the employer but because of third party industrial action the contractor could not in fact gain access. The court held that the employer was not in breach since he had provided the physical route onto the site and the possibility of obstruction by third parties was a risk carried by the contractor.

12.3.4   Time of access

The time when possession is granted will often be of importance. This may be because there are time stipulations in the agreement necessitating early access if they are to be achieved or because the work must be coordinated with other contractors' work. In civil engineering contracts, in particular, the time of access is often important because of the weather; concreting and earthworks are significantly less efficient during the winter than during the warmer, drier summer. In *Freeman v Hensler (1900) Hudson's Building and Engineering Contracts* 4th Edition Vol II p. 292, the date of the contractor's possession was agreed; when the employer delayed the date of possession by such a period of time that work, which was envisaged as summer work, had to be carried out in winter, the contractor recovered for all the additional cost of working in winter. When no date for possession is agreed, it will be implied that the site must be handed over to the contractor within a reasonable time of making the contract: see, for example, *The Queen in Right of Canada v Walter Cabott Construction Ltd* 21 BLR 46 (discussed above).

12.4 Obligation to provide those things necessary to progress the works efficiently

12.4.1 The obligation to issue drawings and instructions in a reasonable time

The drawings and instructions available at the outset of a project are often insufficient to construct the works. Detailed drawings and information will often be required as the work progresses and there will normally be an implied obligation upon the employer to supply this material in sufficient detail and in sufficient time to enable the contractor to build the works. The extent and basis of such obligations are considered in *Merton v Leach* 32 BLR 51. In *Neodox v Borough of Swinton and Pendlebury* 5 BLR 34, Mr Justice Diplock was invited to say what was the implied term in a civil engineering contract concerning the provision of information required to construct the works. He first set out the contract terms which may have affected the answer and continued

> It is clear from these clauses which I have read that to give business efficacy to the contract, details and instructions necessary for the execution of the works must be given by the engineer from time to time in the course of the contract and must be given in a reasonable time. In giving such instructions the engineer is acting as agent for his principals, the Corporation, and if he fails to give instructions within a reasonable time, the Corporation are liable in damages for breach of contract.
>
> What is a reasonable time does not depend solely upon the convenience and financial interests of the claimants [the contractor]. No doubt it is in their interests to have every detail cut and dried on the day the contract is signed, but the contract does not contemplate that. It contemplates further details and instructions being provided, and the engineer is to have time to provide them which is reasonable having regard to the point of view of him and his staff and the point of view of the Corporation as well as the point of view of the contractors.

While these dicta of Mr Justice Diplock are, no doubt, of wide application, his approach does indicate that the term to be implied in each case will depend on the circumstances and on the surrounding express provisions in the contract. When the contract itself states the timing when information shall be delivered that overrides any term which would otherwise be implied.

During the progress of the work, the general rule is that the contractor can decide in what order he will perform the works subject to any express requirements in the contract. He must, however, give adequate notice to the employer of his proposed sequence and timing in order to allow the employer and his designers to supply any information required. While the contractor is entitled to complete the works before the due date for completion stated in the contract (subject to contract terms constraining him from early completion) he is not normally entitled to require the employer to provide information at a rate to enable him to complete early. In *Glenlion Construction v Guinness Trust* 39 BLR 89, Judge Fox-Andrews decided that the contractor was not entitled to demand of the employer that information be supplied which would enable the contractor to complete early. He referred to the following passage in Keating (*Keating's Building Contracts*, Supplement to the 4th Edition, p 6) with approval:

> Sometimes contractors at the commencement of or early in the course of a contract prepare and submit to the architect a programme of works showing completion at a date materially before the contract date. The architect approves or accepts without comment such programme. It is then argued that the contractor has a claim for damages for failure by the architects to issue instruction at times necessary to comply with the programme. While every case must depend upon the particular express terms and circumstances, it is thought that, upon the facts set out, the contractor's argument is bad; and that is the case even though the contractor is required to complete 'on or before' the contract date.

12.4.2   Provision of adequate work opportunity

Often the contractor can gain access to the site and has adequate space and drawings but still cannot progress the work. This may be because necessary preparatory works to be done by others have not yet been completed; if the work performed by those others is delayed, then the contractor will be forced into delay. Whether or not the contractor can recover additional payment for this delay will depend upon the express terms of the agreement or, if none, the existence of an implied term, either to the effect that his employer will bear the risk of such delays, or that his employer will provide him with sufficient work to enable him to complete the work efficiently. The question of whether or not such a term should be implied arose in *Martin Grant & Co Ltd v Sir Lindsay Parkinson & Co Ltd* 29 BLR 31. The project here was a major housing development in Islington. Parkinson was the main contractor and Grant was Parkinson's subcontractor, employed to do the formwork for the development. Grant knew that there were provisions in the main contract allowing the architect to extend the time for performance of the works because of delays and that, in most instances, the main contractor would not be compensated for these delays. The project was, in fact, delayed by a very considerable time and the subcontract works lasted for about five years rather than the two years originally contemplated. As a result Grant was forced to work inefficiently. However, there was no express term in the subcontract allowing Grant to be compensated for this delay, so they sought to imply the following term which appeared in their pleadings:

> It was an implied term of the said sub-contract that ... the Defendants [Parkinson] would make sufficient work available to the Plaintiffs [Grant] to enable them to maintain reasonable progress and to execute their work in an efficient and economic manner.

Lord Justice Lawton made the following comments:

> [Counsel for Grant] appreciated that that implied term could not arise on what has been called the *Moorcock* principle, namely it was not necessary for the efficacy of the performance of the contract; and he also seems to have accepted, as far I have followed his argument, that it could not be said to be implied on the basis that it was the obvious but unexpressed intention of the parties. The way he put his case was that that kind of term was to be implied by reason of the relationship of the parties, namely a contractor making a contract with a sub-contractor .... Is there a general rule of law implying such a term as was pleaded? The first observation to make is that building disputes have been regularly tried in this court all my professional lifetime and long before. If there were a general rule to the effect set out in the [alleged implied term], it is surprising that it has never been recognised before. [Counsel for Grant] has told us that there is no trace in the reported English cases of any such general rule, nor is there in the standard text books. That, of course, does not conclude the matter by any means because it was accepted by [Counsel for Parkinson] that the relationship between contractor and sub-contractor by implication of law does give rise to obligations on each side. There is, for example, by implication of law, an obligation to cooperate with one another. But the degree of cooperation will depend, in my judgment, upon the express terms of any contract which the parties may have made.

At this point Lord Justice Lawton referred to the express terms of the subcontract which acknowledged that delays may be incurred but which did not provide for the subcontractor to be compensated for this event. He then concluded

> It seems to me, having regard to the express terms and for the reasons I have indicated, that there is no room for this implied term. What I have had to consider is whether the term pleaded arises as a matter of law because of the relationship between contractor and sub-contractor in the circumstances of this case. I am firmly of the opinion that it does not.

12.5 The employer's obligation to obtain permits

Permits are frequently required before certain classes of work can commence. The question of which party must obtain these permits is a matter of construction of the contract and, in many cases, the construction is assisted by a consideration of the question: who is best placed to procure the permit? For instance, permits relating to the movements or use of specific items of plant to be used on site are clearly to be obtained by the contractor who supplies the plant unless the contract states otherwise.

If, for any reason, the employer must cooperate with the contractor in obtaining the permit it is submitted that the employer will be obliged to cooperate reasonably. Often, however, the employer is best placed to obtain the permit in question; here the obligation will fall upon him or her, unless the contractor has expressly undertaken to obtain it. In some situations, the employer is the only party realistically capable of obtaining the permit; here it is submitted that it will be an implied term that the permit will be obtained at the time when the work is to commence. A contractor employed to build a structure, for example, is entitled to expect that planning permission for the development will have been obtained before the date set for commencement of working.

In the Canadian case of *Ellis Don Ltd v The Parking Authority of Toronto* 28 BLR 98, the contractor had to construct a car park in Toronto within a specified time. Before excavation could commence, a permit was required from the City Building Department and, on a true construction of the contract, it was held that it was the employer's responsibility to procure this permit. In fact, the permit was not issued until about eight weeks after the envisaged start date and, although the contractor was able to perform some preliminary work without the permit, the delay to his programme was about seven weeks. Mr Justice O'Leary said

> There was an implied warranty on the part of the defendant not to interfere with the progress of the work, and the failure by the City to fulfil its obligation to obtain the necessary excavation permit in time, certainly interfered with the progress of the work.

He based his decision, *inter alia*, upon the New York decision of *Weeks v Rector of Trinity Church in the City of New York* (1900), 67 NY Supp 670, where Mr Justice Rumsey said (at pp. 672–673):

> The obligation upon the plaintiff to proceed promptly and diligently with this work gave to him the right to enter upon the premises, and involved necessarily an obligation on the part of the defendant that he should not be interfered with while he was engaged in completing the contract, and also an obligation on the part of the defendant that if the law required any act to be done by it before the work could be commenced under the contract, it would perform that obligation . . . . It being made by the law the duty of the defendant to procure this permit, there arose . . . an implied obligation that it would procure the permit within the time necessary to enable the plaintiff to proceed with his work diligently and promptly, as he had agreed to do in his contract.

He also cited the English case of *Porter v Tottenham UDC* [1915] 1 KB 776 where Lord Justice Pickford said (at p. 795)

> It does not seem to me, from a contract of this kind, that there can be implied more than this: that when the time comes which is stipulated in the contract for doing the work, and before which it cannot be done, there will be authority in the defendants to allow it to be done.

12.6 Obligation to appoint certifiers, nominated subcontractors, etc.

The contract will often require or envisage that the employer will appoint a certifier who is to administer the contractor. Often the contract is unworkable if a certifier is not in place and there will normally be implied an obligation for the employer to nominate someone to act in this capacity reasonably quickly.

Also some contracts envisage that subcontractors are to be nominated to undertake certain aspects of the work and there will be an implied undertaking on the employer's part to make the nomination in reasonable time and in accordance with the terms of the contract. This matter is dealt with in Section 13.4.

13

Subcontracting in construction

13.1 Introduction

Subcontracts are widely used in the construction industry, particularly for work with a specialist element, such as air-conditioning systems or cladding to buildings. In principle there is no legal difference between a subcontract and a main contract. But the use of subcontracting in the construction industry has introduced a number of practices, such as 'nomination', incorporation of the main contract terms into the subcontract, pay-when-paid provisions and others which merit discussion.

13.2 Privity and the contractual chain

13.2.1 Privity: the principle

Consider the situation where the employer (E) engages a contractor (C) to construct a piece of work and the contractor subcontracts it to a subcontractor (SC); he in turn sub-subcontracts it to a sub-subcontractor

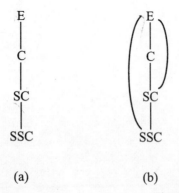

(a)   (b)

Fig. 13.1: Chains of contracts

(SSC) and the result is the chain of contracts shown in Fig. 13.1(a). (The vertical lines in the figure refer to contractual relationships.)

The 'doctrine of privity' is an important rule of contract law in this regard. This doctrine is derived from the principle that only those who have provided consideration to a contract (see Section 5.9) are entitled to sue upon that contract. Accordingly, only the two parties to the contract can rely on the contractual relationship which comes into existence. The corollary of this is that a party may look only to those with whom it is in a direct contractual relationship for a contractual remedy. Parties who have a direct contractual relationship are said to stand in a position of *contractual privity*.

Consequently, in the case of the contractual situation described in Figure 13.1(a), E cannot obtain a remedy from SC or SSC despite the interest that E has in the work performed by them since there exists no contractual privity between E and SC or between E and SSC. If SC or SSC has performed the work badly E will have to seek a remedy from C. (C cannot, of course, avoid liability by subcontracting to SC, unless the contract between E and C allows C to do so.) However, the law allows parties to make more than one agreement with regard to the same subject matter; accordingly, the situation shown in Figure 13.1(b) may exist where the normal chain of contracts are supplemented by additional agreements which create a contractual relationship between parties who would not normally be in such a relationship. Such contracts are often termed 'direct warranties' or 'collateral warranties'.

The doctrine of privity, therefore, operates to prevent anyone relying on a contract unless they are a party to that contract, even if that person has an important interest in the proper performance of that contract. The leading case of *Tweddle v Atkinson* (1861) 1 B&S 393 involved a contract between two relatives by which they agreed to provide a benefit to a third relative. One of the contracting relatives died and the survivor refused to bestow the agreed benefit, whereupon the aggrieved third relative sued upon the contract. His action was dismissed, despite his obvious interest in having the contract performed, because he was not a party to the contract. Many situations arise in construction where one party has an important interest in the proper performance of a contract to which he is not a party. For instance, where an employer lets out a building contract to a contractor and the contractor lets out the electrical work to a subcontractor, the employer has an important interest in the proper performance of the work; the question arises, how can the employer safeguard his or her interests?

13.2.2 How may an employer control subcontracted work?

If in the situation described in Figure 13.1(a), SC or SSC are undertaking work then E will have no contractual right to control their performance of the work, though the employer may always eject them from site (though if he does this he should expect action from C unless such an ejection is justified under the main contract). There are, however, a number of practical ways in which the employer can provide some degree of control over subcontracted work even though the party undertaking the work and the employer have no contract. First, the employer will normally insist that the main contract provides the employer or his or her agent with a right to object to the appointment of proposed subcontractors (often there is a requirement for any objection to be reasonably based). The contract is typically worded so that the contractor must seek the approval of the employer or his or her agent before taking on any subcontractor. This helps both to maintain an accurate record of the subcontracts and to ensure that only subcontractors which are apparently competent are employed. If a subcontractor is employed without prior approval the employer will be entitled to eject the subcontractor from the site whether or not the subcontractor has breached any term of the contract and, indeed, the subcontractor may be entirely innocent. In this situation, the subcontractor will have to seek a remedy from the contractor based on the contractor's breach of contract, as a term is generally implied into contracts that the contracting parties have authority to enter into the contract.

Second, the main contract usually contains terms authorising the employer or his or her agent to issue instructions to the contractor on the mode of performance of the contract. If the work is sublet, and the subcontractor appears to be undertaking the work in such a way that there is a risk that the contract specification may not be attained the employer may issue an instruction concerning the performance of the work. A failure by the subcontractor to comply with the instruction will be a breach by the main contractor of his obligations under the main contract. If corrective action is not taken immediately, the employer will be able to halt the works. If the subcontractor continues with the works in defiance of these instructions (on the basis, for example, that his subcontract with the main contractor does not oblige him to take instructions from the employer) the employer is entitled to eject him from the site. Again, the subcontractor's remedy (if any) will be against the main contractor.

13.2.3 Creating a direct contract between the employer and the subcontractor

If in the situation described in Figure 13.1(a), SC or SSC have performed the work in a manner which does not accord with the contract between E and C, E cannot seek a remedy against them; so E will seek the remedy from C. If a remedy cannot be sought against C, for instance if C becomes bankrupt or takes his or her assets out of the country, E is left without a remedy. It is of benefit to the employer, therefore, to establish a contractual relationship, a direct warranty, between himself and SC and SSC. Such a warranty may arise as an express agreement or as a warranty of quality.

Express direct warranty
The employer may write into the main contract a requirement that the contractor obtain a written warranty from any proposed subcontractor in favour of the employer; this warranty will establish a contractual bond between the employer and the subcontractor. The warranty will normally be worded such that the subcontractor agrees that he will perform the

works such that the main contract will not be breached and if he is in breach of this obligation the employer may sue him as if he, the subcontractor, were the main contractor. This requirement for the main contractor to obtain the warranty may readily be enforced if the main contract is worded such that the employer may refuse to approve the appointment of any subcontractor if the subcontractor fails to provide a warranty in the required form. One matter that must be clarified in this regard is what consideration does the employer provide for the warranty agreement? Often, the employer's consideration is the approval but often (and this provides more security for the employer) a deed is executed or a nominal fee (of say £1) is also provided by the employer to the subcontractor to make sure that sufficient consideration is provided.

Warranty of quality
A warranty of quality arises where it is fair to assume that a subcontractor is making an undertaking intended to be acted upon by the employer and where sufficient consideration can be found to support the existence of a contract. The leading case is *Shanklin Pier Ltd v Detel Products* [1951] 2 KB 854. The plaintiffs in this case were the owners of a pier. During repainting works the manufacturer of a brand of bituminous paints represented to the plaintiff that their paint was suitable for the work. As a result of this the plaintiff instructed their contractor to place an order with the defendant paint manufacturer. The paint failed and the plaintiff owner sued the paint manufacturer on the basis of their representation. The court held that there was a contractual warranty subsisting whereby the paint manufacturer warranted that their paint was suitable. The consideration supplied by the owner was the undertaking to instruct its contractor to place a contract with the manufacturer.

The limits of this principle are, however, well demonstrated by *Independent Broadcasting Authority v EMI Electronics Ltd and BICC Construction Ltd* 14 BLR 1. This concerned the liability of EMI and BICC for the collapse of the Emley Moor television mast. EMI were the main contractor and BICC were nominated subcontractors. There was no express direct warranty agreed between IBA, the employer, and BICC but IBA claimed that a representation made by BICC during the project constituted a warranty. The facts were these: the Emley Moor tower was one of a series of masts. When the first of these to be built reached a height of some 850 ft it began to oscillate wildly. As a result, the IBA suggested to BICC that the design of the towers should be investigated and in reply BICC wrote that they were 'well satisfied that the structures will not oscillate dangerously'. The judge at first instance, Mr Justice O'Connor, held that this assurance amounted to a contractual warranty (he found consideration to support the contract). The Court of Appeal agreed with him. Since the Emley Moor tower did, in fact, collapse, BICC were therefore in breach of contract according to the judge and the Court of Appeal. The House of Lords, however, disagreed. Viscount Dilhorne said

> If this is right, then it would seem to me to follow that any representation, whether made innocently, negligently or fraudulently, which is intended to

be acted on and which is acted on creates a contractual relationship. I do not think that this can be right.

His Lordship relied upon statements made by Lord Moulton in *Heilbut Symons & Co v Buckleton* [1913] AC 30 that a contract of the type alleged 'must be proved strictly. Not only the terms of such contracts but the existence of an *animus contrahendi* [willingness to contract] on the part of all the parties to them must be clearly shown'.

However, in the circumstances of the *IBA v BICC* case the assurance, though not amounting to a contractual warranty, was fatal to BICC's defence, since it amounted to a misrepresentation within the principles of negligence laid down in *Hedley Byrne & Co Ltd v Heller & Partners Ltd* [1964] AC 465 (see Section 18.4.4) and was, according to the House, made negligently. If, however, the assurance had not been made negligently then it would have been crucial to the success of the IBA's claim against BICC to determine whether or not the assurance amounted to a contractual warranty.

The Subcontractor's perception of the direct warranty
In theory a direct warranty may also be to the advantage of SC and SSC in some cases if worded appropriately. For instance, while E cannot sue SC in the situation described in Figure 13.1(a), neither can SC sue E. But if C goes into liquidation before C pays SC, SC may benefit from a direct contract with E. However, the terms of the typical direct warranty are fairly one-sided. They might read

> WHEREAS the employer and the main contractor have entered into an agreement ('the main contract') that the main contractor will perform all those works described as [describe] AND WHEREAS the subcontractor has and is deemed to have full knowledge of the terms of the said main contract AND WHEREAS the subcontractor has agreed with the main contractor that the subcontractor will undertake that part of the said works known as [describe] NOW it is HEREBY AGREED between the employer and the subcontractor that the latter will perform those works which he has agreed to undertake in full compliance with the main contract terms and will be liable to the employer for all losses suffered by the employer in the event that the subcontractor fails to perform the works in full compliance with the main contract. BUT in no event will the employer become liable to the subcontractor for payment or for any other claim howsoever framed, except in respect of the £1 fee to be paid by the employer to the subcontractor as consideration for this agreement.

13.2.4 Additional work undertaken by the subcontractor at the employer's request

In some circumstances an additional obligation will arise outside the scope of the original agreement which will operate to circumvent the privity rule. If the contract between the employer and the contractor specifies a particular scope of work and yet the employer directly asks the subcontractor to undertake work outside that scope he or she may be liable to the subcontractor for the value of that extra work if the request was given in circumstances where it was reasonably to be inferred that the additional work was to be paid for directly by the employer.

A direct request by the architect or engineer under the contract to the subcontractor will not normally bind the employer as neither will have the authority to bind the employer unless they have been expressly clothed with such authority.

13.2.5 Negligence liability

When the employer makes a representation to the subcontractor (e.g. concerning conditions on site) or the subcontractor makes a representation to the employer (e.g. concerning the suitability of a particular construction technique) a liability may arise between them in negligence under the principle of *Hedley Byrne v Heller and Partners* [1964] AC 465 (see Section 18.4.4).

13.2.6 Possible future amendments to the privity rule

The strict application of the privity rule has received a good deal of criticism. Contracts are often made with the clear intention of bestowing a benefit upon a third party (see, for example, *Tweddle v Atkinson* (1861) B & S 393 referred to above). When one contracting party becomes incapable of or refuses to enforce the contract for the benefit of the third party, the third party (who cannot sue) loses the benefit. Having reviewed criticism, the Law Commission (Consultation Paper No 121, 1991) have recommended that legislation be introduced to allow some classes of third party to enforce the agreement. In their paper the following recommendation appears (paragraph 5.10):

> We provisionally recommend that a third party should be able to enforce a contract in which the parties intend that he should receive the benefit of the promised performance and also intend to create a legal obligation enforceable by him. From this it follows that the creation of a right in a third party should not be inferred from the mere fact that he will derive benefit from performance of the contract.

Therefore, the key to the third party's right to enforce the agreement is the intention of the contracting parties at the time of making the contract that he be entitled to do so. In paragraphs 5.11 and 5.12 the Law Commission suggest

> Whether or not a contract is intended to create a legal obligation enforceable by the third party is to be derived from the terms of the contract and the surrounding circumstances . . . . Furthermore it is the objectively determined intentions of the parties which matter rather than their private thoughts.

In other words the contract has to be construed in the normal way.

A number of matters which affect construction industry contracts have not been addressed in the paper. These include the situations where there is a power for a certifier to make binding certificates and where there is an arbitration clause, particularly one where the arbitrator is empowered to 'open up review and revise' the certifier's decisions. There is no indication in the paper regarding whether a third party with an entitlement to enforce the agreement is to be bound by the certification and arbitration provisions.

The current recommendations are provisional and final recommendations will not be published until comments have been received and considered. Even in their final form they will not become law until enacted by Parliament during which process further amendments may be made. Since neither the form of these amendments nor the timetable for legislation can be predicted the full impact of these changes on the privity rule cannot be assessed at the present time. The effect on construction contracts may be minimal.

13.3   The right to discharge contractual obligations by vicarious performance

13.3.1   The general right to delegate non-personal contractual obligations

General principles

Subcontracting is a species of delegation of contractual responsibilities. As regards the relationship between the employer and the contractor the fundamental question is: may the contractor delegate the performance of his contractual obligations to a third party? It matters little to the employer whether that delegation is administered through a subcontract or through some other means, such as a gift by the third party to the contractor. The rule of privity means that the employer cannot sue the delegee directly, and the formation of a direct warranty between the employer and the delegee is not barred by the lack of a subcontract between the contractor and the delegee. In the commercial world, however, subcontracting is the almost invariable means of such delegation, but the courts normally talk in more general terms such as delegation or of vicarious performance.

In *Southway Group Ltd v Wolff and Wolff* 57 BLR 33, Lord Justice Bingham emphasised that here, as elsewhere in contract law, the objective intention of the parties is paramount in deciding whether an obligation may be vicariously performed:

> Whether a given contract requires personal performance by A, or whether (and if so to what extent) A may perform his contractual obligations vicariously, is in my opinion a question of contractual construction. That does not mean that the court is confined to a semantic analysis of the written record of the parties' contract, if there is one. Such is not the modern approach of construction of a commercial contract. It means that the court must do its best, by reference to all admissible materials, to make an objective judgment of what A and B intended in this regard.

In practice the intention of the parties is often expressed in the terms of the contract. Indeed, most standard form contracts contain clauses relating to subcontracting, normally restricting its use unless and until approval has been obtained from the employer's agent (see Section 13.3.2). However, some contracts are silent on the matter and in such cases one important indicator of the objective intention of the parties is the subject matter of the contract.

Vicarious performance of contractor's obligations

The general rule appears to be that a contractor, who has been employed to undertake work, may subcontract that work out provided that the particular skills of that contractor are not being relied upon by the employer. To draw a broad distinction we might say that where the contractor's obligation is to achieve a specified result (e.g. to place and compact 20 000 m³ of crushed rock) then the contractor may subcontract the work out. But where the obligation involves a personal discretion (for example to exercise reasonable skill and care in the planning and design of a building suitable for the employer's headquarters), the work may not be subcontracted without the consent of the employer. In the traditional scheme of construction, where the design and construction aspects of a project are separated, we may say as a generalisation which may require refinement in particular cases that the planning and design work may not be sublet, while the construction work may be.

A number of decided cases illustrate this. In *British Waggon Co v Lea* (1880) 5 QBD 149, the Divisional Court held that a contractor who agreed to repair wagons could perform the contract by getting those repairs performed according to the specification by a third party. However, in *Moresk Cleaners v Hicks* 4 BLR 50 an architect was sued for professional negligence in the design of a roof. He sought to defend himself by claiming to have delegated the design of certain elements of the roof to the contractor and was held not to be entitled to treat this as a defence. He was not entitled to delegate the work as it involved design to a reasonable standard, rather than compliance with a defined specification. In *Southway Group Ltd v Wolff and Wolff* 57 BLR 33, the work contained in the contract for the refurbishment of a warehouse was very loosely specified (not even the location of key areas of the structure such as the core had been agreed). This was because the employer was acquainted with an employee of the contractor and relied upon his skill and knowledge to provide a suitable result. The Court of Appeal decided that for those aspects of works where the employer was relying upon the personal discretion of the contractor's employee, no vicarious performance was permitted.

Vicarious performance of employer's obligations

It is submitted that the general test for the right to have contractual obligations vicariously performed is identical for both contractors and employers and derives from the true construction of the contract.

In the case of the delegability of the employer's obligations, however, a difficulty has arisen following the case of *Linden Gardens Trust Ltd v Lenesta Sludge Disposals Ltd and others* 57 BLR 57. Here the court suggested that in the normal course of events an employer could assign his right to have a construction contract performed on the basis that the employer's obligations were purely mechanical and it matters little to the contractor who performs them (details of this argument are set out in Section 15.2.2). It may be said that an obligation which is assignable may *necessarily* be vicariously performed (though normally, of course, when there is an assignment there is nothing to be performed by the assignee except the receipt of the benefit assigned, because only benefits may be assigned).

The Court of Appeal in making its remarks, it is submitted, was not considering the typical situation of a construction contract; the obligations of an employer under such a contract may often be substantial and, in part, personal. To that extent they are not assignable. If the judges' arguments in Linden Garden are generally followed, the effect will be that most of the obligations which an employer undertakes under a construction contract will be vicariously performable, unless there is a prohibition in the contract which forbids such a delegation.

It is submitted that it is appropriate to return to the general test suggested above which may be applicable to delegation by both contractors and employers. The test is: what is the intention of the parties, objectively construed, using the words of the contract and the surrounding circumstances? It is submitted that very few construction contracts studied in this way would lead to the conclusion that *all* the employer's obligations be freely delegable.

13.3.2   Express contractual restrictions on subcontracting

Where approval is required
Most construction contracts require that a contractor who wishes to subcontract work out must obtain the prior consent or approval of the employer or his agent (e.g. the architect or engineer). Often the contract provides that this consent or approval should not be unreasonably withheld. But if the contract is silent on the question of whether the employer must act reasonably in approving subcontractors what is the position? It appears that there is no obligation for the employer to act reasonably. In *Leedsford Ltd v Bradford Corporation* 24 BLR 45 an item in the bills read: 'Artificial stone ... the following to be obtained from the Empire Stone Company Limited, 326 Deansgate, Manchester or other approved firm.' The plaintiff contractor sought approval for the supply to be obtained from a firm other than the one named but the architect refused. The plaintiff ordered the specified stone, which was more expensive than that supplied by the firm (whose name they had submitted for approval), and then sued for the difference in price, on the grounds of breach of contract for failure reasonably to approve an alternative supplier. The Court of Appeal rejected the plaintiff's claim. Lord Justice Singleton said:

> It appears to me that there is good reason for saying, upon the authority of that decision [*Viscount Tredegar v Harwood* [1929] AC 72], that in these circumstances the words 'or other approved firm' do not add anything to the rights of the plaintiff contractors. If that be right, there is no obligation upon the architect to approve any firm suggested to him other than the Empire Stone Company Limited. If he acts honestly it can be said that there is no more to be done. It is not a case in which he has to act reasonably in considering whether to approve or not.

Prohibitions against assignment and their effect on the right to subcontract
The law relating to assignment is dealt with in Chapter 15, but one aspect of this subject needs to be considered here because of its overlap with subcontracting. When there is a prohibition against assignment in a

contract, the courts may construe this to produce a prohibition against vicarious performance. For example, in *Linden Gardens Trust Ltd v Lenesta Sludge Disposals Ltd and others* 57 BLR 57 the Court of Appeal considered the following prohibition in the JCT form:

> 17(2) The Contractor shall not without the written consent of the Employer assign this Contract, and shall not without the written consent of the Architect (which consent shall not be unreasonably withheld to the prejudice of the contractor) sublet any portion of the Works . . .

The court heard that the terms 'assignment' and 'subcontracting' were often confused and used interchangeably by commercial people. They agreed that the prohibition was not upon an *assignment* of the contract (which was unassignable in any event), but upon *vicarious performance*. In support of this construction Lord Justice Nourse said:

> With regard to clause 17(2), I think it clear that the presence of the prohibition against subletting 'any portion' of the works, coupled with the absence of a prohibition against subletting the whole of them, requires the words 'shall . . . not assign this contract' to be construed as meaning 'shall not sublet the whole of the works'.

Accordingly care should be taken when scanning contracts to check for restrictions on subcontracting. A restriction on assignment may suffice to achieve that effect.

13.4 Nominated subcontractors

13.4.1 General

Many construction contracts contain provisions which allow the employer to instruct the contractor to enter into a subcontract with a named (or 'nominated') subcontractor or supplier. The aim of this power is to ensure that the employer can choose specialist subcontractors without becoming contractually liable to that subcontractor for payment etc., although it may follow on from nomination that the subcontractor is required to execute a direct warranty in favour of the employer. However, as noted in the example given in Section 13.2.3 the terms of the warranty are generally designed to protect the employer against the default of the subcontractor; they rarely cause the employer to become liable for the subcontractor's payments, access etc., for which the subcontractor must seek redress against the main contractor.

One important point that should also be noted is that there is some concern whether the traditional system of nomination offends against the European Directives on competition. This throws doubt on the enforceability of such provisions.

13.4.2 Failure of nomination provisions to provide the employer with the sought-after benefits

Because the system of nomination attempts to achieve two apparently incompatible aims, namely avoidance of liability while maintaining control of specialist work there are a number of problems associated with the system. In *Bickerton v North West Metropolitan Regional Hospital Board* [1970] 1 WLR 607, Lord Reid said of nomination (at p. 611):

> The scheme for nominated subcontractors is an ingenious method of achieving two objects which at first sight might seem incompatible. The employer wants to choose who is to do the prime cost work and to settle the terms on which it is to be done, and at the same time to avoid the hazards and difficulties which might arise if he entered into a contract with the person whom he has chosen to do the work.

One of the problems has been that the courts have been unwilling to make a contractor liable for the work of a nominated subcontractor when the contractor has little control over it. Disquiet was expressed in the House of Lords both in *Bickerton v NW Metropolitan Regional Hospital Board* [1970] and *Gloucestershire County Council v Richardson* [1969] 1 AC 480.

In *Richardson* the contractor was obliged to enter into a contract by which a nominated supplier supplied concrete columns. The terms of the supply contract were negotiated by the employer and they limited the supplier's liability to replacement of defective columns: consequential losses were excluded. The contractor had no right to object to the nomination. The columns were defective. It was held that the contractor should not be liable for latent defects. In this case, the Law Lords appeared to be very much influenced in reaching this conclusion by the lack of control which the contractor had (e.g. see the dicta of Lord Wilberforce at pp. 507–508).

In *Bickerton* a specialist subcontractor was nominated to provide mechanical services in a building. However, almost immediately upon commencement of the works, they went into liquidation and the liquidator refused to complete the work. The House of Lords agreed with the main contractor's contention that

- the contractor was entitled to a reasonably rapid re-nomination and to damages for delay awaiting a re-nomination
- the contractor was not liable to reimburse the employer when the subcontractor's liquidation caused the employer to expend additional monies in getting the works completed using a different subcontractor.

The House of Lords appear to have made this decision primarily upon the consideration that the terms of the main contract neither entitled nor required the contractor to carry out the works which were to be performed by nominated subcontractors. They said that, although the contractor was responsible for the nominated subcontractor, such responsibility could exist only where a nominated subcontractor was, in fact, in existence. Accordingly, if the first nominated subcontractor went into liquidation, another must be nominated.

In *Fairclough Building v Rhuddlan Borough Council* 30 BLR 26 the Court of Appeal decided that where the first nominated subcontractor leaves the work in a defective state the re-nomination subcontract must include a requirement to remedy the defective work. If it does not it is an invalid re-nomination. The judgment of the court at page 44 reads

> If defects are found in main contract work the contractor will have to put it right pursuant to his overall obligation to perform the contract. So also in

the case of work which he has elected to have performed by a subcontractor. He has, however, no obligation to do nominated subcontractor or prime cost work. [Counsel for the employer] submitted that remedial work was not nominated subcontract work but we do not follow this. The nominated subcontractor is obliged to produce work which satisfies the subcontract. If he does some work which does not satisfy the contract he is obliged, if he stays, to cure the position.

An examination of these cases and the ratios of subsequent decisions (including *Percy Bilton v Greater London Council* [1982] 1 WLR 794, yet another House of Lords decision on the same standard form as was considered in *Richardson* and *Bickerton*) show, however, that the House of Lords has laid down no generally applicable principles, apart from exhibiting an unwillingness to saddle a contractor with liability to an employer when the cause of the breach which occurs may be said to be attributable to the employer's failure to nominate a viable and competent subcontractor. Each case will, it is submitted, turn on its own contract terms.

13.4.3   The contractor's liability for design work undertaken by a nominated subcontractor

Under a typical construction contract the contractor is employed to build, not to design. On occasions, however, design obligations are written into the agreement and, in these cases, there is no doubt that the contractor is obliged to carry out such design obligations. However, it sometimes happens that a contractor is obliged, by the terms of his contract, to employ a nominated subcontractor and that subcontractor's obligations include some design work. To what extent is the main contractor liable to the employer for the nominated subcontractor's breaches of design obligations? This point was raised in the Irish case of *Norta Wallpapers (Ireland) Ltd v John Sisk & Sons (Dublin) Ltd* 14 BLR 49 [1978] IR 114. The facts were that the employer, Norta, instructed Sisk, the contractor for the construction of a wallpaper factory, to enter into a nominated subcontract with Hoesch, a specialist factory builder, for the construction of the superstructure. Some time after opening, the factory began to leak because the design of the roof-lights was negligent. The design was undertaken by Hoesch and was approved by the employer's engineer; the contractor, Sisk, had no involvement in this work. When the leak was discovered, however, Norta found themselves unable to sue Hoesch, since there was no contractual privity between them, so they claimed against Sisk. Mr Justice McMahon, at first instance, and the Irish Supreme Court, on appeal, held that the question of the extent of the contractor's obligations to the employer for the nominated subcontractor's work was governed by the implied terms in the agreement between the employer and contractor. In general, the contractor is liable for the nominated subcontractor's failure to supply materials of merchantable quality or their bad workmanship. Mr Justice McMahon, however, thought that different considerations applied when the problem was the faulty design of the subcontractor and particularly where the main contractor had no opportunity to object to the nominations or had no real involvement in the design. The Supreme Court of Ireland affirmed this view.

The House of Lords faced a similar problem in *IBA v EMI and BICC* 14 BLR 1 and, while they agreed that *Norta v Sisk* had been correctly decided they felt that the important consideration was the contractor's lack of opportunity to become involved. Lord Fraser of Tullybelton said (at page 46)

> The question in the instant case is exactly the same [as that raised in *Norta*], but in my opinion the answer is different. Although the facts in *Norta* were very like those in the present case, they are distinguishable in the respect that, before the contract between Norta and Sisk was made, Norta's engineers had already approved the German company's design and specification and Norta had promised that the order for the superstructure would be given to them at a price which was also agreed. Sisk thus were given no option either as to the identity of the subcontractor or as to the design or price of the superstructure. In the present case, although EMI had no option but to appoint BICC as subcontractor for the mast, they were not bound to accept any particular design at any particular price. If they had checked BICC's design and had considered it unsatisfactory they would have been entitled to insist on its being improved. That is not a mere theoretical possibility, as is shown by the fact that on a previous occasion, in 1958, when EMI had tendered to IBA for the erection of a lattice mast at Mendlesham, they had expressly accepted 'over-all responsibility' for the mast including its design and they had then told BICC that they wished to arrange for a check on the structural design as an additional safeguard. That procedure could I think have been repeated in 1963 if EMI had wanted.

The position thus appears to be

- a contractor will be liable for the faulty designs of a nominated subcontractor, if he expressly agrees to be liable for them and he has the ability to control the design work
- but a contractor will not be liable for the nominated subcontractor's faulty designs if he has no right to object to the nominations and has no control over the design work.

13.4.4   Should the system of nomination be used by employers?

The system of nomination was devised by the professional advisers of employers in order to achieve a particular set of benefits. However, as the cases of *Bickerton* and *Richardson* show, the effect is often to leave the employer liable to or with no effective right of action against the contractor. Unless the employer has a direct warranty with the subcontractor or unless a warranty of the type found in *Shanklin Piers v Detel* (see Section 13.2.3) exists then the employer has no action at all. This can be a costly situation for an employer to find himself in. Accordingly, it might well be asked whether the benefits of nomination are worth the risk? I cite here the opinion of Keating in this regard (5th edition, p. 294) which I find convincing:

> The reasons advanced in favour of nomination are that it gives the employer the choice of a specialist contractor, it enables him to obtain the best price

for specialist works and it enables him to have the advantage of design work which his professional advisers cannot carry out. None of these arguments are valid save the first. Even here the employer can issue a list of subcontractors any of whom he will approve. The rest is a matter of tendering procedure. Nomination can be avoided if specialist works are described in terms of performance specification and the main contractors invited to tender are given sufficient time to make their own enquiries among specialist subcontractors.

If the employer wishes, however, to nominate a subcontractor it is strongly advised that he takes a warranty from the subcontractor concerning the subcontractor's performance during the works and as to the quality of the work provided.

It is also advised that the employer has regard to the current uncertainty about whether the system of nomination is contrary to European Community competition law, as mentioned in Section 13.4.1. If this is so, the traditional nomination system will be rendered unenforceable, and alternative methods of achieving the results sought will need to be employed.

13.5   Terms of the subcontract

Generally the same rules of contract apply to subcontracts as they do to main contractors. Because of the network of contracts on a project, subcontracts are often written with specific reference to the main contract. Often they contain a term which expressly incorporates 'the terms of the main contract insofar as these are consistent with the subcontract' or some other such phrase. Often the payment provisions and claims procedures are closely linked. For example 'pay when paid clauses' are common and it is often a duty of the contractor to seek to claim on behalf of his subcontractor.

13.5.1   Incorporation of the terms of the main contract into the subcontract

It is often a term of the subcontract that the terms of the main contract apply to the subcontract. This is a convenient device for ensuring that when the subcontractor is in default, thereby causing the contractor to be liable to the employer, the contractor can recover the same damages from the subcontractor as he owes to the employer. When such a result is achieved the contracts are said to be 'back-to-back'. On occasions, the way in which a main contract clause might apply to the subcontract is not clear. The court will attempt to produce a result which accords with the intention of the parties. For example, in *Geary, Walker & Co Ltd v W Lawrence & Son* (1906) HBC 4th Edition Vol ii p. 382, the subcontract provided that the terms of payment would be the same as those for the main contract. The main contract provided for a limit on the retention monies but that limit exceeded the value of the subcontract; the Court of Appeal decided that the subcontract clause was to be construed as involving repayments in the same proportion as the subcontract price bore to the main contract price.

13.5.2   Pay when paid clauses

Since the main contractor often budgets to make the subcontractor's payment out of sums paid by the employer to the main contractor for the subcontract work, the contractor may be embarrassed if the employer refuses or is unable to pay and yet the contractor cannot establish a bona fide claim against the subcontract. Therefore many subcontracts contain a provision whereby the contractor is not obliged to pay for work until he is paid for the work by the employer. These appear to be effective.

13.5.3   Contractor's obligation to pursue claims on behalf of the subcontractor

Subcontracts often contain provisions where the subcontractor is entitled to make a claim for additional payments, upon which happening, the contractor is obliged to pursue the claim against the employer, based on the terms of the main contract. This involves a similar device to 'pay when paid' clauses since only upon the proof by the contractor of the subcontract claim is the subcontractor entitled to be paid. Problems may arise when the main contractor and employer reach an agreement concerning the valuation of a claim but the contractor fails to inform the subcontractor. Here the subcontractor may be kept in the dark about the agreement. Under many standard form subcontracts, the main contractor is obliged to do all things reasonable to secure the benefits of the main contract for the subcontractor; any failure to do so will thus be a breach of the subcontract. Acts by the main contractor, such as the making of a clandestine agreement with the employer about matters which affect the subcontractor's right to be paid will be inconsistent with the subcontract and hence will be a breach for which the subcontractor may recover damages.

14

Certificates issued under construction contracts

14.1 Introduction

14.1.1 The use of certificates in the administration of construction contracts

Certificates are widely used in the administration of construction contracts to indicate that some event, such as the completion of some element of work, has, in the opinion of the certifier, been performed; or that some sum is, in the opinion of the certifier, due to the contractor. The precise effect of any particular certificate will depend upon a proper construction of the contract terms under which it was issued and the form in which it is issued, but some general points, illustrating the approach of the courts to the validity and meaning of certificates, may be made.

14.1.2 Certifiers

The certifier is the person authorised to issue certificates under the contract. While there is no reason, in principle, why different persons should not be authorised to issue certificates, usually only one certifier is named and this promotes control over the administration of the project. The certifier tends to be known by a variety of names in the various forms of contract commonly used: as the architect in the JCT contracts, as the engineer in the ICE contracts and other contracts issued by engineering institutions, and as the supervising officer in the GC/Wks/1 contract. Generally, the functions of these various certifiers are similar under each of these forms of contract, though the effect of the issue of any individual certificate will depend on the precise contract terms under which it is issued.

The responsibilities and obligations of the certifier when issuing certificates are discussed in Section 26.2.

14.1.3 The meaning and use of the word 'certificate'

The important feature of a certificate is that it is to affect the rights of the parties to the contract in some respect. It is therefore to be issued fairly and in good faith having appropriate regard to the terms of the contract. Certification is not to be a purely administrative process to be undertaken in the interests of one party.

The term 'certificate' or its derivatives (to certify, certification, etc.) are commonly used in construction contracts. But, it is submitted, this word has no intrinsic significance. What is important is the meaning of the words in their context; in particular they should express the concept of certification rather than use the word 'certification'. Accordingly, a contractual provision requiring a named person to make a 'decision' or 'determination' or to issue a 'formal instruction' may well have the same legal effect as if the word certify was used. While the term 'certifying' may suggest a more formal process than, say, 'making a decision' the two may, in an appropriate contractual setting, be equivalent. An important practical example of this is the requirement in Clause 66 of the ICE Contract for the Engineer (the person charged with issuing certificates) to give a decision when requested to do so by one of the parties. Such a decision is an important step in the process of reaching arbitration and, most crucially, a party to the contract who disagrees with the engineer's decision has only three months in which to commence proceedings. It is submitted that, in this case, no formal distinction can be drawn between such a decision and a certificate and that such a decision is subject to the same rules as a certificate.

In this chapter, therefore, the term 'certificate' should be read as including all 'decisions', 'determinations' (and so on) of the certifier which, according to the contract, affect the rights of the parties under the contract and are expressly or impliedly to be made fairly and honestly.

14.1.4 Withdrawal of certificates

All matters relating to the issue of certificates are governed by the terms of the contract and this applies equally to the withdrawal of a certificate. It often happens in practice that a certifier will, after issuing a certificate, purport to withdraw it. Clearly, if he is entitled to do so by express terms in the contract, he may withdraw a certificate. If no such express powers are included it appears that he may not. In *CM Pillings v Kent Investments Ltd* 30 BLR 80 at p. 86 Lord Justice Kerr dealt with such a possibility:

> On 11th October 1984 the architects threatened to withdraw or cancel the certificates which they had recently issued . . . in fact the certificates were not withdrawn, if indeed there is any such power under the contract.

This suggests that an express power of withdrawal of certificates is required if such a purported withdrawal is to be effective.

14.1.5 The status and legal nature of certificates

A question which is of considerable importance is the legal nature of a construction contract certificate. At one stage the court decided that a certificate of payment due was in many respects equivalent to a cheque in that no 'set-off' was allowed. This means that provided a contractor had a certificate purporting to entitle him to a stated sum, the employer was obliged to pay that sum in full even though the employer had a contra-claim against the contractor. In *Modern Engineering v Gilbert Ash* [1974] AC 689 the House of Lords rejected this view and emphasised the principle that if the owner had a bona fide and supportable claim against the contractor, the employer can deduct the value of that claim from the sum described in the certificate unless the contract obliges him in terms to pay the full amount.

A second question which often arises is the ability of the contractor to receive payment if work has been performed under a contract where payment is to be made on a certificate but no certificate has, in fact, been issued. In *Panamena Europa Navigacion v Leyland & Co* [1947] AC 428 the House of Lords decided that in these circumstances the contractor can recover if the certifier insists on unreasonable preconditions, or if he acts improperly in any other way.

A further problem that sometimes arises is when the certificate contains an error and shows the incorrect amount. Must the employer pay the amount certified or must he pay the proper amount as substantiated by the contractor? In *Lubenham Fidelities v South Pembrokeshire District Council* 33 BLR 46 this situation arose. Here the contract was the JCT 80, Clause 35 of which allowed arbitration on certificates during the project. In addition, the contract terms assumed that any errors in one certificate would be rectified in subsequent certificates. Therefore, the Court of Appeal said that the employer's obligation was to pay the amount certified and not to look behind the certificate. The judgment of the court included the following statement (at page 55):

> Whatever the cause of the under-valuation, the proper remedy available to the contractor is, in our opinion, to request the architect [the certifier] to make the appropriate adjustment in another certificate, or if he declines to do so, to take the dispute to arbitration under clause 35. In default of arbitration or the issue of a new certificate the conditions themselves give the contractor no right to sue for the higher sum. In other words we think under this form of contract the issue of a certificate is always a condition precedent to the right of the contractor to be paid.

The contractor's case included arguments based on *Panamena* and on *Modern Engineering v Gilbert-Ash*. The court thought that neither was relevant. *Panamena* was irrelevant since in the instant case the employer had not procured the incorrect certificate, they had merely acquiesced in its issue. Further, there was no arbitration clause in *Panamena* so that there was no possibility of remedying the situation by reference to an arbitrator. By raising an argument based on *Modern Engineering v Gilbert-Ash* the contractor sought to show that the certificate was not sacrosanct but could be adjusted. The Court of Appeal contented themselves (at page 58) with the view that set-off was an entirely different matter from the issue then before the court.

14.2 Types of certificate

Under the standard forms of contract a wide range of certificates may be issued with a wide range of names and apparent purposes and effects.

Thus, for instance, under the JCT 80 contract the architect may issue
certificates of Practical Completion (Clause 17.1), Completion of Making
Good Defects (Clause 17.4), Frost Damage (Clause 17.5), Partial Possession
(Clause 18.1), Liquidated Damages (Clause 24), Loss and Expense upon
Determination (Clause 27.4.4.), Interim Certificates for Payment (Clause
30.1), Final Certificate (Clause 30.8) and of Failure to Complete by a
Nominated Subcontractor (Clause 35.15).

Given the large number of different types of certificates that may be
issued, any classification will have, of necessity, to be crude.

14.2.1   Interim payment certificates

The effect of interim certificates on payment
Many contract forms require the contractor to submit an account to the
certifier at times stated in the contract and the certifier will then consider
this account and issue a certificate stating the sum which, in his or her
opinion, is due under the contract and which the employer must pay.
Generally, the figure certified will be an approximate estimate and is rarely
binding upon the employer or contractor unless the contract clearly makes
it so. Thus, while an interim certificate creates a debt due which may be
assigned (see *Workman Clark & Co v Lloyd Brazileno* [1908] 1 KB 968), an
employer may resist payment on the grounds that he or she reasonably
believes that the certificate overvalues the amount due to the contractor.

In *CM Pillings & Co v Kent Investments Ltd* 30 BLR 80 the contract was for
the extension of a large house. The form of contract provided for the issue
of interim certificates. Interim certificate 12 was issued for £105 000 but
was not paid. The contractor applied to the court for summary judgment
and the employer made a cross-application for a stay to arbitration. The
question at issue was whether there was a real dispute over the amount
certified or whether the employer had simply refused to pay. If there was a
dispute it had to be heard before the arbitrator. Apparently, the employer
had been concerned about the expenditure and appointed a new quantity
surveyor to investigate the matter and had refused, in the mean time, to
pay. The contractor argued that if he wished to withhold payment he, the
employer, would have to set out his reasons. Lord Justice Kerr said

> I turn to the first issue as to whether there is an arguable dispute as to
> the correctness of certificate No. 12 which the employers raise in this case.
> The submission made by [counsel] for the contractor was that there was no
> such dispute; there was merely an allegation by the employers that the figure
> appeared to be wrong, without any reasons given to substantiate this, so that
> in effect all they were doing was disputing that amount and raising a question
> mark over it. [Counsel for the contractor] submitted that that will not do, as
> shown by some of the remarks in judgments of this court in *Ellis Mechanical
> Services Ltd v Wates Construction Ltd* 2 BLR 60, [1978] 1 Ll Rep 33n. What
> was said (and I do not propose to read it) is that employers, and of course
> it equally applies to head contractors and subcontractors depending on the
> terms of the contract, cannot simply say 'I want to investigate the accounts'
> as it is put by Lord Denning MR and much to the same effect by Lawton
> and Bridge LJJ. That is not sufficient to entitle them to keep a contractor
> out of his money. On balance, however, I think that there is just enough in

this case to make it arbitrable, in the sense that there is just sufficient material to entitle the employers to say that they have raised a bona fide arguable contention that certificate No 12 is open to challenge.

However, in *Lubenham Fidelities* (see Section 14.1.5) it was held that the employer had to pay the full sum stated on the face of the certificate even though it had been certified by mistake. The reasoning turned, in that case, on the fact that interim arbitration was available.

The effect of interim certificates on claims that the work does not comply with the specification
Interim certificates will, in general, have no significant effect on a claim by the employer against the contractor for poor work except to show, as a matter of evidence, that the works appeared on cursory inspection to be in order. The main standard contract forms expressly provide that this is so. Clause 60(8) of ICE 6th Edition allows the engineer to correct previously issued certificates and Clause 30.10 of JCT 80 specifically states that only the Final Certificate shall have effect as 'conclusive evidence that any works, materials or goods to which it relates are in accordance with the Contract'.

14.2.2 Completion certificates

Contracts often call for the certifier to certify that part or all of the works are completed. The word 'complete' suggests absolute completion according to the contract drawings and specification. Since this is often difficult to achieve in practice, most standard form contracts require a certificate to be issued when the works are 'substantially complete' (see ICE 6th Edition, Clause 48) or 'practically complete' (see JCT 80, Clause 17.1). The effect of such a certificate is normally to start a period of time running during which any defects which manifest themselves are to be remedied by the contractor. The issue of this certificate also often entitles the contractor to a proportion of the retention monies. These matters are to be determined by a construction of the contract and no general guidelines can be laid down.

14.2.3 Final Certificates

Certificates expressed to be 'Final' Certificates are often issued under construction contracts (see e.g. Clause 30 of the JCT 80 Contract). The intended effect of such a certificate is that it should be conclusive evidence concerning those matters which fall within its scope. However, as with all certificates, its true effect can only be determined by reference to the precise terms under which it is issued. It is submitted that clear words must be expressed in the contract before such a certificate has any conclusive effect.

Note, however, that while the JCT contract states that a Final Certificate becomes conclusive unless arbitration or other proceedings have been commenced within defined time limits, the court has a discretion to extend this period by virtue of Section 27 of the Arbitration Act 1950. In *McLaughlin & Harvey Plc v P & O Developments Ltd* 55 BLR 105 Mr Justice Gatehouse said, (relying on dicta of Lord Bridge in *Comdel Commodities v Siporex Trade SA* No. 2 [1991] AC 148) that in his judgment 'there is jurisdiction [provided by Section 27] to extend the time-limit imposed by Clause 30.9.3'.

14.3   Recovering payment without a certificate

Even where, upon a true construction of the contract, the issue of a certificate is a condition precedent to the right to be paid, the contractor may, nonetheless, recover his payment if either the certifier or the employer has acted improperly. The leading case is *Panamena Europa Navigacion (Compania Limitada) v Frederick Leyland & Co Ltd* [1947] AC 428. Here the contract required the surveyor, Dr Telfer (who was the certifier under a shipbuilding contract), to certify that the work was satisfactory. He insisted, however, on receiving additional information before certifying, namely 'such information as to labour, materials, dock and crainage charges as to enable a rapid and accurate appreciation to be made of the position'. The contractor did not supply the information, no certificate was issued, and the contractor sought to recover payment without a certificate. Lord Thankerton said (at pp. 433–436)

> There is no dispute that this information was only required by Dr Telfer because of the view held by him that his function of certification was not confined to passing the actual quality of the work done but that he was also entitled to consider the manner in which the work had been carried out, and, in particular, whether there had been reasonable economy in time, labour and materials. Dr Telfer declined to proceed with the matter unless he was provided with the information to which on his erroneous view of the contract, he held himself entitled . . . . This means that an illegitimate condition precedent to any consideration of the granting of a certificate was insisted on by Dr Telfer and the appellants [shipowners]. It is almost unnecessary to cite authority to establish that such conduct on the appellant's part absolved the respondents [contractors] from the necessity of obtaining such a certificate, and that the respondents are entitled to recover the amount claimed in the action.

14.4   Ineffective certification

The discussion in previous sections has proceeded on the basis that the certificate itself has been

- made by the person authorised by the contract to make it and has been made in authorised circumstances
- made in the correct form
- made honestly and fairly
- issued to the parties to the contract

In general, a certificate must be made in the manner prescribed by the contract, in good faith and communicated to the parties; otherwise it is ineffective. Accordingly if, for example, a certificate is issued which in the normal course of events would have been conclusive as to some matter, is issued improperly, then it is not conclusive as no proper certification has, in fact, taken place.

14.4.1 Certificate not made by authorised person or made in circumstances other than those authorised by the contract

Certificate issued by the wrong person
If a person is named as certifier under the contract only that person, and no other, may issue a certificate. A certifier may obtain the assistance of others (e.g. quantity surveyors) to value the amount payable but he or she must certify personally. An example where the certifier was assisted in drawing up the document is given by *Anglian Water Authority v RDL Contracting* 43 BLR 98. Here the named engineer under the contract and only that person was entitled to make a decision under Clause 66 of the Conditions of Contract. A document said to be a Clause 66 decision was attacked by the contractor on the grounds that, while it had been signed by the engineer, it had, in fact, been drafted by an assistant. Judge Fox-Andrews said

> In the commercial world many decisions are made by people such as [the Engineer] who append their signature to letters drafted by others. It would require compelling evidence to establish in such circumstances that the decision was not that of the signatory.

Certificate issued in unauthorised circumstances
If the certificate is issued in respect of matters which fall outside the certifier's jurisdiction as determined on a proper construction of the contract, or if the certificate is issued outside any time limits specified in the contract then the certificate will be ineffective.

14.4.2 Certificate made in an incorrect form

General observations on the necessary form for a certificate
For a certificate to be validly made it must comply with any requirements expressed in the contract. However, construction contracts rarely set out any detailed requirements. In practice certificates are often issued on standard forms published by the institutions who publish the standard form contracts and are designed specifically to be used with those contracts. However, unless the contract expressly says so, it seems that it is not necessary to issue the certificate in any particular form: see *Elmes v Burgh Market Co* (1891) Hudson's Building Contracts (4th Edition) Vol II, p. 170. A document (or oral statement), to be a certificate, must, however, clearly be the result of a certifying process, though the word certificate (or any derivative) need not, it seems, be used. The courts have, however, advised certifiers to use that word.

Token Construction v Charlton Estates 1 BLR 48 is a case of importance in relation to the required form of certificates and merits some study. It illustrates a number of points which are relevant to this topic. In particular it shows that to be valid a certificate must be the result of a 'certifying process', served, and clear and unambiguous.

The certificate must be the result of a 'certifying process'   The architect in *Token Construction* wrote a letter which was subsequently said to be a certificate issued under Clause 16 of the Contract. Lord Justice Edmund Davies said

> That clause [i.e. Clause 16] required him to 'certify' in writing. While no set form of certificate is provided, unlike that under Clause 21(a) and (b), it must clearly appear that the document relied upon is the physical expression of a certifying process. One should, therefore, have some regard to the factors of 'form', 'substance' and 'intent' of which Mr Justice Devlin spoke in the admittedly different circumstances of *Minster Trust Ltd v Traps Tractors Ltd* [1954] 1 WLR 963. Or, to adopt a passage in Hudson (10th Edition, p. 479), the document should be the expression in a definite form of the exercise of the ... opinion ... of the ... architect ... in relation to some matter provided for by the terms of the contract. And, as [counsel for the employer] accepted, it must be free from ambiguity.

Lord Justice Stephenson stated that the important factor was not the wording used but the manner and appearance of the process:

> I do not think there is any magic in the word 'certify' and although the architect acting under Clause 16 would be wise to use it, 'confirm' or 'express' might do equally well.

The certificate must be served   Lord Justice Edmund Davies said

> [counsel for the employer] stresses that clause 16 imposes no requirement whereby 'the Architect certifies in writing' his opinion must be served upon any particular person, and is thus unlike, for example, clause 21(a), which requires the architect to issue interim certificates to the 'contractor'. Nonetheless I have some difficulty in thinking that there would be a sufficient compliance with Clause 16 if the architect certified in writing and then locked the document away and told no-one about it. [Counsel for the employer]'s submission is that it is enough if the party entitled to take advantage of the document (i.e. the employer) is made aware of its effect. My doubt as to the correctness of his view persists.

Lord Justice Edmund Davies did not decide the last point raised in the above passage ('its validity does not now call for necessary determination'). It is submitted however that his doubt is soundly based. If a certificate is to be valid it must surely be served *at least* upon all parties to the contract whose rights it may *adversely* affect. Neither of the other Lords Justice decided this point, though all three noted the problem. A reading of their judgments suggests that their difficulty here related to the construction of the particular contract before them. Clause 21 required the certificate to be served on the contractor but Clause 16 was silent, thereby suggesting that the parties may have agreed that no service was required under Clause 16.

However, it is submitted that the 'no ambiguity' point discussed below, on which the judges were unanimous, entails a requirement for service unless the contract expressly says otherwise. Otherwise a certificate would have to be clear and unambiguous and yet need not be served.

The certificate must be clear and unambiguous   Where a certificate may significantly affect the rights of the parties it must be clear, as illustrated by the following dicta of Lords Justice Edmund Davies and Roskill:

> Certifying under clause 16 can, as in the present case, have consequences highly important to both parties. There should, accordingly, be no need to resort to any process of *inferring* in order to determine whether it has taken place, yet I find it inescapable in the present case. While the letter does in truth refer to clause 16, it does not purport to constitute a certifying thereunder. It ought not to be so regarded by mere implication. (per Lord Justice Edmund Davies)

> It is important to appreciate that the architect, when acting or purporting to act under ... any ... clause or condition in the contract, is exercising power which affects the contractual rights of the parties to the contract by varying those rights in one or more ways as the parties have agreed should be the case. It is therefore of crucial importance that any exercise of power by the architect should be done clearly and unambiguously so that the parties know where they are and should not be left in doubt. (per Lord Justice Roskill)

One case which is often cited as authority for the proposition that a certificate, such as a Final Certificate under the standard building contract, need not be expressed to be such, is *London Borough of Merton v Lowe and another* 18 BLR 130. The facts need to be considered, however, in understanding the decision. The plaintiff was the owner of a swimming pool. The defendant was the architect appointed under the building contract for the swimming pool. The contract provided for the issue of a Final Certificate which, unless challenged within a short time, became binding in respect of workmanship. The defendants issued such a Final Certificate even though they should have known that there were defects in the roof. As a result of issuing the Final Certificate in these circumstances they negligently caused the plaintiff's potential right of action against the contractor to lapse. The claim was thus one for professional negligence and, in particular, negligent certification. It was the architect's defence that the document which the parties have taken to be the Final Certificate (and which the architect described as a Final Certificate in their letter which accompanied the certificate) was, in fact, defective and hence could not have been relied upon by the contractor as a valid defence. While, in principle, this is, no doubt, a sound defence argument, such chicanery is likely to colour the court's view of the validity of the document. But, more importantly, in the circumstances everyone involved realised that what was being proffered was intended to be a Final Certificate. Lord Justice Eveleigh said

> In relation to that final certificate it was submitted on behalf of the defendants that the certificate was not a final certificate, and therefore would not have been available as a defence for the contractor against a claim made by the plaintiff. It is said it was not a final certificate because it did not bear those

words upon it; it did not, on the face of it, state that it was a final certificate. It is said that it was not a final certificate because it did not comply, in its content, completely with that which has to be put upon a final certificate. It is said that although the words 'final payment' appeared upon it, that was no indication it was a final certificate because a final payment in a building contract may often have to precede the time for the issue of a final certificate.

And it is said that this certificate was issued very much out of time. It should have been issued, according to the terms of the contract, I think I am right in saying, within six months of the end of the defects liability period. It matters not. It should have been issued some years before it actually was.

According to the terms of the contract – I forbear from reading them; they appear in the papers and in the judgment of the learned judge – the certificate should have been issued earlier; and it was the duty of the architect to issue it. But on the facts of the case what happened was this: the contractors called for the certificate, the plaintiffs asked the architect not to issue it, there was still some electrical work to be done, and it was not until May 1973 that the plaintiffs agreed, on the advice of the architect, that the certificate could be issued. In the correspondence between the Council [the plaintiff] and the architects relating to this matter they speak of the issue of the final certificate; and in the covering letter enclosing the certificate with which we are concerned the defendants say to the contractors: 'We are enclosing the final certificate.'

I take the view that the plaintiffs, in an action brought by them against a main contractor, could not have been heard to say that this document was not a final certificate. It goes against all common sense. In my view it goes against the rules of law, too. They would have been estopped from so contending, in my view. The fact that the words 'Final Certificate' did not appear upon it seems to me to be wholly irrelevant in the present circumstances. They appeared so strongly in the covering letter that the two must be read together.

14.4.3 Certificate not made honestly and/or fairly

A certifier need not afford the parties an opportunity to be heard before he or she issues a certificate but he or she must act honestly and fairly. The certifier must, when issuing a certificate, be independent. In *Hickman v Roberts* [1913] AC 229 an architect was clearly operating under the influence of the employer and so his Final Certificate was set aside. In this case the contract provided that the architect's decision should be final and that payments should be made on the architect's certificate. The architect delayed issuing the certificates and the contractor commenced an action to recover sums which they said were due. The House of Lords found that the architect 'did not act with sufficient firmness to enable him to decide questions according to his own opinion, those questions affecting the issue of certificates and the interim amounts thereof. Instead of doing so, my Lords, he accepted the instructions or order of the owners and their solicitors upon that topic' (per Lord Shaw). Accordingly the House of Lords held that in these circumstances the employer was precluded from setting up as a defence either that the certificate was a condition precedent or that the certificate was conclusive as to the value of the works.

Likewise, any collusion with either party will cause the certifier's certificates to be set aside.

14.4.4   Certificate not communicated

A certificate to be effective must, it seems, be communicated to both parties. Merely for the certifier to sign it is insufficient: *London Borough of Camden v Thomas McInerney* (1986) 2 Constr LJ 293.

15

Assignments of contractual benefits

15.1 Introduction

15.1.1 Assignments relating to construction

An assignment is the transfer by a party to a contract of some or all of his or her benefits under that contract. In construction the following are common examples of assignments:

- where a contractor assigns sums due to him under the contract (e.g. retention monies) as security for advances of money or goods from financiers or suppliers
- where a developer who has employed a contractor to construct a building, and who lets it out on a full repairing and insuring (FRI) lease, assigns the benefits of the construction contract to the tenants so that those tenants can get any defects in the building repaired by the contractor
- where the owner of the benefit of a collateral warranty wishes to pass on that benefit as part of the transfer of rights in a property to which the warranty relates. For example, where an architect or engineer has given a collateral warranty in favour of a tenant in a building and that tenant wishes to transfer his interest by sale or lease he might transfer his interest in the collateral warranty as part of the transfer.

In recent years the question of assignability in relation to construction contracts and design warranties has increased in significance. Following *D & F Estates v Church Commissioners* [1989] AC 177 it became clear that actions for defective work stood little chance of success unless they were based in contract. In the context of changing property ownership, the only mechanism for the new owner to obtain a contractual right to sue a contractor for defective work is to have that right specified under the contract assigned to him. In parallel with this development, the practice of taking collateral warranties from designers and contractors has grown up and these are often assigned.

For these reasons the question of assignment has great commercial significance. Unfortunately, very few cases relating to construction have been decided and as a consequence detailed principles and their applications to construction industry contracts are not well established.

15.1.2 Terminology

In the law relating to assignment, the party who transfers the contractual benefit is known as the assignor, while the person who receives the benefit is known as the assignee. The person who has an obligation to provide the benefit is known as the debtor. Thus before the assignment the debtor owes the benefit to the party who becomes known as the assignor. Following the assignment the debtor owes the benefit to the assignee.

15.2   Contractual benefits and burdens

15.2.1   Only benefits may be assigned

In each of the examples given in Section 15.1 the transfer which is termed an 'assignment' relates only to the benefit of the contract; indeed, the basic rule is that only benefits may be assigned. The burdens may not be assigned. But, as will be seen below, the mere fact that something may be classified as a benefit does not always entitle the person to whom it is owed to assign it.

15.2.2   Benefits which depend on the person to whom they are owed are not assignable

One benefit of a contract is the right to call for its performance. But, where the performance depends in some degree upon the nature or character of the person to whom that performance is to be rendered, then assignment of such a benefit is not permitted. Such contracts are said to be personal in nature. They include contracts for personal service and contracts where some personal intervention is involved. In *Linden Gardens Trust v Lenesta Sludge Disposals Ltd and others* 57 BLR 57 Lord Justice Staughton approved the following statement which appears in Chitty on Contracts (26th Edn) Vol 1 para. 1416:

> The benefit of a contract is only assignable in 'cases where it can make no difference to the person on whom the obligation lies to which of two persons he is to discharge it'.

In the same case Lord Justice Nourse considered the assignability by an employer of a construction contract. He suggested that the right to have a construction contract performed is generally assignable on the basis that any performance which the employer needs to render is purely mechanical and is not affected by the identity of the person who undertakes it:

> The benefit of a contract, while it is unperformed, is the right to require its performance by the other party. Where a building contract contains no provision to the contrary I see no reason why the employer should not ordinarily be able to assign to a third party the right to require its performance by the contractor .... The employer's ability, in the ordinary

way and where there is no provision to the contrary, to assign to a third party the right to require performance of a building contract is not specifically established by any authority which has been cited to us. It is, however, effectively recognised by the decision of the House of Lords in *Tolhurst v The Associated Portland Cement Manufacturers (1900) Ltd* [1903] AC 414 . . . The obligations of the employer under a building contract are to make the site available to the contractor and to pay him the price. Neither obligation, the first as a matter of common sense and the second on the authorities (see for example *Tolhurst*), is in itself capable of making the performance of the contract personal to the employer. It will only become so if the other terms of the contract or the circumstances of the case show that that was what the parties intended.

However, in most instances the obligations of the employer are far greater than simply to make the site available and to pay the price. Normally, significant cooperation is required between the employer and the contractor to construct the project (see Chapter 12), including the employer's nomination of a certifier to administer the project and to take decisions which are often binding upon the parties. The identity of the person who performs the employer's obligations is clearly not always (or even usually) a matter of indifference to the contractor.

In *Linden Gardens Trust v Lenesta Sludge Disposals Ltd and others* 57 BLR 57 Lord Justice Staughton provided an example at p. 77 which illustrates this (even though he also felt that the right to have the contract performed should be assignable):

> A contract that A will build a house for B, and follow his instructions on such variations as the contract may allow, cannot be converted by assignment into an obligation to follow the instruction of C.

While the employer rarely issues instructions personally, it is common for him to be empowered to do so through an agent, normally an architect or an engineer. Normally, identical legal results are produced whether an employer acts personally or through an agent. If we take the above quote and replace 'his instructions' by 'the instructions of his appointed agent' we arrive at the scheme of the typical construction contract. This should produce the same result, that is a prohibition on the assignment of the right to require a performance of the contract.

15.2.3   Transfer of the burden of a contract

In some circumstances a contracting party may discharge his burden without performing the contract himself. There are two methods of achieving this: through novation or through vicarious performance. Neither, however, ranks as an assignment.

Novation of contract
A burden under the contract may be transferred with the consent of the other party to the contract. But such a transfer does not rank as an assignment but as a 'novation of contract', where a new contract comes into existence. In *Linden Gardens Trust v Lenesta Sludge Disposals Ltd and others* 57 BLR 57 Lord Justice Staughton described 'novation' as:

... the process by which a contract between A and B is transformed into a contract between A and C. It can only be achieved by agreement between all three of them, A, B and C. Unless there is such an agreement, and therefore a novation, neither A nor B can rid himself of any obligation which he owes under the contract. This is commonly expressed by the proposition that the burden of a contract cannot be assigned unilaterally. If A is entitled to look to B for payment under the contract, he cannot be compelled to look to C instead, unless there is a novation. Otherwise B remains liable, even though he has assigned his rights [i.e. benefits] under the contract.

In *Tolhurst v Associated Portland Cement* [1902] 2 KB 660 at 668, Lord Justice Collins expressed the matter as follows:

A debtor cannot relieve himself of his liability to his creditor by assigning the burden of the obligation to someone else. This can only be bought about by the consent of all three, and involves the release of all three.

If we consider the process to take place in two stages the matter becomes readily recognisable as a matter of contractual discharge and formation. First, the two contracting parties agree to dissolve their contract. Then one of those parties enters into a new agreement with a third party.

Vicarious performance

In some situations a party may discharge his burden by getting others to perform the contract work. This is known as 'vicarious performance' and occurs, for example, when a contractor subcontracts the work out.

Vicarious performance differs radically from assignment proper, since here the original contractor remains liable for the work of his subcontractor. So, while he may discharge his burden, in the sense that he does not physically perform the work, he does not discharge his liability for that work. This may be contrasted with the situation where there has been an assignment proper of a contractual benefit: here the person who owes the benefit may set up as his defence to liability the fact that he has paid the benefit over to the person to whom it was assigned. The question of vicarious performance and its main form, subcontracting, is dealt with in Chapter 13.

15.2.4 Classification of benefits

It is on occasion important to distinguish between different classes of benefit. Sometimes the assignability of a benefit will depend upon its nature, and provisions restricting the assignability of benefits in a contract may only be effective in respect of some classes of benefit. In *Linden Gardens Trust Ltd v Lenesta Sludge Disposals Ltd and others* 57 BLR 57 Sir Michael Kerr explained the distinction between the term 'benefit' used in its wider and narrower senses:

... the term 'benefit' can also be used in a wider or narrower sense in the context of assignability.

In the wider sense one speaks of 'assigning the benefit of a contract'. The 'benefit' is the right to call on the 'debtor' to perform the relevant obligations for the benefit of the assignee. Such an assignment is permissible in relation to contracts which involve no obligations of a personal nature, which would preclude assignment, and which contain no prohibition against assignment. *Tolhurst v Associated Portland Cement Manufacturers Ltd* [1902] 2 KB 660 (CA) and [1903] AC 414 provides a notable example. A contract concluded with the Plaintiff for the supply of chalk from certain quarries for fifty years was held to be assignable to a successor of the original contracting company, because, on its true construction, there was nothing in the contract which involved a personal element so as to preclude the assignment of the benefit of the contract, in the sense of the supply of chalk, to a different company. There was also nothing in the contract which expressly prohibited assignment, and this is crucial for present purposes. Thus, Lord MacNaughten said at page 420: 'It seems to me that the contract is to be read and construed as if it contained an interpretation clause saying that the expression "Tolhurst" should include "Tolhurst" and his heirs, executors, administrators and assigns, owners and occupiers of the Northfleet Quarries, that the expression "the company" should include the company and its successors and assigns, owner and occupiers of the Northfleet Cement Works and that the words "his" and "their" should have a corresponding meaning. That, I think, was the plain intention of the parties.'

That was a case in which the 'benefit of the contract' was assigned.

But one may also speak of the assignment of a contractual 'benefit' in a narrower sense even in relation to contracts which are personal in their nature. One is then referring to the assignability of benefits arising *under* the contract, which are narrower than the benefit of the performance of the contract as a whole. Such benefits will be choses in action or proprietary rights arising incidentally from the terms of the contract. In his article in the *Modern Law Review,* from which Lord Justice Staughton has quoted, Professor Goode refers to them as 'fruits of performance' which can be assigned, as distinct from the right to the performance of the contract as a whole which cannot. Some illustrations are discussed in paragraph 1416 of *Chitty* to which Lord Justice Staughton also refers. For instance, while contracts between publishers and authors are clearly personal in their nature and therefore unassignable, there would be nothing to preclude an assignment by the author of his right to royalties, or by the publisher of his entitlement to copyright (if he has it) as an item of property. But the benefit *of* the contract is unassignable if it is a personal contract.

As well as the examples given in the above quote, a further practical application of this classification may be seen in Section 15.4, relating to the effect of prohibitions on assignments contained in contracts.

15.3 Legal and equitable assignments

An assignment may be legal or equitable. A legal assignment is one which complies fully with the requirements of Section 136 of the Law of Property Act 1925. An equitable assignment is one which does not comply but which is still recognised by the law as sufficient to create an enforceable assignment, because to fail to do so would be inequitable. The main practical difference between the two types is that when there has been a legal assignment the assignee can sue in his own name without any reference to the assignor; whereas in the case of an equitable assignment the assignee must sue in the name of the assignor or, if the assignor refuses to cooperate, the assignor must be made a defendant in the action.

15.3.1   Legal assignments

Section 136(1) of the Law of Property Act 1925 states that:

> Any absolute assignment by writing under the hand of the assignor . . . of any debt or any other legal thing in action, of which express notice in writing has been given to the debtor, trustee or other person from whom the assignor would have been entitled to receive or claim such debt or thing in action, is effectual in law . . . to pass and transfer from the date of such notice–
>
> (a)   the legal right to such debt or thing in action:
> (b)   all legal or other remedies for the same: and
> (c)   the power to give a good discharge for the same without the concurrence of the assignor

The section, though expressed in somewhat dated language, clearly requires that a legal assignment be absolute; that is, the whole of the relevant debt or benefit must be transferred, with no rights remaining, to the assignor in the benefit assigned. Accordingly, unless the contract provides for sums to be paid in instalments, part of the overall contract price may not form the subject of a legal assignment unless clearly defined. Furthermore, the assignment must be in writing and express notice of the assignment must be given in writing to the debtor.

An example of a legal assignment is where retention monies under a contract, which are not yet due, are assigned in writing with notice to the employer.

15.3.2   Equitable assignment

An equitable assignment occurs whenever it is clear that the assignor intends to transfer a contract benefit to the assignee. No writing is normally required. There is an exception (due to the provisions of Section 53(1) of the Law of Property Act 1925) in the case of an assignment of an equitable interest. An equitable interest is one which is not owned with full legal formality. An example is the beneficiary's ownership of trust property which is legally vested in the trustees (trust being a type of ownership where one party, known as the trustee, holds property for the benefit of another party, the latter being known as the beneficiary).

A common example of an equitable assignment is where a subcontract term states that the subcontractor is due part of the retention monies held by the employer. One such clause considered by the courts reads

> 11(h) If and to the extent that the amount retained by the employer in accordance with the main contract includes any retention money the contractor's interest in such money is fiduciary as trustee for the subcontractor.

This is held to operate as a valid equitable assignment to the subcontractor of the relevant portion of the retention monies, which created a trust in favour of the subcontractor (see *Rayack Construction v Lampeter Meat* 12 BLR 30, *Re Arthur Sanders Ltd* 17 BLR 125 and *Wates Construction (London) Ltd v Franthom Property Ltd* 53 BLR 23).

Notice to the debtor is not necessary for an equitable assignment. However, the assignee is at risk if the debtor is not notified because a dishonest assignor may subsequently assign the same property to another assignee and the question of which assignee takes priority must be addressed. The rule is that priority as against other assignees depends on the order in which the debtor receives notice of assignment, not upon the dates of assignment. Accordingly, putting the debtor on notice at the earliest opportunity makes good sense.

15.3.3   Assignment of remedies

Section 136(1b) provides that on legal assignment 'all legal and other remedies' are transferred along with the debt. In *Herkules Piling and Hercules Piling v Tilbury Construction* (1992) CILL 770, Mr Justice Hirst had to decide whether or not an arbitration clause had been assigned. The case arose from an arbitration award, where the appellants, Hercules and Herkules, were two companies forming part of the same group of construction companies. At some point Herkules' (K's) assets had been transferred to Hercules (C). These assets included the benefits of a construction contract that K had entered into with the respondent, Tilbury Construction. The question arose whether the transfer to C had included the transfer of the right to arbitrate (this matter was apparently of importance in relation to the costs payable in the arbitration proceedings). Mr Justice Hirst construed the transfer agreement and decided that it did not form an absolute assignment within the ambit of Section 136(1) but that it did rank as an equitable assignment. But on the question of the assignment of the arbitration agreement he held that 'the arbitration clause, standing on its own confers discrete rights and obligations upon the two parties thereto' and therefore the assignor could not assign its right to arbitrate. If, however, the assignment had been a legal assignment the situation would have been different 'since Section 136 in terms stipulates that all attendant remedies are transferred; and in consequence, in the case of a legal assignment, the assignor no longer has any legal standing to institute the arbitration (*Cottage Club Estate v Woodside* [1928] 2 KB 463)'.

For the situation where the assignee is the defendant and upon the debtor's right to insist on arbitration, see *The League* [1984] 2 Ll Rep 259.

15.4   Prohibitions against assignment

15.4.1   Are prohibitions against assignment valid?

In the recent case of *Linden Gardens Trust Ltd v Lenesta Sludge Disposals Ltd and others* 57 BLR 57 it was decided that a term in a contract prohibiting assignment does have *an* effect (see Section 15.4.2). However, Lord Justice Staughton in his judgment suggested that he had some misgivings concerning the enforcement of such prohibitions; and while he found himself bound by precedent to acknowledge that they were at least partly effective, the possibility remains that the House of Lords might, at some time, declare otherwise. Lord Justice Staughton said:

If I were free from authority, I should be inclined to think that a prohibition on assignment in a contract was ineffective. Seeing that assignment cannot increase the obligation or alter it in any way, but only change the person who is to benefit from it, there are no very powerful reasons for allowing it to be prohibited.

After considering several possible objections to his own views, including for example, the possibility that 'the original creditor may be indulgent and his assignee ruthless', he continued

These points do not seem to me, either separately or together, sufficient reason to allow the assignment of a benefit under a contract to be prohibited. After all, the benefit is a piece of property, a chose in action: and in general it is desirable that property should be transferable.

He then went on to examine several authorities, including the Court of Appeal case of *Helstan Securities Ltd v Hertfordshire County Council* [1978] 3 All ER 262 which allowed the prohibition to have effect. He concluded that he was bound to follow that authority.

15.4.2   Construction of terms in the contract forbidding assignments

A classification of benefits
A clause purporting to prohibit assignment may, on its true construction, be held to prohibit none or only certain classes of benefit. In his judgment in *Linden Gardens Trust Ltd v Lenesta Sludge Disposals and others* 57 BLR 57 (quoted in Section 15.2.4), Sir Michael Kerr distinguished between the term 'benefit' used in its wider and narrower senses. We may distinguish:

- 'benefit used in its wider sense':
  the right to require the performance of the contract
- 'benefit used in its narrower sense':
  the right to pursue accrued causes of action under the contract
  the right to property arising from the contract (e.g. sums of money due under the contract)

In the case of *Helstan Securities Ltd v Hertfordshire County Council* [1978] 3 All ER 262, for instance, it was decided that the prohibition clause in that contract prevented the contractor from assigning all benefits due under the contract including sums of money due. In *Linden Gardens* on the other hand a clause purportedly prohibiting the employer from assigning the contract was held to mean that he could not assign the right to have the contract performed but that he may assign accrued causes of action under the contract.

Commonly used prohibition clauses
It is common in construction contracts for provisions to be included forbidding assignment of the contract. For instance the ICE Contract 6th Edn., Clause 3 reads:

Assignment
Neither the Employer nor the contractor shall assign the contract or any part thereof or any benefit or interest therein or thereunder without the prior

> written consent of the other party which consent shall not unreasonably be withheld.

Such clauses are probably effective to prevent the assignee taking an interest which he can enforce against the debtor. In *Helstan Securities Ltd v Hertfordshire County Council* [1978] 3 All ER 262, for example, the clause was worded in very similar terms, reading that the contractor should not 'assign the contract or any part thereof or any benefit or interest therein or thereunder without the written consent of the employer'. In *Helstan* a road contractor had purportedly assigned to the plaintiffs amounts due for the works, but it was held that the plaintiffs could not recover.

Some clauses are, however, more loosely drafted and may be ineffective in preventing assignments. In *Linden Gardens Trust Ltd v Lenesta Sludge Disposals Ltd and others* 57 BLR 57 the Court of Appeal heard two cases together (which may be called *Linden Gardens* and *St Martin's*). In each case the contract was the JCT (Joint contracts tribunal) form and the prohibition subclauses read

> 17(1) The Employer shall not without the written consent of the Contractor assign this Contract
> 17(2) The Contractor shall not without the written consent of the Employer assign this Contract, and shall not without the written consent of the Architect (which consent shall not be unreasonably withheld to the prejudice of the contractor) sublet any portion of the Works . . .

The court addressed the question of what each of the subclauses meant. In the case of subclause 17(2) they agreed that the prohibition was not on *assignment* of the contract, but on *vicarious performance*. In support of this construction Lord Justice Nourse said

> With regard to clause 17(2), I think it clear that the presence of the prohibition against sub-letting 'any portion' of the works, coupled with the absence of a prohibition against sub-letting the whole of them, requires the words 'shall . . . not assign this contract' to be construed as meaning 'shall not sub-let the whole of the works'.

Subclause 17(1) caused more difficulty. Lord Justice Nourse considered whether the word 'assignment' was used in the same sense in both subclauses and decided that it was not. His argument was as follows

> The benefit of a contract, while it is unperformed, is the right to require its performance by the other party. Where a building contract contains no provision to the contrary I see no reason why the employer should not ordinarily be able to assign to a third party the right to require its performance by the contractor . . . . Against that background what is the effect of 17(1) of the JCT contract? Once it is established that without that provision the employer would very likely have been able to assign to a third party the right to require its performance by the contractor, it can in my view only be construed so as to prohibit him from doing just that. The word 'assign' is apt to describe the fullest disposal of rights which can be made and the words 'this contract' independently suggest that what is in view is the contract as a whole. While I recognise that so to construe 17(1) is to give it a wider effect than I have given to 17(2), I do not think that it can be intended to do no more than prohibit the employer from subcontracting his obligations under the contract. It is important to emphasise that Clause

17(1) does not have the internal context which I have identified in 17(2). I therefore conclude that the effect of Clause 17(1) is to prohibit the employer from assigning to a third party *the right to require the performance of the contract by the contractor*. [Emphasis added].

Lord Justice Nourse said that the right to require performance of the contract was unassignable, yet he held that the employer could assign 'its accrued causes of action for substantial damages against the contractor'. Sir Michael Kerr took the same view as Lord Justice Nourse on the extent of the prohibition against assignment. He presented his argument for deciding that the clause prohibited the assignment of the right to require the performance of the contract but not the assignment of accrued causes of action in the following way

> Contracts for the construction or alteration of buildings may or may not be personal in their nature, as discussed in the judgment of this court in *Southway Group Ltd v Wolff* 57 BLR 33. Into which category a particular contract falls depends on the true construction of the terms of the contract: *per* Lord Justice Bingham at page 53, in line with the principles discussed and applied in *Tolhurst*. Although the obligations of employers will usually involve a lesser personal element than those of the contractors, I do not think that one can generalise the answer to the question of proper categorisation. However, in the present case this question is conclusively resolved by the express provision precluding assignment of 'this contract' by the employer and contractor without the other's consent. If there had been a similar provision in the *Tolhurst* contract, then the decision would have had to go the other way. The benefit of the contracts, in the sense of the benefit of the right to call for their performance, is therefore not assignable in the present case, although I agree with the analysis in the judgment of Lord Justice Staughton that what was *intended* to be precluded by the prohibitions against assignment was probably no more than vicarious performance of the contractual obligations on either side, which would be referred to as 'subcontracting' in the case of the contractor. In any event, however, on their true construction the contracts do not preclude the assignment of benefits arising *under* the contracts. Thus, the contractors were not precluded from entering into factoring agreements which involved the assignment of sums payable to them. Similarly, I do not see why a prohibition against assignment of 'this contract' should preclude the assignment of claims for damages under the contract, at any rate when the causes of action have accrued. Both are choses in action, and in neither case would their assignment involve an assignment of 'this contract'.

Lord Justice Staughton was unable to agree with the other judges on the degree of prohibition created by clause 17(1). He would have allowed the employer to have assigned the right to have the building contract performed. He argued that if Clause 17(2) was merely a prohibition on vicarious performance, then Clause 17(1) must be given the same meaning.

In the cases under discussion, the employers, as building owners, disposed of interests in the buildings and made agreements with the persons taking those interests whereby the benefits of those contracts were assigned to the new owners. In the first case (*Linden Gardens*) it was held that, since the breach occurred before the assignment, the claims were validly assigned even though the assignor was unaware of the extent of the breaches at the time of the assignment. The assignee's right to claim was, however, limited to that amount which would have been recovered by the assignor if there had been no assignment. In the second case (*St Martin's*), however, the purported assignment had been made before the breaches of contract and hence, in that case, nothing had been assigned.

15.4.3   The effect of the prohibition on the assignor–assignee relationship

A prohibition in the contract against assignment cannot be set up by the assignor against the assignee. In *Linden Gardens Trust Ltd v Lenesta Sludge Disposals Ltd and others* 57 BLR 57 Lord Justice Staughton approved the following extract from an article by Professor Goode in the Modern Law Review 42 MLR 553 at page 555

> The prohibition is for the benefit of the debtor, not the assignor or his trustee in bankruptcy; and if the debtor does not seek to invoke it, or has no legitimate interest in so doing, it is not for the assignor to do so.

15.5   Recovery by the assignee

15.5.1   The general test

In *Linden Gardens Trust Ltd v Lenesta Sludge Disposals Ltd and others* 57 BLR 57 a question which was addressed was the quantum of damages that the assignee could recover. Lord Justice Staughton said

> the assignee can recover no more damages than the assignor could have recovered if there had been no assignment, *and if the building had not been transferred to the assignee*. [Lord Justice Staughton's emphasis]

15.5.2   Set-offs

An assignee will take the benefit of a contract assigned to him 'subject to all rights of set-off and other defences which were available against the assignor'(Lord Justice James in *Roxburghe v Cox* (1881) 17 Ch D 520 at 526). Thus, for example, if the employer has a claim on the retention monies the contractor may only assign those monies subject to the employer's claim. When the assignee takes action for assigned benefits the debtor may raise defences which he would have against the assignor at the date of the notice of the assignment including rights of set-off.

15.6   Assignment of warranties

The benefits which a contractor will assign generally relate to sums of money or other identifiable property. Such assignments cause no difficulty providing they do not fall foul of prohibitions in the contract from which they derive. The benefits which an employer wishes to assign however often relate to *rights* under the contract rather than identifiable parcels of property. For example employers often attempt to transfer the benefit of a warranty that a building has been properly designed or constructed.

The question of the assignability of warranties has taken on an enhanced importance since 1988, when, following *D&F Estates v Church Commissioners* [1989] AC 177 it was decided that actions for defects in buildings, which have not resulted in actual damage to persons or property other than the building itself, could be pursued only by contractual action. Since then, collateral warranties have proliferated in the construction industry and their assignability has, therefore, become a matter of some importance.

A bare right to litigate cannot be assigned. Thus, for instance, if a contractor has constructed a defective building and the employer has a right to sue for those defects, the employer may not simply sell his or her right to sue. In *Linden Gardens Trust Ltd v Lenesta Sludge Disposals Ltd and others*, for example, Lord Justice Staughton said that 'Where the assignment is of a cause of action for damages, the assignee must of course have a sufficient proprietary right, or a genuine commercial interest, if the assignment is not to be invalid'. While the question of what might constitute a 'genuine commercial interest' still remains open, we may at least say, following *Linden Gardens*, that accrued rights of action may be assigned provided there is no prohibition in the contract and the person taking the assignment has a real interest in the building or other property. This, of course, raises the question whether or not a 'right' has 'accrued' in any particular instance (see Section 2.5.3).

16

Consultancy contracts

16.1 Formation

Design and consultancy contracts are formed in the same way as any other contract, by an offer and an acceptance leading to agreement. In practice, the formation of the contract tends to involve fewer detailed negotiations than a construction contract. It typically involves an exchange of letters referring to a standard form of conditions or a standard scale of fees such as those forms published by the Association of Consulting Engineers (the ACE) or the Royal Institute of British Architects (the RIBA). It should be noted that while consultants and designers will typically contract on the standard form produced by their professional institution, this general practice is, in itself, insufficient to make those conditions part of the contract without the agreement of the client, unless that particular client and consultant habitually contract on the basis of the form of contract in question. In *Sidney Kaye, Eric Firmin & Partners v Leon Joseph Bronesky* 4 BLR 1 Lord Justice Cairns observed

> The Conditions of Engagement [published in this case by the RIBA] do not by themselves constitute a contract at all; they can have no operation as between an architect and his client except by incorporation in a contract.

16.2 Terms of the contract

When an agreement is made on the basis of some written terms, those terms govern the contract. If no terms of contract are expressly agreed, the Supply of Goods and Services Act 1982 will supplement the agreement as will a variety of terms implied into the contract to give it business efficacy.

Unless the parties expressly agree otherwise the principal obligations of the consultant will normally be to exercise reasonable skill and care in and about the performance of the work covered by the agreement. This obligation is usually included specifically in the standard terms of appointment published by the various professional bodies; if the contract contains no express terms stating the standard of care to be exercised a requirement to exercise reasonable skill and care will be implied into the contract by Section 13 of the Supply of Goods and Services Act 1982. The failure to exercise reasonable care and skill is known as 'professional negligence'.

In some cases, the consultant's obligation will be of a higher standard than simply exercising reasonable skill and care. This may arise in two ways: first, the express terms of the contract may require some higher standard of care; or second the factual matrix may imply into the contract some enhanced standard of care. For instance, in *Greaves (Contractors) Ltd v Baynham Meikle & Partners* 4 BLR 56 a contractor agreed to design and build a warehouse and subcontracted the design to a firm of structural engineers. It is well known that when the contractor designs and supplies a building to the employer he will impliedly warrant that it is fit for its purpose. The design produced by the structural engineer and according to which the warehouse was built was not, however, fit for the purpose and cracks began to develop during the operation of the warehouse. The engineers were sued by the contractor and defended by alleging that their, the designers', obligation to the contractor was only to use reasonable skill and care. The court, however, held that, in all the circumstances of the case, a term was implied into their agreement that their design would enable the building to be reasonably fit for its purpose.

The requirement that the consultant shall exercise reasonable skill and care in and about the performance of the work covered by the agreement raises two important questions:

- Against which standard is the exercise of the reasonable skill and care to be measured?
- What is the scope of the work covered by the agreement?

These questions are addressed in the following sections.

16.3   The requirement that the consultant exercise reasonable skill and care: the standard to be applied

16.3.1   Professional negligence: a failure to exercise reasonable skill and care

Lawyers normally tend to regard the term 'negligence' as relating to the tort of negligence. Tort involves an obligation which arises independently of contract (tort is discussed in Chapters 17 to 21). However, 'professional negligence' is used to indicate *either* a breach of a term in a contract requiring the professional to exercise reasonable skill and care *or* a breach of a duty owed by a professional in tort. The reason for this dual use is that the duty owed in both cases is identical (see Section 19.1.2). Accordingly, the material in Chapter 19 which deals with breaches of duties of care in the tort of negligence is relevant in determining whether there has been a breach of a contractual obligation to exercise reasonable skill and care; consequently reference should be made to that chapter.

Professional people are said to be professionally negligent if they have failed to use reasonable skill and care in and about the performance of their work. It is important to note that professionals are not in breach of their duty merely by making an error or by providing bad advice:

they will be in breach only if they have failed to use reasonable skill and care.

The question whether a professional person has used reasonable skill and care must be answered in the light of all the circumstances existing at the time. Since all the circumstances must be considered and because every situation is different it is impossible to draw up simple rules. For instance we cannot reduce the law to rules such as 'engineers who design to a lower standard than the relevant code of practice are in breach'. To formulate rules in this way is to concentrate on a single aspect of the professional's behaviour rather than, as the law requires, to look at all the circumstances.

16.3.2 Common professional practice

The standard of care required from people who hold themselves out to be skilled in a particular profession is expressed in the summing up of Mr Justice McNair to the jury in the medical negligence case of *Bolam v Friern Hospital Management Committee* [1957] 1 WLR 582. The 'man on the top of the Clapham omnibus' referred to is simply the legal equivalent of 'the average person in the street'.

> In the ordinary case which does not involve any special skill, negligence in law means a failure to do some act which a reasonable man in the circumstances would do, or the doing of some act which a reasonable man in the circumstances would not do; and if that failure or the doing of the act results in injury, then there is a cause of action .... But where you get a situation which involves the use of some special skill or competence, then the test as to whether there has been negligence or not is not the test of the man on top of the Clapham Omnibus, because he has not got this special skill. The test is the standard of the ordinary skilled man exercising and professing to have that special skill. A man need not possess the highest expert skill; it is well established law that it is sufficient if he exercises the ordinary skill of the ordinary competent man exercising that particular art.

In this context, the dissenting decision of Lord Justice Bingham in *TE Eckersley and others v Binnie & Partners and others* (1988) CILL 388 (the Abbeystead disaster main trial) is worth studying. Binnie & Partners had been found negligent and it was clear that Lord Justice Bingham thought that they had been made a scapegoat. So he made a forthright statement of the duties owed by consultants and designers:

> a professional man should command the corpus of knowledge which forms part of the professional equipment of the ordinary member of his profession. He should not lag behind other ordinarily assiduous members of his profession in knowledge of new advances, discoveries and developments in his field. He should have such awareness as an ordinarily competent practitioner would have of the deficiencies in his knowledge and the limitations in his skill. He should be alert to the hazards and risks inherent in the professional task he undertakes to the extent that other ordinarily competent members of his profession would be alert. He must bring to any professional task he undertakes no less expertise, skill and care than other ordinarily competent members of his profession would bring, but need bring no more. The standard is that of the reasonable average. The law does not require of a

professional man that he be a paragon, combining the qualities of polymath and prophet.

In deciding whether a professional man has fallen short of the standards observed by ordinarily skilled and competent members of his profession, it is the standard prevailing at the time of the acts or omissions which provides the relevant yardstick. He is not to be judged by the wisdom of hindsight.

A point which comes across clearly from both the above quotations is that what constitutes reasonable care in the context of professional practice is not to be judged according to the standard that a reasonable man would expect from such a professional but from the standard that other members of that profession would consider appropriate. The plaintiff must therefore establish that what the defendant has done, or failed to do falls below this standard. In the New Zealand case of *McLaren Maycroft Co v Fletcher Development Co Ltd* [1973] 2 NZLR 100, for instance, the defendant failed to make boreholes which led to difficulties on site because of swampy materials found there. The plaintiff's actions failed, however, because he failed to demonstrate to the court that sinking boreholes in such cases was the (or a) recognised practice among New Zealand engineers at that time.

This emphasis on 'common professional practice' rather than 'reasonable professional practice' raises a number of difficulties which are outlined below.

Where the 'common professional practice' is clearly unreasonable
While the courts place themselves to a large extent in the hands of professional witnesses in applying common professional practice as the relevant standard of care, they always reserve the right to find that such practice is, in fact, negligent. An example of this is found in the case of *Lloyds Bank v EB Savory & Co* [1933] AC 201 in which a bank had made insufficient inquiries to safeguard against fraudulent passing of cheques. Lord Wright remarked

It is argued that this is not the ordinary practice of bankers and that a bank is not negligent if it takes all precautions usually taken by bankers. I do not accept the latter proposition is true in cases where the ordinary practice of bankers fails to make due provision for a risk fully known to those experienced in the business of banking.

Where there are a number of schools of thought
The concept of 'common professional practice' needs some refinement when there are a number of schools of thought. In *Maynard v West Midlands Health Authority* [1984] 1 WLR 634 it was held that, providing that the defendants could show that they had followed a recognised school of thought, they would not be negligent.

Research or innovative work
One feature of professional work is that it often contains an element of research or innovative work. Examples of this include site investigation and the design for projects which requires an extension to existing practice and in which there is, therefore, no 'common professional practice'. In *IBA v*

EMI and BICC 14 BLR 1 it was held that engineers undertaking such work had a duty to think the problem through. They discharged their burden by paying consideration to the potential problems as other members of their profession would have considered to be reasonably sufficient.

The status of codes of practice

Codes of practice, whether drawn up under the direction of the British Standards Institute, some equivalent foreign committee, or by the relevant professional bodies may be considered to comprise a formal statement of what is considered 'good practice'. The difference between 'good practice' and 'common professional practice' appears not to be very great. This is, no doubt, because when published statements of good practice are readily available to all professionals there is no excuse for any professional designing to any lower standard. Hence a failure to follow the provisions of such a code may be prima facie evidence of negligent activity. Mr Justice Beattie said in *Bevan Investments Ltd v Brackhall & Struthers* (No 2) [1973] 2 NZLR 45:

> I am of the view that bearing in mind the functions of codes, a design which departs substantially from them is *prima facie* a faulty design, unless it can be demonstrated that it conforms to accepted engineering practice by rational analysis.

In recent years, a number of professional societies have drawn up standards of practice for their members. In *Lloyd Cheyham & Co v Littlejohn & Co* QBD 30 Sep 1985 the status of the 'Statements of Standard Accountancy Practice' (SSAPs) prepared by the governing committees of the accountancy professions was discussed. The plaintiff alleged that since the defendant had not complied with the relevant SSAP he was, therefore, in breach of his duty of care. Mr Justice Woolf rejected this, saying that a departure from the terms of the SSAP did not necessarily involve a breach of the duty of care. He continued, however, 'They are very strong evidence as to what is the proper standard which should be adopted and regarded as constituting a breach of duty'.

An important point here is the possibility of justifying a departure from the code. If a consultant or designer can demonstrate that (in the light of the information available to them at the time) he took a decision which could be justified he will not be in breach of his duty. An engineer, it is submitted, is always entitled to use his own judgement to override the provisions of a non-compulsory code. Some 'codes' such as the building regulations have force of law (see Section 3.3) and must be complied with; however, 'codes of practice', such as those published by the British Standards Institution do not have force of law and the engineer is entitled to take a different view. However, if the engineer does decide to depart from the code he should record his reasoning.

Work of a highly specialised nature

The standard of 'common professional practice' is difficult to apply unless one is clear which profession one holds oneself out to belong to. For example, a specialist in a highly technical aspect of engineering causes a difficulty: who do we call as an expert witness to prove that the professional has exercised a standard equivalent to the common professional practice? If the professional was employed to undertake novel pieces of site investigation, do we measure his or her performance against that of a general engineer, a civil engineer, a geotechnical engineer or a site investigation specialist? In *Maynard v West Midlands Regional Area Health Authority* [1985] 1 All ER 635 it was said that 'a doctor who professes to exercise a special skill must exercise the ordinary skill of his speciality'. The most satisfactory test is probably to ask: what level of skill did the professional hold himself out as possessing? He should be judged against that standard even if his skill is so remarkably rare that he is the only example: the court will in these circumstances have to extrapolate to decide whether he has attained the 'common professional practice'.

Inexperienced professionals
In *Wilsher v Essex Area Health Authority* [1987] 2 WLR 425 the court said that the standard of care to be expected from doctors should not depend upon their training or their experience but the task which they perform. Lord Justice Mustill said that the legitimate expectation of the patient to expect a standard of care appropriate to his or her condition was paramount. Thus an inexperienced doctor who attempts a specialist operation must expect to be judged against the standard of the specialists who are qualified to undertake such work. Much design work in the construction industry is performed by junior engineers, architects or surveyors who are normally graduates but may have little practical experience and this case shows that whatever the actual level of experience of the engineer, the standard required is that of a reasonably experienced member of their profession.

Recently published advances
There is an obligation upon the professional to keep abreast of new developments (see the statement of Lord Justice Bingham in *TE Eckersley and others v Binnie & Partners and others* (1988) CILL 388 quoted above). To what extent must a professional take into account recent advances in his or her discipline? In *Crawford v Charing Cross Hospital* (1953) The Times 8 December, the Court of Appeal held that a professional need not read every article appearing in the professional literature, and need not adopt techniques advocated in those articles until such techniques become accepted practice in the relevant discipline.

16.4 Examples of consultancy activities which may result in professional negligence

16.4.1 General consultancy

Construction professionals carry out a wide range of activities ranging from design to giving advice and supervising work. Whenever it is alleged that a professional has been professionally negligent it will be appropriate to test that allegation by reference to the common professional practice. In cases where professional negligence is alleged it is usual for expert witnesses to attend the trial to state whether, in their opinion, the defendant has failed to exercise that level of skill and care which could be expected from members of the relevant profession.

16.4.2   Surveys; collecting and investigating information

The practical aspects of this area of law are best grasped by considering a particular area of work for illustrative purposes. One such area which often causes difficulties in construction is 'ground investigation', where professionals and contractors obtain information about the subsoil to enable the foundations of a building or other groundworks to be designed. The following cases show the approach adopted by the law, though it should always be remembered that, in order to determine whether a professional has been negligent, all the circumstances must be taken into account.

In *Batty v Metropolitan Property Realisations Ltd* [1978] QB 554, the court said that someone developing a site may be negligent if he fails to investigate adjacent sites for evidence of geological faults which may affect his development. In *Balcomb v Wards Construction (Medway) Ltd* (1980) 259 Estates Gazette 765 there was held to be a potential duty to investigate the history of a site. In the New Zealand case of *Bowen v Paramount Builders (Hamilton) Ltd* [1977] 1 NZLR 394 the builder was held to be negligent for failing to take additional precautionary measures when the soil conditions which manifested themselves should have alerted him to the fact that his initial design was inadequate. Accordingly if, as they so often do, ground conditions on site indicate that additional site investigation or a revised design is required, the engineer should be prepared to take the decision to perform the necessary work or alterations.

An additional point, and one that frequently arises in practice, is the problem of information supplied by others relating, for example, to the ground conditions on a particular site. Many sites that are currently being developed have been built on in the recent past and records of earlier investigations exist. To what extent is the designer of the new works entitled to rely on information passed to him? The answer to this is provided by the general legal requirement that he, the engineer, must exercise reasonable skill and care. In *Moneypenny v Hartland* (1824) 1 C&P 378 for instance, the architect and engineer of a bridge were held liable for failing properly to examine the foundations soils. Chief Justice Abbott said

> if a surveyor did not inform himself by boring or otherwise, of the nature of the soil of his foundation, and it turned out to be bad ... and if he went upon the information of others, which now turns out to be false or insufficient, he must take the consequences; for every person, employed as a surveyor, must use due diligence.

Of course, the designer is often not in a position to investigate all aspects of the materials he works with. However, he still has a duty to perform the level of research which he, as a reasonably competent professional, should. In *Sealand of the Pacific v Robert C McHaffie Ltd* (1974) 51 DLT (3rd) 702, for instance, it was held that a designer should not, where he should reasonably suspect a problem, simply rely on claims made by the manufacturer or supplier.

16.4.3   The preparation of reports

Reports are frequently produced in the construction industry. For example, an engineer may produce a report on the ground conditions on a particular site or a surveyor may produce a report outlining the likely expenditure to be anticipated in connection with a particular project. When the report is accurate no liability arises. When, however, it is inaccurate, the professional who produced the report may be liable. The chief area of concern relates to his or her potential liability to the client; if the report is produced without due care and skill, the professional will have to recompense the client for any losses suffered by the client as a direct result of that negligence.

In some cases a professional will even owe a duty to those that read his or her report and rely upon it to their financial disadvantage, despite the lack of a contractual relationship between them. This is an exception to the general legal rule that contracts are the only mechanism for regulating economic relations and compensating economic loss. In *Candler v Crane, Christmas and Co* (1951) 1 All ER 426, for instance, accounts were prepared for a company in order to attract investors. The accounts were negligently prepared and the investors who relied on them suffered a loss as a result. Lord Justice Denning said that the accountants owed a duty not only to their client, but also

> to any third person to whom they themselves show the accounts, or to whom they know their employer is going to show the accounts, so as to induce him to invest money or take some other action on them. But I do not think the duty can be extended still further so as to include strangers of whom they have heard nothing and to whom their employer without their knowledge may choose to show their accounts.

This statement indicates quite clearly the classes of person to whom professionals owe a duty of care when preparing a report.

Exclusion clauses and disclaimers
When a professional makes a mistaken recommendation in a report, whether orally or in a document, it may have substantial financial consequences if relied upon. Professionals may attempt to exclude or limit their liability in two direct ways. First, they may agree to perform work only on the basis that their liability is limited in some way. Second, they may include a disclaimer in their report. These techniques for reducing potential liability are discussed in Chapter 24.

16.4.4   Supervision of work

An engineer's duty to supervise work depends on the terms in his contract with his client; but the terms in other contracts such as that under which the contractor is undertaking the work will be a factor in understanding his own contract. It is generally the case that an engineer or architect who is engaged to supervise the work is not obliged to watch every detail of the work as undertaken by the contractor. For instance in *McLaren Maycroft Co v Fletcher Development Co Ltd* [1973] 2 NZLR 100 the consulting engineer was, it was argued by the plaintiff, negligent in his supervision of contractors who were excavating swampy material and filling in a site which was subsequently used to build houses. The contractor decided in this case to test his method of working by driving lorries over the filled ground to see if any problems occurred. The court held that the engineer's responsibility was to ensure that the contractor was using proper methods and to make checks from time to time to ensure that the contractor was adhering to them. He did not have to watch every pass of the lorries.

In *East Ham Borough Council v Bernard Sunley & Sons Ltd* [1966] AC 406 at p. 443 Lord Upjohn referred to the volume and degree of supervision typically to be exercised by an architect supervising building works (and the same, no doubt, applies to the case of an engineer supervising engineering works) and stated that an architect is entitled to take reasonable decisions concerning how to apply his limited supervisory resources.

> As is well known, the architect is not permanently on the site but appears at intervals, it may be of a week or a fortnight, and he has, of course, to inspect the progress of the work. When he arrives on site there are many very important matters with which he has to deal: the work may be getting behindhand through labour troubles; some of the suppliers of materials or the subcontractors may be lagging; there may be physical trouble on the site itself, such as, for example, finding an unexpected amount of underground water. All these are matters which may call for important decisions by the architect. He may in such circumstances think he knows the builder sufficiently well and can rely upon him to carry out a good job; that it is more important that he should deal with urgent matters on the site than that he should make a minute inspection on the site to see that the builder is complying with the specifications laid down by him .... It by no means follows that, in failing to discover a defect which a reasonable examination would have disclosed, the architect was necessarily thereby in breach of his duty to the building owner so as to be liable in an action for negligence. It may well be that the omission of the architect to find the defects was due to no more than an error of judgment, or was a deliberately calculated risk which, in all the circumstances of the case, was reasonable and proper.

It should, however, be clearly understood that cases like those described above are mere instances of the operation of the general principle that reasonable skill and care should be exercised. The level of supervision required is thus determined by the details of the case. If the engineer knows that special problems are likely to arise then additional supervision is required. And if the engineer's contract with the client requires him to watch every movement on site, he will be liable if problems occur because he has failed to do this.

16.5 The scope of a consultancy agreement

16.5.1 The extent of the work which the consultant/designer has agreed to perform

If the consultant contracts on the basis of one of the standard forms of appointment published by one of the professional institutions, the scope and extent of the consultant's obligations will be as set out in that form.

Often, however, the requirement for the consultant to act as certifier will not be explicitly stated, though it may be implied by the factual matrix, particularly if the construction contract which runs in parallel with the consultancy agreement contains certification provisions.

Typically conditions published by professional bodies will contain a scale of fees so that if the scope of the work increases or decreases, the remuneration will also be increased or decreased in line with the changes in the scope of the work. If a lump sum fee is agreed and there is a possibility that the scope of works may increase during the currency of the project, the agreement should say how the remuneration is to be affected. In *Gilbert & Partners v R Knight* 4 BLR 9, for instance, a surveyor agreed to undertake certain surveying and supervisory services in connection with work to be done on a dwelling house. In the letter which set out the appointment the surveyor wrote 'As agreed, I confirm that my fee for carrying out this work is to be £30.' The homeowner was obviously pleased with the work as it progressed because she continued to order more and more so that although the price for the work began at £662 it quickly rose to £2283. The surveyor continued to supervise and control the extra work without mentioning the possibility of increasing his fees until he eventually submitted an invoice for £135. The homeowner refused to pay any more than £30. The surveyor sued. Lord Justice Davies put the position as follows:

> Of course in the ordinary way if one employed a professional man to give professional services it is a necessary implication, unless anything to the contrary is expressly said, that the employer (to use that word) will pay a reasonable remuneration for those services. But in this case the cardinal point is that there had been this previous agreement to do some work for a lump sum of £30, and I for myself cannot see that there is any necessary implication that, when the work was going to be extended, or increased, in the absence of any express mention of it Mrs Knight [the homeowner] should be liable to make any further payment to the plaintiffs. If [the surveyor] had said in 1966:
> 'Well, now, look here, I have only agreed to do the other work for £30; if you want me to do this extra work I shall have to have a further figure or scale fees.'
> Mrs Knight (this is pure speculation) might have done one of two things. She might have said:
> 'If that is going to be added to the cost of it I am not going on.'
> Alternatively, she might have said:
> 'We have the builder: no doubt he will be very pleased to do this extra work: I will carry on with the builder without your intervention at all.'
> What she *would* have said we do not know.

The court held decided that the surveyor could not recover more than the £30.

16.5.2   Whether or not a piece of work falls within the consultant's brief

In *Richard Roberts Holdings Ltd and another v Douglas Smith Stimson Partnership and others* 46 BLR 50, the plaintiff was the owner of a dyeworks and the defendant was the designer of alterations to that factory. There was no engineer on the project and the dispute concerned a piece of specialist plant, namely the lining of an effluent tank. The architect did not believe they were responsible for the tank lining and did not charge any fee for work associated with the lining. Nonetheless they did seek quotations from suppliers of tank linings and commented on quotations received. Judge Newey said: 'The architects argue that in seeking quotations from suppliers, they were acting "informally", so as to help [the employer] to perform its part of the project. The comments contained in their letters were merely intended to be helpful'. The tank lining failed shortly after being put into service. The employer sued them for professional negligence. '[The employers] submit that the architects were acting as architects for the dyehouse projects as a whole. If they had wished to limit their role, they should have done so expressly and in writing. They cannot realistically claim to have been bystanders so far as the choice of lining was concerned.'

Judge Newey decided that the architects were responsible:

> In my view the architects were employed by Holdings to act as architects for the creation of the Hinckley Dyeworks. They were not responsible for the equipment, such as dye mixing machines and pipes, which [the employer's] staff would design and fix for themselves .... The lining was I think an integral part of the tank. The architects did not know about linings, but part of their expertise as architects was to be able to collect information about materials of which they lacked knowledge and/or experience and to form a view about them. If the architects felt that they could not form a reliable judgment about a lining for the tank, they should have informed [the employer] of that fact and advised them to take other advice, possibly from a chemist.

16.5.3   The duration of the consultant's obligation.

During the project

A question of some importance relates to the nature and extent of the consultant's obligation in terms of time. If, for instance, an architect designs a detail at the commencement of the project which was done at the time with reasonable skill and care, but which, by the end of the project, is known by the architect to be inadequate; and if the architect then fails to remedy the problem, what is the position? Is the architect entitled to claim as a defence that at the time the work was done it was not negligent? In *London Borough of Merton v Lowe* 18 BLR 130, Sir William Stabb said

> I am now satisfied that the architect's duty of design is a continuing one, and it seems to me that the subsequent discovery of a defect in the design, initially and justifiably thought to have been suitable, reactivated or revived the architect's duty in relation to design and imposed on them the duty to take such steps as were necessary to correct the results of that initially defective design.

A continuing duty after the end of the project?

In the trial at first instance in *TE Eckersley and others v Binnie & Partners and others* (1988) CILL 388 the judge suggested that the designer of construction works might be responsible for continuing to consider the works and their safety in the light of new advances in understanding. On appeal to the Court of Appeal the matter was not formally decided. Lord Justice Bingham touched on the matter and said

> What is plain is that if any such duty at all is to be imposed, the nature, scope and limits of such a duty require to be very carefully and cautiously defined. The development of the law on this point, if it ever occurs, will be gradual and analogical. But this is not a suitable case in which to launch or embark on the process of development because no facts have been found to support a conclusion that ordinarily competent engineers in the position of [Binnie] would . . . have been alerted to any risk of which they are reasonably unaware at the time of handover.

The imposition of such a continuing duty upon designers would be a new departure in the law of professional negligence. If it is decided that it applies it would require that designers would have to keep records in such a fashion that the results of advances in knowledge of materials, geology and general engineering could be assessed for many years after the works were completed.

16.6   Termination of the agreement

Most standard form contracts contain provisions for terminating the consultancy agreement. If no termination provisions are agreed, can the client terminate a consultant's appointment at will? In *Thomas v Hammersmith Borough Council* [1938] 3 All ER 201, Lords Justice Slesser and Mackinnon appear to have decided that when an architect is appointed he is, unless the terms of the contract provide otherwise, to be allowed to complete the project which he commences. And if he is prevented from so doing this will be a breach of contract entitling him to damages for the loss of profit which he would have earned. Lord Justice Slesser said

> I entertain no doubt that the architect would have been entitled to reasonable remuneration for the work which he had already done, and also to damages for the loss of remuneration which he had been prevented from earning until the work was finished . . . . Although this contract . . . would contain no express term to this effect, I think that it would be implied that the Council, having employed the plaintiff to build their town hall, agreed with him that they would not prevent him from doing the work, and so prevent him from earning his remuneration.

In *Edwin Hill & Partners v Leakcliffe Properties Ltd and another* 29 BLR 43 counsel for a party who had terminated an architect's appointment, in circumstances where there was no expressly agreed terms concerning termination, submitted that the agreement could be terminated at will. Mr Justice Hutchinson said

> while it may be true that architects are usually employed on terms which give the building owner a right to terminate their employment on payment of an agreed sum for the work they have done, the ordinary rule, it seems to

me, in the absence of such an express term is that formulated in *Thomas v
Hammersmith Borough Council.*

This suggests that the client should resist the temptation to appoint a
consultant on an informal basis if there is a possibility that project may
not proceed or if it is anticipated that a change of consultant may be made
at some time in the future. The client should be careful to include express
terms relating to termination.

16.7 Delegation of consultancy and design services to another

Under a construction contract the contractor's obligation is to achieve a
particular end. This end is normally set out in the drawings, specifications
and contract documents; or in the case of an informal contract, it will be
to provide the employer with a piece of construction which is fit for its
purpose. Accordingly, the employer is not disadvantaged if the contractor
subcontracts out or delegates some of the work because the employer can
look to the contractor to perform the contract or to pay for its non-
performance in any event.

In the case of design or other such consultancy contracts the same
considerations do not apply. Often the consultant has been chosen because
of his or her experience, skill or reputation in a particular area and clients
would be rightly annoyed to find that the work which they had entrusted
to a particular consultant had been delegated or subcontracted out. In
addition, and more importantly from a liability point of view, since the
consultant's obligation is not normally to achieve a particular end (as is
the case with a contractor) but to exercise reasonable skill and care, the
consultant could, by delegating the work to an apparently competent
delegate, avoid liability to the client; the client would then be forced
to seek redress from the delegate who may be impecunious. Because
the client is disadvantaged if design or consultancy work is delegated,
the rule that a consultant may not delegate (or at least that he or she
retains full responsibility for that work) has been established. (The general
question of what work may or may not be delegated is discussed in Section
13.3.)

In *Moresk Cleaners v Hicks* 4 BLR 50 an architect who was sued for
professional negligence in the design of a roof defended himself by
claiming to have delegated the design of certain elements of the roof
to the contractor. Sir Walter Carter QC did not accept this as a defence.
He observed

> So here was the design of the building being delegated by an architect to this
> firm of contractors, who owed no duty to the building owner and who were
> simply contractors who were trying to get what they hoped no doubt would
> be a profitable contract to construct this structure. In my view the defendant
> had no power to delegate this duty of design at all. It is said in the defence
> that it was an implied term of the defendant's employment that he should
> be entitled to delegate certain specialised design tasks to qualified specialist
> subcontractors. I am unable to make any such implication. In my view if a
> building owner entrusts the task of designing a building to an architect he is
> entitled to look to that architect to see that the building is properly designed.

The architect has no power whatever to delegate his duty to anybody else, certainly not to a contractor who would in fact have an interest which was entirely opposed to that of the building owner.

In *Nye Saunders & Partners v Alan E Bristow* 37 BLR 92 the question of delegation arose in the context of an estimate for the likely cost of building work. The plaintiffs were a firm of architects and they claimed in their action to be entitled to fees for a substantial amount of design work they had performed for the defendant client. At an early stage in the project the architect, who was entrusted with the whole design and consultancy package, had consulted a quantity surveyor who, after substantial analysis, suggested a likely cost of approximately £240 000. However, the figure rose, in particular because of the high rate of inflation at the time (1974) and a revised estimate of £440 000 eventually emerged. The client was shocked as he could not afford this and he decided not to proceed with the work, terminating the architect's agreement. The architect sued for fees to date and the client defended by alleging that the architect had been professionally negligent in not providing him, the client, with a reasonable estimate accounting for inflation. The architects claimed that they reasonably delegated this task to a competent quantity surveyor. Lord Justice Stephen Brown did not find this to be an answer:

> It is argued firstly that Mr Nye [the architect] discharged his duty completely by simply taking the step of consulting a quantity surveyor . . . . Of course it was a very sensible and prudent step for Mr Nye to take to consult a quantity surveyor who is an expert in computing costs. But in my judgment he cannot avoid responsibility for the fact that he did not draw the attention of his client to the fact that inflation was not taken into account. The duty rested fairly and squarely upon Mr Nye and it cannot be avoided by, as it were, seeking to move the responsibility on to [the quantity surveyor].

However, in *Investors in Industry v South Bedfordshire District Council* 32 BLR 1, the architect was held entitled to rely on the advice of another consultant because of the terms of the architect's contract with the client. That contract was based on the RIBA Conditions of Engagement, Clauses 1.22 and 1.23 of which envisaged that the architect should advise on the need to appoint independent consultants and that, on their appointment, should co-ordinate their work. Lord Justice Slade considered the liability of the architects for the work undertaken by such a consultant:

> the RIBA Conditions, in our judgment, clearly contemplate that where a particular part of the work involved in a building contract involves specialist knowledge or skill beyond that which an architect of ordinary competence may reasonably be expected to possess, the architect is at liberty to recommend to his client that a reputable independent consultant, who appears to have the relevant specialist knowledge or skill, shall be appointed by the client to perform this task. If following such a recommendation a consultant with these qualifications is appointed, the architect will normally carry no legal responsibility for the work to be done by the expert which is beyond the capability of an architect of ordinary competence; in relation to the work allotted to the expert, the architect's legal responsibility will normally be confined to directing and co-ordinating the expert's work in the whole. However, this is subject to one important qualification. If any danger or

problem arises in connection with the work allotted to the expert, of which an architect or ordinary competence reasonably ought to be aware and reasonably could be expected to warn the client, despite the employment of the expert, and despite what the expert says or does about it, it is in our judgment, the duty of the architect to warn the client. In such a contingency he is not entitled to rely blindly on the expert, with no mind of his own, on matters which must or should have been apparent to him.

Part 3

Torts in construction

The law of tort in construction

17.1 Introduction

17.1.1 Preliminary note

In Chapters 4 to 16 the role of contract in construction was examined. In Chapters 17 to 21 the law of tort will be examined and, in particular, the tort of negligence in construction. Before studying these matters in detail it is useful to consider a number of preliminary matters.

17.1.2 The distinction between contract and tort

Contract and tort both fall within the purview of what is generally termed the law of obligations. The 'obligation' in question relates to a 'duty situation' which exists between the defendant and a (successful) plaintiff. In the case of a contract, the *duty* is established by agreement while in tort the law imposes the duty because the relationship or proximity between the parties warrants it. An obvious example is furnished by the tort of battery: if one person attacks another then an action in battery will lie, even if (as usual) there was no agreement that the attacker would not make an attack. The *duty* here is imposed by law not by agreement.

17.2 Important torts

Torts play a significant role in construction law. The tort of negligence is of prime importance but others are, on occasion, also of importance. The following are examples.

17.2.1 Trespass to land

The law of trespass protects landowners from having their land directly invaded by persons who have no licence or invitation to come on the land. A common example of possible trespass in the construction industry is the oversailing of tower crane booms. There is a legal maxim which says that the ownership of land includes ownership of the air above and the ground below that land. According to this maxim the operator of an oversailing tower crane is trespassing, a view supported by the courts. In *Anchor Brewhouse Developments Ltd v Berkeley House (Docklands Developments) Ltd* (1987) 284 EG 625, for instance, Mr Justice Scott said

> What is complained of in the present case is infringement of air space by a structure positioned on a neighbour's land. The defendant has erected tower-cranes on its land. Attached to each tower crane is a boom which swings over the plaintiff's land. Each boom is part of the structure on the defendant's land. The tort of trespass represents an interference with possession or right to possession. A landowner is entitled, as an attribute of his ownership of the land, to place structures on his land and thereby reduce into actual possession the airspace above his land. If an adjoining owner places a structure on his (the adjoining owner's) land that overhangs his neighbour's land, he thereby takes into his possession air space to which his neighbour is entitled. That in my judgment is trespass.

17.2.2   Nuisance

Nuisance is a tort which protects the interests of occupiers of land from interference by their neighbours. If, for instance, a neighbour allows substances such as poisons, dust, noise and vibration to escape from his land, his neighbours' enjoyment of their land occupancy is impaired. It is the role of the law of nuisance to restrict the activities which may be undertaken on land in the light of the effect of those activities on neighbours. Neighbours are often adversely affected by the various activities undertaken by construction companies, particularly during the construction process itself, but also when materials are mined, stored or during the operation of heavy plant. The role of the tort of nuisance and its closely allied tort, the rule in *Rylands v Fletcher*, will be examined in Chapter 21.

17.2.3   Breach of statutory duty

The phrase 'breach of statutory duty' bears a number of meanings in the law of tort. It may mean a breach of civil law duty imposed by a statute. For instance, the Occupiers' Liability Acts 1957 and 1984 impose a duty upon those in control of premises to have regard for the safety of those who enter onto those premises and a breach of such a duty may be termed a breach of statutory duty.

In addition, lawyers speak of a breach of statutory duty even where the statute specifies no civil redress, but where the courts infer the imposition of a civil duty. Thus, for example, a number of rules relating to safety on building sites, known as Construction Regulations, are laid down as subordinate legislation. These regulations are framed in criminal law terms, yet it is common for an injured construction worker to cite, in his tortious claim, breaches of the Regulations. The Court of Appeal decision in *Groves v Lord Wimborne* [1983] 2 QB 402 is the authority for the inference of a tortious remedy in such a case.

17.2.4   Retention of title clauses: the tort of conversion

It is common for suppliers to provide materials to contractors before being paid for them. There is a danger inherent in this if the contractor goes into receivership before the materials have been paid for, especially if they have been delivered to site and incorporated into a building. A device used by many suppliers is to write 'retention of title clauses' into the supply contract whereby the ownership of the materials does not pass to the contractor until payment has been made in full. The effectiveness of such clauses was established in *Aluminium Industrial Vaasen BV v Romalpa Aluminium* [1976] 1 WLR 676. When a retention of title clause is used, the ownership of the materials remains in the original supplier and any person interfering with the materials will be liable to the supplier in the tort of 'conversion'. Relevant cases which may be consulted are *Burden (UK) Ltd v Scottish Timber Products Ltd* [1981] Ch 25, where the situation where the materials are already incorporated into a building is discussed, and *W Hanson (Harrow) Ltd v Rapid Civil Engineering Ltd and Usbourne Developments Ltd* 38 BLR 106, where the effect of a clause in the construction contract entitling the employer to use 'any materials of the contractor' and on the potential effect of the employer paying the contractor for those materials under the construction contract is discussed.

17.3   The uses of the term 'negligence': contractual and tortious negligence

Law students typically learn of 'negligence' as a tort, a breach of an obligation which exists independently of a contractual agreement. The term 'negligence' in the context of professional negligence, however, is used both in relation to the breach of contractual as well as tortious obligations (see Sections 16.3.1 and 19.1). This terminology has arisen because it has been established in a long series of cases that professional people offering services owe the same standard of care to their clients in contract as they owe to those to whom they owe a tortious duty; in both cases they must not be 'negligent'. Their obligation is to use reasonable skill and care in both cases (see also the Supply of Goods and Services Act 1982 which enacts this in respect of their contractual obligations). A consultant may often owe a co-terminous and co-extensive obligation to his or her client in contract as in tort. This is important in a number of situations and in particular in regard to limitation, discussed in Section 2.5.

Negligence and the duty of care

18.1 The elements of the tort of negligence

The tort of negligence involves the breach of a duty to take care imposed by the law and owed by the defendant to the plaintiff, which results in damage to the plaintiff. There are three principal elements to the tort of negligence each of which a plaintiff must prove in order to succeed:

- the plaintiff must show that the defendant owed the plaintiff a 'duty of care' at the time of the alleged negligent act or omission
- the plaintiff must show that the defendant breached that 'duty of care'
- the plaintiff must show that the breach of duty caused damage to the plaintiff.

These three elements are usually abbreviated to 'duty, breach, damage'. One of the difficulties which faces students of the law of negligence is that these elements appear to overlap considerably and in many cases appear simply to be different ways of looking at the same thing. This is particularly true in the case of 'duty' and 'damage'; the question of whether a duty is owed can, as will be seen, be answered only in the light of a knowledge of the type of damage allegedly caused. But the confusion also affects the question of 'breach'; breach is the failure to exercise reasonable care. But the question of what constitutes reasonable care is, of course, intimately related to the question of the type, magnitude and risk of damage that is likely to be caused by the behaviour complained of.

18.2 The species of tortious negligence

Two species of tortious negligence have been evolved by the courts.

18.2.1 *Donoghue v Stevenson* negligence

Whenever a person undertakes an activity which, if done carelessly, is likely to result in personal injury or property damage to another, then the first must exercise reasonable care (and, if appropriate, reasonable skill) in performing that activity. If reasonable care is not taken and, as a result, another suffers personal injury or property damage, then the first is liable for this loss and any other loss (e.g. loss of earnings) directly flowing from it. This species of negligence is derived from the decision in *Donoghue v Stevenson* [1932] AC 562.

Note that the essence of this species of negligence is 'careless acts leading to physical damage'.

18.2.2   *Hedley Byrne v Heller* negligence

Whenever people hold themselves out as skilled and provide advice which they intend or expect another to rely upon, and upon which that other does reasonably rely, then if that advice is carelessly formulated, they are liable for any damage which ensues, whether it be economic loss or physical damage. This species of negligence is derived from the decision in *Hedley Byrne v Heller and Partners* [1964] AC 465.

Note that the essence of this species of negligence is 'reasonable reliance on another's advice leading to loss'.

18.2.3   Are the species of negligence really distinct?

A substantial amount of case law has been decided concerning the exact limits of these species of negligence and the circumstances in which each is appropriate. Although these two heads have been treated as distinct categories, it should be pointed out that the courts have seemed reluctant to make a sharp distinction. They have tended to treat *Hedley Byrne* as a subset of the general tort of negligence as represented by *Donoghue v Stevenson*. Certainly, the two types of negligence share many features. The same basic elements are required in each case and these are explored in the following sections.

18.3   The duty of care

People often exhibit carelessness resulting in damage to others. But even in such cases they are not necessarily negligent in the legal sense. The law restricts the situations in which a person is liable for his or her careless activities using the concept of a 'duty of care' (i.e. a 'duty to take reasonable care'). Unless a plaintiff can establish that the defendant owed him the relevant duty of care he cannot recover for his damage on the basis of the tort of negligence.

In the construction industry many examples may be cited where carelessness normally leads to liability or alternatively normally does not do so.

18.3.1   Where carelessness normally leads to liability

An example of the situation where carelessness normally leads to liability is where a part of a structure collapses injuring someone (e.g. *Sharpe v ET Sweeting & Son Ltd* [1963] 1 WLR 665). Another is the careless preparation of a house surveyor's report on behalf of a building society: the prospective purchaser (who will normally have contributed to the cost of the survey and report) who relies on the report will often be able to sue the surveyor even though there is no contract between them because a tortious duty of care comes into existence (see *Smith v Bush* [1990] AC 831).

18.3.2 Where carelessness normally does not lead to liability

An example of the case where liability typically does not arise is when a certifier negligently fails to certify monies due to the contractor; here the contractor will not normally have an action in negligence against the certifier (see *Pacific Associates v Baxter* 44 BLR 33). Another is illustrated by the case of *The University of Glasgow v William Whitfield and John Laing Construction Ltd* 42 BLR 66 where it was held (at page 83 of the BLR report) that the contractor under a traditional building contract does not owe the architect a duty of care to warn him that his design is inadequate.

These two situations where respectively liability normally does or does not arise are distinguished by the existence, or not, as the case may be, of a duty of care. It is important to note that the existence or not of a duty of care depends not upon the type of situation but upon all the facts of each individual case; that is why the above examples were qualified by 'normally' and 'usually'. In the following sections we shall examine what circumstances must prevail before a duty of care comes into existence.

It is often suggested that, under the law of negligence, in a given set of circumstances 'A owes B a duty of care'. This formulation causes a good deal of confusion because it is not adequately qualified. The correct formulation is, it is submitted, that 'A owes B a duty of care in respect of harm of type C occasioned by activity of type D'. Thus in any given situation A may owe B a duty in respect of some matters but not owe such a duty in respect of others. In order to analyse the concept of a duty of care, therefore, it is necessary to focus on three separate aspects of the situation:

- Who *may* owe whom a duty (i.e. if all other criteria are met)?
- In respect of which types of harm/loss experienced by the plaintiff can a duty exist? Broadly speaking, the chances of a duty of care arising are greatest when the plaintiff experiences personal injury and least when the plaintiff's only loss is a purely economic one.
- As a result of what activities undertaken by the defendant can a duty exist? The likelihood of a duty existing are greatest when the plaintiff's loss is caused by the direct activities of the defendant; it is least when it is alleged that the defendant omitted to do something.

18.4 Who may owe whom a duty of care?

18.4.1 *Donoghue v Stevenson* negligence: the neighbour principle

Prior to 1932, negligence did not exist as a single tort but as a number of separate torts each of which had been independently established in the courts. To determine, before then, whether a party owed another a duty of care it was necessary to examine the decided cases in order to determine whether the facts fell within an established category. In 1932 the single tort of negligence was established in the case of *Donoghue v Stevenson* [1932] AC 562. This is the famous 'snail in a ginger beer bottle case' in which the plaintiff attended a café in Paisley for a drink with a friend who bought her a ginger beer, which was provided in an opaque bottle. The proprietor bought the bottles direct from the manufacturer. Half the contents of the bottle were poured out and the plaintiff drank it. She refilled her glass with the remaining ginger beer and out of the bottle came the decomposed remains of a snail. The plaintiff suffered gastro-enteritis. She sued the manufacturer of the ginger beer, with whom she clearly had no contract. She alleged that he owed her a duty of care. In that case Lord Atkin laid down a general principle against which it was possible to determine whether or not a duty was owed without reference to previous cases. Lord Atkin said

> The rule [of morality] that you are to love your neighbour becomes in law, you must not injure your neighbour; and the lawyer's question, Who is my neighbour? receives a restricted reply. You must take reasonable care to avoid acts or omissions which you can reasonably foresee would be likely to injure your neighbour. Who, then, in law is my neighbour? The answer seems to be – persons who are so closely and directly affected by my act that I ought reasonably to have them in contemplation as being so affected when I am directing my mind to the acts or omissions which are called in question.

The House of Lords found that the plaintiff was a 'neighbour' as far as the manufacturer was concerned; the latter had a duty to look out for her safety when undertaking his manufacturing operations and was liable when he failed to do so and thereby caused her damage.

This 'neighbour principle' has been extremely influential in the modern law. However, it is an extremely wide principle being unlimited as to the types of persons, the type of activity and the type of damage for which negligence will provide a remedy. The courts have taken Lord Atkin's dictum as a guide rather than as definitive statement of the law. For instance Lord Reid in *Home Office v Dorset Yacht Co* [1970] AC 1004 said: 'The well-known passage in Lord Atkins' speech should, I think, be regarded as a statement of principle. It is not to be treated as if it were a statutory definition. It will require qualification in new circumstances.' The qualifications placed upon the dictum have generally focused upon the type of activity and the type of damage for which recovery in negligence is permissible. It remains, therefore, an accurate statement of the law on who *may* owe whom a duty of care, but not on whether a duty will be owed in a particular case.

The case of *Bourhill v Young* [1943] AC 92 provides an example of the case where the outer limits of the neighbour principle were tested. The activity which caused the damage in that case was clearly a careless act and the damage was physical. The only question which remained was whether the plaintiff might owe the defendant a duty of care in principle. The facts were these: the plaintiff witnessed the aftermath of a fatal motor accident in which the defendant had been negligent and in which the defendant himself had been killed. The plaintiff, a pregnant woman, suffered nervous shock and miscarried her baby. The House of Lords held that the defendant was not liable. The plaintiff and her damages were simply not reasonably foreseeable to the defendant, and in the terminology of *Donoghue v Stevenson* she was not a 'neighbour' of the negligent driver. Since there was no neighbour relationship, no duty of care existed and hence no liability in negligence.

18.4.2   The plaintiff's harm

The law, in its attempt to keep the ambit of the tort of negligence under control, has subdivided the types of damage into a number of categories. If sufficient proximity to establish a 'neighbour' relationship exists and the relevant breach is established, the recoverability for the ensuing loss will be as follows.

1   *Personal injury*   damages for this are always recoverable.
2   *Damage to property*   this is always recoverable providing the 'property' in question was not supplied by the defendant in the first place (the rationale for this being that when the defendant provides the property, the rights of the parties, if any, should be dealt with by contractual obligations – the law of tort will not assist those who fail to extract contractual safeguards).
3   *Damage to another's economic well-being resulting directly from personal or property damage*   again this is almost always recoverable: the classic example is loss of earnings resulting from personal injury.
4   *Damage to the plaintiff's financial well-being when the loss does not flow from personal injury or property damage suffered by the plaintiff*   this is termed pure economic loss and is rarely recoverable unless the rule in *Hedley Byrne v Heller* applies.

18.4.3   The definition of 'damage to property'

In (2) above the distinction was drawn between damage to property which exists independently of the defendant and that which the defendant supplies himself. In the latter case the law does not treat the damage as damage to property, but as an example of the supply of a defective product. The remedy for the supply of a defective product is an action for economic loss which lies in contract, and only in contract. No action lies in negligence. This principle was established beyond doubt by a seven-member court in the House of Lords case in *Murphy v Brentwood* [1990] 3 WLR 414, 50 BLR 1, where Lord Bridge offered the following rationale, which is quoted at some length because of the importance of this principle for construction law:

> *Dangerous defects and defects of quality*
> If a manufacturer negligently puts into circulation a chattel containing a latent defect which renders it dangerous to persons or property, the manufacturer, on the well known principles established by *Donoghue v Stevenson* [1932] AC 562, will be liable in tort for injury to persons or damage to property which the chattel causes. But if a manufacturer produces and sells a

chattel which is merely defective in quality, even to the extent that it is valueless for the purpose for which it is intended, the manufacturer's liability at common law arises only under and by reference to the terms of any contract to which he is a party in relation to the chattel; the common law does not impose on him any liability in tort to persons to whom he owes no duty in contract but who, having acquired the chattel, suffer economic loss because the chattel is defective in quality. If a dangerous defect in a chattel is discovered before it causes any personal injury or damage to property, because the danger is now known and the chattel cannot safely be used unless the defect is repaired, the defect becomes merely a defect in quality. The chattel is either capable of repair at economic cost or it is worthless and must be scrapped. In either case the loss sustained by the owner or hirer of the chattel is purely economic. It is recoverable against any party who owes the loser a relevant contractual duty. But it is not recoverable in tort in the absence of a special relationship of proximity imposing on the tortfeasor a duty of care to safeguard the plaintiff from economic loss. There is no such special relationship between the manufacturer of a chattel and a remote owner or hirer.

I believe that these principles are equally applicable to buildings. If a builder erects a structure containing a latent defect which renders it dangerous to persons or property, he will be liable in tort for injury to persons or damage to property resulting from that dangerous defect. But if the defect becomes apparent before any injury or damage has been caused, the loss sustained by the building owner is purely economic. If the defect can be repaired at economic cost, that is the measure of the loss. If the building cannot be repaired, it may have to be abandoned as unfit for occupation and therefore valueless. These economic losses are recoverable if they flow from breach of a relevant contractual duty, but, here again, in the absence of a special relationship of proximity they are not recoverable in tort. The only qualification I would make to this is that, if a building stands so close to the boundary of the building owner's land that after discovery of the dangerous defect it remains a potential source of injury to persons or property on neighbouring land or on the highway, the building owner ought, in principle, to be entitled to recover in tort from the negligent builder the cost of obviating the danger, whether by repair or by demolition, so far as that cost is necessarily incurred in order to protect himself from potential liability to third parties.

One potential problem associated with the definition of property damage and pure economic loss concerns what was called the 'complex structure' theory by Lord Bridge in the earlier case of *D & F Estates v Church Commissioners for England* [1989] AC 177. This describes the situation where a structure is complex, that is where it comprises a number of distinct parts. It was postulated that a defect in one part of a structure (say in the foundations) might lead to damage in another part (say a wall supported on the foundation). In this case no recovery in negligence could be made against the contractor who built the foundation because this is purely economic loss and is recoverable only in contract. However, under the complex structure theory, it might have been possible to recover for the damage to the wall because the contractor's negligence in respect of the foundations has led to damage to *other property* owned by the plaintiff, namely the wall.

This theory was dealt with at some length in a number of speeches in *Murphy* because, since it had first been suggested in *D & F Estates*, it had put the law into a state of uncertainty. Lord Bridge (who first suggested the theory in *D & F Estates*) dismissed his own theory in the following manner:

> The reality is that the structural elements in any building form a single indivisible unit of which the different parts are essentially interdependent. To the extent that there is any defect in one part of the structure it must to a greater or lesser degree necessarily affect all other parts of the structure. Therefore any defect in the structure is a defect in the quality of the whole and it is quite artificial, in order to impose a legal liability which the law would not otherwise impose, to treat a defect in an integral structure, so far as it weakens the structure, as a dangerous defect liable to cause damage to 'other property'.
>
> A critical distinction must be drawn here between some part of a complex structure which is said to be a 'danger' only because it does not perform its proper function in sustaining the other parts and some distinct item incorporated in the structure which positively malfunctions so as to inflict positive damage on the structure in which it is incorporated. Thus, if a defective central heating boiler explodes and damages a house or a defective electrical installation malfunctions and sets the house on fire, I see no reason to doubt that the owner of the house, if he can prove that the damage was due to the negligence of the boiler manufacturer in the one case or the electrical contractor on the other, can recover damages in tort on *Donoghue v Stevenson* [1932] AC 562 principles. But the position in law is entirely different where, by reason of the inadequacy of the foundations of the building to support the weight of the super-structure, differential settlement and consequent cracking occurs. Here, once the first cracks appear, the structure as a whole is seen to be defective and the nature of the defect is known. Even if, contrary to my view, the initial damage could be regarded as damage to other property caused by a latent defect, once the defect is known the situation of the building owner is analogous to that of the car owner who discovers that the car has faulty brakes. He may have a house which, until repairs are effected, is unfit for habitation, but, subject to the reservation I have expressed with respect to ruinous buildings at or near the boundary of the owner's property, the building no longer represents a source of danger and as it deteriorates will only damage itself.
>
> For these reasons the complex structure theory offers no escape from the conclusion that damage to a house itself which is attributable to a defect in the structure of the house is not recoverable in tort on *Donoghue v Stevenson* principles, but represents purely economic loss which is only recoverable in contract or in tort by reason of some special relationship of proximity which imposes on the tortfeasor a duty of care to protect against economic loss.

Lord Oliver made the following observations in support of the above statement:

> My Lords, I agree with the views of my noble and learned friend, Lord Bridge of Harwich, in this appeal that to apply the complex structure theory to a house so that each part of the entire structure is treated as a separate piece of property is quite unrealistic. A builder who builds a house from foundations upwards is creating a single integrated unit of which the

individual components are interdependent. To treat the foundations as a piece of property separate from the walls or the floor is a wholly artificial exercise. If the foundations are inadequate the whole house is affected. Furthermore, if the complex structure theory is tenable there is no reason in principle why it should not also be applied to chattels consisting of integrated parts such as a ship or a piece of machinery. The consequences of such an application would be far-reaching. It seems to me that the only context for the complex structure theory in the case of a building would be where one integral component of the structure was built by a separate contractor and where a defect in such a component had caused damage to other parts of the structure, e.g. a steel frame erected by a specialist contractor which failed to give adequate support to floors or walls. Defects in such ancillary equipment as central heating boilers or electrical installations would be subject to the normal *Donoghue v Stevenson* principle if such defects gave rise to damage to other parts of the building.

18.4.4 The recovery of pure economic loss: reliance negligence

There is, however, one area of negligence in which it is settled that pure economic losses can be recovered. When people hold themselves out as having some special skill or knowledge and provide advice to another in the expectation that that other will rely upon that advice, they will be liable if any loss, including economic loss, is suffered as a result. This category is of some importance in relation to construction professionals who prepare reports and designs.

This head of liability was initially established in the case of *Hedley Byrne v Heller and Partners* [1964] AC 465 and has been treated by the House of Lords as correct on many occasions. In *Hedley Byrne* the court, while extending the defendant's duty of care in respect of economic loss, still sought to place substantial limits on those to whom such a duty was owed. Their Lordships were not prepared to allow liability for negligent misstatements generally but only where certain conditions were met. Lord Reid said

> It seems to me that there is good sense behind our present law that in general an innocent but negligent misrepresentation gives rise to no cause of action. There must be something more than mere misstatement . . . [Lord Reid then examined a number of earlier authorities including dicta from Lord Haldane's speech in *Robinson v Bank of Scotland* [1916] SC 154 in which Lord Haldane speaks of a duty of care arising when there is a special relationship . . . He [Lord Haldane] speaks of other special relationships and I can see no logical stopping place short of all those relationships where it is plain that the party seeking information or advice was trusting the other to exercise such a degree of care as the circumstances required, where it was reasonable for him to do that, and where the other gave the information or advice when he ought to have known that the inquirer was relying on him.

Lord Morris said

> My Lords, I consider that . . . it should now be regarded as settled that if someone possessed of a special skill undertakes, quite irrespective of contract, to apply that skill for the assistance of another person who relies upon such

skill, a duty of care will arise. . . . Furthermore, if, in a sphere in which a person is so placed that others could reasonably rely on his judgment or his skill or on his ability to make careful inquiry, a person takes it on himself to give information or advice to, or allows his information or advice to be passed on to, another person who, as he knows or should know, will place reliance on it, then a duty of care will arise.

18.4.5 *Donoghue v Stevenson* compared with *Hedley Byrne*

Reliance by the plaintiff on the defendant is an important factor in the formulation of the *Hedley Byrne* type of negligence and it is often termed 'reliance negligence' as opposed to the 'carelessness negligence' which corresponds with the wide *Donoghue v Stevenson* type liability. That the two types of negligence, though stemming from the same original source, are distinct is seen in the speech of Lord Reid in *Hedley Byrne*. He said that while *Donoghue v Stevenson* was 'a very important decision' he did not think that 'it has any direct bearing on this case'. 'The law', said Lord Reid, 'must treat negligent words differently from negligent acts'. So when the alleged negligent activity is a deed, the rule in *Donoghue v Stevenson* will apply and the standard of care will be that of the reasonable person. When the activity complained of consists of words or some other communication the rule to be applied will be found in *Hedley Byrne* and the standard of care will be related to the skill of the defendant (see Section 16.3).

18.4.6 Acts and omissions

The duty imposed by the law of negligence is to avoid causing harm to one's neighbour; it does not extend to conferring benefits upon him. Accordingly, omissions rarely give rise to a cause of action, so that in general there is no duty at common law for one person to prevent another from suffering harm unless, of course, the first person caused the danger to begin with. If a person is in danger, another person may, in effect, stand by and watch without liability. An example of this is provided by *Smith v Littlewoods Organisation Ltd* [1987] All ER 710 where Lord Goff held that in English law there is no duty to prevent another inflicting harm on a third person.

   The rule concerning omissions is not applicable, however, if the defendant places himself in a special relationship with the plaintiff so that he owes the plaintiff a duty to act positively. A number of such situations arise in relation to the construction industry.

Failure to supervise

If an engineer fails to provide an adequate level of supervision and, as a result, damage is sustained, he or she may be found liable although this will depend on all the relevant circumstances. The level of supervision is a function of the importance of the work and the supervisor has the obligation 'to ensure that the work is properly and expeditiously carried out, so as to achieve the end result as contemplated in the contract' (per Judge Stabb in *Sutcliffe v Chippendale & Edmondson* 18 BLR 149 at 162).

The fact that the supervision fails to detect all defects is not, however, of itself, proof of negligence: see Section 16.4.4.

Failure to warn of danger

A difficult question arises in connection with whether a professional person has a duty to warn of possible danger. The question can be answered in terms of whether that professional has assumed this responsibility towards the plaintiff. Thus in the normal course of events a contractor will be responsible for the safety of his work-force and it will not be for the engineer or architect to warn of danger (beyond what is required by safety legislation – see Section 18.5.4). If, however, the engineer imposes a particular sequence of working upon a contractor which involves keeping elements of structure in a dangerous condition, then the engineer will be required to provide reasonable warnings.

In *Clayton v Woodman & Son (Builders) Ltd* 4 BLR 65 the plaintiff was a workman injured in the collapse of some masonry following the visit of the architect to the site. It was alleged that the architect ought to have issued a variation as the work as originally designed could not readily have been constructed in safety but that he refused. It was said that the collapse was occasioned by his failure to vary the works. Lord Justice Pearson pointed out that the role of the architect was to advise the client and he, the architect, was entitled to assume that the contractor would execute the work safely and that he owed no duty to the contractor or to the men working on site. Lord Justice Pearson dealt with a variety of possible arguments which might be set up on behalf of the injured workman:

> It can be suggested that the fault of the architect was in not advising the builder, through his existing representative on site, the plaintiff, as to how the work required by the specification should be executed. If he had done so, the architect would have been stepping out of his province and stepping into the province of the builder. It is not right to require anyone to do that: and it is not in the interests of the builder's workpeople that there should be a confusion of functions as between the builder on the one hand and the architect on the other. I would hold that it was plainly not the architect's duty to do that. It will be observed that he had at any rate no pre-existing duty to do that. He was not asked to give any advice and he did not profess to give any such advice, and I cannot see that it can be regarded as a fault that he did not step out of his province and advise the builder in what manner the builder should carry out his own building operations. . . . If I had thought that there was some evidence that the architect directed the workman to do something dangerous – that is to say something which the architect knew or ought to have known would be done in such a manner that it would be dangerous – then it might well be that some duty would have been imposed on the architect.

In *Clayton v Woodman* the architect was found not to be liable, although the court clearly left it open for an architect or engineer to be found liable if they assumed such liability by giving advice as to the mode of undertaking the construction or if they directed that work, which was inherently dangerous, should be undertaken. An example of where the architect was made liable was in *Clay v A J Crump & Son Ltd* 4 BLR 80.

Here the architect allowed a wall to be put into a dangerous condition. When it collapsed the architect was found jointly liable in negligence with the contractor.

18.5 Duty imposed by statute

In a number of instances a duty is imposed by statute where it would not be imposed at common law, or alternatively the statute may impose a higher standard of care than would be imposed at common law. There are a number of important statutes and these are mentioned very briefly below.

18.5.1 The Defective Premises Act 1972

In 1970 the Law Commission suggested (Law Commission Report No. 40: 'Civil Liability of Vendors and Lessors for Defective Premises') that a short statute be passed in order to improve the position of purchasers of defective houses. The concern was that the law failed to provide adequate safeguards. The law of contract rarely applied and the law of negligence failed, it was thought, to establish any significant safeguards against losses other than physical injury. The legislation resulting from the Law Commission's recommendations was passed in June 1972. However, the efforts of the legislators were too late; for shortly before the Act received its Royal Assent, the Court of Appeal delivered its judgment in *Dutton v Bognor Regis UDC* [1972] 1 QB 373, which suggested that the law of negligence provided substantial protection for subsequent purchasers. Indeed greater protection appeared to be provided by the common law than was provided by the Act. This the Court of Appeal achieved by, in effect, characterising defective buildings as physically damaged buildings. This approach was later reiterated by the House of Lords in *Anns v London Borough of Merton* [1978] AC and *Junior Books v Veitchi* [1983] 1 AC 520. The practical effect of these developments in the common law was that the Defective Premises Act was largely ignored since by Section 6(2) of the Act the duties it created were additional to all other duties and did not supersede them.

In recent years, however, the position has changed radically and the Defective Premises Act has once more taken on significance. Since the decision of the House of Lords in *Murphy v Brentwood* [1990] 3 WLR 414, which caused the law to revert to its pre-*Dutton* position, the Defective Premises Act 1972 has re-acquired the significance which the Law Commission originally assumed it would have. It has once more become an important statute providing duties of care where none would exist under the common law.

The application of the Act
The Act applies only in the following cases:

- Where the work in question was undertaken on or after 1 January 1974: Section 7(2).

- Where the construction in question relates to a dwelling: Section 1(1). Note that the Act applies equally whether the work concerns the erection, conversion, or enlargement of the dwelling.
- Where an 'approved scheme' is not used: Sections 2(1) to 2(6). Section 2 enables the Secretary of State to approve a scheme which in effect operates as a scheme of insurance. Only one such scheme has been approved, the NHBC Scheme, though this lost its approved status in 1979 (see *Keating's Building Contracts*, 5th Edition, p. 362). The NHBC Scheme continues to operate its insurance function. However, since it has lost its approved status, the Defective Premises Act applies to all dwellings constructed since 31 March 1979.

(Note: the NHBC (The National House Building Council) is a very important participant in UK Construction. It is a voluntary body with representatives of the Royal Institute of British Architects, the Royal Institute of Chartered Surveyors, the Building Societies Association, the Consumers Association, local authorities and others. It is a non-profit-making organisation which keeps a register of builders and developers. Registration involves the acceptance of inspection during construction, the use of construction to standards laid down by the NHBC, the vendor must offer the purchaser an agreement in the NHBC standard form and warrant that an NHBC standard Notice of Insurance cover will be issued. As a result, the builder warrants that the dwelling has been constructed to NHBC standards and undertakes to remedy, at his own expense, any defect notified within two years of the issue of the Notice of Insurance Cover, except where the defect arises from design details provided by the purchaser. The principal safeguards available to the purchaser are, however, provided by the NHBC. They provide cover for major defects notified up to ten years from the date of issue of the Notice of Insurance. The precise wording of the agreements should be consulted in each individual case as exceptions apply.)

The duty
Section 1 of the Act imposes a duty of care owed to owners of the premises by all those who have undertaken work upon it. In the absence of this statute the principal builder may, under the usual rules of negligence or contract, owe a duty of care to the first occupier or purchaser of the property. But if the property is then sold, the necessary relationship to establish a cause of action under the usual rules of law (especially following *Murphy v Brentwood* [1990] 3 WLR 414) disappears. The Defective Premises Act thus provides additional protection for the subsequent purchaser of a defective domestic property in these circumstances. Section 1(1) provides

> A person taking on work for or in connection with the provision of a dwelling (whether the dwelling is provided by the erection or by the conversion or enlargement of a building) owes a duty
> (a) if the dwelling is provided to the order of any person, to that person; and
> (b) without prejudice to paragraph (a) above, to every person who acquires an interest (whether legal or equitable) in the dwelling;

> to see that the work which he takes on is done in a workmanlike, or as the case may be, professional manner, with proper materials and so that as regards that work the dwelling will be fit for habitation when completed.

The period of limitation in this case is to be six years running from the date when the dwelling was completed; but if a person returns to the building to rectify defective work a new period of six years begins to run in respect of that rectified work from the date when it was undertaken: Section 1(5).

18.5.2　The building control legislation

In Section 3.3 the statutory requirements relating to compliance with the Building Regulations were discussed. It was seen that those who produced construction work which failed to comply with the Regulations are liable under the criminal law.

There is, however, a potential additional head of claim, under Section 71 of the Health and Safety at Work etc. Act and Section 38 of the Building Act 1984. This is not available at the present date since neither of these sections, both of which contain identical wording, are yet in force and there is no indication that they will be activated. These sections provide that a 'breach of duty imposed by the Building Regulations shall, so far as it causes damage be actionable, except insofar as the Regulations provide otherwise'. Unfortunately the definition of 'damage' for the purpose of this section given in Section 71(4) of the 1974 Act is unclear in scope and is said to include 'the death of, or injury to, any person' but fails to deal with property damage or economic loss. The fact that the 1974 Act is concerned solely with safety, and the purposes for which Building Regulations may be made under the 1984 Act do not include the safeguarding of building investment, suggests that the duty established by Sections 71 and 38 is restricted to personal injury cases. Since the sections are currently ineffective no actions may be brought at this time. However, when (and if) it becomes law the principal advantage of bringing an action under this rule is that, apparently, no duty needs to be established. Once the breach (i.e. the contravention of the Building Regulations) and the consequent damage are proved, the duty automatically arises. Since the Building Regulations are framed in detailed technical terms, the breach may readily be identified unlike many normal negligence cases where the reasonableness of the defendant's behaviour is always relevant.

18.5.3　The Consumer Protection Act 1987

The Consumer Protection Act 1987 is designed principally to protect consumers in product liability situations, that is where a product is supplied which contains a defect which causes personal injury or damage to the property of a consumer. Its importance for construction is that its drafting appears to be wide enough to include building work. The terms 'product' and 'goods' are defined in Section 1(2) and Section 45(1) respectively as:

product: . . . any goods or electricity and . . . includes a product which is comprised in another product, whether by virtue of being a component part or raw material or otherwise

goods: . . . substances, growing crops and things comprised in land by virtue of being attached to it and any ship, aircraft or vehicle.

According to these definitions, buildings are not excluded, although Section 46(4) does exclude situations where the supply of goods refers to a supply of goods comprised in land where the supply includes the creation or disposal of an interest in land. Accordingly, where a builder sells a house he will not be affected by this Act, although he may well be caught by the Defective Premises Act 1972 discussed above.

In Section 2(1) of the 1987 Act it is provided that

Where any damage is caused wholly or partly by a defect in a product, every person to whom subsection (2) . . . applies shall be liable for the damage.

Those to whom Subsection (2) applies are the producer of the product, any person holding himself out as the producer of the product, the importer of the goods into the EC and in some cases, the supplier of the product. Important definitions are those of 'defect' in Section 3(1) and 'damage' in Section 5(1). A defect exists for the purposes of the Act where 'the safety of the product is not such as persons generally are entitled to expect' and damage means 'death or personal injury or any loss of or damage to any property (including land)'. These definitions confine the ambit of the Act considerably for construction work. No liability is established for pure economic loss and no liability will be created unless the defect renders the structure or other building unsafe.

18.5.4 The safety legislation

Construction has an appalling safety record. Accordingly, it is right that there should be extensive and strict control of safety on construction sites. The topic of safety is outside the scope of this book but because of its practical importance the principal pieces of legislation should be mentioned: see Section 3.4.1. In particular, note the new EC Directives (due to come into force on 1 January 1993) which impose additional obligations regarding safety on all those involved in construction.

Breach of the duty of care in negligence

19.1 Introduction

19.1.1 Preliminary note

In Chapter 18 it was seen that a plaintiff must prove three elements in order to show successfully that a defendant was negligent in the sense understood by the law of tort. The first element, the duty of care, was discussed and the rules for determining whether or not such a duty existed were set out and explained. In this chapter the second element of the law of negligence is discussed. This involves asking whether the person who owes a duty is in breach of that duty.

19.1.2 Negligence in contract and tort

In this chapter we shall focus on negligence in the tortious sense. We have seen (in Chapter 16) that a consultant or a designer operating under a contract normally owes to his or her client a contractual obligation to exercise reasonable skill and care. This obligation, though contractual in nature, is indistinguishable from the standard of care owed by such a professional in tortious negligence whenever a duty of care is established. Consequently this chapter provides the answer to two questions:

- If A owes B a duty of care in the tort of negligence, what activities by A constitute a breach of that duty?
- If A owes B a contractual obligation to exercise reasonable care and skill, what activities by A constitute a breach of that obligation?

In practice the answer may be different in the case of tortious and contractual obligations since in tort the obligation is to avoid causing harm whereas in contract there will be positive obligations, such as the obligation to provide certain advice or warnings. However, wherever an obligation or duty exists, whether in tort or contract, the test for breach is identical.

This is illustrated by comments made in *North West Water Authority v Binnie & Partners* QBD (unreported December 1989). This action arose from the Abbeystead disaster where a valve house exploded causing death or injury to a number of visitors and damage to the equipment located in the building. The actions for personal injury and the fatal injuries had already been heard and Binnie & Partners, the designer, had been found liable in negligence. The client, the water authority, then decided to sue Binnies for property damage. They alleged that, since they had already been found liable for negligence, Binnies could not now claim that they were not negligent in this new action. Binnies sought to show, however, that this new action raised entirely new questions to those which prevailed in the earlier case. But Mr Justice Drake observed

> So I gave notice to [counsel for Binnie] at an early stage ... that I would like him to tell me what practical as opposed to theoretical differences there would be in the two sets of litigation. He pointed out that the issue between the [personal injury] plaintiffs and Binnies was in tort, whereas the action between Binnies and the Water Authority lies in contract.... But I asked to be shown the contract and to have pointed out to me any way in which the contract in practice would modify or give rise to different issues from liability in tort. I was given no satisfactory answer.

19.2   The test of breach of duty

The basic test whether or not a party is in breach of his or her duty of care is did the defendant act reasonably in all the circumstances? This is, in essence, a question of fact in each case. This means that in the days when civil actions were tried by juries, the question of whether the defendant was in breach of his or her duty of care was a question that would have been left to the jury. In order to answer it, all the relevant circumstances must be considered. Accordingly, it is impossible to reduce the law to rules such as 'drivers who speed are in breach' or 'engineers who design to a lower standard than the relevant code of practice are in breach'. To formulate rules in this way would be to focus on one particular aspect of the defendant's behaviour rather than to look at all the circumstances of the case.

There are a number of factors which help us in establishing whether or not the defendant had acted reasonably in any particular instance. These include the magnitude of damage which is likely to result, the cost of avoiding that damage, the utility of the defendant's acts and whether it is necessary to act in an emergency situation or whether ample time is available for careful consideration. Each of these matters is discussed below.

While the question of the breach itself involves the answer to a question of fact, it also involves a comparison against a standard, and the level of that standard is a matter of law. The requirement that the defendant must act reasonably must thus take into account any relevant skill that the defendant professes to possess. Thus an engineer designing a bridge will not be judged against the standard of the average reasonable person in society, for the average reasonable person knows very little about bridge design. Rather, the engineer will be judged against a higher standard of care. The question of the 'standard' of the duty is of considerable importance in the law relating to construction consultants and designers.

19.3 The standard of care

The law of negligence requires that those who owe duties of care to their neighbours should act reasonably. This does not mean that each person should act in accordance with a test of reasonableness which depends on his or her own personal characteristics. Rather, the test is applied objectively: one should exhibit the level of care as one might expect from a 'reasonable person'. Each person, whatever his or her own deficiencies, must attain the standard of the reasonable person. It is no defence to assert, said Lord Denning in *Nettleship v Weston* [1971] 2 QB 691, that 'I was doing my best and could not help it, if one's incompetent best is not good enough'. The rationale for applying an objective test is first that by indulging in contact with the world at large one is holding oneself out to be a reasonable man or woman and/or second that other members of the community have a right to expect that others will act in a reasonable manner.

Where the plaintiff does not hold himself out, except for his mere presence, as possessing any particular attributes, skills or shortcomings, he will be required to exercise the skill and care of the reasonable person. In the field of construction law, however, many persons act within spheres that require particular skills. If one holds oneself out to be a skilled person, the rule is that one is then judged by the standard of the reasonable competent member of that profession or trade. The fact of 'holding oneself out' is the key to understanding the standard of care, since even a person who is ignorant of the skills necessary for a particular task will be required at law to exhibit those skills if he or she holds themselves out to be able to perform the task. Technicians will thus be required to exhibit the skills of a competent engineer if they advertise themselves as being able to perform engineering work. Young graduate engineers who set up in business as engineers competent to undertake work in a certain area must exhibit the skill typical of a reasonably experienced engineer in that area even though they have no relevant practical experience at all.

The question of the standard of care arises both in the context of contractual and tortious negligence. It is discussed in detail in Chapter 16 (Section 16.3) which deals with the obligations of professionals under their consultancy contracts.

19.4 Factors affecting the reasonableness of the defendant's behaviour

Lord Atkin's famous dictum in *Donoghue v Stevenson* (see Section 18.4.1) suggests that we must take reasonable care to avoid acts or omissions which we can reasonably foresee would be likely to injure our neighbours. Thus even where injury is foreseeable, a defendant is not charged with an absolute duty to avoid such injury, merely to take reasonable care to avoid it. In asking whether the defendant has taken reasonable care, the law takes into account a number of factors including the magnitude of the risk, the cost of avoidance, and the utility of the defendant's activity.

19.4.1 The magnitude of the risk

The magnitude of the risk (which is a function both of the probability of harm occurring and the gravity of harm which may occur) arising from the defendant's activities is always important in determining whether or not such activities can give rise to a claim in negligence. Lord Oaksey pointed out in *Bolton v Stone* [1951] AC 850 that 'Life would be almost intolerable if [the ordinary careful person] were to attempt to take precautions against every possible risk which he can foresee'.

In *Haley v London Electricity Board* [1965] AC 778 the level of risk which the defendant had to guard against was debated in quantitative terms. In this case a blind person sustained injury by falling into an excavation opened up for road works in London. These works were fenced-off so that sighted people could readily take precautions. It was submitted by the defendants that the risk of a blind person coming along was so slight that they were not unreasonable in failing to protect the blind person especially. The court was presented with statistics showing the number of blind people in London and the likelihood that such people would be on that pavement during the course of the works. The court found that even though the risk was small it was not so small that the defendants could ignore it.

19.4.2 The cost and practicality of avoiding the harm

The law will not impose upon defendants a duty to go to extraordinary efforts to avoid harm arising in the course of activities which, themselves, are reasonable.

19.4.3 The utility of the defendant's acts

The general contribution of the defendant's acts to society is an important factor. The greater the value to society, the less likely it is that the defendant will be found negligent. In *Daborn v Bath Tramways* [1946] 2 All ER 333, for example, the damage was caused by an ambulance during the war. Lord Justice Asquith considered that the importance for the whole community of the activity which it was alleged was negligent had to be taken into account. He pointed out that

> In determining whether a party is negligent, the standard of reasonable care is that which is reasonably to be demanded in the circumstances. A relevant circumstance to take into account is the end to be served by behaving in this way or that. As has often been pointed out, if all the trains in the country were restricted to a speed of five miles an hour there would be fewer accidents, but our national life would be intolerably slowed down. The purpose to be served, if sufficiently important, justifies the assumption of abnormal risk. . . . In considering whether reasonable care has been observed, one must balance the risk against the consequences of not assuming that risk.

19.4.4 Emergencies

People are often required to act in the heat of the moment. It is clear that in an emergency situation the question of whether or not they have acted reasonably is to be decided taking this into account. Thus, for instance, an engineer who has only a very short time to evaluate a situation and recommend appropriate action will not be judged on the same basis as one who has abundant opportunity to analyse and consider the situation with his or her professional colleagues. The test to be applied remains that of the reasonable engineer in all the circumstances.

19.5   Organisation and systems failures

It is often difficult for a plaintiff to show that a professional person has not exercised reasonable care. The plaintiff's difficulties are, however, eased significantly if the damage is attributable not to a shortcoming in a professional's judgement, but in the organisation and system that he or she operates. Examples of the form that such failures may take include failures to ensure that staff are of adequate qualification and experience, failures to perform adequate checks on work done and failures to provide adequate communications. An example of the last category of failure occurred in *Sutcliffe v Thackrah* [1974] AC 727 where an architect failed to supply the quantity surveyor who was drawing up an interim certificate with details of defective work and was consequently found to be professionally negligent.

20

Negligence: the requirement for resulting damage before action

Liability under the tort of negligence cannot arise unless damage flows from the breach. This idea is expressed by some lawyers in the following way: 'there can be no negligence in the air'. Thus if a person acts in flagrant breach of a duty of care there is no negligence until the plaintiff is injured. The sense of this rule is readily appreciated when one considers the case, say, of someone driving carelessly through a crowded shopping street. It is clearly not open to everyone who is potentially at danger to sue in negligence. Otherwise, the whole population of the street could sue. The law of negligence restricts the right to sue to those who actually suffer some damage.

There are a number of rules concerning the damage which occurs and which transforms 'negligence in the air' into negligence which the law recognises. These may be briefly stated as follows:

1   The damage must be of a type for which the law allows recovery in the circumstances. In general this means that the damage must be personal injury or property damage (as defined after *Murphy v Brentwood* [1990] 3 WLR 414). If, however, the plaintiff can bring himself within the rule in *Hedley Byrne v Heller* [1964] AC 465, pure economic loss will also be recoverable.
2   The defendant's breach must have caused the damage. Even if a causal link is proved, however, the defendant will be liable only for damage which is not too remote.
3   The plaintiff's damage must be of a type foreseeable by a reasonable defendant.

These rules are examined in Chapter 22 as many of the principles of this branch of the law are common to the tort of negligence and to breaches of contract.

21

The law of neighbours:
nuisance and *Rylands v Fletcher*

21.1 Introduction

The torts of nuisance and *Rylands v Fletcher* are concerned with protecting a person's enjoyment of or rights over land. This is a matter of some importance in the field of construction since the performance of the work and the structures which result often inconvenience or disturb those who occupy neighbouring land.

Neighbours often complain of dust, smoke, noise, bright lights, vibration, blocking up of accesses, loss of support to their land, the behaviour of workmen and so on during construction works, particularly in crowded city centres. On occasions the interference can be very substantial indeed as when chemicals leak out from the site and pollute neighbouring properties or when stored water floods adjacent land. The law's role is to balance, on the one hand, the rights of those who own land to do as they wish upon that land and to develop it for the greater public good and, on the other, the rights of those affected by the interference that such use causes. The study of the torts of nuisance and *Rylands v Fletcher* involves an analysis of how the courts have approached this balancing act.

21.1.1 Preliminary definitions

Nuisance may be defined in the following terms:

> A person commits a nuisance when he is responsible for a state of affairs which causes a physical injury to neighbouring land or which causes the occupier of that land to experience unreasonable interference with his enjoyment of the land.

The tort of *Rylands v Fletcher* is derived from the rule laid down in the case of the same name in 1868. In the course of his judgment in *Rylands v Fletcher* [1868] LR 3 HL 330, Mr Justice Blackburn stated the rule:

> [a] person who for his own purposes brings on his lands and collects and keeps there anything likely to do mischief if it escapes, must keep it at his

peril and, if he does not do so, is prima facie answerable for all the damage which is the natural consequence of its escape.

On appeal to the House of Lords this judgment was affirmed in the terms quoted above but the additional requirement was imposed that the bringing of the thing likely to do mischief if it escapes must involve a 'non-natural use' of the defendant's land (per Lord Cairns).

The two torts clearly overlap; the principal distinctions are as follows.

1 The liability in *Rylands* is much stricter than nuisance. Once the defendant has brought a thing on his land so that he comes within the rule in *Rylands v Fletcher*, he is prima facie liable if it escapes irrespective of whether or not he has been negligent or indeed whether or not he could foresee the damage that an escape could cause. In nuisance, however, the role of negligence is of much greater significance; it emerges through the requirement that the interference should not be unreasonable.

2 Nuisance, while producing a less strict liability, applies to a wider range of interferences. In the case of *Rylands* the 'things' must be physical things, they must be accumulated and they must involve a 'non-natural use' of land. These limitations do not arise in the law of nuisance. Intangibles, such as noise and vibrations, are covered by nuisance; no accumulation is necessary and the defendant's use of land may be perfectly natural.

In short, *Rylands v Fletcher* liability is substantially stricter than nuisance liability but it applies to a much smaller range of situations.

21.1.2   Remedies for the torts of nuisance and *Rylands v Fletcher*

The torts of nuisance and *Rylands v Fletcher* are not actionable without damage. Both, however, are dependent upon the defendant causing a state of affairs to exist. In both cases the state of affairs which may cause the damage can be recognised and, hence, it is possible for a plaintiff to obtain a court order (a *quia timet* injunction) before any damage occurs if it appears to the court that damage is likely to occur. This injunction will order the defendant to cause the state of affairs which is likely to lead to damage to cease.

21.2   Nuisance

21.2.1   The elements of nuisance

The tort of nuisance arises when the defendant interferes with the plaintiff's enjoyment of his or her land. The nature of this interference may be classified into two distinct categories:

● a physical injury to the land
● an interference with the enjoyment of the land.

Lord Westbury, in the case of *St Helen's Smelting Co v Tipping* [1865] 11 HL Cas 642, drew the distinction between these two categories as follows:

> it appears to me that it is a very desirable thing to mark the difference between an action brought for a nuisance upon the ground that the alleged nuisance produces material injury to the property, and an action brought for a nuisance on the ground that the thing alleged to be a nuisance is productive of sensible personal discomfort. With regard to the latter, namely, the personal inconvenience and interference with one's enjoyment, one's quiet, one's personal freedom, anything that discomposes or injuriously affects the senses of the nerves, whether that may or may not be denominated a nuisance, must undoubtedly depend greatly on the circumstances of the place where the thing complained of actually occurs. If a man lives in a town, it is necessary that he should subject himself to the consequences of those operations of town, it is necessary that he should subject himself to the consequences of those operations of trade which may be carried on in his immediate locality, which are actually necessary for trade and commerce, and also for the enjoyment of property, and for the benefit of the inhabitants of the town and for the public at large. . . . I think, my Lords, that in a case of that description, the submission which is required from persons living in society to that amount of discomfort which may be necessary for the legitimate and free exercise of the trade of their neighbours, would not apply to circumstances the immediate result of which is sensible injury to the value of the property.

In the case of physical (i.e. material) injury to property, therefore, the person who causes such injury is prima facie liable in nuisance and he or she may not generally raise the defence of reasonable use of land. In the case of interference with the enjoyment of property, however, the reasonableness of the defendant's conduct in all the circumstances is relevant. Typical matters which the courts might consider to be relevant are the seriousness of the interference, the duration of the interference, the locality, the motivation of the defendant, whether the defendant's use of his or her land is ordinary and the impracticability of avoiding the interference. A matter which the courts have not seen fit to consider as relevant (save in so far as the nature of the locality is generally considered to be relevant) is whether the plaintiff moved to the nuisance.

21.2.2 Nuisance arising during normal construction works

The above quoted statement made by Lord Westbury during *St Helen's Smelting* indicates clearly that when the interference complained of is an interference to the enjoyment of land the test of liability is whether the interference is, in all the circumstances, reasonable. If it is, then no nuisance has been committed.

Construction work, as we had noted already, is often responsible for causing substantial inconvenience to those who occupy adjacent land. It is, in such cases, important to understand the position that the law adopts. One important and well-known case provides a useful illustration. In *Andreae v Selfridge & Co* [1938] 1 Ch 1, the defendants undertook the construction of a very large department store on Oxford Street in the 1930s, which proceeded in a number of phases. The plaintiff, who carried on business as a hotelier nearby, complained that the construction was causing a nuisance. The plaintiff first argued that the works were wholly unusual, consisting as they did of deep basements and high steel frame construction. Sir Wilfred Greene MR dismissed this argument:

> As time goes on new inventions and new methods enable land to be more profitably used, either by digging down into the earth or by mounting up into the skies. Whether, from other points of view, that is a matter which is desirable for humanity is neither here nor there; but it is part of the normal use of land, to make use, upon your land, in the matter of construction, of what particular type and what particular depth of foundations and particular height of building may be reasonable, in the circumstances, and in view of the developments of the day. I am unable to take the view that any of these operations was of such an abnormal character so as to justify treating the disturbance created by it, and the whole of the disturbance created by it, as constituting a nuisance.

Sir Wilfred then stated that, in appropriate circumstances, it was permissible to use pneumatic hammers in order to effect the demolition of the existing structure. However, he accepted that the amount of dust which emanated from the site was excessive and he found that there was an actionable nuisance on this basis. He went on to make a number of general observations:

> Those who say that their interference with the comfort of their neighbours is justified because their operations are normal and usual and conducted with proper care and skill are under a specific duty, if they wish to make good that defence, to use that reasonable and proper care and skill. It is not a correct attitude to say: 'We will go on and do what we like until somebody complains.' That is not their duty to their neighbours. Their duty is to take proper precautions, and to see that the nuisance is reduced to a minimum. It is no answer for them to say: 'But this would mean that we should have to do the work more slowly than we would like to do it', or 'it would involve putting us to some extra expense.' All those questions are matters of common sense and degree, and quite clearly it would be unreasonable to expect people to conduct their work so slowly or so expensively, for the purpose of preventing a transient inconvenience, that the cost and trouble would be prohibitive. It is all a question of fact and degree, and must necessarily be so. . . . The use of reasonable care and skill in connection with matters of this kind may take various forms. It may take the form of restricting the hours during which work is to be done; it may take the form of limiting the amount of a particular type of work which is being done simultaneously within a particular area; it may take the form of using proper scientific means of avoiding inconvenience. Whatever form it takes, it has to be done, and those who do not do it must not be surprised if they have to pay the penalty for disregarding their neighbours' rights.

The position, then, appears to be: it is acceptable to undertake construction works even if this causes inconvenience to one's neighbours provided that one uses reasonable care and skill in order to protect the neighbours' enjoyment of their. land. Today, fumes, dust, noise and other such inconveniences should be minimised by the use of dust shields, noise shields and other measures which may reasonably be employed.

21.2.3   Nuisance caused by withdrawal of support owed to neighbouring land

Since the law of nuisance concerns all the various ways in which one's acts may affect the integrity of, and enjoyment of, adjacent land, it follows that the law concerning support for neighbouring land comes within the ambit of nuisance. It is, however, as we shall see, a curious feature of the English law of support that one owes a duty to support adjacent land by minerals but not by water. In the case of mineral support (by soil, rock and so on) the duty to support comes into being when the support has been provided for longer than twenty years. One may, however, abstract water from one's land with impunity at any stage even though this causes settlement of the neighbouring land.

Mineral support

In *Charles Dalton v Henry Angus and Company* [1881] 6 App Cas 740 two dwelling houses were built independently on the edge of their owners' land, thereby requiring support from the adjacent soil. After each had been standing for more than twenty years the plaintiff's house was converted into a factory in 1849. The internal structure was modified whereby internal walls were removed and the new structure caused a greater weight to pass onto the foundations adjacent to the neighbour's land. Consequently the requirement for support from the adjacent soil increased. This conversion was made openly. Twenty-seven years later, the plaintiff's neighbours engaged a contractor to demolish the house, and to make an excavation; the contractor was bound by the contract to shore up the plaintiff's land and make good any damage. The contractor employed a subcontractor upon similar terms. When the excavation was commenced by the subcontractor, the plaintiff's heavily loaded foundation was deprived of support, it sank and the structure collapsed. The plaintiff sued the owner of the land upon which the excavation was made and the contractor. It was held that they were liable in nuisance.

Water support

In climatic conditions such as those which exist in the UK, the water table is generally close to the ground surface, usually one or two metres below it. If the water table is lowered for any reason, the effective stresses in the soil increase which will cause settlements and this may, in turn, result in damage to structures and buildings. The ground water may be lowered in a number of ways including the deliberate pumping in order to provide a water supply or to facilitate the construction of ground works. A problem arises when the water table in one parcel of land is lowered as a result of the abstraction of water from a nearby parcel of land. The fact that soil layers tend to lie in roughly horizontal strata which are interconnected means that the effects of abstraction can be felt over a wide area, especially when pumping from permeable soils such as gravels and sands.

The lowering of ground water through abstraction may be thought of as the withdrawal of water support. However, the law treats the withdrawal of water support and the withdrawal of mineral support very differently. It allows one to abstract water from one's own land, irrespective of the consequences. The reason for this appears to be the long-established historical right to abstract water. The courts' approach to this situation is illustrated by the case of *Langbrook Properties Ltd v Surrey County Council and others* [1969] 3 All ER 1424. Here the plaintiff developers owned a site at Sunbury-on-Thames which they were developing by erecting shops, offices and residences. During the construction of the M3 motorway, there was a need to divert an aqueduct and in order to do this a number of excavations needed to be made adjacent to the plaintiff's development. In order to keep the excavations dry, dewatering was undertaken by pumping. As a result some of the plaintiff's buildings, including a thirteen-storey office block, experienced differential settlements. The plaintiff sued the county council as agents for the Ministry of Transport for the M3 construction, the statutory water authority and two contractors who were carrying out the work. Mr Justice Plowman held that one has an unfettered right to abstract water from one's land and hence no action in nuisance could lie against any of the defendants who were each acting within their rights. In the subsequent case of *Stephens v Anglian Water Authority* [1987] 1 WLR 1381 the plaintiff attempted to circumvent the rule of the law of nuisance by suing in negligence. The Court of Appeal, however, reaffirmed a landowner's right to abstract water whatever the damage to his or her neighbour's property.

Note: Landowners will often require a licence to abstract water.

21.2.4   Liability for failure to remedy a nuisance situation

In many situations a nuisance situation may be created without any act of the person who occupies or controls the land. The law is that once the occupier is aware that a nuisance situation has developed, there is an obligation to take reasonable remedial action. Thus when an occupier of a site lets out work to a contractor and later finds that the contractor is causing a nuisance, the occupier must take reasonable steps to abate that nuisance. The same rule applies whether the nuisance is caused by trespassers (see *Sedleigh Denfield v O'Callaghan* below) or by purely natural causes (see *Leakey v National Trust* below).

In *Sedleigh Denfield v O'Callaghan* [1940] AC 880 a local authority trespassed on the defendant's land and caused a nuisance by placing a grid incorrectly on a culvert which they had installed in a ditch. The defendant came to know of the nuisance. The grid caused flooding which damaged the plaintiff's land. The House of Lords held the defendant liable. Lord Wright said

> The liability for a nuisance is not, at least in modern law, a strict or absolute liability. If the defendant by himself or those for whom he is responsible has created what constitutes a nuisance and if it causes damage, the difficulty now being considered does not arise. But he may have taken over the nuisance, ready made as it were, when he acquired the property, or the nuisance may be due to a latent defect or to the act of a trespasser, or stranger. Then he is not liable unless he continued or adopted the nuisance, or, more accurately, did not without undue delay remedy it when he became aware of it, or

with ordinary and reasonable care should have become aware of it. This rule seems to be in accordance with good sense and convenience.

In *Leakey and others v National Trust for Places of Historic Interest or Natural Beauty* [1980] 1 QB 485 the defendants owned and occupied a conical hill. Homes belonging to the plaintiffs stood at the foot of the hill. Although there was some evidence that some parts of the hill had, in the distant past, been steepened by human activity, it was accepted for the purposes of the appeal that the hill was in its purely natural state. In 1976 a very dry summer, followed by a very wet autumn, caused the Keuper marl from which the hill was formed to slip and to encroach upon the plaintiffs' property. The defendants refused to remedy the problem on the grounds that since the hill was in a purely natural state its slippage was a natural event for which they bore no liability. However, the Court of Appeal unanimously decided that the National Trust was liable.

21.2.5 Defences

The principal defences to actions in nuisance when facts normally sufficient to constitute a nuisance are established are those of common law right and of statutory authority.

Much construction work is carried out under statutory authority and the limits of this defence thus have an important effect on the liability of those such as local authorities, the majority of whose works are constructed in pursuance of their various statutory powers. The leading authority on the question of statutory authority is *Manchester Corporation v Farnworth* [1930] AC 171 which involved the building and subsequent operation of a power station which was sanctioned by statute. The plaintiffs claimed that their fields and the crops thereon were destroyed by fumes emitted from the defendants' power station. The defendants pleaded that the Manchester Corporation Act 1914 entitled them to erect the power station. Viscount Dunedin said

> The serious character of the nuisance naturally makes one reflect on the magnitude of the nuisance which would be caused by stations far bigger than this one, and that such stations are likely in the near future to be established is certain. That brings me to say a word or two on what I conceive to be the well settled law on such matters. The cases are numerous. . . . I believe their whole effect may be expressed in a very few sentences. When Parliament has authorised a certain thing to be made or done or done in a certain place, there can be no action for nuisance caused by the making or doing of that thing if the nuisance is the inevitable result of the making or doing so authorised. The onus of proving that the result is inevitable is on those who wish to escape liability for nuisance, but the criterion of inevitability is not what is theoretically possible but what is possible according to the state of scientific knowledge at the time, having also in view a certain common sense appreciation which cannot be rigidly defined, of practical feasibility in view of situation and of expense . . . the defendants have not discharged the onus incumbent on them.

The category of common law right to create what would otherwise be an actionable nuisance is of very limited ambit, but includes the line of cases on water abstraction which decide that it is lawful to abstract water from one's own land, and that any damage caused by such abstraction is no nuisance (see Section 21.2.3).

21.3 The rule in *Rylands v Fletcher*

21.3.1 Elements of the tort in *Rylands v Fletcher*

The rule in *Rylands v Fletcher* has already been defined in the introduction to this chapter. In regard to this definition the following questions may be asked: What 'things' fall within the rule? What is meant by 'collects and keeps there'? What constitutes an 'escape'? What is meant by 'non-natural use'? These questions are addressed below. First, however, it is instructive to examine the facts of the case which caused the court to establish the new head of liability which is now known as the rule in *Rylands v Fletcher*.

In order to improve the water supply to their mill in Lancashire the defendants sought to construct a reservoir. They obtained a permit to build on the land of a local landowner, Lord Wilton. Lord Wilton had also granted mining rights to the plaintiffs, and the mines extended close to the location of the proposed reservoir. The defendants engaged reputable engineers to perform the reservoir construction. During the course of that construction the engineers came across disused mine shafts (which in fact connected to the plaintiffs' mine) and attempted to seal them. But they did not seal them properly. When the reservoir was filled, the seals did not hold back the water and the plaintiffs' mine was inundated. Lord Cairns put the matter like this:

> My Lords, the principles on which this case must be determined appear to me to be extremely simple. The defendants, treating them as the owners or occupiers of the close on which the reservoir was constructed, might lawfully have used that close for any purpose for which it might in the ordinary course of the enjoyment of land be used; and if, in what I may term the natural use of that land, there had been any accumulation of water, either on the surface or underground, and if, by the operation of the laws of nature, that accumulation of water had passed off into the close occupied by the plaintiff, the plaintiff could not have complained that that result had taken place. If he had desired to guard himself against it, it would have laid upon him to have done so, by leaving, or by interposing, some barrier between his close and the close of the defendants in order to have prevented that operation of the laws of nature. . . . On the other hand if the defendants, not stopping at the natural use of their close, had desired to use it for any purpose which I may term a non-natural use, for the purpose of introducing into the close that which in its natural condition was not in or upon it, for the purpose of introducing water either above or below ground in quantities and in a manner not the result of any work or operation on or under the land – and if in consequence of their doing so, or in consequence of any imperfection in the mode of their doing so, the water came to escape and pass off into the close of the plaintiff, then it appears to me that that which the defendants were doing they were doing at their own peril; and, if in the course of their doing it, the evil arose to which I have referred, the evil, namely, of the escape of the water and its passing away to the close of the plaintiff and injuring the plaintiff, then for the consequence of that, in my opinion, the defendants would be liable.

What 'things' fall within the rule?
The 'thing' must be tangible. It is not, however, necessary that it be dangerous. In the case of *Rylands v Fletcher* itself the thing in question was water which is not inherently dangerous except when it is accumulated in large quantities. The test is whether the thing will cause mischief if it escapes.

What is meant by 'collects and keeps there'?
It is necessary that the defendant brings the thing onto his or her land and collects it there. Note, however, that if things naturally on the land such as rock and soil escape through the agency of something which has been accumulated (for example explosives) this may also be caught by the rule.

What constitutes an 'escape'?
Viscount Simon said in *Read v Lyons* [1947] AC 156 that the appropriate test of escape is for there to be an 'escape from a place where the defendant has occupation or control over land to a place which is outside his occupation or control'.

What is meant by 'non-natural use'?
This requirement considerably restricts the ambit of the rule in *Rylands v Fletcher*. But there is considerable uncertainty as to the test to be applied. In *Rylands*, Lord Cairns seemed to suggest that a wide range of things might be considered not naturally on land, including, for example, grazing cattle. This would indicate that, for instance, the accumulation of fuels and other potentially dangerous substances on a construction site would be within the ambit of the rule. This wide interpretation of non-natural use does not, however, appear to have found favour in the courts on subsequent occasions when the matter has come for decision. In the Privy Council in *Rickards v Lothian* [1913] AC 263 the plaintiff had experienced damage because a water tap in a property above that owned by the plaintiff overflowed. The action was based on the rule in *Rylands*. Lord Moulton observed

> The provision of a proper supply of water to the various parts of a house is not only reasonable but has become, in accordance with modern sanitary views, an almost necessary feature of town life. It is recognised as being so desirable in the interests of the community that in some form or other it is usually made obligatory in civilised countries. Such a supply cannot be installed without causing some concurrent danger of leakage or overflow. It would be unreasonable for the law to regard those who install or maintain such a system of supply as doing so at their peril, with an absolute liability for any damage resulting from its presence even when there has been no negligence.

21.3.2 Is the rule in *Rylands v Fletcher* important for modern construction?

The approach of the modern courts to the meaning of 'non-natural use' tends to suggest that the normal accumulation of building materials, fuel for construction, water stored for use in the construction and so on probably constitutes a 'natural use' of land. This may readily be justified in economic terms, for while such accumulations are primarily for the benefit of individual employers in the accomplishment of their construction work, that construction itself benefits society generally in the same way that the provision of water supply benefits society. The fact that the courts are likely to find that most accumulations on site, even if they are liable to do damage should an escape occur, involve a natural use of land, suggests that the rule in *Rylands v Fletcher* is of little significance in the construction industry today. The torts of nuisance and negligence, it might be suggested, will supply a remedy in appropriate cases. The basic problem is that the purpose the 'rule' is to serve has never been clearly identified and defined. Therefore, the law has tended to drift back to nuisance and negligence, the aims of which are clear and sustainable. The fact remains, however, that the decision in *Rylands* itself remains in force and if facts sufficiently similar to those of the original decision were to recur, all courts except the House of Lords would be obliged to follow it.

Part 4

Miscellaneous topics in construction law

Damages for breach of contract and breach of tortious obligations

22.1 Introduction

'Damages' is the term used by the law to indicate the compensation awarded by a court or other tribunal to a party who has succeeded in his or her case. It is a sum of money which stands in the place of the loss which the successful party has experienced as a result of the breach of the duty owed by the other party.

Generally speaking, the question of the damages to be awarded as a result of the breach of tortious and contractual obligations requires the same considerations, although the object of awarding damages in each case is slightly different. Damages in contract are awarded to place the innocent party in the position he or she would have been in had the contract been completed; damages in tort are awarded to put the innocent party in the position he or she would have been in if nothing had happened, that is to say, if the tort had not occurred.

22.2 Causation

22.2.1 General observations

Plaintiffs who allege negligence or breach of contract must show that the defendants not only owe them a duty (whether in contract or tort) and are in breach of that duty, but that they have caused damage for which they can recover. This involves a consideration of three matters:

- Is there a causative link between the damage suffered and the breach of the duty or obligation?
- Is the damage sufficiently proximate to the breach for a reasonable person to be able to say that it was the breach which caused it?
- Is the damage of a type which is reasonably foreseeable?

The first question relates to the physical reality ('Did the defendant in fact cause the damage?') and is often answered by expert evidence. The second and third questions are posed by the law in order to limit the liability of defendants to those plaintiffs who are most immediately and most significantly affected by the breach of duty. Unless all three questions can be answered in the affirmative the plaintiff will be unable to recover the loss as damages.

22.2.2   The 'but for . . .' test

The test used to determine whether the plaintiff's damage has been sustained as a result of the defendant's breach is often termed the 'but for . . .' test. In *Cork v Kirby Maclean Ltd* [1952] 2 All ER 402 Lord Denning remarked that 'If the damage would not have happened *but for* a particular fault, then that fault is the cause of the damage; if it would have happened just the same, fault or no fault, the fault is not the cause of the damage'. A clear example of this is found in *Barnett v Chelsea and Kensington Hospital Management Committee* [1969] 1 QB 428 where a doctor refused to treat a patient and the patient later died. The doctor was, however, found not liable because by the time the patient presented himself for treatment he was so ill that no treatment was possible. Accordingly it could not be said that *but for* the doctor's failure to treat the patient, he would not have died.

This particular rule is often of importance in construction. For example, a person who buys a plot of land upon which to construct a building may afterwards employ a ground investigation contractor to survey the site; if the contractor fails to detect bad ground conditions the owner may feel aggrieved when he finds the bad ground during the construction phase of the works. But what is the site-owner's loss? He may have to spend a considerable sum in geotechnical improvement; but the ground investigation contractor did not cause this loss – he merely failed to recognise that it was an inevitable occurrence. If, however, the site-owner had not, at the time of the ground investigation, yet bought the site, and relied upon the ground investigation in buying it, then he can argue that the site investigation contractor has caused the loss; but he will have to show that he would not have bought the site if he had known of the bad ground – otherwise the loss would again have been suffered in any event and so the ground investigation contractor could not have caused it. In this type of case it is often difficult for the site-owner to prove causation against the ground investigation contractor in respect of the general cost of the site or the works. However, consider the following heads of claim which may, in appropriate circumstances, be successfully pursued.

- If the ground investigation contractor's report, having failed to identify problems on the site, suggested a certain system of operations on site which had to be drastically revised when the problem came to light, the ground investigation contractors might well be said to have caused the costs of delay and disruption suffered in excess of those which would have been expended if the bad ground had been identified at the outset.
- If expensive ground works or foundations are required, because of the bad ground conditions; and, if there was sufficient space on site to build on more suitable ground, if only the site-owner had known of the

poor ground conditions in the current location, he might successfully argue that he would have erected the building in that more favourable location and hence would have saved money overall in so doing.

- If the site-owner had known the additional cost of the work due to the bad ground conditions he would not have commenced construction but would have used the site for a different purpose which in all the circumstances would have been a sounder investment, then he may claim that the contractor has caused him loss.

In the situations outlined it will be observed that what the site-owner is attempting to do is to identify a loss for which he can say: 'but for the ground investigation contractor's ineffective survey I would not have to pay this cost'. He will not be able to recover except those losses for which he can show that the 'but for' test applies. The onus will be upon the plaintiff to show that his loss would not have been sustained but for the defendant's breach and this will be a question of fact to be proved by evidence.

22.2.3   Complicating factors

Usually the 'but for . . .' test is adequate to determine causation. However, in some instances where more than one cause contributes to the plaintiff's damage there are complicating factors which must be considered. These will not be dealt with here in any detail. They include pre-existing conditions (e.g. the property in respect of which a negligence claim is made was already damaged: see, for example, *Performance Cars v Abraham* [1962] 1 QB 33), the situation where there are multiple causes (e.g. the contractor negligently constructs work which has been negligently designed by another person) and subsequent interventions (e.g. the property in respect of which a negligence claim is made is subsequently damaged: see, for example, *Jobling v Associated Dairies* [1982] AC 794 and *Baker v Willoughby* [1970] AC 467).

22.2.4   Third party 'contribution' to the plaintiff

Normally the plaintiff will sue for losses which he has actually incurred. Indeed, the general rule is that he is only entitled to sue for those losses he has actually experienced. But in a number of situations a plaintiff who receives what might be loosely termed a 'contribution' from a third party, and hence suffers no actual financial loss, is still entitled to sue for substantial damages. One such situation is where the plaintiff is insured and his loss is made good by an insurance company.

A construction industry problem which has caused some recent debate is where an employer has a building constructed and then sells it with defects at the full market rate without warranting its good condition or, alternatively, lets it out at the market rate on a full repairing and insuring lease. In such a case the employer, under the construction contract, has suffered no loss. That loss falls on the buyer or tenant, as the case may be. But does this mean that the employer's good fortune in making the deal on the terms he did allows the defaulting contractor to avoid any financial liability for his breaches of contract? In short, may the employer still sue the contractor for the full value of the defects in the building? In *Linden Gardens Trust Ltd v Lenesta Sludge Disposals* 57 BLR 57 Lord Justice Staughton discussed this issue:

> When a plaintiff's initial loss has subsequently been made good by someone other than himself, the general rule is that he can recover only nominal damages. But there are certainly exceptions. An obvious example, which occurs every day, is when a plaintiff has been compensated by his insurers; nevertheless he may sue in his own name and recover substantial damages, although he may be bound to pay them over to his insurers. Another example is to be found in the case of *Design 5 v Keniston Housing Association Ltd* 34 BLR 92. There the loss of the counter-claiming defendants had been or would be made good by a grant from the Department of the Environment. It was held that the defendants could nevertheless recover substantial damages. Judge Smout QC regarded the test as being whether the recovery was *relevant* to the harm suffered, or whether it was *res inter alios acta* [meaning an irrelevant third party intervention which should not affect the rights of the plaintiff]; money received by way of insurance or benevolence was merely an example of a recovery that was not relevant . . .
>
>   . . . I find it difficult to suggest a comprehensive definition of the circumstances in which compensation derived from some third party is irrelevant . . . It may be that one has to fall back on what Viscount Haldane, the Lord Chancellor, said in *British Westinghouse Electric and Manufacturing Co v Underground Electric Railways of London* [1912] AC 673 (at page 688): 'The quantum of damages is a question of fact, and the only guidance which the law can give is to lay down general principles which afford at times but scanty assistance'.
>
>   In the particular case of damage to a building which is later sold, in my judgment there is no rule of law that the damages must necessarily be nominal. If, however, a subsequent owner also has a claim in his own right in respect of the same damage, the law must find some solution to prevent double recovery. It may be that in such a case one should consider which is the more appropriate plaintiff to recover on the facts.

22.3   Remoteness and foreseeability

When discussing limits on the recoverability of damages for breaches of duty, lawyers tend (though this is not invariably the case) to consider the rules for breaches of tortious and contractual obligations separately; for tort, the test of 'remoteness' is used while for contract the test of 'reasonable foreseeability' is used. In practice, however, both amount very much to the same thing.

22.3.1   Tort: the remoteness test

In *Overseas Tankship (UK) Ltd v Morts Dock & Engineering Co (The Wagon Mound (No 1))* [1961] AC 388 the defendants negligently allowed oil to escape from their ship. The oil spread across the water in the harbour. The plaintiffs owned a wharf into which the oil drifted. The plaintiffs were undertaking welding work in their wharf and, after receiving advice that the oil was not flammable, they continued to weld. The oil did, however, catch fire and the wharf was badly damaged. The plaintiffs sued for this damage. The Privy Council held that the damage was not reasonably foreseeable since at that time it was thought that such oil could not catch fire while floating on water. The damage which occurred had to be of foreseeable type if it was to be recoverable. It was of no assistance to the plaintiffs that the defendants could foresee some damage to the plaintiffs' wharf from, say, oil pollution.

22.3.2 Contract: reasonable foreseeability

In *Hadley v Baxendale* [1854] 9 Ex 341 the Court of Exchequer handed down what has become the classic statement on the damages which may be recovered as a result of a breach of contract:

> Where two parties have made a contract which one of them has broken, the damage which the other party ought to receive in respect of such breach of contract should be such as may fairly and reasonably be considered as either arising naturally i.e. according to the usual course of things, from such breach of contract itself, or such as may reasonably be supposed to have been in the contemplation of both parties at the time they made the contract as the probable result of such breach of it.

There are two distinct heads (or limbs as they are normally called). The first relates to the damage which may be recovered in the general case, while the second, often termed 'special damages', which can be recovered only if the plaintiff advises the defendant at the time of making the contract that he may experience these losses in the event of a breach.

Clearly the limbs of *Hadley v Baxendale* are associated with what may be termed 'foreseeability'. The first limb allows damages to be recovered if they are objectively foreseeable; the second limb allows damages which are deemed to be foreseeable by virtue of the fact that they have been mentioned at the time the duty arises. In *The Heron II* [1969] 1 AC 350 Lord Reid explained the test of foreseeability that would be applied:

> The crucial question is whether, on the information available to the defendant when the contract was made, he should, or the reasonable man in his position would, have realised that such loss was sufficiently likely to result from the breach of contract to make it proper to hold that the loss flowed naturally from the breach or that loss of that kind should have been within his contemplation.

22.4 Allegations by the defendant that cost of remedial works or of consequent losses are irrecoverable

22.4.1 Allegations that the plaintiff has failed to mitigate his or her loss

The defendant is liable for losses which flow from the breach and which are reasonably foreseeable. This rule is, however, subject to an important qualification, often called 'the duty to mitigate', meaning the plaintiff's duty to mitigate the loss he or she experiences as a result of the defendant's breach. If, for instance, a contractor is wrongfully ejected from the site by the employer on the first day of the project, the contractor's loss is, on first impression, the whole of the anticipated profit from the project.

However, rarely will the contractor be able to claim this sum in full, for he will have a duty to mitigate. In practice this means that he must put his men, plant and the other resources to work elsewhere. If the market is good for contractors he will readily find that they can be put on work as profitable as the project from which they have been evicted. It will, in such circumstances, be difficult for the contractor to claim more than the cost of the preliminary work which he has undertaken in maintaining his resources, moving them to site for the project and removing them again. If, however, the construction market is in a depressed state the contractor might not be able to obtain any work except at low prices, and there will in this case be an additional measure of damages which will be based on the difference in the prices for work agreed with the defaulting employer and the lower prices forced on the contractor by the breach of the defaulting employer.

Lord Haldane in *British Westinghouse Electric and Manufacturing Co v Underground Electric Railways of London* [1912] AC 673 put the rule as follows:

> The fundamental basis [of the general rule] is thus compensation for pecuniary loss naturally flowing from the breach; but this first principle is qualified by a second, which imposes on a plaintiff the duty of taking all reasonable steps to mitigate the loss consequent on the breach, and debars him from claiming any part of the damage which is due to his neglect to take such steps.

However, Sir John Donaldson, in *The Solholt* [1983] 1 Ll Rep 605, pointed out that to say that the plaintiff is under a duty to mitigate is slightly misleading. He has no duty to do anything, but he can claim damages only insofar as that damage could not have been avoided by his reasonable mitigation of it. What is reasonable in each case is a question of fact. In *Payzu Ltd v Saunders* [1919] 2 KB 581, for instance, the defendants refused to honour a contract to supply certain goods to the plaintiff, but they then said they would supply the goods if the plaintiff paid on terms more favourable to the defendants. The Court of Appeal held that, if that was the most appropriate way for the plaintiff to mitigate his loss, it was reasonable to expect him to obtain the goods from the party in breach at the increased price.

22.4.2 Allegations that the plaintiff has had the remedial works carried out to negligent excess

It often happens that an employer who finds defects in his building calls upon a consultant to advise him both as to the necessary remedial works and as to the liability of the parties involved in the construction of the works. If that consultant advises him to undertake certain remedial works the employer is, generally, entitled to rely upon that advice and to carry out those works. He may then subsequently sue the party or parties liable for the cost of the remedial works. On occasions, however, the defendants object to the magnitude of damages claimed; they claim, in effect, that the plaintiff employer has expended an excessive amount on remedial works which it would be unreasonable for him to claim against them.

One recent case where this argument was raised was *The Board of Governors of the Hospital for Sick Children v McLaughlin and Harvey plc and others* (1987) Constr LJ Vol 6 No 3 p. 245. This case involved the new cardiac wing for the Great Ormond Street Hospital which was built between 1977 and 1980. Shortly after the construction was finished a beam collapsed and the hospital commenced actions against the contractor, the architect and the structural engineer. In order to investigate the damage the hospital engaged an expert, Dr Christie, who made extensive recommendations concerning remedial works which were necessary to ensure that the building was safe. These recommendations had already been implemented at the date of the trial. The defendants, however, considered that the remedial works were excessive and an issue arose as to the amount that the hospital could recover. Judge Newey held that the crucial factor was whether or not Dr Christie's advice was negligent. This was relevant because, if the hospital had acted on negligent expert advice (and had executed more remedial works at a greater cost than was reasonable), this was not something the defendants could have foreseen. His Honour indicated in the following passage that a defendant should foresee that a plaintiff will consult experts and act on their advice:

> The plaintiff who carries out either repair or reinstatement of his property must act reasonably. He can only recover as damages the costs which the defendants ought reasonably to have foreseen that he would incur and the defendant would not have foreseen unreasonable expenditure. Reasonable costs do not, however, mean the minimum amount which, with hindsight, it could be held would have sufficed. When the nature of the repairs is such that the plaintiff can only make them with the assistance of expert advice the defendant should have foreseen that he would take such advice and be influenced by it.

If that expert advice is negligent, however, that may break the chain of causation so that the defendant might not be responsible for the cost incurred on negligent advice. His Honour made the following comments:

> Since the hospital were acting on Dr Christie's advice, if he were negligent that would break the chain. . . . Dr Christie's remedial proposals, requiring the removal of one slab level, removal of services, extensive excavations, greatly enlarged reinforced pile caps, reinforcement of pile rafts and many additional piles, were undoubtedly extensive and expensive. They were the product of caution and a resolve not to leave anything to chance, which could be reasonably avoided. . . . Dr Christie . . . was the engineer in actual charge of the remedial works. In my judgment his proposals were within the range of those which an ordinary competent engineer would have adopted. He was not negligent.

In *Frost and another v Moody Homes Ltd & others* (1989) CILL 504, a case decided by Judge Newey subsequent to the *Governors of the Hospital for Sick Children* case, however, the situation was different. In *Frost v Moody* a home-owner sought advice concerning cracks which had developed in the house. The advice he received was to install expensive new foundations to remedy the damage. However, it seemed that the advice was over-cautious and that the house had never been in peril. All that was required was redecoration to cover up the existing cracking. Accordingly, the owners could not recover the cost of installing the new foundations. Judge Newey said

> To recommend new foundations at a cost of £60 000 or more was in those circumstances not to be perfectionist as was the plaintiff's engineer in the *Governors of the Hospital for Sick Children* case, but to fail to exercise the care to be expected of the ordinary competent engineer.

These two cases highlight the dilemma which many employers face when defects are found. Employers naturally wish their advisers to err on the side of caution when recommending appropriate remedial works, but if those recommendations are far too cautious they will not be able to recover the cost of implementing them.

22.4.3   Allegations that the remedial works constitute betterment

The term 'betterment' refers to the situation where an employer who discovers defects in the work is alleged to have remedied it to a higher standard than required by the original contract. The law on this point is succinctly set out by Judge Newey in *Richard Roberts Holdings Ltd and another v Douglas Smith Stimson Partnership and others* 46 BLR 50:

> If the only practicable method of overcoming the consequences of a defendant's breach of contract is to build to a higher standard than the contract had required, the plaintiff may recover the cost of building to that higher standard. If, however, a plaintiff, needing to carry out works because of a defendant's breach of contract, chooses to build to a higher standard than is strictly necessary, the courts will, unless the new works are so different as to break the chain of causation, award him the cost of the works less a credit to the defendant in respect of betterment.

22.5   Where the sums recoverable are quantified by the contract

Parties often include, in their agreement, clauses which regulate what 'compensation' (to use a broad term) is to be paid in certain circumstances. The circumstances may amount to a breach or they may simply be an event which is catered for in the contract. Where the level of compensation is set for breaches, the compensation is referred to as 'liquidated damages', that is to say damages for breach of contract which are of a liquidated or ascertained amount. When the event which triggers the compensation is not a breach of contract the sums payable are not properly classed as damages, for the payment is made under contract terms, not in breach of contract terms.

22.5.1   Where the contract provides for additional sums in circumstances which do not amount to breach

Typical examples of where the contract provides for payment in certain circumstances which do not amount to a breach are as follows.

Variations to work ordered in accordance with the contract
One common feature of construction is that the design often changes during the currency of the works or the extent of the work changes from

what was anticipated at the time of making the contract. Most construction contracts contain a 'variations clause' which entitles the employer or his or her certifier to vary the works and to value the variation so that both the work and the price are changed. Such contracts tend to provide rules for computing the value of variations.

Loss and expense clauses
Construction efficiency tends to be highly dependent on the availability of information, access to the site, access to workfronts, storage, work space, interference by other contractors, subcontractors and so on. A single contract price can yield high profits or result in significant losses depending on the site conditions and hence many contracts contain 'loss and expense' provisions which provide a contractual mechanism whereby the contractor can receive additional remuneration if he is adversely affected by specified causes.

If no loss and expense provision (or similar provisions such as those in a re-measurement contract, which allow increases in rates for work done in circumstances which were not envisaged at the time of making the contract) is included in the contract, the contractor whose work is delayed and disrupted must rest any claim on a breach of contract and seek to recover damages for breach. The problem here is that the contract must show that 'availability of information, access to the site' and other factors which he claims have hampered his work are covered by appropriate contractual terms. If there are express terms covering these matters then no problem exists; but otherwise it will be necessary to show that such terms are implied in the contract.

While such clauses do not relate to breaches of contract it seems that many of the same considerations will apply in computing the financial consequences. For instance, if a variation is ordered the contractor will, it is submitted, have an obligation to re-plan his work so that it will proceed with reasonable efficiency.

22.5.2 Liquidated damages clauses

Liquidated damages are all those sums which have been reduced to a fixed sum by the contract and which are payable upon the breach of contract by the party required to make the payment. They may be contrasted with 'unliquidated damages' which have not been reduced to a defined sum and which are the normal damages recoverable upon a breach of contract.

Liquidated damages are used in a variety of situations including

- liquidated damages for delay: expressed as a certain amount of money per unit of time (e.g. per hour, per day, per month, etc.).
- liquidated damages for inefficiency in the completed works: many projects for power and process plants include machinery which is designed to produce a specified output for a specified input (e.g. of power for a power station, chemicals for a chemical plant). The

contractor is often responsible for installing equipment which meets the specification. Any shortfall in the plant efficiency will often be dealt with by liquidated damages.

A number of rules have been defined by the courts in connection with liquidated damages:

- a liquidated damages clause may not be used to penalise a breach excessively and the sums payable may be no greater than a sum representing a genuine pre-estimate of the likely damages which would normally flow from the breach. Accordingly if it is clear that a liquidated damage clause is a penalty clause then the courts will not enforce it but will treat the damages as unliquidated and will assess them (see *Dunlop Pneumatic Tyre Company v New Garage and Motor Company* [1915] AC 79).
- a liquidated damages clause may be used to limit the damages payable. In *Temloc v Errill Properties Ltd* 39 BLR 30, for instance, the word 'nil' had been inserted as the rate of liquidated damages in a standard printed form of contract. The Court of Appeal decided that this meant that the rate was £0 and that this was 'an exhaustive agreement as to the damages which are or are not to be payable by the contractor in the event of his failure to complete the works on time' (per Lord Justice Nourse).

22.6   Practical aspects relating to the quantification of damages/claims

In practice, a number of difficulties arise in quantifying a claim for damages or a claim under the contract. First, the plaintiff must show the basis on which the damages are recoverable; second, he or she must prove the precise loss sustained (and in so doing must attribute each item of loss to a breach); third, there are difficulties quantifying some types of damage such as inconvenience.

22.6.1   Identifying the basis of quantification

The decided cases show a range of techniques used by the court to determine the measure of damage which the plaintiff is entitled to recover. If, for instance, a contractor fails to perform part of a building contract it may be appropriate to assess the damage on the basis of the amount that the employer's property is less valuable by reason of the contractor's failure to perform; or alternatively it may be appropriate to assess the damage on the basis of the cost to the employer to have the work executed which the contractor failed to perform.

The cases show that the courts do not lay down precise rules for computing damages. They provide simple principles and it is for the plaintiff to show that his method of calculating the damage for which he contends is reasonable. In *Radford v Defroberville* 7 BLR 35 Mr Justice Oliver said that the starting-point for the applicable principle was the statement by Baron Parke in *Robinson v Harman* [1848] 1 Exch 850 that

The rule of common law is, that where a party sustains a loss by reason of a breach of contract, he is, so far as money can do it, to be placed in the same situation, with respect to damages, as if the contract had been performed.

Mr Justice Oliver then went on to say that the measure of damage could not be determined in the abstract and that the court does not disregard the hopes and aspirations or the individual predilections of the particular plaintiff in applying that basic principle.

22.6.2 Remedying defective work: is the appropriate measure of damage the diminution in value or cost of the work?

The question of the appropriate method of computing damages for defective work is of great importance in construction law. Various bases for calculation may be suggested including the diminution in value of the building and the cost of repair. Often the building experiences only a small diminution in value despite the defective work whereas the cost of remedying that work is very costly. In such a case the contractor will attempt to have damages calculated on a diminution basis while the employer will seek to recover the cost of the remedial work.

In *East Ham Borough Council v Bernard Sunley Ltd* [1966] AC 406, Lord Cohen said

> the learned editors of *Hudson's Building and Engineering Contracts*, 8th Edition (1959) say at p. 319 that there are in fact three possible bases of assessing damages, namely (a) the cost of reinstatement; (b) the difference in cost to the builder of the actual work done and work specified; or (c) the diminution in value of the work done due to the breach of contract. They go on: 'There is no doubt that *whenever it is reasonable* for the employer to insist upon reinstatement the courts will treat the cost of reinstatement as the measure of damage'.

Non-compliance with the specification may have a number of practical effects and it is suggested that it is not possible to decide how damages should be calculated without a consideration of these effects. These may be classified as follows:

- it may render the construction different from what was agreed (e.g. by installing artificial stone paving instead of natural stone)
- it may render the works unsafe (e.g. poorly secured cladding)
- it may render the works less valuable (e.g. the type of concrete used will reduce the working life of a building or increase maintenance costs)
- it may be unimportant both from aesthetic and engineering points of view (e.g. where the contract requires stone from Quarry A to be used but practically identical stone from Quarry B is used instead).

It is suggested that in the first and second situations reinstatement costs may reasonably be recovered. In the third, the difference in cost or diminution in value heads are more appropriate unless reinstatement is less costly. In the fourth, the difference in cost head is the fairest since, although the employer has not suffered a direct loss, it would be wrong to allow the contractor to benefit from his breach.

Reinstatement costs are never easy to calculate. The valuation of the economic effect of the inclusion of substandard materials in a structure is even more difficult and expert evidence concerning the engineering consequences will be required.

If the employer has already remedied non-compliant work or replaced the material on the advice of his or her experts the question of whether such expenditure was reasonable is to be answered by asking whether the advice received was negligent or not. The employer will be entitled to rely on non-negligent advice: *The Board of Governors of the Hospital for Sick Children v McLaughlin and Harvey plc and others* (1987) Constr LJ Vol 6 No 3 p. 245.

22.6.3   The time at which the loss is to be calculated

In *East Ham Borough Council v Bernard Sunley & Sons Ltd* [1966] AC 406 a building was handed over to the employer in 1954. Defects were later discovered and these were rectified in 1960 and 1961. In 1954 the cost would have been £17 000 but in 1960/1 it was £21 000. The House of Lords, having decided that reinstatement costs were appropriate, then decided that the 1960/1 costs were the proper quantification of damages.

22.6.4   Proving the loss

In some situations in construction, the precise cause and effect for each individual loss is difficult to establish. The reason for this is obvious to those who are regularly involved in the planning of construction work: the interactions and interrelationships between individual items are complex. This complexity may be shown on a very detailed network representation of the project, but even this does not allow the precise cause and effect relating to each change in the work to be computed because the network may be altered in the light of these changes. Since the networks will not be updated continuously but at discrete times it will not be possible to trace through individual causes and effects.

This has been recognised in *Crosby v Portland UDC* 5 BLR 121. Here the arbitrator had made an award based on a claim document which had been divided in a series of individually headed claims. In his award, however, he had granted certain sums or extensions of time in respect of certain identified heads of claim. In one part, however, he awarded an aggregate sum and an overall extension of time for a number of claims without saying how much each contributed to the total. He explained his method in the award:

> The result, in terms of delay and disorganisation, of each of the matters referred to above was a continuing one. As each matter occurred its consequences were added to the cumulative consequences of the matters which had preceded it. The delay and disorganisation which ultimately resulted was cumulative and attributable to the combined effect of all these matters. It is therefore impracticable, if not impossible, to assess the additional expense caused by delay and disorganisation due to any of these matters in isolation from the other matters.

Mr Justice Donaldson was invited to decide whether this approach was permissible. He described the situation:

> Since, however, the extent of the extra cost incurred depends upon an extremely complex interaction between the consequences of the various denials, suspensions and variations, it may well be difficult or even impossible to make an accurate apportionment of the total cost between the several causative events. An artificial apportionment could of course have been made; but why, they ask, should the arbitrator make such an apportionment which has no basis in reality? I can see no answer to this question. . . . Provided he ensures there is no duplication, I can see no reason why he should not recognise the realities of the situation and make individual awards in respect of those parts of individual items of the claim which can be dealt with in isolation and a supplementary award in respect of the remainder of these claims as a composite whole. That is what the arbitrator has done.

In *Borough of Merton v Leach* 32 BLR 51 a similar point arose, this time in respect of the JCT form contract. Mr Justice Vinelott (on page 102 of the BLR report) followed the approach of Mr Justice Donaldson in *Crosby v Portland*. Recently the case of *Wharf Properties v Eric Cumine Associates* 52 BLR 1 has been decided by the Privy Council. This case involved a set of pleadings which, by all accounts, was wholly unparticularised. Their Lordships advised that '[the present] case, whilst of obvious importance to the parties because of the sums involved, raises no question of any general importance'. However, the following statement is of value:

> Their Lordships are wholly unpersuaded by [counsel's] submission that the two cases of *J Crosby and Sons v Portland UDC* and *L B Merton v Stanley Hugh Leach Ltd* provide any basis for saying that an unparticularised pleading in this form ought to be permitted to stand. Those cases establish no more than this, that in cases where the full extent of extra costs incurred through delay depend upon a complex interaction between the consequences of various events, so that it may be difficult to make an accurate apportionment of the total extra costs, it may be proper for an arbitrator to make individual financial awards in respect of claims which can conveniently be dealt with in isolation and a supplementary award in respect of the financial consequences of the remainder as a composite whole. This has, however, no bearing upon the obligation of a plaintiff to plead his case with such particularity as is sufficient to alert the opposite party to the case which is going to be made against him at the trial.

22.6.5 Damages for inconvenience and distress

One of the important heads of damage in small domestic construction and surveying cases is inconvenience and distress. While damages for the frustration due to the messiness of the work or its duration are apparently not recoverable (see for instance *Hutchinson v Harris* (1978) 10 BLR 19), if there is inconvenience and distress to people living in the property then modest damages may be recovered. Lord Denning said in *Perry v Sidney Phillips and Sons* [1982] 1 WLR 1297:

> it seems to me that Mr Perry is entitled to damages for all the vexation, distress and worry he has been caused by reason of the negligence of the surveyor.

All this worry and distress may nowadays be the subject of compensation. Not excessive, but modest compensation.

In *Watts and Watts v Morrow* 54 BLR 86, it was said that damages are not normally available for 'distress, frustration, anxiety, displeasure, vexation, tension or aggravation' but that moderate damages are allowable for 'physical inconvenience and discomfort caused by the breach and mental suffering directly related to that inconvenience and discomfort' (per Lord Justice Bingham).

22.6.6   Interest claims

Claims pursued in arbitration or litigation tend to take a considerable time to be resolved, usually years rather than months. One effect of this is that successful claimants or plaintiffs are kept out of their money for a significant time and they should, therefore, be paid interest as compensation. However, the only general 'right' that a party has to claim interest is found in discretionary powers under the Supreme Court Act and the Arbitration Act. If the contract contains a clause relating to payment of interest then this prevails (see for instance *Morgan Grenfell (Local Authority Finance) Ltd v Seven Seas Dredging Ltd (No 2)* 51 BLR 85 which focused on the construction of the rather loosely worded interest provisions in the ICE 5th Edition contract).

In order for plaintiffs in the construction industry (and contractors in particular) to recover sensible sums as interest there have been a number of attempts to recover interest as damages under the contract. In other words the interest is not claimed *on the* damages, but *as* damages. The general rules regarding the recoverability of damages were stated in *Hadley v Baxendale* (1854) 9 Ex 341 (above). However, the best that can be said for the state of the law at the moment regarding the recoverability of interest as damages is that it is unclear and contradictory.

One would have thought that in the construction industry it was perfectly foreseeable that in the usual course of things, and without any special knowledge, the result of late payments which were properly due would be that the party kept out of his money would need to raise money to bridge the shortfall (and hence would have to pay interest) or that he would have less to invest (and so would lose interest). However, interest does not seem to be recoverable as general damages since the court would not impute to the parties' knowledge that damages flowed naturally from a delay in payment; see the Court of Appeal decision in *President of India v Lips Maritime Corporation* [1987] 3 WLR 572.

23

Joint and vicarious liability

23.1 Introduction

One of the striking features of construction is the large number of parties often involved in a piece of work. There may be an employer, main contractor, several subcontractors each with overlapping responsibilities, numerous consultants each interacting with one another and each being a potential contributor to any damage which follows, employees acting recklessly while about their employer's business and so on. It is therefore a matter of some practical importance to ask how liability is apportioned when damage is caused by more than one person, or is caused by one person under the control of another.

23.2 Joint and several liability

23.2.1 Independent and joint liability

When the plaintiff's damage has been caused by the breach of more than one defendant, the liability of those defendants may be described as independent or joint.

Independent liability refers to the situation where the defendants are not operating in concert and different elements of damage are caused by each of the defendants. In this situation, each defendant is liable only for the damage which he himself has caused. A typical example is where the plaintiff sues two consultants for negligence in respect of design defects where the breaches of each have resulted in different elements of damage.

Joint liability arises where more than one defendant is responsible for the same damage. Two situations may be distinguished. First, where more than one defendant participates in the act or event which results in the damage; for example where two consultants jointly write a negligent report which causes loss to the client who relies upon it. Second, where there are several independent breaches which are concurrent and lead to the damage; for instance where a consultant produces an inadequate design for a piece of reinforced concrete structure and the contractor then fails to supply the specified reinforcement for that piece of structure.

23.2.2   Joint liability: all defendants are liable for the plaintiff's loss

In practice the distinction between the two types of joint liability is of little importance and will not be discussed here. The basic principle is that in cases where more than one defendant is responsible for breaches leading to the plaintiff's damage each is liable for the full amount of damage suffered by the plaintiff, although, as we shall see in Section 23.3, those who have been sued successfully can seek a contribution from the other responsible parties.

Cassell & Co Ltd v Broome [1972] 1 All ER 801 involved a number of defendants, each of whom had contributed to a serious libel. Some defendants had acted recklessly and wilfully in the publication and therefore became liable to 'exemplary damages', a form of damages not normally available, but designed to punish the defendant rather than to compensate the plaintiff. However, not all the defendants sued fell in this category and the House of Lords decided that when an award of joint damages is made, the sum to be awarded must be in the lowest sum recoverable by the plaintiff against each of the defendants individually. They allowed individual additional assessments to be made against the individual defendants but these were to be the individual responsibility of each defendant and, unlike the 'lowest sum', could not be recovered from the defendant of the plaintiff's choice. Most reported cases of joint liability concern defendants each of whom is liable in tort and there seems to be little authority for the situation where one or more has a contract with the plaintiff, the terms of which diminish their liability in damages (see, however, Subsection 2(3) of the Civil Liability (Contribution) Act 1978, dealt with in Section 23.3). If the *Cassell* principle applies, plaintiffs should have regard to the likely basis of calculation of damages against each of the defendants before indiscriminately joining them all in the same action. In *Cassell*, Lord Hailsham advised

> plaintiffs who wish to differentiate between the defendants can do so in various ways, for example, by electing to sue the more guilty only, by commencing separate proceedings against each and then consolidating, or, in the case of a book or newspaper article, by suing separately for ... [the different libels alleged to have been committed, each of which had different levels of seriousness].

23.2.3   Typical situations giving rise to joint liability

Situations which give rise to joint liability in construction are common and include the following.

* Where two defendants act independently so that their breaches of duty cause the same damage; here, both are responsible for the full damage.
* Where two or more persons act in concert; for example where persons act together in a common adventure such as a partnership or joint-venture. Here, they are each liable for all the breaches of contractual and tortious duties by those acting in concert.
* Where a tort is committed by a person who is acting on behalf of

another and with the assent of that other; here both the person who actually commits the tort and his or her principal are liable.
- Where a person is acting in the course of his or her employment and commits a tort; here, both he or she and the employer are jointly liable. In this case the employer's liability is styled 'vicarious liability' and does not depend on any culpability on his or her part.

The effect of a number of defendants being responsible for the damage is that the plaintiffs will often seek to recover their damages not from the most guilty but from the most solvent defendant. This may throw an unfair burden on that defendant, and while the defendant against whom proceedings have been brought, may seek a contribution (see Section 23.3) from the other defendants it may turn out to be a permanent burden if the other defendants simply cannot pay their proportion of the damage.

23.3 Contribution and apportionment

The Civil Liability (Contribution) Act 1978 Section 1 provides that joint defendants who are sued can claim a contribution from the others in proportion to their liability. Section 2 of the Act entitles the court to apportion liability between defendants. The general principles are contained in Subsections 1(1) and 2(1) of the Act. Section 2(3) sets out the principal grounds upon which a potential contributor can defend in the event that the court takes the view that he or she has contributed to the damage.

1 Entitlement to contribution
(1) Subject to the following provisions of this section, any person liable in respect of any damage suffered by another person may recover contribution from any other person liable in respect of the same damage (whether jointly with him or otherwise).
2 Assessment of contribution
(1) Subject to subsection (3) below, in any proceedings for contribution under section 1 above the amount of the contribution recoverable from any person shall be such as may be found by the court to be just and equitable having regard to the extent of that person's responsibility for the damage in question. . . .
(3) Where the amount of the damages which have or might have been awarded . . . against the person from whom the contribution is sought was or would have been subject to

(a) any limit imposed by or under any enactment or by any agreement made before the damage occurred;
(b) any reduction by virtue of Section 1 of the Law Reform (Contributory Negligence) Act 1945. . . .

The person from whom the contribution is sought shall not . . . be required to pay . . . a greater amount than the amount of those damages as so limited or reduced.

The Contribution Act thus clearly makes provision for a contributor to set up a contractual limitation provision or a contributory negligence defence (see Section 23.6) in response to contribution proceedings.

23.4   Vicarious liability for torts

Vicarious liability exists when one person A is liable for the torts of another B. This liability is generated if two conditions are met:

- A and B have a special relationship (such as a contract of employment) whereby A exercises a degree of control over the activities of B
- the tort is related in some way to the special relationship between A and B.

The most common situation where vicarious liability arises is where an employee commits a tort; here the employer becomes vicariously liable. The rationale for vicarious liability derives from social considerations. A commercial enterprise involves profit and risk; it would not be right to allow the employer to take the profits and transfer his risks onto the public. If members of the public or other workers are injured by an employee who is engaged making a profit for his employer, the injury has been caused by the enterprise and should be compensated for by the entrepreneur. The law provides the plaintiff with a choice. They may take action against the employee or the employer and usually choose the latter.

The law recognises a distinction between employees and independent contractors. Independent contractors cannot be controlled by their 'employer' and so no vicarious liability attaches to the employer for acts of independent contractors. Accordingly, the distinction between employees (servants) and independent contractors is an important and fundamental one since servants attract vicarious liability for their employees, while independent contractors do not. The precise test to be applied in order to distinguish between independent contractors and employees is not always clear. Lord Denning said in *Stevenson Jordan & Harrison v MacDonald Evans* [1952] 1 TLR 101:

> The test usually applied is whether the employer has the right to control the manner of doing the work. A simple test is suggested: if the employer can only control *what* is done, the employee is an independent contractor and his torts do not make the employer liable. If, however, the employer can control *the way in which it is to be done* then the employee is a servant and the employer will be vicariously liable for his torts. However, the nature of the relationship must depend on all the circumstances and control is only one, though an extremely important, factor.

An employee does not attract liability to his or her employer for every negligent act; only those which are referable to the employment relationship subsisting between them. One problem is to determine whether what is done by an employee, albeit an unauthorised act, is referable to the relationship of employment. For instance, in *Whatman v Pearson* (1868) LR 3 CP 422 a contractor allowed his workmen an hour for lunch but they were not permitted to go home or to leave their horses and carts unattended; one workman, however, went slightly out of his way in order to go home for lunch and he left his horse in front of his house. The horse ran off and damaged the plaintiff's property. The question was whether the employer was vicariously liable and this turned on whether or not the workman was acting in a way which was referable to his employment. The court decided that this was properly left to the jury for their decision and that they could justifiably decide that the employer was vicariously liable.

23.5 Liability for the actions of independent contractors

The general rule is that an employer is not liable for the acts of an independent contractor. In *Honeywell and Stein Ltd v Larkin (London's Commercial Photographers) Ltd* [1933] All ER 77 Lord Justice Slesser said

> It is well established as a general rule of English law that an employer is not liable for the acts of his independent contractor in the same way as he is for acts of his servants or agents, even though these acts are done in carrying out work for his benefit under the contract.

However, there are a number of important exceptions.

Whenever an employer authorises the independent contractor to commit a tort, the employer cannot avoid liability for it because he or she has, in effect, acted in concert with the contractor. Thus in *Ellis v Sheffield Gas Consumers Co* (1853) 2 E&B 767 the defendant gas authority had authorised a contractor to make excavations in the street, the result of which was a spoil heap. The plaintiff fell over this and was injured. The defendants were liable as they had authorised the nuisance.

There are a number of situations where the law characterises the employer's duty as 'non-delegable' in which case the employment of an independent contractor, no matter how reputable or skilled, will not enable the employer to avoid his or her liability. There appears to be no consistent rule about which types of activities might be so characterised. Duties which have been held to be non-delegable include employers' duty to provide a safe workplace for their employees. There is also a class of such duties classified under the head of 'hazardous activities'. In *Salsbury v Woodland* [1970] 1 QB 324 Lord Justice Widgery said that an employer was not liable simply because the work was hazardous; it had to be attended by some special hazard such that an employer could not reasonably avoid his or her liability by employing an independent contractor. Examples which are of relevance to the construction industry and which have been held to be attended by special hazards include working on the highway (*Holliday v National Telephone Co* [1899] 2 QB 392) and ground works adjacent to a neighbouring property which threaten to undermine its foundations (*Angus v Dalton* [1888] 6 App Cas 740) or work such as metal welding which may cause fire (*Honeywell and Stein Ltd v Larkin Brothers (London Commercial Photographers) Ltd* [1933] All ER 77).

23.6 Contributory negligence

Contributory negligence refers to a situation where the defendant has caused the plaintiff's damage but where that damage is exacerbated by the failure of the plaintiff to take sensible and proper care of himself and his property. The classic case of this in law is of a motor accident victim who was not wearing a safety belt and where the failure to wear a belt has added to his injuries; in this situation the damages which the defendant will have to pay are reduced to account for the contributory negligence of the plaintiff. Note that the plaintiff's act or failure to act does not have to amount to negligence itself; it is enough if it contributes to the damage.

The law on contributory negligence is contained in the Law Reform (Contributory Negligence) Act 1945 which provides in Subsection 1(1):

> Where any person suffers damage as a result partly of his own fault and partly of the fault of any other person or persons, a claim in respect of that damage shall not be defeated by reason of the fault of the person suffering the damage, but the damages recoverable in respect thereof shall be reduced to such an extent as the court thinks just and equitable having regard to the claimant's share in the responsibility for the damage.

> Provided that
> (a) this subsection shall not operate to defeat any defence arising under a contract;
> (b) where any contract or enactment providing for the limitation of liability is applicable to the claim, the amount of damages recoverable by the claimant by virtue of this subsection shall not exceed the maximum limit so applicable.

One area of current interest and development is whether the law of contributory negligence applies to contractual claims, as opposed to whether a contractual defence may be set up as allowed for in the proviso to Subsection (1). The current position appears to be that it does so only where the obligation which is sued upon would have arisen in negligence as well as in contract: see the Court of Appeal's decision in *Forsikringsaktieselskapet Vesta v Butcher* [1988] 3 WLR 565. This case was appealed to the House of Lords ([1989] AC 852) but the point was not decided. The situation described by the Court of Appeal would appear to apply to consultancy contracts in which advice is provided in circumstances which would also be covered by a negligence duty under the principles of *Hedley Byrne v Heller* [1964] AC 465. The Law Commission has, however, recommended ('Contributory negligence as a defence to contract', Working Paper 114, August 1990) that whenever the plaintiff's loss is partly attributable to his or her own behaviour, damages should be apportioned as appropriate, even if the duty is a strict one. This report may influence the judiciary but a change in the law may have to wait for legislation.

Avoiding, limiting and insuring against liability risks for construction and consultancy work

24.1 Introduction

Construction typically involves large sums of money. Some contracting firms who undertake the work are financially powerful and can sustain the consequences of a large claim made against them. However, many are not and will wish to limit or reduce their potential liability somehow. In the case of consulting firms this is also true; they will often find it difficult to meet a large claim made against them. There are a variety of methods used by organisations in the construction industry to reduce or limit their liability, including

- insurance
- exclusion clauses, limitation clauses and disclaimers
- indemnity and contingency clauses.

In addition to these formal procedures, organisations often adopt informal methods such as checking systems (including quality assurance) which are designed to minimise the risk of liability. In this chapter these various methods of minimising liability risk will be examined.

24.2 Insurance

24.2.1 General introduction and terminology

Construction involves many risks and it is an important aspect of the management process in construction to control and manage these risks. One important way in which this can be achieved is through insurance.

Insurance is effected by contract between 'the insurer' and 'the insured', so that upon the happening of some event the insurer will pay to the insured an amount calculated in accordance with the contract terms. There are a number of specialist terms used in insurance which need to be understood.

1 *Insurable interest* an insured may only take out insurance if he or she has an insurable interest, that is if he or she will suffer a loss if the

event insured against happens. Thus, for example, a developer may insure against accidental fire on his own site; but he has no insurable interest in fires which may affect another developer's work.

2 *Policy and premium* insurance contracts need not be in writing. However, they normally are, and are contained in a document called a policy. The insured party provides a sum of money known as the premium as consideration for the insurance cover he or she receives.

3 *Indemnity and non-indemnity policies* a non-indemnity policy is one in which the sum payable by the insurer is fixed in advance. An example is life assurance (the term 'assurance' is typically used for non-indemnity policies) where the named person or persons receive a set sum on the happening of the insured event, namely the death of the insured. An indemnity policy is one where the amount payable depends upon the amount of loss actually experienced by the insured upon the happening of the insured event. This is the typical situation in construction insurance contracts; thus, if an engineering consultancy has 'professional indemnity' cover, the insured event will be a successful claim made against the practice and the amount payable will be the value of that claim.

4 *Utmost good faith (uberrimae fidei)* a contract of insurance is valid only if the insured party has disclosed to the insurer every fact which is 'material' to a proper assessment of the insurer's risk. A material fact is therefore one which would cause a prudent insurer to consider whether or not to offer the insurance on the terms currently offered. If there has been a 'material non-disclosure', the insurance contract may be avoided by the insurer.

5 *Subrogation* when an insurer pays out under an insurance contract upon the happening of the insured event he or she then becomes entitled to pursue any claim which the insured would have had in connection with that event. An example is where a construction plant belonging to Contractor A is damaged in an accident caused by another contractor B. If the insurer of the plant pays contractor A for the damage, it may then take an action to recover damages from B in A's name. This is known as a right of subrogation.

24.2.2 Contractor's and project insurance

A variety of types of insurance are used in the construction industry. Most construction contracts require the contractor to take out specified types of insurances. In addition a contractor may take out a Contractor's All Risks (CAR) policy which covers him for a wide range of matters. The extent of these policies will be determined by the terms of the policy in each case and, as with all contracts, generalisations should be avoided; the individual contract terms (and, in particular, the exclusion clauses) should be consulted. See, however, *Petrofina (UK) Ltd and others v Magnaload Ltd and others* 25 BLR 37 for a discussion of the principles and application of the rules of subrogation in the context of a Contractor's All Risks policy.

24.2.3 Professional indemnity (PI) insurance

One type of insurance that deserves special mention is the professional indemnity insurance taken out by engineers, architects, surveyors and other professionals. These tend to be annual policies which cover the insured against claims made in the year of cover (but, as with all other insurance contracts, the terms govern the rights and obligations of the parties and generalisations should be avoided). Thus if an engineer designs a bridge in 1985 and is notified of a professional indemnity claim in 1991, the insured will normally be claiming against his 1991 insurers, that being the year in which the claim is made. Problems often arise when consultants change insurers. An example is found in *Patricia Thorman and others v New Hampshire Insurance Company (UK) Ltd and another* 39 BLR 41. Here a firm of architects were informed of potential claims against them in 1982 but were not made aware of the details until 1984. Meanwhile in 1983 they had changed insurance companies; the insurance policies in each case contained an identical clause as follows:

> Section 1 – Professional Liability. The company will indemnify the Insured against loss arising from any claim or claims for breach of duty in the professional capacity stated in the Schedule which is made against them during the period set forth in the Schedule by reason of any neglect omission or error whenever the same was or may have been committed or alleged to have been committed by the Insured or any person now or heretofore employed by the Insured or hereafter to be employed by the Insured during the subsistence of this policy.

Both insurance companies denied that they were the insurers for the claim. The Court of Appeal found that in that particular case the earlier insurance company was the responsible insurer. The question depended, however, on the precise facts and the terms of the policies in question and no general rule may be laid down.

Note: This case also provides a discussion (see, for example, Sir John Donaldson's judgment at p. 54) on a difficult problem which may be faced by professionals: the avoidance of an insurance contract by the insurer on the grounds of material non-disclosure in respect of potential or anticipated claims.

24.3 Exclusion clauses, limitation clauses and disclaimers

24.3.1 The nature of exclusion clauses, limitation clauses and disclaimers

Parties may attempt to exclude or limit their liability for work in two direct ways. First, they may agree to perform work only on the basis that their liability is limited in some way. Second, they may issue a prominent disclaimer of liability in respect of the work. The first method is essentially contractual in nature; the second method is essentially designed to prevent liability arising in negligence, and will not affect the duties assumed by parties under the contract unless the disclaimer is also a contract term.

24.3.2   The interpretation of and validity of exclusion clauses, limitation clauses and disclaimers

The Unfair Contract Terms Act 1977 was introduced to provide some control over exclusion and limitation clauses and disclaimers. These devices are ineffective unless they satisfy the 'reasonableness' test specified by the Unfair Contract Terms Act 1977, Sections 2 and 3 of which provide as follows:

2 Negligence Liability
(1)   A person cannot by reference to any contract term or to a notice ... exclude or restrict his liability for death or personal injury resulting from negligence.
(2)   In the case of other loss or damage, a person cannot so exclude or restrict his liability for negligence except in so far as the term or notice satisfies the requirement of reasonableness.
(3)   When a contract term or notice purports to exclude or restrict liability for negligence a person's agreement to or awareness of it is not of itself to be taken as indicating his voluntary acceptance of any risk.

3 Liability arising in Contract
(1)   This section applies as between contracting parties when one of them deals as consumer or on the other's written standard terms of business.
(2)   As against that party, the other cannot by reference to any contract term
    (a)   when himself in breach, exclude or restrict any liability of his in respect of the breach; or
    (b)   claim to be entitled
        (i)   to render a contractual performance substantially different from that which was reasonably expected of him, or
        (ii)   in respect of the whole or any part of his contractual obligation, to render no performance at all, except in so far as (in any of the cases mentioned in this subsection), the contract term satisfies the requirement of reasonableness.

The requirement of reasonableness in respect of disclaimers placed in reports compiled by professionals was examined in *Smith v Bush* [1990] AC 831. Lord Griffiths, in his speech, gave some useful guidance on the factors to be taken into account when deciding whether a particular clause or notice was reasonable. First, he said that if the professional was in a strong bargaining position relative to the person relying upon the advice, that was indicative of unreasonableness. Second, it is indicative of reasonableness if it would have been practicable to obtain the advice from an alternative source. Third, if the task carried a high risk of failure then that always suggested that a disclaimer would be reasonable. And fourth, the likely financial consequences, the ability of the parties to bear those consequences and the availability of insurance must all be taken into account.

The courts have had to consider whether or not contract clauses pass the test of reasonableness on a number of occasions (e.g. *Rees Hough Ltd v Redland Reinforced Plastics Ltd* [1984] 27 BLR 136 and *Barnard Pipeline Technology Limited v Marston Construction Co Limited* (1992) CILL 743). The decided cases appear to indicate that the court is greatly influenced by the 'overall impression' in the light of all the circumstances operating at the time the agreement was made. In construction cases most parties are large commercial concerns run by managers who are well aware of the dangers of accepting onerous terms which form part of the other party's standard conditions. Because of this it is thought that judges will naturally be inclined to find that terms are reasonable unless it would clearly be unjust to enforce them.

Section 3 of the Act operates only when one party deals as consumer or on the other's written standard terms of business. The question of who can be considered as dealing 'as consumer' and what constitutes 'written standard terms of business' were explored in *The Chester Grosvenor Hotel Company Ltd v Alfred McAlpine Management Ltd and others* (1992) 56 BLR 115. In this case a hotel commissioned a contractor to carry out refurbishments. The contract terms were written by a manager employed by the contractor. The hotel owners argued that their business was as hoteliers not as developers; accordingly, they said, they were dealing 'as consumer' when they entered into the refurbishment contract. The judge, however, decided that since the Grosvenor Hotel was a luxury hotel it needed constantly to be refurbished to maintain its status; 'these contracts were entered into as part of Grosvenor's established practice of refurbishing the hotel. In these circumstances I conclude that these contracts were an integral part of Grosvenor's business, and that in entering into them it did not deal as consumer within the terms of the statute' (per Judge Stannard).

On the question of whether the terms employed amounted to 'written standard terms of business' the contractor argued that since they were modified from project to project to suit the circumstances they were not to be considered standard terms. The judge said 'it does not follow that because terms are not employed invariably, or without material variation, they cannot be standard terms. If this were not so the statute would be emasculated. In my judgment the question is one of fact and degree. . . . What is required for terms to be standard is that they should be regarded by the party which advances them as its standard terms and that it should habitually contract in those terms.'

24.3.3 Disclaimers in reports

Reports are regularly produced in the construction industry. For example, an engineer may produce a report on the ground conditions on a particular site or a surveyor may produce a report outlining the likely expenditure to be anticipated in connection with a particular project. When the report is accurate no liability arises. When, however, it is inaccurate, the professional who produced the report may be liable. The chief area of liability relates to the professional's potential liability to the client; a potential liability will arise if the report is produced without due care and skill and the professional will have to recompense the client for any losses suffered by the client as a direct result of that negligence.

In some cases a professional will even owe a duty to those who read the report and rely upon it to their financial disadvantage, despite the lack of a contractual relationship between them. Often professionals attempt to avoid the possibility of such liability arising by the provision of a prominent disclaimer in the report. These may contain wording such as

> This report has been produced by ... [state name of engineer] ... for ... [state name of the client] ... in accordance with that client's particular requirements. The contents of the report are confidential and other persons are not entitled to use the information contained within it. No liability whatsoever will be incurred to any persons using this report without express permission from ... [state name of engineer].

Such a disclaimer will be ineffective unless it is reasonable as noted above.

24.4   Indemnity and contingency clauses

24.4.1   Indemnity clauses

Indemnities are commonplace in construction industry contracts. In most main contracts the contractor agrees to indemnify and keep indemnified the employer against all losses and claims of a wide variety of descriptions. Such clauses, however, often attract the requirements of the Unfair Contract Terms Act 1977 and regard should be had to whether or not a particular clause meets the 'requirements of reasonableness'. There are other pitfalls for such clauses to be noted also, one of the most important being that explained by Lord Justice Devlin in *Walters v Whessoe Ltd and Shell Refining Co Ltd* 6 BLR 23:

> It is now well established that if a person obtains an indemnity against the consequences of certain acts, the indemnity is not to be construed so as to include the consequences of his own negligence unless those consequences are covered either expressly or by necessary implication. They are covered by necessary implication if there is no other subject-matter upon which the indemnity could operate. Like most rules of construction, this one depends upon the presumed intention of the parties. It is thought to be so unlikely that one man would agree to indemnify another man for the consequence of that other's own negligence that he is presumed not to intend to do so unless it is done by express words or by necessary implications.

24.4.2   Contingency clauses

A contingency clause is one whereby one activity is required only if another specified event occurs. In the case of a contractor–subcontractor relationship an example is a 'pay when paid' clause, which states that the contractor will pay the subcontractor for an element of work within so many days of the contractor receiving payment for it; in other words, the contractor need pay the subcontractor only if and when the contractor gets paid. A contingency clause of this type when appropriately worded is to be construed in accordance with the normal rules of contract construction. It may also, where the Unfair Contract Terms Act 1977 applies, fall foul of the reasonableness requirements and hence be unenforceable.

The resolution of construction law disputes

25.1 Introduction

The object of the laws of contract and tort, which form the core of construction law, is to define the rights and obligations of the parties. The law is presented as a series of rules whose application to a given factual situation often means that a number of interpretations of the legal position are possible. Often the factual background will, itself, also be less than clear. The parties in such situations will, naturally, tend to favour the interpretation which, for them, is best and, unless the interests of all relevant parties coincide, a dispute may ensue. In practice parties usually reach a compromise for a very simple reason; whatever their interests, it rarely lies in pursuing the dispute to the point where it is adjudicated by a tribunal, even if the party is very confident that the interpretation they propose will be accepted by the tribunal. However, there are disputes where such large sums are at stake that it is commercially acceptable to risk having to pay the costs of running the action even if the prospects are not good.

In this chapter the various common methods of pursuing a remedy (assuming that an amicable settlement is not achieved at the outset) will be outlined. The three principal means are

- litigation
- arbitration
- non-binding dispute resolution (Alternative Dispute Resolution: ADR).

Disputes in the law of tort may be resolved in exactly the same way as contractual disputes. The consensual nature of contract often, however, suggests a consensual means of dispute resolution and hence arbitration clauses are popular in contracts. Tortious disputes which cannot be resolved by negotiation are invariably settled by litigation, although the processes of arbitration and ADR are, in principle, available provided all parties agree.

The topic of litigation is vast and complex and will be presented only in the merest outline; the interested reader is advised to consult one of the many works available on this topic.

Non-binding dispute resolution (usually called by its American name, Alternative Dispute Resolution, which for the sake of simplicity will be adopted here also) is one which is currently receiving significant attention. ADR is an umbrella term for a range of processes including conciliation, mediation and mini-trials. Its development may be seen as a reaction to the perceived, and probably actual, inefficiencies inherent in the way disputes are currently dealt with both through litigation and arbitration. The construction industry has traditionally been highly litigious and it is therefore encouraging to see that this industry is at the forefront of ADR developments in this country.

25.2 Litigation

Litigation is the process of dispute resolution operated by the state through the courts. In Chapter 2 the hierarchy of courts operating in the UK was explained. In the case of construction disputes where there is no agreement to arbitrate, the first venue for the dispute to be heard is the County Court for small disputes or the High Court for substantial disputes.

The procedural rules relating to litigation are contained in large, officially produced, books: in the case of the High Court it is the *Rules of the Supreme Court*, colloquially known as the 'White Book' and in the case of the County Court it is the *County Court Practice* or the 'Green Book', the references indicating the colour of the cover for each book.

In both High Court and County Court proceedings, the process is very similar and by way of illustration the High Court process is outlined here.

A writ is issued and served
The party seeking redress will attend (normally through his or her solicitor) an office in the High Court and ask that a formal document (a writ) be issued requiring the party from whom redress is sought to answer the allegations made against him or her. The party seeking redress (the plaintiff) then serves the writ on the other party (the defendant).

A statement of claim is prepared by the plaintiff and served on the defendant
The statement of claim is a document, 'a pleading', which outlines the plaintiff's case against the defendant and the remedy sought by the plaintiff.

The defendant may capitulate or decide to defend
When the defendant sees the case against him he may decide to capitulate, wholly or in part, or to defend the action. If the defendant decides to capitulate he completes a form which he will have received with the writ and statement of claim. If he decides to defend he must answer the allegations by serving a defence, which is also a pleading in the proceedings. Often the defendant will also serve a counterclaim in which he will register a claim against the plaintiff relating to the same subject matter.

Subsequent pleadings and timing
The plaintiff, on receipt of the defence, may serve a reply (the third and, usually, the last pleading) if he wishes, and must supply a defence to counterclaim if a counterclaim is made by the defendant. The timing of the service of the pleadings is set out in the White Book; generally, however, 'extensions of time' are given in construction law cases to enable fuller pleadings to be drawn up since the time limits given in the White Book (normally fourteen days between pleadings) do not allow complex allegations to be investigated.

Summons for directions
When the pleadings have been served, the plaintiff will arrange for a 'summons for directions' to be heard by a judge. The judge will hear representations from solicitors or counsel representing both parties and will set down rules concerning a number of matters relating to the conduct of the proceedings, including

1 *Discovery* the disclosure of the relevant documents which each party possesses.
2 *Expert witness statements* in construction disputes expert witnesses are often called. It is generally convenient if each party can see the expert evidence which the other party will be relying upon in advance of the hearing.
3 *Hearing date and venue* in some disputes the court will fix a date for a hearing. This is very common because of the need to ensure that lawyers, experts and other witnesses are available. However, the numbers of cases which are settled before hearing means that it is essential to double, triple and even sextuple book. As a result it is never certain that the date allocated will be available.

The hearing
The hearing will take place before the trial judge. In the case of construction disputes this will normally be in the Queen's Bench Division of the High Court and will be dealt with as Official Referee's business. Both parties will be represented at the trial of the action by barristers, also called counsel. (Following the enactment of the Courts and Legal Services Act 1990 a committee is currently examining extending 'rights of audience' in the High Court and the other senior courts to people other than barristers.) Counsel will open and present their clients' cases and will examine their own witnesses and cross-examine the opponent's witnesses. Proceedings are adversarial in nature; that is to say, the judge does not take an active role in the proceeding in order to elicit the facts respecting the claims made by the parties. Rather, the judge listens to the arguments and evidence advocated and adduced by each party and decides between them on the basis of the evidence actually provided by the parties.

Judgment
After the hearing the judgment is given by the judge. This is usually spoken from a typed draft, though a written judgment may simply be handed down.

Appeal and execution
If either party is unhappy with the judgment he or she may appeal to the Court of Appeal. The appeal is heard by three Lords Justice of Appeal. In any event, whether or not an appeal is to be made, the judgment must be complied with immediately by the losing party (unless an order for a 'stay of execution' is obtained). If the terms of the judgment are not complied with, the party in default will be ordered to comply and, through a variety of mechanisms and sanctions, execution of the judgment will be compelled.

In practice, construction law litigation will be conducted as Official Referee's business in the Queen's Bench Division of the High Court. Even where the action is begun outside the Official Referee's courts it is normally transferred there in the preliminary stages of the litigation (a useful introduction to practice in the Official Referee's courts is given by His Honour Judge Newey QC in an article published in the *Construction Law Journal*, Vol 6 No 3, 'The preparation and presentation of cases in the Official Referee's courts').

25.3   Arbitration

Arbitration is a system of dispute resolution which operates in parallel with the court system. Parties to a contract may decide that it is more appropriate to have their disputes (existing or future) adjudicated by a privately constituted tribunal than in a public court. In such a case, English law enables them to empower one or more arbitrators to rule upon their disputes in a decision which binds them both.

Arbitration is very common in the field of commercial law, including construction law, and the majority of standard form contracts contain a clause committing the parties to arbitration in the event that disputes arise which the parties cannot resolve by compromise. The fact that arbitration clauses are so common in commercial standard form contracts suggests that there are significant perceived advantages of arbitration relative to, say, litigation in the courts. The following points consider the relative merits and disadvantages of arbitration *vis-à-vis* litigation.

25.3.1   Advantages and disadvantages of arbitration

The technical expertise of the arbitrator and advocates
Many construction disputes turn on technical considerations. It is appropriate, then, that the tribunal and the advocates should be technically qualified. Judges and barristers normally have only legal qualifications. Hence, barristers will often not be able to deal with the technical issues in as efficient a manner as would an appropriately qualified construction professional; and judges will not possess the requisite technical understanding to develop a logical preference for the technical arguments proposed by one party over the other. An arbitrator or advocate in arbitration may, however, be an engineer, an architect or a surveyor as appropriate. If a technically qualified arbitrator is appointed this will

often reduce the time of the arbitration as the arbitrator will readily appreciate the submissions put to him or her on the technical aspects of the case.

Privacy
Court action involving commercial disputes in England will generally be heard in public courts. Privacy is often important since confidential or sensitive information may form part of the evidence; parties may find it convenient to concede certain issues in the privacy of arbitration which could not be conceded in open court for commercial reasons. And they may find it possible to prosecute certain claims for which they have a legal right in arbitrations which would be difficult to pursue for political reasons in open court.

Convenience and comfort
It is of some importance that the hearing be held at a time and place which is convenient for all concerned including the parties, their advisers and witnesses. In court actions, the disputes will be heard in a room at a place decided by the court's 'listing officer' and the exact timing may not be known until shortly before the case is due to be heard. Court proceedings are often held in places where there are only the most basic facilities. Commercial people would prefer to use a comfortable private room, where coffee and lunch may be served and where telephone, fax, photocopying and secretarial services may be provided.

Speed and cost
It is often suggested that arbitration proceedings are speedier and less costly than litigation. This is not always so. A full court hearing may take several years of preliminary pleading and waiting for a judge to hear the case. However, even the most complex arbitrations may be begun in a shorter period than this and, in this sense, arbitration is certainly speedier, especially for longer trials. Whether or not arbitrations last less time in terms of days of hearing is more difficult to say. Certainly in technical disputes there is less need for experts in arbitration; although they tend still to be called in significant numbers and whether less evidence is actually adduced in arbitration is doubtful. Often, arbitrators will not be as skilful as judges in reducing the time taken for hearings. Judges in court will often ask questions which may indicate the matters they believe to be in real dispute, thereby confining the issues upon which submissions need be made. Arbitrators, on the other hand, are generally in a more difficult position. They often do not have the legal skill and training to control the reference using the devices employed by the judiciary. And even if they do, they owe a duty to the parties not to open themselves up to an allegation of technical misconduct; the best way of safeguarding their position in this respect is to sit and listen patiently and only to ask questions which clarify the evidence. This, of course, leads to longer hearings.

Since arbitration often lasts longer than a comparable case in litigation, it is often more expensive. In addition, the court facilities are operated free for the benefit of the public and hence no fees are payable by the parties for the court room or the judges and officials. In arbitration, the arbitrator and the premises must be paid for by the parties.

However, arbitrations may be more efficient than litigation if revised procedural mechanisms are implemented so that they no longer slavishly follow court proceedings in format. Since arbitrators are not bound by the procedural rules of the courts it is possible to devise simple methods of arbitration and some professional institutions have developed short form arbitration rules. It is not uncommon, for instance, to have a 'documents only' arbitration where there is no oral hearing; this can considerably reduce the time and expense of arbitration.

Where more than two parties are involved
Since arbitration jurisdiction is based on contract it follows that non-parties cannot be brought into the arbitration without their consent. It often happens that the subject of the dispute concerns more than two parties. For example A may claim against B; B may raise the defence that C has caused A's damage. In such a situation there are a variety of mechanisms available for the courts to involve more than two parties. Arbitration, which relies on contract, however, cannot be used to cause third parties to submit to the arbitrator's jurisdiction unless that third party is contractually obliged to submit.

The obligation for a third party to submit to the arbitrator's jurisdiction is achieved in a number of standard form subcontracts. Under the terms of these subcontracts, the subcontractor is obliged to have his disputes heard and resolved by the same tribunal as will hear disputes between the employer and main contractor. This allows the main contractor to stipulate that the subcontract dispute be heard in the arbitration but it does not entitle him to bring another party with whom he has no contract into the arbitration.

25.3.2 Principles of arbitration law

Arbitration law is a highly technical subject and a number of comprehensive textbooks are available. Foremost among these is Mustill and Boyd, *Commercial Arbitration*, 2nd edition (1989).

In this section it is impossible to provide anything but the briefest outline of the law. Five important topics have been chosen for discussion:

- The arbitration legislation and its shortcomings
- The requirements of an arbitration agreement
- The terms of the arbitration agreement implied by the Arbitration Acts
- The construction of the arbitration agreement
- Litigation in breach of an arbitration agreement.

The arbitration legislation and its shortcomings
The principles of English arbitration law have been developed in a piecemeal fashion by the courts over the last two or three centuries. The

most important modern sources of law are, however, the Arbitration Acts of 1950, 1975 and 1979. The 1950 Act is the principal piece of legislation. The 1975 and 1979 Acts relate mainly to specific aspects of arbitration law namely international arbitration agreements and appeals against an arbitrator's decisions. The rather haphazard nature of the arrangement of the arbitration legislation is well recognised and many of the provisions are difficult to interpret. Mr Justice Steyn in his Bernstein Lecture in 1990 said: 'Quaintly, for example, our principal statute [the Arbitration Act 1950] provides in its first section for the revocation of the mandate of the arbitrator. There must be a better place to start. And the rest of that statute is not conspicuous for an orderly and logical treatment of the subject'. And as a remark on some of the drafting in the arbitration legislation he said in the same lecture, 'no academic, practitioner or judge has yet fathomed the meaning of Section 5 of that [i.e. the 1979] Act'.

A committee has commenced the work of drafting a new consolidated Arbitration Act which, it is hoped, will set out the existing law in an orderly, easy to follow format. The committee is unusual in that it is not sponsored by Government departments but is working in the private sector, albeit in close co-operation with all the interested parties. It is hoped that the draft Bill will be sponsored by the Government and will be enacted in the first half of the 1990s.

The requirements of an arbitration agreement

An arbitration agreement is the term of a binding contract in which the parties commit themselves to arbitrate disputes. The agreement is often contained in 'the arbitration clause' of construction contracts. In order for the arbitration agreement to be binding on the parties it must be in writing, in terms whereby the parties agree clearly and unambiguously to arbitrate disputes in the event that such disputes arise.

A binding arbitration agreement must be in writing   The requirement for the agreement to be in writing stems from Section 32 of the Arbitration Act 1950 which provides that only written agreements are enforceable.

Ambiguous agreements   For the agreement to be enforceable it must clearly indicate that resolution of disputes by arbitration is available as of right.

Incorporation by reference   Provided that, on a true construction of the document, a sufficient intention is found, incorporation by reference is sufficient. For example in *Modern Buildings (Wales) Ltd v Limmer and Trinidad* 14 BLR 101, a subcontract was placed by letter in the following terms:

> To supply adequate labour, plant and machinery to carry out in full accordance with the appropriate form for nominated sub-contractor (RIBA 1965 Ed).

In fact there was at the time no 1965 edition of the RIBA form. The Court of Appeal held, however, that the words identified the NFBTE/FASS (Green form) contract as being 'the appropriate form'. Since that contract contained an arbitration clause it was incorporated by reference into the agreement and either party could insist that disputes be arbitrated rather than litigated.

The terms of the arbitration agreement implied by the Arbitration Acts

The 1950 Arbitration Act implies terms into arbitration agreements which it covers. Some of these are conditionally implied and operate providing the parties do not express an alternative intention. Some operate to void expressly agreed inconsistent terms.

Conditional terms   Section 14 of the 1950 Act is an example of a term which is implied only if no contrary intention is contained in the arbitration agreement. It provides

> Unless a contrary intention is expressed therein, every arbitration agreement shall, where such provision is applicable to the reference be deemed to contain a provision that the arbitrator or umpire may, if he thinks fit, make an interim award.

See also Section 6 (one arbitrator to be appointed unless number expressly agreed), Section 8 (if two arbitrators to be appointed, they may/will appoint an umpire), Section 12 (powers of the arbitrator and the court in the conduct of the reference), Section 15 (specific performance of contracts relating to land), Section 16 (finality of the award), Subsections 18(1) and (2) (costs), and Section 19A (interest on awards).

Voiding terms   In a number of cases terms included expressly in the arbitration agreement which are inconsistent with the sections of the Act are deemed void. Subsection 18(3), for instance, deals with prior agreements relating to costs. It declares that

> Any provision in an arbitration agreement to the effect that the parties or any party thereto shall pay their or his own costs of the reference or award shall be void.

The construction of the arbitration agreement

Since the arbitration agreement is a term of a contract, its true meaning in law is determined by construing it in accordance with the normal rules of construction. Two matters of importance regularly arise in connection with the construction of these clauses; first, the question whether or not a particular dispute falls within the ambit of the arbitration agreement; and second, what powers does the arbitrator have under the agreement.

Does the dispute fall within the arbitration agreement?   In the case of *Ashville Investments Ltd v Elmer Contractors Ltd* 37 BLR 55, the extent of the arbitration clause was in issue. If the disputes submitted to the arbitrator fell within the ambit of the arbitration clause the arbitrator had jurisdiction. Otherwise he did not. The disputes in question related to a rectification of the contract and allegations of innocent or negligent misrepresentation. The arbitration clause gave the arbitrator power under the contract to hear disputes 'arising . . . in connection with' the contract. The Court of Appeal held that this wording, in the context of the contract before it, was sufficiently wide to include the claims for rectification and misrepresentation. However, they were clear that the issue was one of construction of the clause in the context of the whole agreement and they were not persuaded by argument from one counsel that since similar words in another contract had been held to have a particular meaning then this provided a precedent. Lord Justice May said

> it is a principle of law that the scope of an arbitrator's jurisdiction and powers in a given case depend fundamentally upon the terms of the arbitration agreement, that is upon its proper construction in all the circumstances. However I do not think that there is any principle of law to the effect that the meaning of specific words in one arbitration clause in one contract is immutable and that those same specific words in another arbitration clause in other circumstances in another contract must be construed in the same way.

The arbitrator's powers under the arbitration agreement   The power of the arbitrator is determined by construing the arbitration agreement. The leading case on this in the context of construction contracts is *Northern Regional Health Authority v Crouch* [1984] QB 644. This case has important implications for many arbitrations in the construction industry since it, in effect, states that the role of an arbitrator under the typically worded construction contract is not the same as that of a court and, in particular, that the court does not have the powers which the arbitrator enjoys under the contract. The contract in *Crouch* was under the JCT Form which, like most of the common construction contracts, provides that the certifier's certificates were to bind the parties in the first instance, but that the arbitrator had the power to 'open up review and revise' those certificates. The practice of Official Referees (who handle most construction disputes) had, until that time, been to assume that they had the same powers as were granted to the arbitrator under the contract. The Court of Appeal decided that the court had no such jurisdiction. Lord Justice Browne-Wilkinson said

> In principle, in an action based on contract the court can only enforce the agreement between the parties: it has no power to modify that agreement in any way. Therefore, if the parties have agreed on a specified machinery for the resolution of their obligations, the court cannot substitute a different machinery. So, in this contract the parties have agreed that certain rights and obligations are to be determined by the certificate or opinion of the architect. In an action questioning the validity of an architect's certificates or opinion given or expressed under clauses 22 or 23 of the main contract, in my judgment the court's jurisdiction would be limited to deciding whether or not the certificate or opinion was legally invalid because given, for example, in bad faith or in excess of his powers. In no circumstances would the court have power to revise such certificate or opinion solely on the ground that the court would have reached a different conclusion since to do so would be to interfere with the agreement of the parties. The powers conferred on the arbitrator are of a different kind. Under clause 35(3) he has power not merely to determine disputes on legal rights under the provisions of the contract (including the consequences flowing from certificates or opinions of the architect). In addition, he is given the power to modify those contractual rights by varying the architect's certificates and opinions if he disagrees with them by substituting his own discretion for that of the architect. The

arbitrator has power not only to enforce the contractual obligations but to modify them. ... The parties have never agreed to vest in the court power to vary their contractual obligations even if they could validly so agree. ... Therefore as a matter of principle I reach the conclusion that if this matter were to be litigated in the High Court (whether before the official referee or a judge) the court would not have power to open up review and revise certificates or opinions.

Sir John Donaldson said in the same case:

Arbitration is usually no more and no less than litigation in the private sector. The arbitrator is called upon to find the facts, apply the law and grant relief to one or other or both of the parties. Under a JCT arbitration clause (Clause 35), the arbitrator has these powers but he also has power to 'open up, review and revise any certificate, opinion, decision, requirement or notice'. This goes further than merely entitling him to treat the architect's certificate's opinions, decisions, requirements and notices as inconclusive in determining the rights of the parties. It enables, and in appropriate cases requires, him to vary them and so create new rights, obligations and liabilities in the parties. This is not a power which is normally possessed by any court and again it has a strong element of personal judgment by an individual nominated in accordance with the agreement of the parties.

Sir John then went on to deal with the 'vexed question of what happens if, instead of arbitrating ... one of the parties resorts to the courts ... or both parties agree to waive their rights under the arbitration clause and submit their dispute to the jurisdiction of the courts'. He decided that, even in such a case, the court would not have the power to open up the certifier's decision.

As a result of this case a new verb was coined among construction lawyers, normally used in the passive form: 'to be Crouched'. This happens when the claim of a party requires the certificates of the certifier to be opened up and that party commences litigation proceedings and hence loses its right to arbitrate the dispute. Since the court has no power to open up the certificate it can obtain no relief if opening up the certificate is an essential step in its case; they have been Crouched. In the subsequent case of *Benstrete Construction Ltd v Angus Hill* 38 BLR 115, upon an undefended application, the Court of Appeal gave a very brief judgment to the effect that under the JCT Minor Works Contract the parties were not Crouched by going to court. Sir John Donaldson explained that the terms of the principal standard building and engineering contracts contained what he described as 'an internal arbitration clause which enabled the parties in that arbitration to seek to set aside or revise architects' certificates'. The way in which *Benstrete* has been interpreted by some commentators (e.g. see the commentary on the case in the Building Law Reports) is that when the certificate of the certifier is only to have a provisional effect, rather than to be binding, then the court can exercise the power of the arbitrator.

To mitigate some of the difficulties associated with the decision in Crouch the Courts and Legal Services Act 1990 now provides (as Section 43A of the Supreme Court Act 1981):

In any cause or matter in the High Court in connection with any contract incorporating an arbitration agreement which confers specific powers upon the arbitrator, the High Court may, if all parties to the agreement agree, exercise any such powers.

This enactment is clearly designed to overcome the decision in *Crouch* but is only available when all parties agree and is therefore not likely to overcome the possibility of a party becoming 'Crouched'.

Litigation in breach of an arbitration agreement

The effect of an arbitration clause   An agreement to arbitrate does not prevent the parties from taking their disputes to court. The court always has jurisdiction to try such disputes and any provision which attempted to exclude this jurisdiction would be void. The courts will, however, respect the agreement of the parties if they have agreed to arbitrate disputes and, in the event that one party wishes to arbitrate rather than litigate, the courts will usually stay any court proceedings pending the conclusion of the arbitration proceedings.

Once substantive proceedings (i.e. excluding the seeking of the ancillary relief which only the court is empowered to grant) have commenced in the courts, the right of the parties to insist upon arbitration is lost, unless both agree to arbitrate; once a party has elected to litigate, his or her right to insist on arbitration is gone and so any special powers granted to the arbitrator cannot now be exercised. In the case of arbitration agreements containing an 'open up review and revise' type power, a party who is involved in litigation but now desires a certificate to be altered will be 'Crouched', unless both parties agree to empower the Official Referee to exercise the same powers as an arbitrator.

Staying court proceedings to arbitration   The courts, when faced with a plaintiff who bases his or her claim on matters which are covered by an arbitration clause, has jurisdiction to hear the dispute. If the defendant wishes to have the matter arbitrated, however, the courts will consider whether or not to use their powers under Section 4 of the Arbitration Act to order a stay. Section 4(1) of the Act provides

> If any party to an arbitration agreement . . . commences any legal proceedings in any court against any other party to the agreement . . . in respect of any matter agreed to be referred, any party to those legal proceedings may at any time . . . before delivering any pleadings or taking any other steps in the proceedings, apply to that court to stay the proceedings, and that court or a judge thereof, if satisfied that there is no sufficient reason why the matter should not be referred in accordance with the agreement, and that the applicant, was, at the time when the proceedings were commenced, and still remains, ready and willing to do all things necessary to the proper conduct of the arbitration, may make an order staying the proceedings.

A number of important points are raised by this subsection.

1   A valid arbitration agreement within the meaning of Section 32 of the Act must subsist. Such an agreement must be in writing and it

survives the fall of the other terms in the event that a repudiatory breach is accepted by the innocent party – see *Heyman v Darwins Ltd* [1942] AC 356.

2   The party seeking the stay must show that the dispute falls within the terms of the contract: see *Ashville Investments v Elmer Contractors* 37 BLR 55 discussed above.

3   The party claiming the stay will be defeated if he or she has delivered any pleadings or taken any other steps in the proceedings. In *Eagle Star Insurance v Yuval Insurance* [1978] 1 Ll Rep 357 Lord Denning said that a step in the proceedings 'is a step by which the defendant evinces an election to abide by the court proceedings and waives his right to ask for arbitration'. Before arbitration proceedings have commenced or during the proceedings one or more parties may wish to seek ancillary relief from the courts. For instance, one party may wish to obtain an injunction to prevent the other party from disposing of certain property which the first has some interest in. The arbitrator does not have such power although the courts are given such power specifically by Section 12(6)(h) of the 1950 Arbitration Act. In *Channel Tunnel Group Ltd and another v Balfour Beatty Construction Ltd and others* 56 BLR 18 it was held that a party could obtain an injunction even before any request for arbitration had been made provided the applicant intended to proceed to arbitration.

4   The party seeking the stay must be ready and willing to arbitrate. In *G Dew and Co Ltd v Tarmac Construction Ltd* 15 BLR 22, the party seeking the stay at first denied that there was a contract or an arbitration clause; when the other party began proceedings, the first party changed its mind and attempted to obtain a stay. It was held that the applicant was not at the material times 'ready and willing to do all that is necessary'.

5   The court's power is clearly discretionary and hence the applicant cannot require a stay as of right (compare the situation in international cases discussed in Chapter 27). A number of cases have been decided where the court has refused to grant a stay. A number of situations may be identified. One situation where the court has refused to grant a stay is where to do so would result in two sets of proceedings. In *Taunton-Collins v Cromie* [1964] 1 WLR 633, for instance, a building owner sued his architect for faulty design. The architect defended by saying that the defects were due to faulty construction. The owner then joined the builders as a third party. There was an arbitration clause in the contract between owners and the builders, and the builder applied for a stay. The judge said: 'Our whole judicial procedure would be brought into disrepute if there was a serious possibility of getting conflicting decisions on questions of fact by two different tribunals'. This attitude raises difficult questions in the light of the *Crouch* decision and it may be that the reluctance of the courts to order stays when proceedings are already in the courts will be diminished when the applicant has a material advantage in having his dispute arbitrated.

6   Where fraud is alleged, Section 24(2) of the 1950 Act allows the party against whom the fraud is alleged to have the matter heard before the

court. If the party making the allegation wishes the matter to go to court he or she must at least prove a prima facie case of fraud. In any event, the party applying for the stay must show that the fraud alleged falls within the scope of the arbitration agreement. If it does not, then no stay will be available.

25.3.3   Procedure in arbitrations

It is often suggested that an arbitrator is master of the procedure to be adopted in the arbitration proceedings. This is an overstatement of his or her powers.

First, the arbitration agreement is fundamental to the arbitrator's appointment and, hence, any procedural rules laid down in the agreement must be complied with. A number of special procedures have been developed for use with the various standard form contracts. If the agreement incorporates such a document, the arbitrator *must* follow the procedure stipulated in those agreed rules unless the parties make a subsequent agreement altering the procedure.

Second, a number of rules have been established concerning the arbitration process. It is clear from a long line of decisions that the arbitrator must act fairly in his handling of the proceedings. In *Moran v Lloyd* [1983] 1 Ll Rep 51 misconduct was said to include 'any failure to give a party a reasonable and proper opportunity to put forward his own case and to rebut that of the opposite party'. The need for the arbitrator to act fairly is, perhaps, obvious. Another line of authority suggests a not-so-obvious constraint on the arbitration, that it be conducted along adversarial lines. This means that the hearing is to be run so that each party presents his or her case; it is not for the arbitrator to determine issues of his or her own making and to question the parties in order to adduce evidence which the parties choose not to adduce. This not-so-obvious rule is exemplified by the decision in *Town & City Properties (Development) Ltd v Wiltshire Southern Ltd and Gilbert Powell* 44 BLR 114. In this case the arbitrator appointed under a JCT form of contract decided that he would run the arbitration as an inquisitorial investigation. He held technical meetings with the parties (although one of them objected to this mode of procedure), published a detailed document which he called a 'Preliminary view' upon which he invited comments. When no comments were received he published the same document as an award. The court removed the arbitrator on the grounds that he had misconducted the proceedings in adopting a non-adversarial approach. Sir William Stabb, in his judgment, adopted the following passage from Mustill and Boyd's textbook:

> Unless the parties have agreed to the contrary, expressly or by implication, the arbitrator is required to adopt an 'adversarial' rather than an 'inquisitorial' procedure. Under such a procedure it is not the function of the judge or arbitrator to seek out the truth by engaging in speculation, pursuing enquiries or calling for and examining witnesses. His task is to choose between two alternative versions of the truth, presented to him by the parties.

This view of the law is difficult to reconcile with Section 12(1) of the 1950 Arbitration Act (which was not discussed in the judgment) which provides

Unless a contrary intention is expressed therein, every arbitration agreement shall, where such provision is applicable to the reference be deemed to contain a provision that the parties to the reference, and all parties claiming through them respectively, shall, subject to any legal objection, submit to be examined by the arbitrator or umpire, on oath or affirmation, in relation to the matter in dispute and shall, subject as aforesaid, produce before the arbitrator or umpire all documents within their possession or power respectively which may be required or called for, and do all other things which during the proceedings on the reference the arbitrator or umpire may require.

25.4   Alternative dispute resolution

There is currently a great deal of disillusionment in the construction industry, and indeed in many industries, concerning the traditional methods of dispute resolution. In particular it is thought that they are too expensive, too lengthy and do not promote good commercial relations. In order to overcome some of these perceived difficulties, a number of forms of non-binding dispute resolution techniques have been suggested. These have been pioneered in the USA and are gaining popularity here in the UK. The common perception among industrialists and construction professionals is that litigation is confrontational (not the way to reach compromise) and impenetrable in its jargon and procedures (so that those who should be taking the decisions cannot find out what the real issues are). In order for Alternative Dispute Resolution (ADR) to work, methods have to be established whereby the system is designed to be less confrontational and to be straightforward so that senior executives can be present and can, at an early stage, be presented with the important commercial issues so that they can take a proper commercial view of the way they wish to deal with the dispute.

A number of techniques have been developed. All are non-binding (that is the parties are not bound to follow the resulting recommendation) and, indeed, it may well be that this is one of the keys to their success. If parties feel that they have nothing to lose, but much to gain, they are often prepared to enter into the ADR process. Since the results are non-binding, the expenditure on preparation and legal fees is often greatly reduced; but there is a degree of formality in the process which ensures that thought is given by the parties to preparing their best case.

Some spectacular successes are claimed for ADR in the USA. Philip Naughton QC, an English lawyer, in a recent article (*Constr LJ* Vol 6 No 3) tells of his experiences in observing ADR in the USA and comments: 'There is something almost magical in following the progress of a mediated settlement. ... I have been impressed by how well mediations which looked hopeless actually worked.' These reflections might also be compared with the incredulity of many observers of litigation as they see settlements made 'at the door of the court' on occasion after occasion, the expense and effort of which may so easily have been saved if ADR had been attempted at an early stage.

The following techniques are common in the USA and it is to be hoped that they will soon come to be used in Britain also. There seem to be no standardised definitions (see Sir Lawrence Street's article, *Arbitration* Vol 58 No 2(S), for a discussion on the various definitions used); the following are advanced in order to illustrate the distinctions made between the various techniques rather than to provide universal definitions.

1 *Conciliation* here a third party endeavours to bring the parties to a dispute together in order to discuss and to resolve their dispute. The conciliator does not become heavily involved, does not meet either of the parties in private and it is not his or her function to suggest possible solutions to the dispute. The conciliator is a catalyst rather than a source of energy.

2 *Mediation* here a third party brings the parties to a dispute together. The mediator discusses the issues with them, both in open session and in private discussions with individual parties. The mediator often acts as a messenger who shuttles between the parties with suggestions. While it is not his or her function to suggest solutions, for it is important that the mediator is perceived as impartial and open-minded throughout, he or she is entitled to point out strengths and weaknesses of each party's case.

3 *The mini-trial* this is a short hearing in which each party presents its summary case in an agreed time (usually two hours or less) with short replies to the other party's then following. The panel who are addressed during this procedure consists of an independent third party and representatives of both sides, often senior executives from each disputant who are not connected with the dispute. The panel retires at the end of the presentations and formulates recommendations which can be accepted or rejected by executives from each side. The object of the exercise is to allow both sides to prepare their best points and then to 'run them past' senior executives, who are in the best position to take commercial decisions such as whether to pursue the case or to settle.

An important matter to be considered by those disputants who wish to go to a conciliator or mediator is to set out the limits to the conciliator/mediator's authority to meet parties in private (if any), to make suggestions for compromise (if any), and to lay down ground rules for the protection of information passed to the conciliator/mediator by parties in private.

Numerous articles and other publications are now available on the subject of ADR (for example see *Arbitration*, which regularly carries material on all aspects of ADR). A study of these will indicate the variety of techniques available.

The role of construction professionals in the administration of construction contracts and resolution of construction law disputes

26.1 Introduction

Construction professionals are, of course, very much involved in the administration of construction contracts and the resolution of disputes. Such involvement is often informal, as when they act as the person employed to inspect the works during construction, or when they discuss potential methods of resolving a dispute with other interested parties. They can, however, become more formally involved in the administration of construction contracts and the resolution of construction disputes in a number of ways:

- as the certifying authority under a construction contract
- as an expert witness in proceedings (litigation or arbitration)
- as an advocate
- as an arbitrator (or mediator or conciliator).

26.2 Construction professionals as certifiers under construction contracts

26.2.1 The role of the certifier

Most construction contracts make provision for a certifier who certifies payments, values variations, and who, in addition, acts as the employer's agent. It is well established that such a certifier has two roles: one as certifier and another as the employer's agent. That these separate roles should not be confused was emphasised by Mr Justice Vinelott in *London Borough of Merton v Stanley Hugh Leach* 32 BLR 51. In the paragraph quoted below he describes the position of the architect under the Standard (JCT) Building Contract, but the same will be true of the engineer under the Standard (ICE) Civil Engineering Contract or a certifier/agent under most of the other major standard form contracts:

> It is to my mind clear that under the standard conditions the architect acts as the servant or agent of the building owner in supplying the

contractor with the necessary drawings, instructions, levels and the like and in supervising the progress of the work and in ensuring that it is properly carried out. He will of course normally though not invariably have been responsible for the design of the work. There are very few occasions when a building owner himself is required to act directly without the intervention of the architect. ... To the extent that the architect performs these duties the building owner contracts with the contractor that the architect will perform them with reasonable diligence and with reasonable skill and care. The contract also confers on the architect discretionary powers which he must exercise with due regard to the interests of the contractor and the building owner. The building owner does not undertake that the architect will exercise his discretionary powers reasonably; he undertakes that although the architect may be engaged or employed by him he will leave him free to exercise his discretion fairly and without improper interference by him.

The standard contracts often allow an arbitrator to 'open up, review and revise' the instructions and certificates issued by the architect or engineer as appropriate. This is one of the safeguards which the contractor has under the contract. But the arbitrator's power in this context is to open up the instructions and certificates issued by the certifier in his or her role *as certifier*; the arbitrator cannot review the instructions given by the certifier when he or she acts as the *employer's agent*. In *Merton v Leach* Mr Justice Vinelott said

to the extent that the architect acts as the agent or servant of the building owner in discharging obligations imposed on the building owner by the contract his acts are not subject to review by the arbitrator – though they may found a claim for damages for breach of contract the extent of which will fall to be determined by the arbitrator.

26.2.2   The requirement that the certifier should act fairly

The certifier when acting in his or her capacity as certifier is under a duty to act fairly between the parties. However, there is no obligation upon the certifier to afford a full hearing, or anything like it, to the parties when he or she makes a decision or issues an instruction or certificate. In *Borough of Hounslow v Twickenham Garden Developments Ltd* 7 BLR 81, Mr Justice Megarry said

It seems to me that an architect under a building contract has to discharge a great number of functions, both great and small, which call for the exercise of his skilled professional judgment. He must throughout retain his independence in exercising that judgment; but provided he does this, I do not think that, unless the contract so provides, he need go further and observe the rules of natural justice, giving due notice of all complaints and affording both parties a hearing. His position as an expert and the wide range of matters that he has to decide point against any such requirement: and an attempt to divide the trivial from the important, with natural justice applying only to the latter, would be of almost insuperable difficulty. It is the position of independence and skill that affords the parties the proper safeguards, and not the imposition of rules requiring something in the nature of a hearing.

26.2.3 The duty of care owed by the certifier to his or her client

The role of the certifier has often been characterised as 'quasi-judicial' or 'quasi-arbitral'. From this proposition it has, in the past, been argued that since judges and arbitrators are immune from liability for professional negligence, then so too are certifiers. This argument was decisively rejected in *Sutcliffe v Thackrah* 4 BLR 16. In this case it was held that an architect who negligently over-certified a payment could be sued by his or her client for the loss that the client suffered as a result of the architect's negligence. Lord Morris drew a distinction between the role of a certifier under the contract and the role of an arbitrator:

> The question now arising is whether the respondents were functioning in an arbitral role when they issued the two interim certificates dated 25 May and 1 July 1964. It was with the object of so asserting that by the re-amended defence the pleader denied that the respondents owed any duty to the appellant to use reasonable care in issuing certificates. If this were right the position would be strangely anomalous and illogical. An examination of the RIBA contract shows how manifold are the duties of the architect. Being employed by and paid by the owner he unquestionably has in diverse ways to look after the interests of the owner. In doing so he must be fair and he must be honest. He is not employed by the owner to be unfair to the contractor. If work to a certain specification is to be done under the contract there is neither unfairness nor partisanship in ensuring that the work is properly carried out. It would be unfair to the owner to permit work that is inferior to the contract terms: it would be unfair to a contractor to require work that is superior to the contract terms. So a proper and reasonable discharge of his duties by an architect demands supervision on his part. If by reason of negligent supervision on the part of an architect loss or damage results for an owner it could hardly be contended, and indeed it is not contended, that the architect could escape liability to the owner for such negligent supervision. If this is so – why should he be immune if the interim certificates which he issues incorporate and set out the results of his faulty supervision? The certificates will merely be the expression of and will result from his preceding negligence. If, as I think is agreed, an architect is not acting as an arbitrator when he supervises the work being done neither should he be regarded as an arbitrator if what he does is to certify more than he would have certified had his supervision been careful rather than careless. The same result should follow in a case where the negligent issuing of interim certificates is not the consequence of any negligence.

26.2.4 The duty of care owed by the certifier to the contractor

Frequently the contractor who enters into a long expensive construction contract depends heavily upon the certifier to provide prompt, full certification. Otherwise the contractor can be left nursing a significant amount of negative cash-flow which may, in some cases, cause the contractor to become insolvent.

Can the contractor sue the certifier for losses (such as interest payments) which he experiences as a result of negligently inadequate certification? Clearly, the usual situation is that there is no contract between the certifier and the contractor and so such an action must proceed, unlike the case of *Sutcliffe v Thackrah*, in tort. In *Pacific Associates v Baxter* 44 BLR 33 the

Court of Appeal decided that, in the normal situation, no such action would succeed. The action had to proceed on the basis of the rule in *Hedley Byrne v Heller and Partners* [1964] AC 465 (see Section 18.4.4). However, their Lordships were clear that the requirements of the rule were not made out; in short, the contractor did not reasonably rely on the certifier in the sense required by *Hedley Byrne v Heller* and hence the certifier was not liable to the contractor for negligent certification.

26.3 Where the construction professional is an expert witness

26.3.1 Witness of fact and expert witnesses

The general rule of evidence is that witnesses must state the facts which they perceived and must not give their opinion about what inferences are to be drawn from those facts; it is for the tribunal to draw the appropriate inferences. However, it is recognised that, in some situations, it is of great benefit if evidence of opinion can be adduced. For example, in a technical matter, a witness is often much better placed, either by virtue of his or her training or experience, to decide what inferences may be drawn and, in such cases, opinion evidence is admissible. In *Folkes v Chadd* (1782) 99 ER 589, for instance, the question was whether an earth bank, which had been erected as part of a sea-defence system, contributed to the choking up of a harbour with sand. John Smeaton, the most celebrated engineer of his day, was called to give evidence. An objection was raised by the other party on the grounds that Smeaton was going to give evidence of opinion, not fact. Lord Mansfield said

> The question is, to what has this decay been owing? The defendant says to this bank. Why? Because it prevents the back water. That is a matter of opinion; the whole case is a question of opinion, from facts agreed upon. Nobody can swear that it was the cause; nobody thought it would produce this mischief when the bank was erected.
>
> Mr Smeaton is called. A confusion now arises from a misapplication of terms. It is objected that Mr Smeaton is going to speak, not as facts, but as to opinion. That opinion, however, is deduced from facts which are not disputed – the situation of banks, the course of tides and of winds, and the shifting of sands. His opinion deduced from all these facts is, that, mathematically speaking, the bank may contribute to the mischief, but not sensibly. Mr Smeaton understands the construction of harbours, the causes of their destruction and how remedied. In matters of science no other witnesses can be called. ... I cannot believe that where the question is, whether a defect arises from a natural or an artificial cause, the opinions of men of science are not to be received.

However, opinion evidence should not be admitted if it relates to matters which are clearly within the tribunal's knowledge and understanding. For instance in *Hinds v London Transport Executive* [1979] RTR 103, Lord Denning said of a report:

> Reading through that report, it is quite plain that it is merely giving arguments in favour of the plaintiff on the issues of negligence and causation and so forth. I cannot see that it contains any expert evidence at all. Some people

try to call engineers in these cases but they are of no help to the court. They only give the arguments which counsel can give as well or better.

26.3.2   Who is entitled to be an expert witness?

In construction law cases an expert will normally be a member of the relevant professional body. If the opinion evidence required relates to civil engineering matters, then the expert will normally be a chartered civil engineer; or if the evidence required relates to the layout of a building or building finishes, a chartered architect may be retained. However, there are no formal requirements and the tribunal may accept anyone as an expert witness provided that they have experience and knowledge of the matters in question.

When the matter involves highly technical issues, academics may be instructed. However, there is a tendency to appoint university staff simply because they appear to be well qualified academically and to have published in the relevant field. A client should be careful to ensure that the witness is appropriate – and if the dispute turns upon practical matters, an academic is unlikely to be the most appropriate witness.

In *R v Silverlock* [1894] 2 QB 766 a witness who had no professional qualifications was called to give evidence about whether one piece of handwritten text was in the same hand as the writing in a letter. The witness was, in fact, a solicitor who testified that he had studied handwriting as a hobby for about ten years. Lord Russell of Killowen ruled on the qualities required in expert witnesses before they can be called to give evidence of opinion:

> It is true that the witness who is called upon to give evidence founded on a comparison of handwritings must be *peritus*; he must be skilled in so doing; but we cannot say that he must have become *peritus* in the way of his business, or in any definite way. The question is, is he *peritus*? Is he skilled? Has he had an adequate knowledge? Looking at the matter practically, if a witness is not skilled the judge will tell the jury to disregard his evidence. There is no decision which requires that the evidence of a man who is skilled in comparing handwriting and has formed a reliable opinion from past experience, should be excluded because his experience has not been gained in the way of his business. It is, however, really unnecessary to consider this point; for it seems from the statement in the present case that the witness was not only *peritus*, but *peritus* in the way of his business. When once it is determined that the evidence is admissible, the rest is merely a question of its value or weight, and this is entirely a question for the jury, who will attach more or less weight to it according as they believe the witness to be *peritus*.

26.3.3   The functions of expert witnesses

The work of expert witnesses can be divided into a number of phases. When first consulted by their clients they must give frank advice, indicating the strengths but also the weaknesses of their clients' case and advising on the potential arguments available to 'the opposition' (it is difficult to avoid the use of such language in the context of the adversarial system). Perhaps the client will wish to be reassured that his or her case is good, but that is not the expert's function; if the expert believes that the case is not a strong one he or she should advise the client to attempt to settle without recourse to arbitration or litigation.

The second phase involves experts in 'constructing a case' and in writing a report which summarises their views. They should collate all the available data and arrange it so that their clients' case is seen in the best light and so that appropriate responses are produced to rebut any arguments which may be put forward by the other side. This phase involves imaginative development and arrangement of the facts so that the best possible case can be advanced.

The third phase involves meeting the expert(s) from the other side to agree facts and, if possible, to reach agreement on the implications of those facts. By 'if possible' often means, in practice, 'if appropriate', because the two sides will often be trying to show that different consequences flow from agreed facts. For example, experts may agree that certain ground conditions in fact existed; but they may not be able to agree as to whether or not such conditions were 'reasonably foreseeable by an experienced contractor', since such inferences often form the very substance of the plaintiff/claimant's case or the response by the defendant/respondent.

The fourth and final phase involves presenting the technical case in court. This will normally involve the experts in presenting the report which they have prepared to the tribunal and in answering questions on that report. Their client's counsel will examine them in chief, in order to highlight the significant parts of the report. The opposition counsel will attempt to attack the report and the expert will be expected to defend it.

26.3.4 The neutrality of expert witnesses

The question of the neutrality – or otherwise – of experts is a matter that has received a significant amount of attention, particularly in the criminal law sector where a number of miscarriages of justice have recently been reported. It is often felt that the adversarial nature of the litigation/arbitration process does not allow the expert to express a neutral view. In an article in *Arbitration*, Mr Francis Goodall says ('Expert witness: partisan with a conscience', *Arbitration*, August 1990 pp. 159–161):

> In the preparation of his report, in the meetings with other experts, and in his analysis of the other parties' reports for the benefit of his client's counsel, an expert will be influenced by the realities of the adversarial process towards a report that expresses 'the truth and nothing but the truth' but seldom 'the whole truth'. He will include nothing that he does not believe to be a true or at least reasonably arguable interpretation of the data, and then will express no opinion that he does not genuinely hold; he may make light of or pass over in silence such facts and opinions as may be unhelpful to his client, unless as a matter of practical calculation he thinks a particular omission is likely to backfire on him.
>
> If this acceptance of a certain economy with the truth be thought heretical I would quote no less support than His Honour John Newey QC, an Official Referee who has recently written '... since the procedure in both courts and arbitrations is adversarial, an expert is not obliged to speak out, or write in his report, about matters concerning which he has not been asked

at all, either by his client's opponent's counsel or by the Official Referee or arbitrator' (*Construction Disputes: Liability and the Expert Witness*; Andrea Burns ed., Butterworth & Co. (Publishers) Ltd. 1989: p. 241). In practice it is not often the ascertainable facts that give rise to omissions or equivocations: the facts are on record for all to see, in photographs and technical reports. It is the interpretation of those facts, and the deductions drawn from them, and the discounting of them as not material to the problem, that provide scope for crucial differences of opinion or emphasis. In a report for exchange the expert is entitled to leave unsaid such of his opinions and conclusions as are disadvantageous to his client. That is not to resist telling 'the whole truth'. The opinion of an expert, be he never so eminent, is not 'the truth' even though it is truly his own; so he may keep it to himself if he thinks fit, until such time as someone may question him about it directly.

But Mr Goodall concludes his article with the following statement which should be borne in mind by any expert:

> One of the first things asked of the expert [when he takes the witness stand] is whether he stands by his report or whether he has, for whatever reason, had second thoughts that might make him wish to reconsider any of the opinions he has expressed.
>
> The question is not a formality. It will go hard with the expert witness if there is anything in his report, whether fact or opinion, that he cannot in conscience still support as a perfectly legitimate interpretation of the circumstances, taken overall. That is why in preparing his report he had to be careful to hold his partisanship in check; saying nothing he did not believe to be true, even if he was aware that it was not the whole truth, advancing no interpretation that he did not believe tenable, even though he thought another interpretation more likely.
>
> So long as he has safeguarded his position to that extent, his report can be upheld as being true so far as it goes: but if the witness is directly asked to address matters that he has preferred not to touch upon, or to say which of two possible interpretations he really believes to be the correct one, he has only one course open to him. He must answer the question by declaring his full, true and honest opinion, for the benefit of the tribunal, for the cause of abstract justice and for the sanctity of his own conscience and integrity.

In the *University of Warwick v Sir Robert McAlpine* 42 BLR 1 Mr Justice Garland made the following observations which appear to suggest that the expert should be somewhat more neutral than Mr Goodall would allow:

> It appeared to me that some (but by no means all) of the experts in this case entered into the arena in order to advocate their client's case. This led to perfectly proper cross examination on the basis:
>
> > You have assembled evidence and advanced explanations which you consider most likely to assist your client's case.
>
> It is much to be regretted that this had to be so. In their closing speeches counsel felt it necessary to challenge not only the reliability but also the credibility of experts with unadorned attacks on their veracity. This simply should not happen where the court is called upon to decide complex scientific or technical issues. To a large extent this excessively adversarial approach to expert evidence could have been avoided if experts who had at various times expressed contrary or inconsistent views had dealt with this in their reports giving any necessary explanations. Similarly, where experts alter their views

at a late stage or introduce a wholly new theory or interpretation, the new approach should be reduced to writing and furnished to the other parties at the earliest possible opportunity so that all the relevant experts can give the matter due consideration and, in a proper case, meet in order to define what is common ground and where they differ. ... It is in my view salutary to recall the observations of Lord Wilberforce in *Whitehouse v Jordan* [1981] 1 WLR 246 at page 256:

> It is necessary that expert evidence presented to the court should be, and should be seen to be, the independent product of the expert, uninfluenced as to form or content by the existence of litigation. To the extent that it is not, the evidence is likely to be not only incorrect but self-defeating.

26.4   The construction professional as advocate

Arbitration cases need not be presented by lawyers. Anyone may act as an advocate and in some cases lay advocates may be most appropriate. Before taking on a case would-be lay advocates should familiarise themselves with the procedures of arbitration and should, ideally, have attended a substantial number of hearings and should note well the process and the etiquette.

Often parties will agree in advance that there will be no representation by lawyers and clearly in these situations a lay advocate is not only desirable but also necessary. In no-lawyer arbitrations many of the formalities may be relaxed, though it is preferable if the arbitrator has a sound knowledge of the law; the fact that no lawyers are present does not affect the requirement that the proceedings be conducted fairly and that the decision be made in accordance with the law.

26.5   The construction professional as arbitrator, conciliator or mediator

26.5.1   Introduction

Many construction professionals are appointed as arbitrators, conciliators or mediators. They have a good working knowledge of the industry and often have senior management and technical skills which are often useful in the resolution of disputes. An outline of the law of arbitration was presented in Chapter 25 and Alternative Dispute Resolution (ADR) was briefly introduced. Arbitrators, whether they be construction professionals or lawyers, must follow the same rules relating to acting fairly and must conduct the arbitration in accordance with the rules, if any, agreed by the parties.

It is important that construction professionals are fully versed in the techniques of arbitration, mediation or conciliation before they take an appointment. Professionals should not allow themselves to take a case which they cannot handle any more than they should agree to design a structure for which they have no training. In *Pratt v Swanmore Builders and Baker* 15 BLR 37, Mr Justice Pain had this to say of an arbitrator who had been chosen from the Institute of Arbitrator's panel of arbitrators and who was out of his depth:

This arbitration went wrong from the very beginning. [The arbitrator] was not employed for his knowledge of the law and he is not to be found guilty of misconduct simply because he made one or more mistakes of law. But by allowing his name to be used on the Institute's panel, he held himself out as a skilled arbitrator and he must be held responsible for the arbitration. Although he cannot be made liable in negligence I take the view that it could be misconduct to fail in certain respects to show the elementary skill of an arbitrator.

26.5.2   The scope of an expert arbitrator's power to use his or her specialist knowledge

One matter of importance to construction professionals who act as arbitrators is whether or not they are entitled to use their own specialist knowledge in coming to their decision. Many construction professionals are chosen precisely because they have such knowledge or skill. Yet they are told that the law is that arbitrations must be run along adversarial lines. This issue has not been properly developed in the current textbooks on arbitration law. The following section examines the issue.

Arbitration is consensual; it is governed by the agreement of the parties. The terms of the arbitration agreement are therefore paramount in defining the arbitrator's power to use his own specialist knowledge. Arbitration agreements rarely, however, contain any express guidance on how the arbitrator is to use any such knowledge and so the implied intention of the parties must be sought.

Implied power to use specialist knowledge
When an expert arbitrator is appointed, the law readily implies a power for him to use his expert knowledge. This has been recognised both in regard to regulating the procedure of the arbitration (provided that the terms of the arbitration agreement and the rules of natural justice are complied with) and in reaching an award. Regarding procedural regulation Mr Justice Goff said of the arbitrator in *Carlisle Place Investments Ltd v Wimpey Construction (UK) Ltd* 15 BLR 109:

> Here is an expert arbitrator, an architect, who has knowledge of the technical side of a dispute of this kind and has been appointed for that reason. He has carried out a series of inspections of the site. The case is one which concerns a proliferation of disputes concerning a large number of separate roofs. There is a serious danger that the case may get out of hand and the costs allowed to escalate to an enormous degree. Against that background, the arbitrator has made an order limiting the question of liability to evidence in respect of 25 roofs. I find it impossible to say that the arbitrator should have exceeded his jurisdiction in making such an order.

In relation to the use of the arbitrator's expert knowledge in reaching an award, Mr Justice Branson, in *Jordernson & Co v Stara, Kopperbergs Bergslag Atkiebolag* [1931] 41 Rep 201, said

> Now I think that the fact that this umpire was an expert in the timber trade and was appointed because he was such an expert must not be lost sight of. I think the parties must be taken to have assented to his using the knowledge which they chose him for possessing.

This may be contrasted with the case where a lawyer has been chosen as arbitrator, where it will generally be implied that the arbitrator does not have such authority. In *Mediterranean & Eastern Export Co Ltd v Fortress Fabrics (Manchester) Ltd* [1948] 2 All ER 186, for instance, Lord Goddard said

> If, for instance, a lawyer was called on to act as arbitrator on a commercial contract he would not be entitled, unless the terms of the submission clearly gave him power so to do, to come to a conclusion as to the amount of damages that should be paid without having evidence before him as to the rise or fall of the market, as the case may be, or as to other facts enabling him to apply the correct measure of damage, but, in my opinion, the case is different where the parties select an arbitrator, or agree to arbitrate under the rules of a chamber of commerce under which the arbitrator is appointed for them, and the arbitrator is chosen or appointed because of his knowledge and experience of the trade. There can be no doubt that with regard to questions of quality and matters of that description an arbitrator of this character can always act on his own knowledge.

General and particular knowledge
Although the courts have consistently implied a power for the expert arbitrator to use his or her specialist knowledge, they have also drawn a clear distinction between 'general' and 'particular' knowledge. The former is the general knowledge which persons who engage in that profession or trade are likely to acquire. Particular knowledge relates to 'knowledge of a specific character acquired by [the arbitrator] and peculiar to him rather than such as may be known to experts generally practising in [the same profession or locality]', per Mr Justice Leggatt in *Top Shop Estates v Danino* (1984) 273 EG 197. General knowledge need not be disclosed because, by implication, the parties will intend that the arbitrator will use such knowledge. Special knowledge, on the other hand, if it is to be used to arrive at a finding in the case, must be disclosed, as the parties may wish to make submissions and call evidence on the point in question. The distinction between general and particular knowledge was discussed by Lord Justice O'Connor in *Fox v Wellfair* [1981] 2 Ll Rep 514. He used the following illustration which was related by Lord Justice Dunn in his judgment:

> Lord Justice O'Connor gave a good example in argument. An arbitrator is required to value a bull killed by the negligence of one of the parties. If the expert arbitrator relies on his general knowledge of the value of bulls, including fluctuations in the market known to anyone who studies the market, there is no need to disclose it. But if he has recently sold an identical bull for a certain sum, it is necessary to disclose that fact to the parties.

In *FR Waring (UK) Ltd v Administracao Geral do Acucar e do Alcool* [1983] 1 Ll Rep 45 at 49, Mr Justice Robert Goff also stressed the distinction between general and particular knowledge:

> a trade tribunal such as the coffee trade's Board of Appeal is a tribunal which is fully entitled to take into account, in considering any evidence which is presented to it, its own experience of the trade. If it is the general experience of the trade which is being taken into account this must be

understood, and expected, by any parties who come before the tribunal on an arbitration. Of course, if there was some particular knowledge about the events in question, the facts of the particular case, which were known to the tribunal, independently of any evidence presented before it at the arbitration, and they were going to rely upon that, then it can be said with force that that particular knowledge should be drawn to the attention of the parties to enable them to make any comments upon it. But general knowledge of the trade is something which it is understood that the tribunal may apply in considering the evidence which is presented before it in any particular case.

Arbitrator must not gather evidence

Although the law allows arbitrators to use their 'particular' knowledge, which may to some extent be considered a form of evidence, it is a recurrent theme in the cases that arbitrators must not introduce evidence properly so-called. Rather, they must use their expertise to understand the evidence presented to them. In *Owen v Nicholl* [1948] 1 All ER 707, Lord Justice Tucker stated that in his opinion 'it would be misconduct within the meaning of that word as used in relation to arbitration if the arbitrator introduced into proceedings evidence other than that adduced by the parties'; and in *Fox v Wellfair* [1981] 2 Ll Rep 514, Lord Denning said 'His function is not to supply evidence . . . but to adjudicate upon the evidence given before him'.

Many arbitrators, of course, have no opportunity or inclination to obtain evidence of their own. But some expert arbitrators may visit the subject matter of the dispute and be tempted to perform experiments or to undertake investigations or experiments of their own. In *Top Shop Estates v Danino* (1984) 273 EG 197, the arbitrator undertook a survey of the movement of people outside a shop which was the subject of a rent-review arbitration. Mr Justice Legatt said that the arbitrator was

> acting under a misapprehension of his function as an arbitrator which is not to play the part of Perry Mason where he feels that the submissions or evidence of the parties might usefully be supplemented.

While it may appear to be unduly restrictive not to allow expert arbitrators to undertake simple experiments within their own sphere of expertise, the approach in *Top Shop Estates* appears to be consistent with the view of Mustill and Boyd, judicially approved in *Town & City Properties (Development) Ltd v Wiltshire Southern and Gilbert Powell* 44 BLR 114 (see Section 25.3.3). Arbitrators who wish to do more than simply 'view' the subject matter would be wise in these circumstances to obtain the parties' agreement first.

Unopposed evidence and taking a different view

Although arbitrators must not supply evidence, they may use their specialist knowledge to evaluate it and if they so decide, to reject it. In arbitration, evidence may be adduced upon which basis arbitrators may decide that the version of the facts contended for by both parties are incorrect. They may then use their expertise and experience to supply what they consider to be the correct version. This critical evaluation becomes particularly important when the arbitration is undefended and where, the arbitrator, having applied his or her knowledge and experience, decides that the evidence, including expert evidence, adduced by the claimant is not sufficiently strong to prove the case. The cases show clearly that arbitrators may use their expertise in this way; but, whenever an arbitrator intends to decide against the apparent effect of the evidence, he or she must inform the parties so that they can make legal submissions and if appropriate provide counter-evidence to deal with the view which the arbitrator has formed.

In *Fox v Wellfair* [1981] 2 Ll Rep 514 (which involved an undefended arbitration) Lord Justice Dunn said

> If the expert arbitrator, as he may be entitled to do, forms a view of the facts different from that given in the evidence which might produce a contrary result to that which emerges from the evidence, then he should bring that view to the attention of the parties.

In *The Vimeira (Interbulk Ltd v Aiden Shipping Co Ltd)* [1984] 2 Ll Rep 66) where expert shipping arbitrators decided on a basis not argued by either party, Lord Justice Goff approved Lord Justice Dunn's above-quoted statement and the Court of Appeal remitted the award to the arbitrators for further consideration.

Remedies available when arbitrators exceed their authority to use their specialist knowledge
If arbitrators use their expertise outside the scope of their authority or contravene the rules of natural justice, then they have committed technical misconduct and the aggrieved party or parties may wish to seek a remedy. The method of seeking such a remedy is to apply to the court for an order remitting the award back to the arbitrator for his or her reconsideration or alternatively an order setting the award aside.

International aspects of construction law

27.1 Introduction

27.1.1 The construction industry and private international law

Construction is an international business. British companies have historically exported construction services around the world and while the
British share of the international market has undoubtedly diminished,
the operation of British companies abroad continues to make a major
contribution both to the British domestic economy and to the international
construction market generally. Furthermore, the impact of international
factors upon the British construction industry is set to expand rapidly
as the Single European Market is established at the end of 1992, with
all restrictions on European cross-national competition and co-operation
being abolished. Against this background it is clear that no examination
of English construction law would be complete without a study of the main
aspects of international law as it affects construction. In this chapter the
principal topic will be the question of the law applicable to a contract in
an international context since this is now becoming an area of outstanding
importance.

Whenever a contract is made wholly in a domestic context, that is to
say between English parties in England concerning construction based in
England, there is no doubt that English law applies; likewise when a tort
is committed by one English person upon another in England then the
English law of torts clearly applies. But in the context of international
construction, or in situations where not all the relevant parties are English
or where there is some other international element associated with the
project, it is necessary to decide which law, that is the law of which country,
is to govern the situation. This area of law is known as 'the conflict of laws'
or as 'private international law'. The term 'conflict' relates to the situation
where there is a potential choice of governing law. If the law under each
of these systems of law were identical there would be no problem. It would
not be necessary, for example, to decide which system of law governed a
contract or which country has jurisdiction to entertain a dispute in their
courts. Problems arise, however, because the laws of the different countries

are different; they conflict. And when they do conflict it is often necessary to identify which legal system is to govern.

27.1.2 The topics dealt with in this chapter

The following points will be addressed in this chapter:

- if parties enter into a contract with an international element which system of law (i.e. the law of which country) governs the contract
- if a tort is committed with an international element which system of law is to be applied
- if parties have an arbitration agreement in their contract, how can this be enforced?

27.1.3 General considerations relating to international private law

English private international law seeks answers to the following questions:

- Which system of law will the English court apply in a given situation?
- Which disputes may be tried in English courts?
- Which judgments and awards of foreign tribunals will be recognised and/or enforced in England?

In this chapter the principal focus will be on the first of these questions, the applicable law. A few preliminary points need to be clarified relating to the application of foreign law by the English courts.

First, it often comes as a surprise to non-lawyers that the courts of one country will enforce a foreign system of law. The theory is that they do not enforce another system of law; English courts enforce only English law. But it is English law that if the parties expressly say that their contract is to be governed by Spanish law, then the court in England applies the Spanish rules of law. They apply Spanish *rules* not Spanish *law*; the English courts apply only English law. That this is the case becomes clear when a rule in the foreign system of law conflicts with an English statute or is contrary to English public policy. In such a case the English court will not apply the foreign law rule which offends.

Second, the rule of *countries*, not *states*, are applied. Since it is countries (not states) who have legal systems, it is necessary to apply these in order to meet the expectations of the people involved. For example the law in Scotland often differs from that in England, and the states of the USA, because they all have their own legal systems rank as countries for this purpose. It would be meaningless to apply the 'law of the USA' to a contract. The application of the laws of countries rather than of states ties in also with the theory of the conflict of laws. The theory is that the courts of one country apply the rules of another not because of international comity, but in order to do justice to the parties involved.

Third, parties may (intentionally or inadvertently) make English law the governing law by the simple expedient of failing to plead that some law other than English law governs.

Note that while it is generally assumed that the law specified must be that of a recognised country, Clause 68 of The Channel Tunnel contract between Eurotunnel and Trans Manche Link provides that the contract should be: 'governed by and in accordance with the principles common to both English law and French law, and in the absence of such common principles by such general principles of international trade law as have been applied by national and international tribunals'. (See *The Channel Tunnel Group Ltd and another v Balfour Beatty Construction Ltd and others* 56 BLR 18.)

27.2   The governing law of a contract

27.2.1   Introduction

The question to be asked here is: when a contract is agreed which involves an international element, the law of which country governs the contract? Until 1991 the rules on this were based on a long series of court decisions. However, in 1991, the Contracts (Applicable Law) Act 1990 came into force. This enactment changes the law in respect of new contracts. The new rules, as we shall see, are not greatly different in practice from those laid down at common law and much of the substance of the applicable rules remain as before, even if they trace back to a different source. From a theoretical or philosophical point of view, however, they are very different, being based on the terms of an internationally agreed treaty.

The 1990 statute is based on the 1980 EEC Convention on the Law Applicable to Contractual Obligations, commonly known as the Rome Convention. The convention was designed to make the law relating to the choice of contract law identical across the European Community in order to facilitate free trade. In this chapter the new law will be considered in detail. However, since construction contracts are often of long duration and because many are made under seal with a twelve-year limitation period it is still necessary to consider the common law which may continue to be operational for some time to come. The common law will be dealt with first as it is rather more straightforward than the new rules as well as being first in chronological order.

27.2.2   The English common law rule on the choice of contract

The freedom of the parties to make the contract they want is very important in the consciousness of English law. Accordingly, the common law rule concerning which law is to govern a contract with an international element is determined by asking, 'What law did the parties intend should apply?'

In *Vita Food Products Inc v Unus Shipping Co* [1939] AC 277, the leading case on the right of parties to incorporate the proper law of their choice into their contract, Lord Wright said

> It is now well settled that by English law ... the proper law of the contract is the law which the parties intended to apply.

The 'proper law of the contract' is the law which the court will apply when deciding questions such as the validity of the terms and the meaning (construction) of the terms in the contract.

In order to ascertain which is the applicable law the following questions should be asked, stopping when the proper law has been identified. This procedure may be thought of as a series of hierarchical tiers. A positive answer to question 1 prevails over answers to 2 and 3 and so on down the hierarchy. The questions are as follows.

1   Have the parties expressly agreed upon the governing law? (if so, then that is the proper law)
2   If the parties have not expressly agreed upon the governing law, is there an implied agreement to be found in their contract? (if so, then that is the proper law)
3   If the parties have not expressly agreed upon the governing law, and there is no implied agreement to be found in their contract what is the law with the closest connection with the contract? (that is the proper law)

Where the parties expressly select the proper law of the contract
If the parties express a view concerning the applicable law then that is apparently conclusive. Lord Atkin, in *R v International Trustee for the Protection of Bondholders AG* [1937] AC 500, said

> Their intention will be ascertained by the intention expressed in the contract if any, which will be conclusive.

Most international construction contracts contain an express clause concerning the law which is to govern the contract and frequently parties will contract under English law even though neither they nor the works have any connection with Britain.

Note: The reason for this important role of English law may be explained by first, the principal international standard form (the FIDIC Form) which is based squarely on the Institution of Civil Engineers' Contract, which was drafted within the context of English law, and second, English contract law tends to be neutral in relation to commercial law – it doesn't impose obligations on parties which they haven't imposed upon themselves; it simply enforces their intention.

Where the parties do not select the proper law of the contract
The second question to be asked is: is there an implied intention concerning the governing law in the contract? If none can be found, the third question must be investigated and the system of law with the closest and most real connection must be found.

Question 2: the search for the implied selection of the proper law   Frequently, a contract will be made which is not expressed to be governed by any particular law. In such circumstances, the law looks first for indications in the contract terms that some particular proper law was impliedly selected. In *Jacobs v Credit Lyonnais* (1884) 12 QBD 589, Lord Justice Bowen said that in the absence of an express agreement concerning the applicable law

> the only certain guide is to be found in applying sound ideas of business, convenience, and sense to the language of the contract itself, with a view to discovering the true intention of the parties.

In order to ascertain whether some particular law is implied by the terms of the contract there are a variety of devices used. For instance, the parties often agree that disputes arising under the contract are to be decided by the courts of, or by arbitration in, a particular country. In such a case, the inference is raised that the parties intended that the law of that country should be the governing law. In *Compagnie Tunisienne de Navigation SA v Compagnie d'Armement Maritime SA* [1971] AC 572 Lord Wilberforce said

> An arbitration clause must be treated as an indication to be considered together with the rest of the contract and relevant surrounding facts. Always it will be a strong indication. . . . But in other cases it must give way where other indications are clear.

The courts also seem to be prepared to derive an implied expression of intention from the factual matrix operating at the time of making a contract. In particular, if the contract for which the proper law is sought is a subcontract, the proper law of the main contract will be important if the two are to be operated within the same organisational scheme. In *JMJ Contractors v Marples Ridgeway* 31 BLR 104, Marples Ridgeway had entered into a land reclamation contract based on the FIDIC contract form with an Iraqi governmental organisation. That contract was expressed to be governed by Iraqi law. Marples Ridgeway then subcontracted certain works, that subcontract being signed in Iraq and based on the ICE form of subcontract. No express agreement was made concerning the applicable proper law of the subcontract. The question arose as to what was the proper law as the subcontract contained no expressed intention on this matter. Mr Justice Mervyn Davies held that the proper law of the subcontract was Iraqi law since in this case the subcontract had to be operated in conjunction with the main contract which was itself governed by Iraqi law. In particular, the subcontractor's rights and obligations were closely tied into the main contract (e.g. the subcontractor undertook the like obligations as the main contractor had under the main contract) and the engineer under the main contract had important parallel functions under both subcontract and main contract.

Question 3: the search for the law with the closest and most real connection   If no implied selection can be found the law asks: which is the legal system with the closest connection with the contract? That system will become the proper law. The court, in essence, asks which system of law they would have chosen to govern their contract if they had directed their mind to the question. In *Bonython v Commonwealth of Australia* [1951] AC 201 Lord Simonds said

> The proper law of the contract [is] the system of law by reference to which the contract was made or that with which the transaction has its closest and most real connection.

In *Whitworth Street Estates Ltd v James Miller and Partners* [1970] AC 583 a Scottish company was to convert a factory in Scotland into a warehouse. The contract was agreed in Scotland. The employer was an English company and the contract form was the RIBA contract. The House of Lords held that English law was the proper law for a variety of reasons including that the contract form used was 'redolent of English law'.

In cases decided earlier in the twentieth century the courts appear to have adopted a number of presumptions in deciding which system of law had the closest connection with the contract. They suggested on a number of occasions that the law of the place where the contract was made (the *lex loci contractus*) or the place where the contract was to be performed (the *lex loci solutionis*) should be presumed to be the proper law. Later decisions have not supported the use of such presumptions: see for instance Lord Diplock in *Amin Rasheed Shipping Corporation v Kuwait Insurance Co* [1984] AC 50.

27.2.3 The Rome Convention rules on the choice of law for new contracts

Article 1(1) of the 1980 Rome Convention, now enacted as the Contracts (Applicable Law) Act 1990, provides that 'the rules of this Convention shall apply to contractual obligations in any situation involving a choice between the laws of different countries'. The Convention, it will be observed, applies to *any situation involving a choice* and its operation is not limited to the case where the contract is made in a European Community context. The question of what amounts to a 'contractual obligation' for this purpose is not entirely clear but in time the European Court will, it is expected, develop a community-wide definition.

One of the prime objectives of the Convention is to ensure uniform application of the rules relating to the choice of governing law of contracts across the Community. In order to ensure this, a supplementary treaty, the First Protocol on the Interpretation by the Court of Justice of the European Communities of the Convention on the Law Applicable to Contractual Obligations, authorises the European Court to interpret the Convention on the application by national courts for a ruling. In addition, Article 18 of the Convention provides that the rules shall not be interpreted by national courts with sole regard to their own legal systems but that 'regard shall be had to their international character and to the desirability of achieving uniformity in their interpretation and application'. Lawyers who have to make predictions concerning the way the courts will decide issues will, therefore, study the official Community report on the Convention (the Guiliana-La Garde Report) in order to understand the purposes of, and the background to, the various articles of the Convention.

Where the parties have expressed a choice or where an implied choice can be inferred
The rule, endorsed by the common law, that the parties may, by express choice, determine the governing law is also contained in the Convention. Article 3(1) provides that 'a contract shall be governed by the law chosen by the parties. The choice must be express or demonstrated with reasonable certainty by the terms of the contract or the circumstances of the case. By

their choice the parties can select the law applicable to the whole or a part only of the contract'. The requirement of reasonable certainty will require some clarification by the courts but the intention here appears to be to allow an implied choice, as is allowed under the English common law.

The Convention rules on the choice, express or implied, of the applicable law thus appear similar to those of the common law. However, the Convention imposes a number of restrictions to the unfettered choice of law, particularly in relation to situations where consumers are involved. For example, Article 5 provides that in the case of a consumer contract, that is where goods and services are supplied to a person for a purpose outside the scope of that person's trade or business, the choice of law shall not deprive that person 'of the protection afforded to him by the mandatory rules of the law of the country where he has his habitual residence'. Article 6 deals in a similar vein with employment contracts.

The above restrictions in the case of consumer and employment contracts may not have a significant influence on construction law. One area of potentially greater importance is the rule contained in Article 3(3) which applies to all contracts including commercial contracts. This provides that where all the elements of a contract relate to one country the parties may choose a different law to govern their contract but that choice shall not 'prejudice the application of the laws of that country which cannot be derogated from by contract, hereinafter called "mandatory rules"'. This rule applies only where all the elements of a contract relate to one country, so that if English parties agree to undertake construction works in England but expressly agree that the contract shall be governed by German law, for instance, the courts of the European Community would still apply 'mandatory rules' of English law although German law would generally be applied.

Where no choice of law is expressed
Article 4(1) provides that if there is no choice of law by the parties 'the contract shall be governed by the law of the country with which it is most closely connected'. This rule appears similar to the common law test of 'closest and most real connection' but underlying it is the concept of 'characteristic performance' derived from Swiss jurisprudence. Note also that the reference here is to the *country* rather than the *legal system* which has the closest connection.

In order to guide the identification of the country which has the closest connection, the Convention provides a number of presumptions. It provides that the country with the closest connection shall be the one 'where the party who is to effect the performance which is characteristic of the contract has, at the time of the conclusion of the contract, his habitual residence, or, in the case of a body corporate or unincorporate, its central administration' (in the case of a construction contract the characteristic performance is clearly the construction of the works). And where the contract is made in the course of a party's trade or profession, the country with the closest connection 'shall be the country in which the principal place of business is situated or, where under the terms of the contract the performance is to be effected through a place of business other than the principal place of business, the country in which that other place of business is situated'. However these presumptions shall be 'disregarded if it appears from the circumstances as a whole that the contract is more closely connected with another country'.

Although it appears from the general rule that the country with the closest connection might be the country where the contractor's principal office is situated, the place of construction will, it is suggested, always tend to be an extremely strong contender for the country with the closest connection.

27.2.4 The time at which the governing law is fixed

The common law dealt with the time at which the governing law was fixed in line with the general principles of the English contract law, that is to say once the agreement is made, the proper law is fixed unless the contract is varied. Accordingly, those events which happen after the contract is made cannot affect the proper law of the contract. In *Whitworth Street Estates Ltd v James Miller & Partners* [1970] AC 583, Lord Wilberforce said

> In my opinion, once it was seen that the parties had made no express choice of law, the correct course was to ascertain from all the relevant contemporary circumstances, including, but not limited to, what the parties said or did at the time, what intention ought to be imputed to them on the formation of the contract. Unless it were to found an estoppel or a subsequent agreement, I do not think that subsequent conduct can be relevant to this question.

However, the Rome Convention takes a different stance in relation to this question. When the parties choose the law to govern a contract this can be done 'at any time' (Article 3(2)), presumably including after the contract has been made, and presumably without the need for a formal variation of contract as would be required by English law. In the event that no choice is made, the country with the closest connection provides the governing law; but under the Convention rules this may change throughout the currency of the contract. Article 4 of the Convention does nothing to exclude the possibility that events occurring after the contract is made may be used to establish the country with the closest connection.

27.3 The governing law when a tort has been committed

The underlying law relating to the governing law of torts committed in an international setting has not been addressed in its European context to the same degree as has been the case for contracts. However, there have been a number of *ad hoc* Directives which have been enacted in the field of consumer torts, so that a uniformity of rules throughout the European Community is provided. An example of this is the Consumer Protection Act 1987.

The academic literature on the common law rules and the underlying jurisprudence of the conflict of laws in the field of tort is vast but unfortunately the English cases are rare. The recent decision in *Murphy v Brentwood* [1990] 3 WLR 414, 50 BLR 1 will mean that fewer tort cases will be brought in the area of commercial construction law but, nonetheless, they are still of significant importance. The increased amount of 'design and build' contracting means that concurrent contract and tort claims may be run against contractors, tort claims being made under the *Hedley Byrne v Heller* principle. The problem of mixed tort and contract claims was addressed by Lord Denning in *Sayers v International Drilling Co* [1971] 1 WLR 1176, where he said

> We cannot apply two systems of law, one for the claim in tort, and the other for the defence in contract. We must apply one system of law by which to decide both claim and defence.

He found that Dutch law was the proper law (of the dispute presumably) and applied it both to the contract and tort aspects of the claim.

The mainstream modern law on the governing law of a tort is based on dicta by Mr Justice Willes in *Phillips v Eyre* (1870) LR 6 QB 1. He said

> As a general rule, in order to found a suit in England for a wrong alleged to have been committed abroad, two conditions must be fulfilled. First, the wrong must be of such a character that it would have been actionable if committed in England. . . . Secondly, the act must not have been justifiable by the law of the place where it was done.

This twin-rule approach undermines the *lex loci delicti* (the law of the place where the tort was committed) governing law applied in many countries. Since the *locus delicti* is often fortuitous or would not be imagined by most people to govern their tortious relations its application is apt to lead to injustice.

Mr Justice Willes' statement has been very influential in this branch of the law, but a variety of approaches have been adopted in interpreting its two limbs. Suffice it to say that its application is not always clear. A suggestion made by some writers (e.g. Morris in 1951, in the *Harvard Law Review*) that the action should be governed by the 'proper law of the tort' may overcome some of the difficulties in this area of the law.

27.4 International arbitration agreements

27.4.1 Staying international disputes to arbitration

When there is a 'domestic' contract (i.e. one which involves no international element) the Court has a discretion under Section 4 of the Arbitration Act 1950 to stay litigation proceedings upon the application of either party when there is an arbitration agreement (see Section 25.3.2). In the case of a non-domestic arbitration agreement the Court's power to order a stay is given by Section 1 of the Arbitration Act 1975. In this latter case the stay is granted to the applicant as of right and the Court has no discretion to withhold a stay.

27.4.2 The governing law of arbitration

Dicey and Morris, in their influential book on the conflict of laws, suggest that 'the validity, effect and interpretation of an arbitration agreement are governed by its proper law. The law governing arbitration proceedings is the law chosen by the parties, or, in the absence of agreement, the law of the country in which the arbitration is held' (Rule 58).

Questions may arise as to whether, for instance, the arbitrator has, under the arbitration agreement, the jurisdiction to decide on particular issues. Such questions are determined in accordance with the proper law of the arbitration agreement which is normally, but not necessarily, the same as the proper law of the contract to which it relates.

There has arisen a debate concerning 'de-localised' arbitration; its proponents suggest that arbitrations may be held without reference to the procedural (and indeed they say substantive) rules of a particular country. In the case of construction law this debate has its greatest relevance in relation to arbitrations under the auspices of the International Chamber of Commerce (ICC) which operates from Paris but which claims to be an international body. Such ICC arbitrations are commonly agreed in international construction contracts such as the FIDIC contract. English law, however, appears to require an arbitration to operate under some recognisable system of national law (but see the dicta by Sir John Donaldson in *Deutsche Schachtbau v R'as Al Khaimah National Oil Company (No. 1)* [1987] 3 WLR 1023).

Bibliography

References in this book

Burns A (ed.) *Construction Disputes: Liability and the Expert Witness* Butterworth 1989

Duncan-Wallace I N *Hudson's Building and Engineering Contracts* 10th edn Sweet & Maxwell 1970 (A supplement to this book was published in 1979)

Goff and Jones G *The Law of Restitution* 3rd edn Sweet & Maxwell 1986

Goodall F Expert witness: partisan with a conscience *Arbitration* August 1990 159–61

May A *Keating on Building Contracts* 5th edn Sweet & Maxwell 1991

Mustill M and Boyd S C *Commercial Arbitration* 2nd edn Butterworth 1989

Naughton P Alternative forms of dispute resolution – their strengths and weaknesses *Construction Law Journal* Vol 6 **3** 195–206

Newey L J The preparation of cases in the Official Referees' courts *Construction Law Journal* Vol 6 **3** 216–24

Street L The language of ADR: its utility in resolving international disputes – the role of the mediator *Arbitration* Vol 58 **2** (S) 17–22

Uff J *Construction Law* 5th edn Sweet & Maxwell 1986

Law Commission Consultation Paper **121** 1991

FURTHER READING

Primary sources

Law reports

Reports of decided cases form an extremely important source of construction law in practice; the following specialist series are particularly useful:

- Building Law Reports, published by Longman (five times a year)
- Construction Industry Law Letter published by Legal Studies and Services (Publishing) Ltd (ten times a year)
- Construction Law Journal, published by Sweet & Maxwell (six times a year).

In addition, practitioners follow changes in the general law through general series of law reports such as the Weekly Law Reports, the All England Law Reports and so on. Brief law reports are also published in *The Times* and the *Independent* newspapers.

Statutes

Statutes, subordinate legislation and other similar materials (e.g. European Directives) are published by Her Majesty's Stationery Office and are available at their outlets. Statutes are collected in the series known as Halsbury's Statutes, published by Butterworths in a large number of volumes with a regular updating service.

Construction law and practice

Practical aspects of construction procedure and contracting

Ashworth A *Contractual Procedures in the Construction Industry* 2nd edn Longman 1991

Haswell C K and de Silva D S *Civil Engineering Contracts: Practice and Procedure* 2nd edn Butterworth 1989

Marks R J, Marks R J E and Jackson R E *Aspects of Civil Engineering Contract Procedure* 3rd edn Pergamon 1985

Ramus J W *Contract Practice for Quantity Surveyors* 2nd edn Heinemann Newnes 1989

Turner D F *Standard Contracts for Building* George Godwin 1984

A variety of publications is available outlining contractual procedures in Europe. For a useful introduction see CIRIA publications:

Biggs W D, Betts M and Cottle M J The West German construction industry: a guide for UK professionals *CIRIA Special Publication 68* The Construction Industry Research and Information Association 1990

Meikle J L and Hillebrandt P M The French construction industry: a guide for UK professionals *CIRIA Special Publication 66* The Construction Industry Research and Information Association 1989

Reynolds S D and Sheppard S The Iberian construction industry: A guide for UK professionals *CIRIA Special Publication 67* The Construction Industry Research and Information Association 1989

Construction law

Abrahamson M *Engineering Law and the ICE Contracts* 4th edn Applied Science Publishers 1979 (Note this edition is essentially a commentary which deals with the ICE Contract 5th edn; the new ICE contract 6th edn was published in 1991.)

Cornes D L *Design Liability in the Construction Industry* 3rd edn BSP Professional Books 1989

Duncan-Wallace I N *Construction Contracts: Principles and Policies in Tort and Contract* Sweet & Maxwell 1986

Emden's Construction Law, Butterworth, regularly updated

Galbraith A *Building Law for Students* 2nd edn 1991 Butterworth Heinemann 1991

Powell-Smith V and Sims J *Determination and Suspension of Construction Contracts* Collins 1985

The legal system

Bailey S H and Gunn M J *Smith and Bailey on the Modern English Legal System* 2nd edn Sweet & Maxwell 1991

Foster N *Blackstone's EEC Legislation* 2nd edn Blackstone Press 1991

Steiner J *Textbook on EEC Law* 2nd edn Blackstone Press 1990

Contracts

Furmston M P *Cheshire, Fifoot and Furmston's Law of Contract* 12th edn Butterworth 1991

Smith J C *The Law of Contract* Sweet & Maxwell 1989

Smith J C *Smith and Thomas's Casebook on Contract* 8th edn Sweet & Maxwell 1987

Torts

Hepple B A and Matthews *Tort: Cases and Materials* 4th edn Butterworth 1991

Rogers W H V *Winfield and Jolowicz on Tort* 13th edn Sweet & Maxwell 1989

Stanton K M *Breach of Statutory Duty in Tort* Sweet & Maxwell 1986

Local government and administrative law

Cross C, Bailey S and Jones R (eds) *Encyclopaedia of Local Government Law* Sweet & Maxwell (regularly updated)

Planning and environmental law

Ball S and Bell S *Environmental Law* Blackstone Press 1991

Heap D *An outline of planning law* 10th edn Sweet & Maxwell 1991
Moore V *A practical approach to planning law* 2nd edn (with 1991 revision) Blackstone Press 1991

Companies and partnerships

Mayson S W, French D and Ryan C *Company Law* 8th edn Blackstone Press 1992
Morse G *Partnership Law* 2nd edn Blackstone Press Ltd 1986
Morse G (ed.) *Palmer's Company Law* Sweet & Maxwell (encyclopaedia, regularly updated)

Safety

Encyclopaedia of Health and Safety at Work: Law and Practice Sweet & Maxwell (regularly updated)
Fife I and Machin A *Redgrave, Fife and Machin's Health and Safety* 10th edn Butterworth 1990
Ridley J R (ed.) *Safety at Work* 3rd edn Butterworth–Heinemann 1990

International law

Collins L (ed.) *Dicey and Morris: The Conflict of Laws* 11th edn in 2 Vols (with 4th supplement 1991) Stevens 1987
Morris O H C and North P M *Cases and Materials on Private International Law* Butterworth 1984
North P M and Fawcett *Cheshire and North: Private International Law* 11th edn Butterworth 1987

Dispute resolution

Donaldson Alternative Dispute Resolution *Arbitration* Vol 58 **2** 102–6
Fay E *Official Referees' Business* 2nd edn Sweet & Maxwell 1988
Fridd N and Weddle S *Basic Practice in Courts and Tribunals* Waterlow Publishers 1989
O'Connor P Alternative Dispute Resolution: Panacea or Placebo *Arbitration* Vol 58 **2** 107–15 (and article references)
Rowland P M B *Arbitration: Law and Practice* Institute of Chartered Accountants and Sweet & Maxwell 1988
Steyn Towards a new arbitration act *Arbitration* Vol 58 **2** 79–84.

Index